Slavery
in the
New World

Slavery in the New World

A READER IN
COMPARATIVE HISTORY

Edited by
LAURA FONER
EUGENE D. GENOVESE

PRENTICE-HALL, INC., Englewood Cliffs, N. J.

Current printing (last digit):
10 9 8 7 6 5 4 3 2

C-13-812867-7
P-13-812859-6

Library of Congress catalog card number:
69-17483

Printed in the United States of America

Prentice-Hall International, Inc., *London*
Prentice-Hall of Australia, Pty. Ltd., *Sydney*
Prentice-Hall of Canada, Ltd., *Toronto*
Prentice-Hall of India Private Ltd., *New Delhi*
Prentice-Hall of Japan, Inc., *Tokyo*

TO
FRANK TANNENBAUM

Introduction

The last decade has brought a major attempt by scholars to apply a comparative method to the study of Afro-American slavery. That comparative analysis should have taken so long to be adopted by American historians constitutes a serious criticism of their tendency to parochialism. Slavery in the United States existed simultaneously with slavery elsewhere in the hemisphere—something antebellum Southerners never lost sight of—and the slave trade and the use of colonial slave labor united the history of four continents during a period of 400 years.

Despite the opportunities for comparative study and despite the efforts of a few men like Oliveira Lima and Gilberto Freyre early in the century, Southern slavery continued to be studied as a national problem, and, as Stanley M. Elkins pointed out in 1959, historians of slavery centered their attention on moral debates and persisted in organizing their materials according to old categories and methods. Even the publication of Frank Tannenbaum's seminal essay, *Slave & Citizen* (1947), which contrasted the Iberian and Anglo-Saxon slave systems and raised a new set of questions and hypotheses, failed to shake American historians out of their complacency.

A dramatic change has occurred in the last few years. The mounting tensions of contemporary race relations have added a feeling of urgency to the attempt to reconstruct the Afro-American past. Perhaps this concern has contributed to an increasing willingness to relinquish exhausted categories and to look to new methods, other disciplines, and the experience of black peoples elsewhere in the hope of finding answers to threatening questions. Whatever the explanation, American historians are finally joining historians in the Caribbean, Latin America, and Europe, as well as sociologists, anthropologists, and economists, in the application of the comparative method. The acclaim given to David Brion Davis's prize-winning book, *The Problem of Slavery in Western Culture,* leaves no doubt that this method has triumphed within and without the historical profession.

This development has introduced an invigorating freshness and a new boldness into historical work. The questions posed by many of the recent studies—most notably in Elkins' study of the effects of slavery on black personality—and the contributions made by scholars from other disciplines have produced a welcome tendency to abandon the sterile isolation of history from the social sciences. To acquaint students and nonspecialist scholars with these encouraging trends we have brought together some of the best efforts to apply the comparative method to the study of slavery. Some of the selections are already well known to historians and others, but most are reprinted for the first time and are only beginning to get the attention we think they deserve. We have omitted such important writers as Ulrich Bonnell Phillips, Kenneth M. Stampp, C. R. Boxer, and Gilberto Freyre, simply because their work has been restricted to a single country; we have, in other words, selected only those studies which introduce a direct comparative dimension. The extent to which the subject has become interdisciplinary is demonstrated by the authors herein represented: nine are historians (Tannenbaum, Elkins, Davis, Goveia, H. S. Klein, Genovese, Jordan, Finley and Mörner); three are anthropologists (Mintz, Harris, and A. N. Klein); and three are sociologists (Hoetink, Sio, and Patterson). Important contributions are also being made by such economists and economic historians as Alfred H. Conrad and John R. Meyer, Celso Furtado, and Caio Prado Junior, but their work has so far been generally restricted to single countries with only hints and implications for comparative history.

A few selections discuss slavery outside the Western Hemisphere, but most remain within that framework. Slavery, as a relationship in which one man held property in another's person, existed in many societies, ancient and modern, and a much broader kind of comparative approach will undoubtedly have to be undertaken. In comparing different societies in time and space, and especially in comparing slavery to other dependent labor systems like serfdom, great care needs to be taken. As A. Norman Klein's essay shows, attempts to compare and associate labor systems that are only superficially similar can produce enormous mischief. The race question in modern American slavery alone sets it apart from most other systems and demands the greatest care in analysis. Apart from this most striking feature, other differences, making for contrast rather than comparison, quickly appear. We need especially to distinguish between societies in which slavery existed as one form of capital-labor relationship alongside other and more widespread forms and societies in which slavery was the prevalent capital-labor relationship and the mainspring for the production of a social surplus. The latter cases existed in both ancient and modern times but with a major difference. Whereas in the ancient world slavery developed out of internal economic processes, in the modern world it was imposed from without by expanding European powers that created a system of colonial exploitation on a labor-basis they themselves had long since overturned at home. As Caio Prado Junior observes, "Slavery in the Americas was not affiliated, in the historical sense, with any of the forms of servile labor deriving from the ancient world or the centuries that followed; it derived from an order of events that was inaugurated in the 15th century with the great maritime discoveries and belongs entirely to this order." From this point of view one may accept the line of thought opened by Charles Verlinden, which asserts institutional continuity between Old and New World slavery, and still insist on the prime task of relating the rise of slavery in the New World to the growth of capitalism and the world market. Once implanted, these slave systems generated certain tendencies that were in fundamental conflict with those economic and ideological currents which were developing in the mother countries of Western Europe. These tendencies arose naturally from the master-slave relationship and were common, although in radically different degrees, to all slaveholding areas. The relationship between these two antagonistic sides of the New World slave experience has yet to be explored adequately but will clearly require a world, not merely a hemispheric, perspective.

In general, the following essays speak for themselves. Many of the authors talk directly to each other's points and reply to each other's main arguments. The book is therefore a kind of forum in which debates over the nature of different slave societies are brought together. To insure maximum clarity and usefulness we present all the selections in full, except that of Mörner, and even in that case only material beyond the question of slavery itself has been omitted.

New York and Montreal   LAURA FONER
                                                         EUGENE D. GENOVESE

Contents

I

General Views on
Slavery in the New World

II

Comparative Viewpoints Applied 85

III

On the Debate 219

Slavery
in the
New World

I

General Views on Slavery in the New World

Despite the efforts of Oliveira Lima and a few others to introduce the comparative dimension into the study of Afro-American slavery, few advances were made until 1947, when Frank Tannenbaum published his seminal essay, *Slave and Citizen,* and even then the conservatism of the historical profession, especially in the United States, nearly halted progress until Stanley Elkins dramatically revitalized the discussion in 1959. Elkins focused on the impact of slavery on the personality of the blacks, boldly introduced psychological models into historical analysis, and by implication related the slave background to a variety of current problems. Coinciding as it did with the beginning of the current phase of the black liberation movement, Elkins' book attracted unusual attention and greatly encouraged historians to pursue the comparative method. Each year now brings new books and articles, and, as was to be expected, major ideological battles have been shaping up.

Part One presents representative selections from the two sides of the unfolding debate. On the one side are Tannenbaum and Elkins, who emphasize the differences between Iberian and Anglo-Saxon slave systems, feudal and capitalist cultures, and such institutional influences as those of church and state. On the other side are Harris, Davis, and Mintz,

1

who emphasize the similarities among all modern slave systems and the role of economic and material conditions. Within each group important differences have already appeared—the groups represent general tendencies, not narrowly defined schools of thought. In some ways, for example, Davis and Harris are further apart than are Davis and Tannenbaum. At the present moment, nonetheless, these two general tendencies dominate the discussion.

We have included a brief selection from Tannenbaum's *Ten Keys to Latin America*, rather than from *Slave and Citizen*, because the latter is too tight to excerpt effectively. An essay of only 100 pages, *Slave and Citizen* must be read as a whole; the selection from *Ten Keys* is merely a bare restatement, which cannot possibly substitute for the earlier work. No serious student—not even a beginner—can afford to skip *Slave and Citizen*, and we have proceeded on the assumption that that book will be read before this one. Although Elkins' greatest contribution was made to the theory of slave personality, that topic is not included here. Instead, we have selected his chapter on the social basis of the regimes. The discussion of slave personality has been proceeding much more rapidly than that of other topics and now requires a volume by itself. Fortunately, such a volume is now in preparation and will appear shortly.*

The first sweeping attack on the Tannenbaum-Elkins line of thought came from an anthropologist, Marvin Harris, although Eric Williams had engaged Tannenbaum in testy exchanges along similar lines a good deal earlier. Davis' *Problem of Slavery* broadened the attack considerably and gave it a new turn. Mintz, an anthropologist like Harris, had been quietly going his own way in a series of studies of the Caribbean that emphasized economic rather than institutional forces, and in his review of Elkins, here included, he joined in direct battle. As will readily be apparent, Mintz's contribution is less a review than a review-essay that counterposes one point of view to another. After presenting these two general tendencies, we shall proceed to a series of specific problems in Part Two and then return, in Part Three, to several attempts to review the debates and to assess the present state of work.

---

* Ann J. Lane, ed., *Slavery and Personality: The Elkins Thesis and Its Critics* (Baton Rouge: Louisiana State University Press, forthcoming).

FRANK TANNENBAUM

Slavery, the Negro,
and Racial Prejudice

Frank Tannenbaum was Professor Emeritus in Latin American history at Colum-bia University and the director of Columbia's university seminars program. He wrote extensively on Latin America, especially Mexico, but his works cover a wide range of subjects, including the American labor movement, prison conditions and reform, and United States foreign policy. Professor Tannenbaum had a lifelong interest in comparative history. His book, Slave and Citizen, is generally considered the seminal work in the field of comparative slavery. The following selection is taken from a later book, Ten Keys to Latin America, and is a very brief, necessarily schematic summary of the position which is more fully and subtly developed in Slave and Citizen.

The Negro, like the Indian and the mestizo, has a special place and a unique role in the Latin American complex. Of the 12,000,000 or more Negroes transported by slave traders to the Western Hemisphere between 1500 and 1850, a large proportion went to what are now the Latin American

From Frank Tannenbaum, "Toward An Appreciation of Latin America," in Herbert L. Matthews, ed., *The United States and Latin America* (2nd ed.), pp. 46–52, © 1963 by The American Assembly, Columbia University, New York, New York. Reprinted by permission of Prentice-Hall, Inc., Englewood Cliffs, New Jersey.

nations. In greater or lesser numbers they were to be found in every part of the area from Chile to Cuba. Next to Haiti, the largest proportion probably went to Brazil, although Cuba was a close third. There are certain general features of the Negro's role in Latin America which have influenced both the economic and the social develop-ment of the area. For one thing, in those regions where the Indian disappeared shortly after European conquest, or proved too intractable, Negro labor was used instead. Generally the Negro did not play an important part in those areas where the Indian survived in large

3

numbers—usually settled agricultural regions. The Negro survived and prospered best in tropical parts of America, largely the coastal lowlands. As a laborer he was employed mainly in the cultivation of sugar, cocoa, and other crops that do well in warm moist climates.

The Negroes were purchased as *individuals* by European masters and were therefore closer to and more dependent on the white man. In fact, some Negroes arrived with the early Spanish expeditions. Although they were slaves, they were treated in some ways as superior to the Indian and were used occasionally as foremen or overseers where Negro and Indian labor were found together. Unlike the Indian, who has proved extremely recalcitrant, the Negro was malleable and culturally receptive. He acquired European language, religion, dress, food, and habits with surprising speed, and in those countries where he is numerically important, he has become a significant influence in the economic, political, and, especially, in the cultural life. He has, as the Indian has not, become culturally a European, and in Brazil, Cuba, Venezuela, and Panama won recognition in literature, music, art, and architecture. This has notably been the case in Brazil where some of the greatest figures in the arts, music, and literature have been mulattoes and Negroes.

It is interesting to speculate on the significance of this remarkable turn of events. The slave, branded and chained, has within a relatively short period of time become one of the leading cultural influences among his former masters. Even while slavery was still in existence (it was abolished in Cuba in 1890 and in Brazil in 1888) the mulatto everywhere identified with the Negro either as slave or as a free man,

and the Abolitionist movement in Brazil was to a large extent carried on by mulattoes and by freed slaves.

Unlike the Indian, the Negro found leaders among members of his own race. More than that, he became identified with and sometimes a distinguished participant in the general culture without relinquishing his Negro heritage, whereas among the Indians, neither the mestizo nor even the pure Indian, such as Juárez, who became president of Mexico, identified with the Indian or defended him against the white man.

The Indian had no natural and trusted spokesman of his own race and no interpreter acceptable to the larger community, whereas the Negro had many. The Negro felt at home in some subtle sense even while he was a slave— as the reading of the literature will reveal. The Indian never felt at home with the white man and does not today. But there are other historical influences which help explain the accommodation of the Negro within the Latin American community in a way that has not happened in the United States.

The Negro slave, brought into the Iberian peninsula as early as 1442, fitted into a society where slavery was still in existence. As a result of the many centuries of warfare with the Moors, if not for other reasons, Spanish society accepted slavery as normal, while it had long since died out in Western Europe. At the time the Negro was brought to Spain, there were Moorish slaves, Jewish slaves, and even some native Spaniards were slaves. Captured prisoners could be held for ransom or could be held as slaves, and the laws allowed other reasons for slavery. But the important point is that there was a slave law, an elaborate code, embodied as part of the *Siete Partidas* going back to Alfonso the Wise (1252–84), which endowed the slave with a legal personality, with duties, and with rights. The slave was known to the law as a human being; he could marry, he could buy his freedom, he could change his master if he found one to purchase him, and he could under certain conditions testify in court even against his master. If a slave became a priest, he had to give his master one slave, but if he became a bishop, he had to give him two slaves.

The Negro brought over from Africa became the beneficiary of this body of law. He was not merely a slave—a chattel, as he was under West Indian and American colonial codes—but also a human being with rights enforceable in the king's court. The Negro in Iberia was also converted to the Catholic faith, and the master had to see to it that he came to church. While Catholic doctrine did not oppose slavery as such, it asserted that master and slave were equal in the sight of God, that what mattered was the moral and religious character of man, and that the master must treat his slaves as moral beings, as brothers in Christ. It also emphasized the merits of manumission. Negroes in Spanish and Portuguese colonies were the inheritors of this legal and religious tradition. It is not suggested that slavery was not cruel, nor that in Brazil, Cuba, Venezuela, or Peru abominable and inhuman acts were not committed against Negro slaves. But cruelty was against the law, and unusual punishment could be brought to the attention of the court by a recognized legal protector of the slave. The killing of a slave was treated as murder. The entire atmosphere was different, and manumission was so frequent that there were often more freed Negroes than there were slaves.

The fact that the slave had both a legal personality and a moral status made manumission natural and the abolition of slavery no great shock. The question of the slave's fitness for freedom never arose, and the freed Negro was a free man, not a freedman. He was legally the equal of all other free men. And when slavery was abolished in Brazil, the crowd in the galleries threw flowers upon the members of the Congress, and the people danced in the streets of Rio de Janeiro throughout the night. The question of segregation, so agonizing and so disturbing in our own South, could never have arisen anywhere in Latin America—neither with the Negro nor with the Indian. It is this tradition in Latin America that makes it most difficult for them to understand our problem or our way of dealing with it.

This does not mean there is no racial prejudice in Latin America. It exists against both the Indian and the Negro, but it is a prejudice which has no sanction in the law. It is social and economic and cultural. It is determined more by social status than by a sense that people of color are inferior in nature—though this feeling exists, particularly regarding the Indian. But any Indian, and any mulatto, if he can escape from his poverty, if he can acquire the graces, the language, the manners, the dress, the schooling, and the associations that will admit him into the best society, will have no insuperable difficulties socially, especially if he is wealthy, and can, if he has it in him, be elected to Congress, be a member of the cabinet, or become president of the country. The fact that he is an Indian or a mulatto will not bar him—and there are some instances of mulattoes and a few Indians who have risen to the highest posts politically. In that sense there is no race prejudice. The case is different for the pure black man. In some countries—in Peru for instance, or Ecuador, Colombia, or Venezuela, or perhaps even in Cuba and Brazil—the pure black man so far has not and perhaps cannot rise to the highest political post or really be accepted by the "best" social set. That is the difference between Latin American racial conditions and our own.

I have probably overdrawn the picture. The tolerance is very great, but not absolute. In Cuba, which certainly is as broadly open as any country in Latin America, the numerous social clubs were exclusively white (before Castro); the fact that a Negro rebellion in which 3,000 lost their lives was possible as late as 1911 casts a long shadow on the white-colored complex in that country. In Panama where the Negroes have assimilated into the Spanish tradition, they identify with the middle class and look down upon the thousands of Negroes brought over from the British West Indies during the construction of the Panama Canal. When a Panamanian speaks of the Negro in Panama, these are the people he refers to. Other illustrations could be added, but it remains true that Latin American attitudes toward the Negro are of a different quality than our own.

There is something else that needs adding. In the United States the Negro's opportunities for wealth, education, professional advancement as doctor or lawyer, and for active politics (outside of the South) are very much greater than in Latin America. True enough, this advancement economically and professionally takes place mostly, though by no means entirely, within the colored community. But the way is not closed—in the arts, in the professions, in education, or in opportunities for distinction. The road is narrow and steep, but there is a road. In contrast, in Latin America the road does not

exist. This is too strong a way to put it. Perhaps it would be more accurate to say that the door is shut but not locked. The gap between the "lower" classes—between not only the Indian and the Negro poor, but all the poor, all the illiterate, and all the children of the little rural hut that I saw in Cundinamarka—and the elite in Bogotá, or between the *huasipongo* on a hacienda in Ecuador and the traveled, sophisticated literary people in Quito is so wide that it is almost unbridgeable. That is, in part, because the countries are poor, the wealthy families fewer, and the indigent more numerous.

But there is a more important point. The hierarchical structure of the society, the aristocratic tradition, the essentially castelike way people are grouped and identified, and the paternal concept that the poor must always be poor, that the servant must always remain a servant, has made the gap between "upper" and "lower" very great indeed. Never in the history of the United States has there been such a distance, such a seemingly impossible distance, between our poorest farmer or immigrant and the wealthiest and most self-conscious of our aristocracy—if that word has any real meaning in our culture. This distance is obviously not racial, not biological, nor based on color of skin or place of origin, but it is perhaps even more effective as a dividing line, and perhaps more permanent. It is an ingrained part of the total scheme of things.

We are fooling ourselves—and Latin Americans who speak as if this were not the case are also fooling themselves—if we or they think that what we call democracy is a thing of formal law and constitutional enactment. It has as a background a feeling of equality, or perhaps egalitarianism, "where a man is a man for all that," where no man rides a high horse and is not expected to ride one. At this point American and Latin American society stand wide apart. The difference between the basic conditions of social equality and opportunity in the United States and Latin America is broad and deep—and not really changeable for a long time to come.

STANLEY M. ELKINS

Slavery in Capitalist and Non-Capitalist Cultures

Stanley M. Elkins is Professor of History at Smith College. Slavery: A Problem in American Institutional and Intellectual Life, *from which the following selection is taken, was originally his doctoral dissertation at Columbia University, and its appearance caused a sensation in the historical profession. He has collaborated with Eric McKitrick on a number of important articles on American political, intellectual, and institutional history. They are currently working on a book on early American political and institutional history. The following selection begins with a discussion of the legal status of the slave in the U.S. South and picks up on the comparative dimension on page 15.*

The four major legal categories which defined the status of the American slave may be roughly classified as "term of servitude," "marriage and the family," "police and disciplinary powers over the slave," and "property and other civil rights." The first of these, from which somehow all the others flowed, had in effect been established during the latter half of the seventeenth century; a slave was a slave for the duration of his life, and slavery was a status which he transmitted by inheritance to his children and his children's children.

It would be fairest, for several reasons, to view the remaining three categories in terms of the jurisprudence of the nineteenth century. By that time the most savage aspects of slavery from the standpoint of Southern practice (and thus, to a certain extent, of law) had become greatly softened. We may accordingly see it in its most humane light and at the same time note the clarity with which its basic outlines remained fixed and embodied in law, much as they had been laid down before the middle of the eighteenth century.[1]

That most ancient and intimate of institutional arrangements, marriage and the family, had long since been destroyed by the law, and the law never showed any inclination to rehabilitate it. Here was the area in which considerations of humanity might be expected most widely to prevail, and, indeed, there is every reason to suppose that on an informal daily basis they did: the contempt in which respectable society held the slave-trader, who separated mother from child and husband from wife, is proverbial in Southern lore.[2] On the face of things, it ought to have been simple enough to translate this strong social sentiment into the appropriate legal enactments, which might systematically have guaranteed the inviolability of the family and the sanctity of the marriage bond, such as governed Christian polity

everywhere. Yet the very nature of the plantation economy and the way in which the basic arrangements of Southern life radiated from it, made it inconceivable that the law should tolerate any ambiguity, should the painful clash between humanity and property interest ever occur. Any restrictions on the separate sale of slaves would have been reflected immediately in the market; their price would have dropped considerably.[3] Thus the law could permit no aspect of the slave's conjugal state to have an independent legal existence outside the power of the man who owned him: "The relation of master and slave is wholly incompatible with even the qualified relation of husband and wife, as it is supposed to exist among slaves...."[4] Marriage, for them, was denied any standing in law. Accordingly, as T. R. R. Cobb of Georgia admitted, "The contract of marriage not being recognized among slaves, none of its consequences follow...."[5] "The relation between slaves," wrote a North Carolina judge in 1858, "is essentially different from that of man and wife joined in lawful wedlock ... [for] with slaves it may be dissolved at the pleasure of either party, or by the sale

---

[1] We have a further advantage in regarding the law of slavery in the light of the nineteenth century. Two general developments of that period inspired a great wealth of writing on the subject in the form of commentaries by jurists and *obiter dicta* by judges, as well as a fresh course of marginal legislation bearing on some of slavery's social implications. These developments were the expansion of slavery into the Gulf states and, much more important, the moral pressures being exerted on Southerners both from the North and from abroad. The bulk of the Southern response to this latter fact took the form of various kinds of defenses of slavery, but for Southern jurists it naturally stimulated a re-examination of the legal aspects of their "peculiar institution."

[2] "In all the category of disreputable callings, there were none so despised as the slave-trader. The odium descended upon his children and his children's children. Against the legal right to buy and sell slaves for profit, this public sentiment lifted a strong arm, and rendered forever odious the name of 'Negro-trader.'" Beverly B. Munford, *Virginia's Attitude toward Slavery and Secession* (New York: Longmans, Green, 1909), pp. 101–2.

[3] This may be tested against what did typically happen in cases where restrictions were placed by the seller himself upon the separation of slaves with whom he was obliged, for whatever reason, to part. "In proportion as these restrictions put important limitations on the purchaser's rights and were safeguarded, they lessened the slave's salability." Frederic Bancroft, *Slave-trading in the Old South* (Baltimore: J. H. Furst, 1931), p. 214.

[4] *Howard* v. *Howard*, 6 Jones N.C. 235 (December, 1858), quoted in Helen T. Catterall, *Judicial Cases Concerning American Slavery and the Negro* (Washington: Carnegie Institution, 1926 ff.), II, 221.

[5] Thomas R. R. Cobb, *An Inquiry into the Law of Slavery in the United States of America* (Philadelphia: T. & J. W. Johnson, 1858), p. 246.

of one or both, depending on the caprice or necessity of the owners."[6]

It would thus go without saying that the offspring of such "contubernal relationships," as they were called, had next to no guaranties against indiscriminate separation from their parents.[7] Of additional interest is the fact that children derived their condition from that of their mother. This was not unique to American slavery, but it should be noted that especially in a system conceived and evolved exclusively on grounds of property there could be little doubt about how such a question would be resolved. Had status been defined according to the father's condition—as was briefly the case in seventeenth-century Maryland, following the ancient common law—there would instantly have arisen the irksome question of what to do with the numerous mulatto children born every year of white planter fathers and slave mothers. It would have meant the creation of a free mulatto class, automatically relieving the master of so many slaves on the one hand, while burdening him on the other with that

many colored children whom he could not own. Such equivocal relationships were never permitted to vex the law. That "the father of a slave is unknown to our law" was the universal understanding of Southern jurists.[8] It was thus that a father, among slaves, was legally "unknown," a husband without the rights of his bed,[9] the state of marriage defined as "only that concubinage . . . with which alone, perhaps, their condition is compatible,[10] and motherhood clothed in the scant dignity of the breeding function.[11]

Regarding matters of police and discipline, it is hardly necessary to view the typical slave's lot in the nineteenth century as one of stripes and torture. Indeed, we should probably not stretch the truth greatly were we to

---

[6] Quoted in Catterall, *Judicial Cases*, II, 221.

[7] The few exceptions—none of which meant very much in practice, except perhaps the law of Louisiana—are discussed in Bancroft, *Slave-trading*, pp. 197–221. "Louisiana, least American of the Southern States," writes Mr. Bancroft, "was least inhuman. In becoming Americanized it lost many a liberal feature of the old French *Code Noir*, but it forbade sale of mothers from their children less than ten years of age (and vice versa) and bringing into the State any slave child under ten years of age without its mother, if living. The penalty for violating either prohibition was from $1,000 to $2,000 and the forfeiture of the slave. That would have meant much if it had been strictly enforced" (p. 197). Louisiana's Spanish and French background, plus the fact that in both the legal and social senses slavery in Latin America generally was very different from slavery in North America, may furnish significant clues to some of the idiosyncrasies in the Louisiana code. See below.

[8] *Frazier* v. *Spear*, 2 Bibb (Ken.), 385 (Fall, 1811), quoted in Catterall, *Judicial Cases*, I, 287.

[9] "A slave has never maintained an action against the violator of his bed. A slave is not admonished for incontinence, or punished for fornication or adultery; never prosecuted for bigamy, or petty treason for killing a husband being a slave, any more than admitted to an appeal for murder." Opinion of Daniel Dulany, Esq., Attorney-General of Maryland, quoted in William Goodell, *The American Slave Code in Theory and Practice* (New York: American and Foreign Anti-Slavery Society, 1853), pp. 106–7.

[10] *State* v. *Samuel* (*a slave*), 2 Dev. and Bat. N.C. 177 (December, 1836), quoted in Catterall, *Judicial Cases*, II, 77.

[11] The picturesque charge that planters deliberately "bred" their slave women has never been substantiated, and Avery Craven's point that white women bred about as young and as often as their black sisters is a sensible one. But with no law to prevent the separation of parents and children, and with the value of a slave being much in excess of what it cost to rear him, the temptation to think and talk about a prolific Negro woman as a "rattlin' good breeder" was very strong. See Avery Craven, *The Coming of the Civil War* (New York: Scribner, 1942); 2nd Ed. (Chicago: University of Chicago Press, 1957), p. 84; Stampp, *Peculiar Institution*, p. 249. Frederic Bancroft gives numerous examples of advertisements describing Negro women in just this way. *Slave-trading*, pp. 68–79.

concede Ulrich Phillips' sympathetic picture of a just regime tempered with paternal indulgence on the majority of well-run plantations. Among decent Southerners the remark, "I have been told that he does not use his people well," was a pronouncement of deep social censure.[12] Yet here again what impresses us is not the laxity with which much of the daily discipline was undoubtedly handled, but rather the completeness with which such questions, even extending to life and limb, were in fact under the master's dominion. "On our estates," wrote the Southern publicist J. D. B. DeBow in 1853, "we dispense with the whole machinery of public police and public courts of justice. Thus we try, decide, and execute the sentences in thousands of cases, which in other countries would go into the courts.[13] The law deplored "cruel and unusual punishment." But wherever protection was on the one hand theoretically extended,[14] it was practically canceled on the other by the universal prohibition in Southern law against permitting slaves to testify in court, except against each other, and in any case the courts generally accepted the principle that the line between correction and cruelty was impossible to determine. Thus a Virginia judge in 1827, faced with an indictment against a master "for cruelly beating his own slave," felt bound to decline jurisdiction with the rhetorical demand: "Without any proofs that the common law did ever protect the slave against minor injuries from the hand of the master . . . where are we to look for the power which is now claimed for us?"[15] To the jurist Cobb it seemed clear on principle that "the battery of a slave, without special enactment, could not be prosecuted criminally."[16] Public opinion itself should, it was generally held, deter

---

[12] "There is a public sentiment to which they are amenable; a cruel, neglectful master is marked and despised; and if cruel and neglectful by proxy, he does not escape reprobation." Nehemiah Adams, *A South-Side View of Slavery* (1855), p. 97. Such a man, according to Frederick Law Olmsted, was known as a "nigger-killer." *Journey in the Seaboard Slave States* (New York: Putnam, 1904), I, 120–21.

[13] DeBow, *Industrial Resources* (1852–53), II, 249.

[14] There was, for example, a South Carolina law of 1740 which provided that, "In case any person shall wilfully cut out the tongue, put out the eye, castrate, or cruelly scald, burn, or deprive any slave of any limb or member, or shall inflict any other cruel punishment, other than whipping, or beating with a horsewhip, cowskin, switch, or small stick, or by putting irons on, or confining or imprisoning such slave, every such person shall, for every such offense, forfeit the sum of one hundred pounds current money." Goodell, *American Slave Code*, pp. 159–60.

[15] *Commonwealth* v. *Turner*, 5 Randolph 678 (November, 1827), quoted in Catterall, *Judicial Cases*, I, 150. It was in the same spirit that Judge Ruffin of North Carolina expressed himself in the case of *State* v. *Mann* in 1829. "But upon the general question whether the owner is answerable, *criminalter*, for a battery upon his own slave . . . the Court entertains but little doubt. That he is so liable has never been decided, nor, as far as is known, been hitherto contended. There has been no prosecutions of the sort. The established and uniform practice of the country in this respect is the best evidence of the portion of the power deemed by the whole community requisite to the preservation of the master's dominion. . . . The power of the master must be absolute to render the submission of the slave perfect. I most freely confess my sense of the harshness of the proposition. I feel it as deeply as any man can. . . . But it is inherent in the relation of master and slave. . . . We cannot allow the right of the master to be brought into discussion in the Courts of justice. The slave, to remain a slave, must be made sensible that there is no appeal from his master. . . ." Quoted in Goodell, *American Slave Code*, pp. 171–73.

[16] Cobb, *Inquiry*, p. 90. "This [the Negro's helplessness] is one of the most vulnerable points in the system of negro slavery," Cobb admitted, "and should be further guarded by legislation." *Ibid.*, p. 98.

wanton brutalities. But the final argument was that of self-interest. "Where the battery was committed by the master himself, there would be no redress whatever, for the reason given in Exodus 21: 21, 'for he is his money'. The powerful protection of the master's private interest would of itself go far to remedy this evil."[17]

Even the murder of a slave found the law straining all its resources to avoid jurisdiction.[18] Murder was indeed punishable, but under circumstances peculiar to the state of slavery, not in ways applying to white society, and always under the disabilities which barred the testimony of Negroes in the courts. An act of North Carolina in 1798 provided that the punishment for "maliciously killing a slave" should be the same as for the murder of a free person—but it did not apply to an outlawed slave or to a slave "in the act of resistance to his lawful owner" or to a slave "dying under moderate "correction."[19] The law in South Carolina allowed that in the absence of competent witnesses to the homicide of a slave, the affidavit of the accused was admissible in his favor before a jury.[20] The criminal jurisprudence of Virginia had never known, before 1851, a case of "more atrocious and wicked cruelty" than that of a. man named Souther who had killed his slave, Sam, under the most

lurid circumstances.[21] Yet the conviction was for murder in the second degree, and Souther escaped with five years in the penitentiary. In general, the court's primary care—not only in the killing of slaves by persons other than the master but also in cases where the slave himself had committed murder and was executed by the state— was for the pecuniary interest of the owner. Numerous enactments provided for compensation in either event.[22] It was precisely this pecuniary interest which was at the very heart of legal logic on all such questions. Just as it was presumed to operate against "cruel and unusual punishment," so it became virtually a non sequitur that a man should kill his own slave. The principle had been enunciated very early: "It cannot be presumed that prepensed malice (which alone makes murder felony) should induce any man to destroy his own estate."[23]

The rights of property, and all other civil and legal "rights," were everywhere denied the slave with a clarity that left no doubt of his utter dependency upon his master. "A slave is in absolute bondage; he has no civil

---

[17] *Ibid.*, p. 98.
[18] "It would seem that from the very nature of slavery, and the necessarily degraded social position of the slave, many acts would extenuate the homicide of a slave, and reduce the offence to a lower grade, which would not constitute a legal provocation if done by a white person." *Ibid.*, p. 92.
[19] Goodell, *American Slave Code*, p. 180. There was a law in Tennessee to the same effect and in virtually the same words. See Hurd, *Law of Freedom and Bondage*, II, 90.
[20] Cobb, *Inquiry*, p. 96.

[21] "The negro was tied to a tree and whipped with switches. When Souther became fatigued with the labour of whipping, he called upon a negro man of his, and made him cob Sam with a shingle. He also made a negro woman of his help to cob him. And after cobbing and whipping, he applied fire to the body of the slave; about his back, belly, and private parts. He then caused him to be washed down with hot water, in which pods of red pepper had been steeped. The negro was also tied to a log and to the bed post with ropes, which choked him, and he was kicked and stamped by Souther. This sort of punishment was continued and repeated until the negro died under its infliction." *Souther v. Commonwealth*, 7 Grattan 673 (June, 1851), quoted in Catterall, *Judicial Cases*, I, 224.
[22] See Hurd, *Law of Freedom and Bondage*, I, 253, 296–97, 300.
[23] "An act about the casual killing of slaves" (Virginia, 1669), *ibid.*, I, 232.

right, and can hold no property, except at the will and pleasure of his master."[24] He could neither give nor receive gifts; he could make no will, nor could he, by will, inherit anything. He could not hire himself out or make contracts for any purpose—even including, as we have seen, that of matrimony—and thus neither his word nor his bond had any standing in law. He could buy or sell nothing at all, except as his master's agent, could keep no cattle, horses, hogs, or sheep and, in Mississippi at least, could raise no cotton. Even masters who permitted such transactions, except under express arrangement, were uniformly liable to fines.[25] It was obvious, then, that the case of a slave who should presume to buy his own freedom—he being unable to possess money—would involve a legal absurdity. "Slaves have no legal rights in things, real or personal; but whatever they may acquire, belongs, in point of law, to their masters."[26]

Such proscriptions were extended not only over all civil rights but even to the civic privileges of education and

worship. Every Southern state except Maryland and Kentucky had stringent laws forbidding anyone to teach slaves reading and writing, and in some states the penalties applied to the educating of free Negroes and mulattoes as well. It was thought that "teaching slaves to read and write tends to dissatisfaction in their minds, and to produce insurrection and rebellion";[27] in North Carolina it was a crime to distribute among them any pamphlet or book, not excluding the Bible. The same apprehensions applied to instruction in religion. Southern society was not disposed to withhold the consolations of divine worship from its slaves, but the conditions would have to be laid down not by the church as an institution, not even by the planters as laity, but by planters simply as masters. The conscientious master no doubt welcomed having the gospel preached to his slaves, provided that they should hear it, as J. W. Fowler of Coahoma County, Mississippi, specified, "in its original purity and simplicity." Fowler wrote to his overseer that "in view of the fanaticism of the age it behooves the Master or Overseer to be present on all such occasions."[28] Alexander Telfair, of Savannah, instructed his overseer that there should be "no night-meeting or preaching . . . allowed on the place, except on Saturday night & Sunday morn."[29] Similar restrictions found their way into the law itself. Typical were the acts of South Carolina forbidding religious meetings of slaves or free Negroes "either before the rising of the sun or after the setting of the same," and of Mississippi permitting slaves, if authorized by their masters, to attend

---

[24] Opinion of Judge Crenshaw in *Brandon et al.* v. *Planters' and Merchants' Bank of Huntsville*, I Stewart's Ala. Report, 320 (January, 1838), quoted in Goodell, *American Slave Code*, p. 92.

[25] *Ibid.*, pp. 89–104.

[26] *Ibid.*, p. 88. A substantial number of Negroes did in fact buy their freedom in the ante-bellum South, but this required the full cooperation of their masters. Legally the slave had no claim to the money he may have collected for his own purchase. This highly precarious customary sanction, if such it may be called, should be compared to the fully articulated legal sanction embodied in the Cuban *coartación* (see n. 71 below). For a discussion of hiring-out arrangements which, although not recognized in law, were by no means unfamiliar (and under which the slave appears in practice to have had more initiative than the law theoretically gave him), see Richard B. Morris, "The Measure of Bondage in the Slave States," *Mississippi Valley Historical Review*, XLI (September, 1954), 219–40.

[27] Goodell, *American Slave Code*, p. 321.

[28] Ulrich B. Phillips (ed.), *A Documentary History of American Industrial Society* (Cleveland: Arthur H. Clark, 1910), I, 115.

[29] *Ibid.*, p. 127.

the preaching of a *white* minister. It was a state of things deplored by the Southern churches, for the law had been none of their doing. "There are over TWO MILLIONS of human beings in the condition of heathen," lamented the Presbyterian Synod of South Carolina and Georgia in 1833, "and some of them in worse condition."

In the present state of feeling in the South, a ministry of their own color could neither be obtained NOR TOLERATED. But do not the negroes have access to the gospel through the stated ministry of the whites? We answer, No. The negroes have no regular and efficient ministry: as a matter of course, no churches; neither is there sufficient room in the white churches for their accommodation.[30]

But the church could do nothing. Its rural congregations were full of humane and decent Christians, but as an institution of authority and power it had no real existence.

It is true that among the most attractive features of the plantation legend, dear to every Southerner with a sense of his past, were the paternal affection of the good master for his blacks and the warm sentiments entertained in Southern society at large for the faithful slave. The other side of the coin, then, might appear as something of a paradox: the most implacable race-consciousness yet observed in virtually any society. It was evolved in the Southern mind, one might say, as a simple syllogism, the precision of whose terms paralleled the precision of the system itself. All slaves are black; slaves are degraded and contemptible; therefore all blacks are degraded and contemptible and should be kept in a state of slavery. How had the simple syllogism come into being? That very

strength and bulwark of American society, capitalism, unimpeded by prior arrangements and institutions, had stamped the status of slave upon the black with a clarity which elsewhere could never have been so profound, and had further defined the institution of slavery with such nicety that the slave *was*, in fact, degraded. That the black, as a species, was thus contemptible seemed to follow by observation. This assumption took on a life of its own in the attitudes of the people, and the very thought of such a creature existing outside the pale of their so aptly devised system filled the most reasonable of Southerners with fear and loathing. Quite apart from the demands of the system itself, this may account for many of the subsidiary social taboos— the increasing severity of the laws against manumission, the horror of miscegenation, the depressed condition of the free Negro and his peculiar place in Southern society: all signs of how difficult it was to conceive a nonslave colored class. Nothing in their experience had prepared them for it; such a class was unnatural, logically awry, a blemish on the body politic, an anomaly for which there was no intellectual category.

There should be no such unresolved terms, no such unfactorable equations, in a society whose production economy had had such dynamic and unencumbered origins. Both reason and instinct had defined the Negro as a slave, and the slave as

that condition of a natural person, in which, by the operation of law, the application of his physical and mental powers depends, as far as possible, upon the will of another who is himself subject to the supreme power of the state, and in which he is incapable, in the view of the law, of acquiring or holding property, and of sustaining those relations out of which *relative* rights . . . proceed,

---

[30] Quoted in Goodell, *American Slave Code*, p. 334.

except as the agent or instrument of another. In slavery, strictly so called, the supreme power of the state, in ignoring the personality of the slave, ignores his capacity for moral action, and commits the control of his conduct as a moral agent, to the master, together with the power of transferring his authority to another.[31]

The basic fact was, of course, that the slave himself was property. He and his fellow bondsmen had long since become "chattels personal . . . to all intents, constructions, and purposes whatsoever."[32]

In the slave system of the United States—so finely circumscribed and so cleanly self-contained—virtually all avenues of recourse for the slave, all lines of communication to society at large, originated and ended with the

---

[31] Hurd, *Law of Freedom and Bondage*, I, 42–43. Such language would lead one to suppose that slavery was a condition which, by its very nature, at all times and in all places, should partake of the same legal and social necessities. But the usage of the ancient world, in which slavery was everywhere prevalent, was bound by no such necessities. Nor was slavery defined either with great clarity or great rigidity. There were so many degrees between "total" freedom and "total" slavery that the two tended to lose much of their meaning as opposites. Moreover, the stigma of slavery itself did not strike nearly so deep as in American slavery; in the latter, a man was either one thing or the other—slave or free. See William L. Westermann, "Between Slavery and Freedom," *American Historical Review*, L (January, 1945), 213–27. The difference that this made in the social attitudes of classical times toward slavery was considerable. "The lack in antiquity of any deep abhorrence of slavery as a social and economic evil may be explained in part," according to Professor Westermann, by the fact that "the change of legal status out of enslavement into liberty, by way of manumission, was as constant and as easy in Greco-Roman life as the reverse transition over the short passage from individual freedom of action into the constraints of nonfreedom, and the methods employed for making either transition were many." *Ibid.*, p. 215.

[32] Hurd, *Law of Freedom and Bondage*, I, 303.

master. The system was unique, *sui generis*. The closest parallel to it at that time was to be found in the Latin-American colonies of Spain and Portugal. But the differences between the two systems are so much more striking than the similarities that we may with profit use them not as parallels but as contrasts. In the Spanish and Portuguese colonies, we are immediately impressed by the comparative lack of precision and logic governing the institution of slavery there; we find an exasperating dimness of line between the slave and free portions of society, a multiplicity of points of contact between the two, a confusing promiscuity of color, such as would never have been thinkable in our own country.[33] But before attempting to establish legal and customary classifications on the slave's condition in these places, in some manner corresponding to those we used for the United States, something should be said about the social and institutional setting in which slavery, in Spain and Portugal themselves, was both viewed and practiced.

Although the Spanish and Portuguese trade in Negro slaves would not become of primary importance until about the same period as did that of England, the civilization of the Iberian Peninsula was one in which slavery had long been familiar: laws, customs, and attitudes concerning it had been fixed for centuries. Indeed, the culture and traditions were rich in continuities with classical times—with the Romans

---

[33] Four works upon which I have drawn heavily for my material on Latin-American slavery are Frank Tannenbaum's *Slave and Citizen* (New York: Knopf, 1947), Fr. Dieudonné Rinchon's *La traite et l'esclavage des Congolais par les Européens* (Wetteren, Belgium, 1929), Sir Harry Johnston's *The Negro in the New World* (London: Methuen, 1910), and Fernando Ortiz, *Los Negros esclavos* (Havana: Revista bimestra cubana, 1916).

themselves, who had known all about slavery. Slavery had been considered by Roman statesmen and publicists, and in succeeding centuries by the Latin church fathers. The church of Rome, in its Holy Scripture, preserved and perpetuated traditions in which the Jews of antiquity had not only held slaves but had also made endless rules for their treatment and governance. Many parts of the Justinian Code dealt with slavery. Moors, Jews, and even Spaniards had been held in slavery, a fact implicitly recognized in the codification of Spanish law undertaken in the thirteenth century by King Alfonso the Wise.[34] Thus the situation of the first Negro slaves, who probably came to the Iberian Peninsula about the middle of the fifteenth century, was at the very outset quite different from that of the first slaves to arrive in Virginia early in the seventeenth. For here they found already waiting a legal and social setting incredibly complex, thick with the experience of centuries, and peculiarly fitted to receive and absorb them.

The "logic" of this tradition, biblical and classical in its origins, would have been incomprehensible to publicists of nineteenth-century America, both North and South, even though each drew upon it for their arguments. In it, there was a clear recognition and implicit sanction of slavery; nowhere was it denied (and thus the Southerner was right); at the same time, held as it were in suspension, was the universal presumption that such servitude, violating the divine and natural equality of

man, was "against both reason and nature"[35] (and here, of course, the Northerner was right). But the fact that these two contrary principles could be supported in such illogical equilibrium within the same body of law and custom, made it possible for the system of slavery to exist, both in Spain and in the New World colonies, in a form which differed immensely from that of the United States. That this was indeed possible requires further explanation, for even after a wide-scale plantation order, based on Negro slave labor, had been established in Latin America, the ancient assumptions and legal sanctions governing slavery carried over into it with great tenacity and persistence.[36]

Of all the national states of western Europe, Spain, though dynastically united to a substantial degree late in the fifteenth century (and having even absorbed Portugal in the sixteenth),[37] remained, long into modern times, much the most "medieval." Its agricul-

---

[34] This was a codification (*Las siete Partidas del Rey Don Alfonso el Sabio*) which dealt extensively with slavery and "which in itself," according to Mr. Tannenbaum, "summarizes the Mediterranean legal *mores* of many centuries. ..." *Slave and Citizen*, p. 45.

[35] "Slavery is a condition and institution made in antiquity, through which men, who were naturally free, enslave themselves and submit to the dominion of others against reason and nature." *Las siete Partidas*, quoted in *ibid.*, p. 45 n.

[36] "In Spain, slavery existed before the Indies were discovered. More specifically, we find slavery in Iberia from the remotest times. . . . Spain was never without slaves. It is thus that the discovery of America and the naturally improvised political economy of the conquistadors and colonizers came face to face with the mold of slavery ready-made in the legal structure of the mother country.

"It happened otherwise in North America, where the colonies did not have *ab initio* a true slave law. This issued from the legislation of the colonies themselves. . . . Perhaps it is due to this circumstance that the slave legislation of the English colonies was more severe than the Spanish, and that the master's power to which the slave was subjected in the former was more absolute and uncontrollable." Ortiz, *Los Negros esclavos*, pp. 334–35.

[37] A union which lasted from 1580 to 1640.

ture retained many of the subsistence features characteristic of manorial economy. Its social stability was guaranteed by that standing alliance of church and state upon which every feudal community rested; there, on a national scale, the Inquisition maintained at extravagant cost the dual secular-spiritual concept of society so characteristic of the Middle Ages and so repugnant to every modern idea. Moreover, having to deal with the Moslems on Spanish soil, the Spaniards had built crusades and the crusading temperament into their basic experience, where it actively remained long after the collapse of the other crusaders' states in Asia Minor. This fact had much to do with the failure to develop a banking and commercial class comparable to those existing elsewhere, for the chronic persecutions of the Moors and Jews deprived the kingdom of its most energetic and experienced businessmen. Banking services tended to be performed in very large part by foreigners, and Spanish wealth quickly found its way to places outside the realm. The monarchy's role in all such matters was conceived in a highly paternal and "illiberal" way, and laissez faire was just as unacceptable in economic life as was freethinking in religion.

This royal paternalism was especially notable in colonial affairs and shows a striking contrast to the permissive policies which allowed so wide a latitude of local autonomy in the English colonies. The royal houses of Spain and Portugal had been the first in the race for overseas colonies—the crown and grandees having been rather more oriented to "glory" than to "success"— but they in time found themselves outstripped by the English and Dutch and saw the fruits of their glory dribble away to London, Antwerp, and other successful centers of banking. This lack

of economic efficiency was not unconnected with the very administrative efficiency that permitted the Spanish crown to maintain such rigid control over its American dependencies. The degree of supervision exercised over colonial life by the Council of the Indies at Madrid does not seem to have been sufficiently appreciated.[38] Add to this the power of the church, and the resulting setting may be seen as one hardly favorable to wide-scale enterprise. Even the establishment of great plantations in Cuba, Santo Domingo, Brazil, and elsewhere in the seventeenth and eighteenth centuries did not mean unmitigated capitalism, as would be the case under the free skies of Virginia, Maryland, and the Carolinas. The great difference lay in the fact that other institutional concerns were present besides those involved with production.[39]

No such dramatic transvaluation of social norms as occurred in seventeenth-century England to accommodate the new standards of the bourgeoisie would ever take place in Spain. And nowhere could the chivalric concept of the

[38] Although the crown was not at all liberal in the actual financing of the early explorations, royal supervision in every other respect was simply a matter of policy; not only were all major officials crown-appointed but "routine activities were often regulated in detail by the voluminous legislation of a paternalistic monarchy," according to C. H. Haring. "No large project or change of official policy might be undertaken, no unaccustomed expenditure might be made from the royal treasury except in time of emergency, without first referring it to the Council of the Indies for approval." See C. H. Haring, *The Spanish Empire in America* (New York: Oxford University Press, 1947), pp. 120–23.

[39] The quasifeudal nature of Spanish landholding, carried over to the colonies, is described in *ibid.*, pp. 258–59. "A minority of fortunate landowning creoles lived much like their Spanish ancestors, imbued with similar aristocratic prejudices, and with similar improvidence and lack of foresight." *Ibid.*, p. 258.

hidalgo, the man who did no work with his hands and to whom business was contemptible, persist so tenaciously as in Spain and the Spanish colonies.[40] There, on the other hand, the concept of private property, peculiarly appropriate to the demands of an entrepreneurial class, would not develop with nearly the elaborateness that characterized it elsewhere. In at least one area—the master-slave relationship—this fact had very important consequences. For all the cruelty and bigotry of this quasimedieval society, the balance between property rights and human rights stood in a vastly different ratio—much to the advantage of human rights—from that seen in the American South.

In the colonies of Latin America we are thus able to think of the church, the civil authority, and the property concerns of the planter-adventurer as constituting distinct and not always harmonious interests in society. The introduction of slaves into the colonies brought much discomfort to the royal conscience; when the trade in Negroes became of consequence, the monarchs gave it their growing concern, and it never occurred to them not to retain over it a heavy measure of royal control. Charles V, who had granted the first license to transport Negroes in quantity directly from Africa to America, turned against the principle late in his reign and ordered the freeing of all African slaves in Spanish America.[41] In 1570 King Sebastian of Portugal issued an order to the colonists of Brazil which

forbade the taking of slaves except by "licit means," specifying that in any case they must be registered within two months or all authority over them be forfeited.[42] A century later it had become clear to the monarchs of Spain that both the demands of their colonists for labor and the revenue needs of the royal treasury required that the trade in African Negroes be accorded full legitimacy. But the king in 1679 still had to be assured "whether meetings of theologians and jurists have been held to determine whether it is licit to buy them as slaves and make asientos for them and whether there are any authors who have written on this particular question."[43] Again we find the king of Spain, in a *Real Cédula* of 1693, commanding the captain-general of Cuba to call upon all masters of slaves, and to "say to them in my name that they must not, for whatever motive, rigorously tighten the wage they receive from their slaves, for having been tried in other places, it has proved inconvenient harming the souls of these people. . . ." Since slavery was "a sufficient sorrow without at the same time suffering the distempered rigor of their master," any excesses were to be punished by applying "the necessary remedy."[44] The monarchy made terms when it met with the full force of this new enterprise—new at least with respect to its proportions. But the energy with which it imposed its own terms was drawn both from the ancient sanctions regarding servitude and from

---

[40] On *hidalguismo*, "the sense of nobility," see Américo Castro, *The Structure of Spanish History*, trans. Edmund L. King (Princeton: Princeton University Press, 1954), pp. 628–35.

[41] Haring, *Spanish Empire*, p. 219. It has to be added that one year after Charles' retirement to the monastery of Saint-Just in 1558, slavery and the slave trade was resumed.

[42] Rinchon, *La traite et l'esclavage*, pp. 140–41. This order applied to native Indians.

[43] "Résumé of the Origin of the Introduction of Slaves into Spanish America" (1685), quoted in Elizabeth Donnan, *Documents Illustrative of the History of the Slave Trade to America* (Washington: Carnegie Institution, 1930 ff.), I, 346.

[44] Quoted in Tannenbaum, *Slave and Citizen*, p. 89.

the traditional force of the crown's institutional prerogatives.

The other item in this equation was the presence of a powerful church with needs of its own. A considerable measure of its power as an institution naturally depended upon its position of leadership in matters touching the morals of society. The maintenance of that leadership required the church as a matter of course to insist on a dominant role in the formulation of all policy which might bear on the morality of the slave system and have consequences for the Faith. The terms it made with slavery paralleled those made by the crown and exhibited the same ambiguities. In effect, the church with one hand condemned slavery and with the other came to an understanding with it as a labor system. Its doctrine asserted in general that the practice of slavery and the slave trade was fraught with perils for those of the faithful who engaged in it and that they stood, at innumerable points, in danger of mortal sin. The immoralities connected with the trade compelled again and again the attention of church writers, and it was in this sense that the Franciscan Father Thomas Mercado had denounced it in 1587 as fostering "two thousand falsehoods, a thousand robberies, and a thousand deceptions."[45] More temperately summarizing the most learned opinion of his age, Germain Fromageau, a doctor of the Sorbonne, declared in 1698 that "one can neither, in surety of conscience, buy nor sell Negroes, because in such commerce there is injustice."[46] In any case, as an eighteenth-century prelate, Cardinal Gerdil, categorically stated, "Slavery is not to be understood as conferring on one man the same power

over another that men have over cattle. . . . For slavery does not abolish the natural equality of man. . . ."[47]

At the same time the church, in its character as an institution, functioning in the society of men, could not afford to proscribe slavery as unconditionally immoral, if for no other reason than that the majority of Christendom's overseas dominions would thus have been stained in depravity—a position which, for almost any procedural purposes, would have been absurdly untenable. Its casuists, therefore, readily found sanctions in tradition whereby slavery might exist under the church's official favor. Thus the Council of the Indies, after meetings with theologians, jurists, and prelates of the church, assured the king of Spain that

there cannot be any doubt as to the necessity of those slaves for the support of the kingdom of the Indies . . .; and [that] with regard to the point of conscience, [the trade may continue] because of the reasons expressed, the authorities cited, and its long-lived and general custom in the kingdoms of Castile, America, and Portugal, without any objection on the part of his Holiness or ecclesiastical state, but rather with the tolerance of all of them.[48]

The Jesuits would labor excessively in places such as Brazil to mitigate the evils of slavery; the papacy itself would denounce it in various ways in 1462, 1537, 1639, 1741, 1815, and 1839; at the same time the church "could no more have proclaimed the abolition of slavery," as Fr. Rinchon remarks, "than it could have imposed the eight-hour day or the rate of family incomes."[49]

---

[45] *Ibid.*, p. 62.

[46] From *La dictionnaire des cas de conscience*, quoted in Rinchon, *La traite et l'esclavage*, p. 148.

[47] James J. Fox, "Ethical Aspect of Slavery," in Charles G. Hebermann and others (eds.), *The Catholic Encyclopedia* (New York: Encyclopedia Press, 1913), XIV, 40.

[48] "Minutes of the Council of the Indies" (1685), quoted in Donnan, *Documents*, I, 351.

[49] *La traite et l'esclavage*, p. 158.

Yet in the very act of certifying the practice of slavery, in admitting its economic necessity, and even in holding slaves of its own, the church had, as it were, bargained with the system so that its own institutional needs and its prerogatives in matters of morality might still be maintained at the visible maximum and protected against infringement. The effects of this determination are overwhelmingly evident in the actual workings of slavery in Latin America. They are evident, indeed, at nearly every point in the traffic itself, for the potent hand of the church fell upon the sequence of events long before it terminated in America. It had missionaries on the soil of Africa, proselytizing among the natives and operating great establishments there. It was highly sensitive to the possibility that the Faith, in the course of the trade, might be corrupted.[50] In 1685 the Inquisition, faced with an impending

transaction which would turn over a portion of the trade to the Dutch, sternly urged the king that,

in case any contract is made with the Dutch, you will please to ordain that all necessary orders be provided and issued for the utmost care of the conservation and purity of our Holy Catholic Faith, because one can very justly fear that if the negroes come by way of the Dutch, they may be greatly imbued with doctrines and errors ... and ... this council should advise the inquisitors to exercise special vigilance.[51]

The contract was eventually made, but the Dutchman who received it was forced to take ten Capuchin monks to his African factories for the religious instruction of the Negroes, to support them, and to allow them to preach in public.[52] The Inquisition had a tribunal in the Indies which would punish any "heretic" (meaning Dutch or Flemish) who tried to introduce his creed there during the course of business.[53] Every slave bound for Brazil was to receive baptism and religious instruction before being put on board,[54] and upon reaching port every ship was boarded by a friar who examined the conscience, faith, and religion of the new arrivals. The friar was there "to investigate the individual's orthodoxy just as today the immigrant's health and race are investigated."[55]

It would be misleading to imply that

---

[50] During the first quarter of the sixteenth century there was much royal soul-searching over the problem of what importation policy was most consistent with both the need for slaves and the need for maintaining the purity of the Indies in matters of faith. Nicolas Ovando, the new governor of Española, was forbidden in 1501 to bring in any but *ladinos* (Iberian Christian Negroes). Isabella suspended importations entirely in 1504; in 1505 Ferdinand, after Isabella's death, reintroduced importations of *ladinos*. In 1510, shipments of *bozales* (African Negroes not Christianized but as yet unsullied by Mohammedanism or Judaism) began being made from the Lisbon slave market—this class having been originally excluded. It was never permitted to come to a choice, however, between admitting or not admitting "infidel" slaves (Jewish or Mohammedan; they were always rigidly excluded); it was rather the question of whether they should be fully Christianized before or after importation to the Indies. When the first asiento was made in 1517 for shipments direct from Africa, the matter was automatically settled. José Antonio Saco, *Historia de la esclavitud de la raza africana en el Nuevo Mundo, y en especial en los paises américo-hispanos* (Barcelona: J. Jepus, 1879), pp. 61–69.

[51] "Report of the Council of the Inquisition to the King" (1685), quoted in Donnan, *Documents*, I, 339.
[52] "Minutes of the Council of the Indies" (1685), *ibid.*, pp. 348–49.
[53] *Ibid.*, p. 348. No one, according to the report, had hitherto been rash enough to attempt this.
[54] "[They] are catechised and receive baptism, a rite which has been found to console their minds under their unhappy circumstances." Carl Berns Wadström, *An Essay on Colonisation* ... (London: Darton & Harvey, 1794), p. 125.
[55] Gilberto Freyre, *The Masters and the Slaves* (New York: Knopf, 1946), p. 41.

slavery in the colonies drew its total character from the powerful influence of the church. But it may be asserted that the church, functioning in its capacity as guardian of morals, was responsible for whatever human rights were conserved for the slave within the grim system. What it came to was that three formidable interests—the crown, the planter, and the church—were deeply concerned with the system, that these concerns were in certain ways competing, and that the product of this balance of power left its profound impress on the actual legal and customary sanctions governing the status and treatment of slaves. These sanctions were by no means what they would have been had it been left to the planting class alone to develop them systematically with reference only to the requirements of a labor system. Let us examine them, taking the same rough categories used with respect to the American South: term of servitude, marriage and the family, police and discipline, and property and other civil rights.

Neither in Brazil nor in Spanish America did slavery carry with it such precise and irrevocable categories of perpetual servitude, *"durante vita"* and "for all generations," as in the United States. The presumption in these countries, should the status of a colored person be in doubt, was that he was free rather than a slave.[56] There were in fact innumerable ways whereby a slave's servitude could be brought to an end. The chief of these was the very considerable fact that he might buy his own freedom. The Negro in Cuba or Mexico had the right to have his price declared and could, if he wished, purchase himself in installments. Slaves escaping to Cuba to embrace Catholicism were protected by a special royal order of 1733 which was twice reissued. A slave unduly punished might be set at liberty by the magistrate. In Brazil the slave who was the parent of ten children might legally demand his or her freedom.[57] The medieval Spanish code had made a slave's service terminable under any number of contingencies—if he denounced cases of treason, murder, counterfeiting, or the rape of a virgin, or if he performed various other kinds of meritorious acts. Though all such practices did not find their way into the seventeenth- and eighteenth-century legal arrangements of Latin America, much of their spirit was perpetuated in the values, customs, and social expectations of that later period. It is important to appreciate the high social approval connected with the freeing of slaves. A great variety of happy family events—the birth of a son, the marriage of a daughter, anniversaries, national holidays—provided the occasion, and their ceremonial was frequently marked by the manumission of one or more virtuous servitors. It was considered a pious act to accept the responsibility of becoming godfather to a slave child, implying the moral obligation to arrange eventually for its freedom. Indeed, in Cuba and Brazil such freedom might be purchased for a nominal sum at the baptismal font.[58] All such manumissions had the strong approval of both church and state and

---

[56] "In the Cuban market freedom was the only commodity which could be bought untaxed; every negro against whom no one had proved a claim of servitude was deemed free. . . ." William Law Mathieson, *British Slavery and Its Abolition* (London: Longmans, Green, 1926), pp. 37–38.

[57] Johnston, *Negro in the New World*, p. 89.
[58] What I have said in this paragraph is virtually a paraphrase of the information which Mr. Tannenbaum has collected and so skilfully summarized on pp. 50, 53–54, 57–58 of *Slave and Citizen*.

were registered gratis by the government.[59]

In extending its moral authority over men of every condition, the church naturally insisted on bringing slave unions under the holy sacraments. Slaves were married in church and the banns published; marriage was a sacred rite and its sanctity protected in law. In the otherwise circumspect United States, the only category which the law could apply to conjugal relations between slaves—or to unions between master and slave—was concubinage. But concubinage, in Latin America, was condemned as licentious, adulterous, and immoral; safeguards against promiscuity were provided in the law,[60] and in Brazil the Jesuits labored mightily to regularize the libertinage of the master class by the sacrament of Christian marriage.[61] Moreover, slaves owned by different masters were not to be hindered from marrying, nor could they be kept separate after marriage. If the estates were distant, the wife was to go with her husband, and a fair price was to be fixed by impartial persons for her sale to the husband's master.[62] A slave might, without legal interference, marry a free person. The children of such a marriage, if the mother were free, were themselves free, inasmuch as children followed the condition of their mother.[63]

The master's disciplinary authority never had the completeness that it had in the United States, and nowhere did he enjoy powers of life and death over the slave's body. Under the Spanish code of 1789 slaves might be punished for failure to perform their duties, with prison, chains, or lashes, "which last must not exceed the number of twenty-five, and those must be given them in such manner as not to cause any contusion or effusion of blood: which punishments cannot be imposed on slaves but by their masters or the stewards."[64] For actual crimes a slave was to be tried in an ordinary court of justice like any free person,[65] and, conversely, the murder of a slave was to be prosecuted just as that of a free man would be.[66] Excessive punishments of slaves—causing "contusion, effusion of blood, or mutilation of members"— by plantation stewards were themselves punishable. Although gross violations of the law occurred, the law here was anything but the dead letter it proved to be in our own Southern states. In the important administrative centers of both Brazil and the Spanish colonies there was an official protector of slaves,

---

[59] Johnston, *Negro in the New World*, p. 42.

[60] "The master of slaves must not allow the unlawful intercourse of the two sexes, but must encourage matrimony." Spanish slave code of 1789, quoted in *ibid.*, p. 44. Although slaves were allowed "to divert themselves innocently" on holy days, the males were to be kept apart from the females. *Ibid.*, p. 44.

[61] Freyre, *The Masters and the Slaves*, p. 85.

[62] Johnston, *Negro in the New World*, pp. 44–45. A diocesan synod of 1680 in Cuba issued weighty regulations on this subject which were supposed to supplement and have equal force with civil law. "Constitution 5 established that 'marriage should be free' and ordered that 'no master prohibit his slaves from marriage, nor impede those who cohabit therein, because we have found that many masters with little fear of God and in grave danger of their consciences, proscribe their slaves from marrying or impede their cohabitation with their married partners, with feigned pretexts'; and also prohibited 'that they go away to sell them outside the city, without that they take together husband

and wife.'" Ortiz, *Los Negros esclavos*, p. 349. The church even made some concessions here to African tribal marriage arrangements, to the extent that a slave with multiple wives might— if the first-married wife's identity could not be ascertained—pick out the one he preferred and have his marriage with her solemnized under the sacraments. *Ibid.*, p. 349.

[63] Tannenbaum, *Slave and Citizen*, p. 56.

[64] Johnston, *Negro in the New World*, p. 45.

[65] The sentence, however, was apparently to be executed by the master. *Ibid.*, p. 45.

[66] *Ibid.*, pp. 45–46. The code does not make it clear whether the penalty would be the same against the slave's master as against another person. But in any case the murderer, master or other, was liable to prosecution.

known variously as the syndic, pro-curador, or attorney-general, under whose jurisdiction came all matters relating to the treatment of slaves. His functions were nurtured by a well-articulated system of communications. The priests who made the regular rounds of the estates giving Christian instruction were required to obtain and render to him information from the slaves regarding their treatment, and investigation and the necessary steps would be taken accordingly. These priests were answerable to no one else for their activities. In addition, the magistrates were to appoint "persons of good character" to visit the estates thrice yearly and conduct similar inquiries on similar matters. A further ingenious provision in the Spanish code caused all fines levied, for mistreat-ment and other excesses against slaves, to be divided up three ways: one-third went to the judge, one-third to the informer, and one-third to the "Fines Chest." Finally, the attorney-general and the justices themselves were made accountable to the crown for failure to carry out these ordinances. An implicit royal threat underlay all this; should the fines not have the desired effect and should the ordinances continue to be broken, "I," His Majesty promised, "will take my measures accordingly."[67]

As was implied in his right to purchase his own freedom, the slave in the Spanish and Portuguese colonies had the right to acquire and hold property. This meant something spe-

cific; in Brazil a master was obliged by law to give liberty to his slaves on all Sundays and holidays—which totaled 85 in the year—during which a slave might work for himself and accumulate money for his purchase price,[68] and the Spanish code of 1789 provided that slaves must be allowed two hours each day in which to be employed in "oc-cupations for their own advantage."[69] In many places slaves were encouraged to hire themselves out regularly (there were skilled artisans among them as well as ordinary laborers), an arrange-ment which was to the advantage of both the master and the slave himself, since the latter was allowed to keep a percentage of the wage. Slaves even in rural areas might sell the produce of their gardens and retain the proceeds.[70] For all practical purposes slavery here had become, as Mr. Tannenbaum puts it, a contractual arrangement: it could be wiped out by a fixed purchase price and leave no taint. "There may have been no written contract between the two parties, but the state behaved, in effect, as if such a contract did exist, and used its powers to enforce it."[71] It was a contract in which the master owned a man's labor but not the man.

---

[67] Ibid., pp. 45–46. The liberal code of 1789 was not uniformly enforced at first; Ortiz, indeed, insists—contradicting the earlier his-torian, Saco—that it was widely evaded until well into the nineteenth century. The colonists, however, eventually had to succumb to pressure from the Spanish government, and by the 1840's the code had been written into local police regulations in Cuba. Ortiz, Los Negros esclavos, pp. 363–64, 70. A full translation of the code in its municipal form is in British and Foreign State Papers, 1842–1843, XXXI (London, 1858), 393–99.

[68] It was not even uncommon for ex-slaves who had thus acquired their freedom to become actual slave-holders on their own account. John-ston, Negro in the New World, p. 90.

[69] Ibid., p. 44.

[70] Tannenbaum, Slave and Citizen, pp. 58–61.

[71] Ibid., p. 55. A practical application of this contractual aspect of slavery was the institution of coartación which developed in Cuba in the eighteenth century. This was an arrangement whereby the slave might buy his freedom in installments. He would first have his price declared (if he and his master disagreed, the local courts would determine it), whereupon he made his first payment. After that point, the price could not be changed, and he could at the same time change masters at will, the new master simply paying the balance of his price. See Hubert H. S. Aimes, "Coartación: A Span-ish Institution for the Advancement of Slaves into Freedmen," Yale Review, XVII (February, 1909), 412–31.

As for the privileges of religion, it was here not a question of the planting class "permitting" the slave, under rigidly specified conditions, to take part in divine worship. It was rather a matter of the church's insisting—under its own conditions—that masters bring their slaves to church and teach them religion. Such a man as the Mississippi planter who directed that the gospel preached to his slaves should be "in its original purity and simplicity" would have courted the full wrath of the Latin church. A Caribbean synod of 1622, whose *sanctiones* had the force of law, made lengthy provisions for the chastisement of masters who prevented their slaves from hearing Mass or receiving instruction on feast days.[72] Here the power of the Faith was such that master and slave stood equally humbled before it. "Every one who has slaves," according to the first item in the Spanish code, "is obliged to instruct them in the principles of the Roman Catholic religion and in the necessary truths in order that the slaves may be baptized within the (first) year of their residence in the Spanish dominions."[73] Certain assumptions were implied therein which made it impossible that the slave in this culture should ever quite be considered as mere property,

either in law or in society's customary habits of mind. These assumptions, perpetuated and fostered by the church, made all the difference in his treatment by society and its institutions, not only while a slave, but also if and when he should cease to be one. They were, in effect, that he was a man, that he had a soul as precious as any other man's, that he had a moral nature, that he was not only as susceptible to sin but also as eligible for grace as his master—that master and slave were brothers in Christ.

The Spaniards and Portuguese had the widespread reputation by the eighteenth century—whatever may have been the reasons—for being among all nations the best masters of slaves.[74] The standards for such a judgment cannot, of course, be made too simple. Were slaves "physically maltreated" in those countries? They

---

[72] Fr. Cipriano de Utrera, "El Concilio Dominicano de 1622, con una introducción histórica," *Boletin eclesiástico de la Arquidiócesis de Santo Domingo*, 1938–39, p. 40.

[73] Johnston, *Negro in the New World*, p. 43. Herbert Klein's excellent monograph, "Slavery in Cuba and Virginia: A Comparative History of the First Hundred Years" (M.A. thesis, University of Chicago, 1959), provides a wealth of detail and specific examples, all of which tend to confirm, in a case-study setting, the general assertions of the present work as well as those of Tannenbaum and Johnston. This is particularly true with regard to the ways in which royal and ecclesiastical power was exercised in the Spanish colonies.

[74] "The Spaniards, Portuguese, and Danes are undoubtedly the best masters of slaves," wrote Carl Berns Wadström in 1794. The English and Dutch were in his opinion the worst. *Essay on Colonization*, p. 151 n. The Portuguese and Brazilians "rival the Spaniards for first place in the list of humane slave-holding nations," writes Sir Harry Johnston. "Slavery under the flag of Portugal (or Brazil) or of Spain was not a condition without hope, a life in hell, as it was for the most part in the British West Indies and, above all, Dutch Guiana and the Southern United States." *Negro in the New World*, p. 89. "The Spaniards themselves maltreated their slaves less than did the planters of the Antilles or of North America at a later period." P. Chemin-Dupontès, *Les Petites Antilles* (Paris: E. Guilmoto, 1909), quoted in *ibid.*, p. 42 n. Moreau de Saint-Méry, writing of the slaves of Spanish Santo Domingo, remarks, "To their masters they are more like companions than slaves." *Topographical and Political Description of the Spanish Part of Saint-Domingo* (Philadelphia, 1796), quoted in *ibid.*, p. 42 n. The French planters of Haiti and the Americans of Georgia both complained that the Spanish code of 1789 would (and did) induce their slaves to escape to the Spanish dominions. *Ibid.*, p. 46.

could, conceivably, have been treated worse than in our own nineteenth-century South without altering the comparison, for even in cruelty the relationship was between man and man.[75] Was there "race prejudice"? No one could be more arrogantly proud of his racial purity than the Spaniard of Castile, and theoretically there were rigid caste lines, but the finest Creole families, the clergy, the army, the professions, were hopelessly

"defiled" by Negro blood;[76] the taboos were that vague in practice. Was there squalor, filth, widespread depression of the masses? Much more so than with us—but there it was the class system and economic "underdevelopment," rather than the color barrier, that made the difference. In these countries the concept of "beyond the pale" applied primarily to beings outside the Christian fold rather than to those beyond the color line.[77]

We are not, then, dealing with a society steeped, like our own, in traditions of political and economic democracy. We are concerned only with a special and peculiar kind of fluidity—

[75] Most writers and students do seem to think that the system was "milder" in the Spanish colonies and in Brazil, but nobody has ever claimed that it was a life of ease and comfort. An interesting summary of observers' opinions on this and other points is Margaret V. Nelson, "The Negro in Brazil as Seen through the Chronicles of Travellers, 1800–1868," *Journal of Negro History*, XXX (April, 1945), 203–18. See also James F. King, "Negro History in Continental Spanish America," *Journal of Negro History*, XXIX (January, 1944), 7–23. "The fact is," as Donald Pierson remarks, "that slavery in Brazil [and, one might add, in Spanish America as well] was both mild *and* severe." The severe side of it, indeed, is discussed with very disagreeable particulars by Arthur Ramos in his *Negro in Brazil* (Washington: Associated Publishers, 1939), pp. 20–22. It could further be pointed out that comparisons, when made, were made most frequently with the British colonies of the eighteenth century, especially the British West Indies. In the United States, on the other hand, by (say) 1850, slavery in a "physical" sense was in general, probably, quite mild. However, even if it had been milder here than anywhere else in the Western Hemisphere, it would still be missing the point to make the comparison in terms of physical comfort. In one case we would be dealing with the cruelty of man to man, and, in the other, with the care, maintenance, and indulgence of men toward creatures who were legally and morally *not* men—not in the sense that Christendom had traditionally defined man's nature. It is for our purposes, in short, the *primary* relationship that matters. Masters and slaves in Brazil, according to João Ribeiro, "were united into families, if not by law, at least by religion." Quoted in Donald Pierson, *Negroes in Brazil* (Chicago: University of Chicago Press, 1942), p. 81.

[76] Even the legendary corruption of the Spanish upper classes was apparently biracial in the New World. Beye Cisneros of Mexico City, during the course of the debates on the Spanish constitution of 1811, declared, "I have known mulattoes who have become counts, marquises, *oidores*, canons, colonels, and knights of the military orders through intrigue, bribery, perjury, and falsification of public books and registers; and I have observed that those who have reached these positions and distinctions by reprehensible means, have been granted the corresponding honors without repugnance, despite their mixed blood. . . ." James F. King, "The Colored Castes and American Representation in the Cortes of Cádiz," *Hispanic American Historical Review*, XXXIII (February, 1953), 56. The looseness of practice which permitted such frequent "passings-over" was actually commended by the acting Captain-General of Venezuela in a dispatch to the Secretary of State for the Indies in 1815; "The State greatly gains," he wrote, "for the increase of the upper class, even though it be artificial, is to its interest." J. F. King, "A Royalist View of the Colored Castes in the Venezuelan War of Independence," *ibid.*, XXXIII (November, 1953), 528. See also Richard M. Morse, "The Negro in São Paulo, Brazil," *Journal of Negro History*, XXXVIII (July, 1953), 290–306.

[77] "The thing that barred an immigrant in those days was heterodoxy; the blot of heresy upon the soul and not any racial brand upon the body." Freyre, *The Masters and the Slaves*, pp. 40–41.

that of their slave systems—and in this alone lay a world of difference. It was a fluidity that permitted a transition from slavery to freedom that was smooth, organic, and continuing. Manumitting slaves, carrying as it did such high social approval, was done often, and the spectacle of large numbers of freedmen was familiar to the social scene. Such opportunities as were open to any member of the depressed classes who had talent and diligence were open as well to the ex-slave and his descendants. Thus color itself was no grave disability against taking one's place in free society; indeed, Anglo-Saxon travelers in nineteenth-century Brazil were amazed at the thoroughgoing mixture of races there. "I have passed black ladies in silks and jewelry," wrote Thomas Ewbank in the 1850's, "with male slaves in livery behind them. . . . Several have white husbands. The first doctor of the city is a colored man; so is the President of the Province."[78] Free Negroes had the same rights before the law as whites, and it was possible for the most energetic of their numbers to take immediate part in public and professional life. Among the Negroes and mulattoes of Brazil and the Spanish colonies—aside from the

swarming numbers of skilled craftsmen —were soldiers, officers, musicians, poets, priests, and judges. "I am accustomed," said a delegate to the Cortes of Cádiz in 1811, "to seeing many engaged in all manner of careers."[79]

All such rights and opportunities existed *before* the abolition of slavery; and thus we may note it as no paradox that emancipation, when it finally did take place, was brought about in all these Latin-American countries "without violence, without bloodshed, and without civil war."[80]

The above set of contrasts, in addition to what it may tell us about slavery itself, could also be of use for a more general problem, that of the conservative role of institutions in any social structure. The principle has been observed in one setting where two or more powerful interests were present to limit each other; it has been tested negatively in a setting where a single interest was free to develop without such limits. The latter case was productive of consequences which could hardly be called, in the classical sense of the term, "conservative."

---

[78] *Life in Brazil, or the Land of the Cocoa and the Palm* (New York: Harper, 1856), p. 267.

[79] King, "The Colored Castes and American Representation in the Cortes of Cádiz," p. 59. See also Irene Diggs, "Color in Colonial Spanish America," *Journal of Negro History*, XXXVIII (October, 1953), 403–26.
[80] Tannenbaum, *Slave and Citizen*, p. 106.

SIDNEY W. MINTZ

Slavery and Emergent Capitalisms

Sidney W. Mintz is Chairman of Yale University's Department of Anthropology and general editor of the Yale Caribbean Series. He is the author of Worker in the Cane: A Puerto Rican Life History *(1960) and of many articles on Caribbean society. The following selection was originally published in the* American Anthropologist *as a review essay of Stanley Elkins'* Slavery. *It is reprinted here under a title suggested by the author.*

A good book dealing with slavery in the Americas is always welcome. The enduring passion in American historiography to treat the War between the States almost exclusively as a military and political conflict has often obscured the slaves, their owners, and the ancient institution which joined them. Elkins' book on slavery is a good one, and in addition to all enlightenments, it may refresh the memories of some soldiering intellectuals badly in need of refreshment.

But the appropriateness of this book for students of culture goes beyond

questions of historiography. Slavery is more than a matter of economics, more than solely a means of controlling the labor of others. It was one of man's most important inventions, and it has been part of the institutional system of myriad societies. Tylor wrote: "The greatest of all divisions, that between freeman and slave, appears as soon as the barbaric warrior spares the life of his enemy when he has him down, and brings him home to drudge for him and till the soil."[1] That "greatest of all divisions" involves in every historical instance a way of life, a conception of the human condition, an ideology of society, and a set of economic arrangements, in short, a cultural apparatus,

From Sidney W. Mintz, "Review of Stanley M. Elkins' *Slavery*," reproduced by permission of the American Anthropological Association from the *American Anthropologist*, LXIII: 579–87 (June, 1961), and the author.

[1] *Anthropology* (London: Watts and Co., 1946), II, 156.

by which slaves and masters are related. The economic arrangements which bound slave and master postulated that the master had the right to appropriate something which was the slave's—his time, or the products of his labor, his skill, often his children, perhaps his life. All definitions of the slave condition contain as a nucleus the idea of the property rights of one person in another. In certain circumstances, such rights take the form of capital. For the anthropologist, whether or not the slave is a capital good, a source of capital accumulation, a commodity, or something else and beyond these, is very relevant. Kroeber has written that "The fundamental thing about culture . . . [might be] the way in which men relate themselves to one another by relating themselves to their cultural material."[2] The relationships between slaves and masters in any particular historical instance are an illustration. As for capital, it may be viewed concretely, as some store used to undertake fresh production, or as a social aspect of the productive process. ". . . capital is not a thing," states Marx,[3] "but a social relation between persons, established through the instrumentality of things." And he adds, in a peculiarly relevant footnote: "A negro is a negro. In certain circumstances he becomes a slave. A mule is a machine for spinning cotton. Only under certain circumstances does it become capital. Outside these circumstances it is no more capital than gold is intrinsically money, or sugar the price of sugar. . . . Capital is a social relation of production." The similarity between Kroeber's definition of culture and Marx's definition of capital springs

from no common intent other than to describe something in human behavior. Both definitions indicate the relevance of the phenomenon of slavery for anthropology. Especially important is the degree to which a particular mode of slavery is primarily economic, or embedded within a code of behavior such that the economic rationale is submerged or secondary. All slavery may be slavery, but not all slaveries are the same, economically or culturally.

Through slavery, human beings, their labor, their lives—that is, their production and reproduction—are transformed into things. In capitalistic societies these things are commodities; in part-capitalistic societies they are part-commodities. Where the kind of social and technical organization is such that it is not possible readily to appropriate a worthwhile portion of the product of others by enslavement, the goals of slavery, when it occurs, will not be directed to the maximization of profit. Where servitude is total, the kind and degree of appropriation will vary, according to what the level of technical development and the accompanying institutional apparatus, including the economic system, make possible.

In this hemisphere introduced Western slavery lasted nearly four centuries; it involved the enslavement, unremitting labor, and, often, violent death, of some ten to twenty million persons. Those numbers are merely the supposed minimum and maximum of creatures forcibly enslaved and do not include those others born into slavery. This was just possibly the greatest acculturation event in human history, beyond its spectacular significance demographically. It is still not enough noticed how mightily the labor of the slaves contributed to the growth

[2] *Anthropology* (New York: Harcourt, 1948), p. 68.

[3] *Capital* (New York: International Publishers, 1939), I, 791.

of industrial capitalism; and even Elkins curiously neglects the work of Eric Williams[4] and others on this theme.

An institution moribund or dead in the mother countries was spread through the subtropical lowlands of the New World, particularly on the Atlantic periphery, with varying vigor and at different times. In the Danish, Dutch, English, French, Portuguese, Spanish, and Swedish colonies, and in the United States, the slave trade and slavery played a key role in the economic development of the capitalist metropolises. Edgar Thompson[5] has shown how this Western industrial slavery, slavery within capitalism, was basic to a pioneer institution, the plantation. The developmental problem was one of bringing into production tracts of fertile land available for the asking, or little more, but in the absence of an adequate labor supply. The need and economic advisability of such development grew swiftly as plantation products were transformed from the luxuries of the rich into the daily necessities—sugar, coffee and the like—of the proletarian poor in the mother countries.

But from the point of view of the entrepreneur, free labor would not do for plantation development, since land was free. Freemen provide opportunities for the garnering of entrepreneurial profit when they have no access to the means of production (particularly land), at any price they can pay, and must instead sell their labor at the market price. In the absence of coercion from above, and of organization below, this price is

determined by supply and demand; and, where supply far exceeds demand, the price is low. Such is the situation which that much-neglected encyclopedic ethnologist, H. J. Nieboer, called one of "close [sic] resources."[6] But the pioneer situation prevailing in the New World lowlands was one of ample free land and scarce labor; the entrepreneur could appropriate neither profit from the employment of needful laborers, nor rent from scarce resources. And in contrast Nieboer called this situation one of "open resources." Or as Thompson put it,[7] in one instance two would-be employers chase one laborer; in the other, two would-be laborers chase one employer. The baldness and simplicity of this formula ought not to rule out its usefulness for understanding the economic grounds for slavery in the New World.

Yet not all New World situations gave slaves the same status, used them in the same ways, treated them with equal cruelty or kindness. It is this variation which caught Elkins' eye. Following a critique of American writing on slavery, he is led to ask his central questions. What set slavery in the United States apart from slavery elsewhere in the New World? Was the impact of North American slavery on the slaves' lives and personalities different from that which it had on slaves in other New World countries and colonies, and if so, why? Having asked the questions, Elkins answers them, fully and eloquently. The core of his argument (pp. 37–80) makes fine reading. He contrasts the slavery systems, and the surrounding institutional apparatuses, in the ". . . liberal, Protestant, secularized, capitalist culture of

---

[4] *Capitalism and Slavery* (Chapel Hill: University of North Carolina Press, 1944).

[5] "The Plantation," unpublished doctoral dissertation (Chicago: Department of Sociology, University of Chicago, 1932).

[6] *Slavery as an Industrial System* (The Hague: Martinus Nijhoff, 1900), pp. 420–22.

[7] "The Plantation," p. 21.

America . . . " with the ". . . conservative, paternalistic, Catholic, quasi-
medieval culture of Spain and Portugal
and their New World colonies" (p. 37).
Elkins' omission of the word "capitalist" from this second list of adjectives
is crucial. Having stated his terms, he
finds largely what Frank Tannenbaum[8]
found before him. In North America,
slavery as an industrial system was
able to develop unhampered by pre-
existing institutions and cultural usages
affecting the definition of the slaves'
place in society; in Latin America,
this was not so. In the first case, slaves
as commodities were at their fullest
defined, while in the second, the complete commercialization (read "dehumanization") of man was prevented by
the prior claims of Church, monarchy,
and tradition—that is, by the culture.

In a subsequent portion of his book,
Elkins contrasts the slaves' experience
of slavery in North America with the
concentration camp experience of
Europeans under Nazism, concluding
that, in their effects on personality,
these two historical events share much.
A final chapter compares the abolitionist movement in North America
with that of Britain, and explains differences in the end of slavery in the
British colonies and in North America
in terms of the different positions of
the abolitionists with relation to national institutional frameworks.

In comparing North American
slavery with that of Latin America,
Elkins adds to Tannenbaum's earlier
(1947) treatment. Tannenbaum puts
his emphasis heavily on whether a
particular society ". . . accepted the
doctrine of the moral personality of
the slave and made possible the gradual
achievement of freedom implicit in

such a doctrine,"[9] and on the role of a
universalistic religion—in this case,
Catholicism—in protecting the slaves
from complete dehumanization. Tannenbaum avoids, however, the question
of differing levels of capitalist development within those countries and
colonies which had slavery. In a recent
discussion on the same subject,[10] he
explicitly rejects "economic determinism" as an explanation of the
difference in systems of slavery in Latin
America and in North America. But
while Elkins has put economics into
the argument he also, like Tannenbaum, circumvents critical evidence
on the interplay of economic and
ideological forces. It is a historical
mistake to treat slavery in Latin
America as a single social phenomenon,
even for purposes of broad comparison.
One relevant example is that of Cuba,
of which Elkins might have said more
than he does. William Law Mathieson[11]
wrote:

Spanish slavery in the West Indies was a
century older and lasted considerably longer
than that of any other European Power.
It began and it ended as probably the worst
in the world; but there was an intermediate
period, happily of great length, during which
its reputation for mildness was fully
deserved.

If the institutional framework of the
society was what kept intact the slaves'
moral personalities, what happened
to it in the case of Cuba, at the beginning and at the end? A look at R. R.
Madden[12] will suffice to reveal what
happened in Cuba to those rosy institu-

---

[8] *Slave and Citizen* (New York: Knopf, 1947).

[9] *Ibid.*, p. viii.
[10] "Race Relations in Caribbean Society,"
in V. Rubin, ed., *Caribbean Studies: A Symposium*
(Mona, Jamaica: Institute of Social and Economic Research, 1957), pp. 60–66.
[11] *British Slavery and Its Abolition* (London:
Longmans Green, 1926), p. 34.
[12] *The Island of Cuba* (London: Chas. Gilpin,
1849).

tional arrangements which protected the slaves, once slavery became part of an industrial plantation system, as it had much earlier in the British and French West Indies, in North America, and elsewhere. Institutional restrictions may have hampered the maturation of slave-based agricultural capitalism in Cuba; but that they could not prevent it is painfully clear in the record. In the mid-nineteenth century, Cuban slavery dehumanized the slaves as viciously as had Jamaican or North American slavery.

On the one hand, then, there was in the case of some Latin American societies an economic change which conditioned radical changes in the slaves' status. Yet again, on the other hand, the argument that there was no working tradition of a slave society in the non Catholic New World countries is open to attack. The British West Indies are a good case in point. Tannenbaum and now Elkins argue that in North America there was absent any legal, institutional, or traditional background for slavery, though Elkins is willing to grant (pp. 41, 47) that the Barbadian (and later, Jamaican) slavery experience may have influenced the form slavery took in North America. In fact, there was an English legal, and to some extent even institutional, background for British West Indian and North American slavery. Madden[13] notes that ". . . a commission was appointed by Queen Elizabeth in 1574 to take steps for the manumission of English slaves, even while her Majesty's fleet was ravaging the coast of Africa for negro ones." In 1537, the House of Lords rejected a bill for the manumission of villeins,[14] and there is docu-

mentary evidence, according to the same author, in the form of surveys, court rolls, and manumissions, proving the existence of sixteenth-century villeinage. It is true that the villeins are estimated to have numbered but one per cent of the population, but this meant thousands of persons.

The Rev. G. W. Bridges, a proslavery racist writer of nineteenth-century Jamaica, cannot be entirely discounted when he writes:

The negro slave-code, which, until lately, governed the laboring classes of Jamaica, was originally copied from that of Barbados; and the legislature of that colony resorted, for a precedent, to the ancient villeinage laws, then scarcely extinct on British ground. They copied thence the principles which ruled, and the severity which characterized, the feudal system under the Saxon government.

Not 70 years prior to the settlement of Barbados, a remarkable badge of servitude had been imposed on British subjects, by the statute against vagabonds, which adjudged them, expressly and absolutely, to positive slavery; inflicting violent punishments on the disobedient, stigmatizing runaways by branding, and, for the second offence, decreeing death. The same law empowered the master to rivet an iron ring around the neck of his slave, affixing the penalty of ten pounds upon the person removing it; and it repeats the word *"slave,"* so odious to British ears, no less than 38 times.

Such remained the effective law of England in the year 1553; and it was only 30 years after that period that Barbados fell into the possession of the Lord High Treasurer. The enactments regarding negro slaves in the colonies were therefore, naturally enough, transcribed from these late precedents at home, where the name and character of slavery was thus familiar.[15] (I: 507–508, *The Annals of Jamaica*, London, John Murray, 1827).

In commenting on this quotation, no

---

[13] *A Twelvemonth's Residence in the West Indies* (London: Jas. Cochrane, 1835), II, 131.

[14] E. Lipson, *The Economic History of England* (London: Adam and Chas. Black, 1945), I, 130.

[15] *The Annals of Jamaica* (London: John Murray, 1827), I, 507–8.

less an authority than L. C. Gray concludes: "It appears probable that colonial lawyers seeking precedent for their legislation found it in this statute, as well as in other vagrancy laws."[16]

Slaves had numbered 9 per cent of the population in the Domesday Book, but slave status had been gradually assimilated to villeinage thereafter. Villeinage at its simplest involved an obligation to enforced labor, both regular and extraordinary (the *precariae*), as well as contributions in kind or in money to the lord; normally the villein had no legal security, but some protection in custom and tradition, and in manorial courts. By and large, Elkins does not deal with these data or provide ample evidence that there was no precedent in England for North American slavery. His argument peters out in a footnote (p. 38), where he mentions medieval villeinage in England, noting that "the legal suppression of personality was never present in villeinage." This latter statement comes as no surprise. Slavery of the particular British West Indian, North American, and nineteenth-century Cuban sort probably had no precedent, legal or otherwise, anywhere in modern times.

The question, then, does not seem to hinge on the presence of a tradition in one case and its absence in another, but on the effective transfer of a tradition in one case and its nontransfer—or incomplete transfer—in another. The Spanish colonies in the New World were no more and no less pioneer settlements than were Barbados, Jamaica, and North America. Why did metropolitan institutions travel effectively with the south Europeans, only ineffectively with the north Europeans? It

is hard not to suppose that the economic and political structures of the metropolises, and not only their religious and other ideological systems, were probably important. England's tradition of representative government meant that, like as not, slave laws would be made by slave-owners, and so they were. In the Spanish colonies, such laws emanated from the mother country. But Elsa Goveia shows that when Cuba's slave-owners became politically powerful, as plantation slavery there became capitalistic in a fuller sense, they handily defeated the intent of the 1789 laws designed to ameliorate the slaves' condition, and humanitarian tradition, universalistic religion, and past practice did not prevent them.[17] This was the same year in which free commerce in slaves was decreed by the Spanish Crown for Cuba, Santo Domingo, and Caracas (Venezuela).

Puerto Rico provides a double example of the economic onslaught upon institution and tradition. The Crown invited Puerto Rico to name a representative to the central governing council of the Empire in 1808, a move expressly designed to reduce separatist pressures accompanying the growth of a plantocracy on the island. Don Ramón Power, first delegate to the council, carried 22 propositions with him, intended to give Puerto Rico's merchant and landed classes greater freedom of action. One such proposition lay at the basis of a whole series of forced labor laws, by which freemen squatters on Crown lands were driven by force onto the plantations.[18] These laws were revoked in 1873, at the same time that

---

[16] *History of Agriculture in the Southern United States to 1860* (Washington: The Carnegie Institution, 1933), I, 343.

[17] "The West Indian Slave Laws of the Eighteenth Century," *Revista de Ciencias Sociales*, IV (1960), 81.

[18] See Sidney W. Mintz, "The Role of Forced Labour in Nineteenth Century Puerto Rico," *Caribbean Historical Review*, II (1951).

the emancipation of the slaves was decreed. As for the slaves and their condition in this 65-year period, much the same occurred as in the case of Cuba. A series of repressive laws was passed, more and more limiting the slaves' legal, social, and economic status. These laws were paralleled by a rising tempo of slave revolts and outbreaks on the plantations. Neither physical type nor nonslave status protected the landless Puerto Rican creole from the plantocrats in the period 1808–1873; and José C. Rosario and Justina Carrión reveal how the doctrine of the moral personality of the slave was conveniently forgotten as the plantations expanded.[19] When Herman Merivale compared Puerto Rico and Jamaica in 1839, he was fully justified in writing:

The tropical colonies of Spain were commonwealths in an epoch when those of most other nations were mere factories; they are now rapidly acquiring the degrading characteristics of factories, while ours, we hope, are advancing toward the dignity of commonwealths.[20]

Yet another case worth examining is that of French Saint-Domingue; it is dealt with in a paper by Wallace Katz,[21] which stresses the relationship between metropolitan authority and the local power of the planters. But the cases noted earlier should be sufficient to make the point.

The upshot of these arguments is that there *was* a legal precedent for slavery in the north European colonies,

and that the institutional apparatus of the south European countries did *not* always protect the slaves—or for that matter, the freemen—in their slaveholding colonies. Notable differences between these two kinds of colonial situation were the varying effectiveness of metropolitan political control and the differing rates of emergence of capitalist plantations. Furthermore, the principal powers which had colonies in the New World differed in the degree to which representative or self-government was possible on the local level. Representative government and quasi-autonomous legislatures were apparently firmer in the British colonies than in the French, firmer in the French colonies than in the Spanish.

The slave plantation, producing some basic commodity for the mother country, was a special, emergent capitalist form of industrial organization, which appeared earlier, and with more intensity, in the colonies of the north European powers than in the colonies of Spain. (Omitted here are the earliest Spanish plantation experiments in Santo Domingo, Cuba, and Puerto Rico, which soon disappeared.) Industrial slavery of this sort effected a more complete dehumanization of the slaves than did other forms of slavery. (And, of course, even domestic slavery in Jamaica, Saint-Domingue, or the American South was less crushing in its impact on the individual than field slavery.)

The differentials in growth of the slave plantations in different colonies are to be understood as resulting from different ecologies, differential maturation of metropolitan markets and industries, and different political relationships between creole governing bodies and the metropolitan authorities. The rate of growth of the slave plantation, then, did not hinge on matters of

---

[19] *El Negro* (Rio Piedras, Puerto Rico: University of Puerto Rico, 1940), pp. 113–20.

[20] *Lectures on Colonization and Colonies* (London: Oxford University Press, 1928). See also, Sidney W. Mintz, "Labor and Sugar in Puerto Rico and Jamaica, 1800–1850," *Comparative Studies in Society and History*, I (1959), 273–80.

[21] "Slavery and Caste," *King's Crown Essays*, VI (1959), 13–34.

race, civil liberties, protection of the rights of individuals slave and free, or the presence or absence of one or several religious codes.

The rates at which existing norms of behavior with reference to "social inferiors" were changed or reversed depended to a considerable extent on the power of the planter class in the creole society, and on its capacity to influence or to immobilize political decisions made in the metropolis. The power of the planter class of course varied. But the capital for plantation development usually originated in the metropolis, and the moral force of capital's sacred right to reproduce itself was felt in turn in metropolitan legislatures.

It needs noticing at the same time that the south European countries and their colonies gave up slavery later than did those of northern Europe. Spain's Antillean colonies, Cuba and Puerto Rico, for instance, declared emancipation respectively in 1880 and in 1873 (not in 1867, the date Tannenbaum gives for both.[22]) From this vantage point, it might appear as if the north European powers earlier recognized the moral failure of slavery and responded selflessly. By and large, this does not appear to have been the case; the difference seems to have been more economic and political than purely ideological. Once emancipation was accomplished, moreover, there is a striking similarity between the south European and the north European colonies and countries in their adjustments to freedom. Jamaica, British Guiana, and Trinidad imported Indian indentures and the record of their employment is not pretty. Cuba, having achieved emancipation at last in 1880 (followed by six years of "guardianship"

for the ex-slaves!) imported Chinese— approximately 125,000—with few institutional protections of any sort, and judiciously kept the price of free labor low by massive importations of Haitians and Jamaicans thereafter. W. Kloosterboer[23] has demonstrated that, where slavery came to an end too soon—that is, before the labor pool had increased to a "closed resources" level—various sorts of forced labor arrangements, usually justified by "vagrancy" laws, were put in force.

These laws have lingered longest, not in countries of a particular institutional background, but in those of a particular level of economic and demographic development. A prime example—as south European as one would like—is provided by Harris[24] for Mozambique; Kloosterboer[25] deals with a similar theme for Angola. In much of contemporary Latin America, indigenous peoples are still driven into wage labor by an array of laws which permit no feasible economic alternatives. Would it be too cruel a jest to say that the south European ideology recognized the moral personality of the slaves but could not adjust to the idea of the moral personality of the freedmen? Be that as it may, it does appear true that capitalism matured more rapidly in the colonies of the north European powers. Emancipation appears to have been an aspect of this maturation. Without questioning the motives of the abolitionists, it needs to be asked again whether the growing awareness of the dignity of freedom may not have been accompanied by an equal awareness

---

[22] "Race Relations in Caribbean Society," p.62.

[23] *Involuntary Labour since the Abolition of Slavery* (Leiden, The Netherlands: E. J. Brill, 1960), pp. 191–202.

[24] "Labor Emigration among the Moçambique Thonga," *Africa*, XXIX (1959), 50–65.

[25] *Involuntary Labour since the Abolition of Slavery*, pp. 67–78.

that free workers produce and consume dramatically more than slaves, other things being equal.

An investment in slaves, after all, means that capital is being held in a particularly inelastic form. Whether or not this will be brought home to the slave-owner depends on the degree to which he considers his human chattels an investment. On the plantations, ecological conditions and the nature of the crops grown meant that the slaves were substantially nonproductive—in terms of maximizing a cash profit—for some part of the year. Unlike the wage earners of early capitalism, slaves represented a cost, diminishing capital when they were not working, to the entrepreneur. This helps to explain the truly desperate efforts of slave-owners to increase their profit margins by compelling slaves to grow their own food-stuffs, by enabling them to become artisans, by renting them out in labor gangs, and so on. In the less capitalistic slavery situations in the New World, circumstance minimized the business-man's view, the deliberate purchase of slaves with the intention of expanding production and hence profit, the borrowing of capital at interest in order to buy slaves, and the other practices associated with the developed slave plantation. The very definitions of idleness, stupidity, and even humanity differed accordingly. On the capitalistic slave plantation, humanity was an obstacle to maximization. In other, less economically committed situations, this was not necessarily the case. The degree of social commitment to a capitalistic mode of production based on slavery is an essential aspect of the analysis of slave status. It is for this reason that even in situations where slaves were used for gain, such use alone does not adequately permit predictions about slave status. M. G. Smith's careful and

important institutional comparison of Jamaican and Zaria (Nigeria) slavery[26] fails of its purpose—which was to obviate interpretations ". . . based on economic determinism . . ."—when he notes but does not fully examine such features of Zaria society as its lack of dependence on overseas markets, its stable economy, the religious motivation and military form of enslavement, and so on.

When Elkins turns to compare North American slavery and the concentration camp experience in recent western European history, his treatment is most of all provocative. It seemed effective to this reviewer, especially to the extent that it deals with the shock effects on human personality of certain cruelly repressive episodes, but much less effective as culture-historical analysis. The author is concerned with the stereotype of "Sambo": ". . . docile but irresponsible, loyal but lazy, humble but chronically given to lying and stealing; his behavior was full of infantile silliness and his talk inflated with childish exaggeration . . ." and so on (p. 82). Why, asks Elkins, is this stereotype of the Negro people so strong, and so exclusively North American? He finds his answer in the trauma of enslavement, and it is in this connection that the concentration camps, and the behavior of their inmates, are discussed.

But only for the shortest of time-spans, in cultural terms, was the concentration camp an institution. Its purpose very soon came to be the annihilation of its inmates. The intent of slavery, much to the contrary, was to perpetuate a population in a given status, and to some extent it succeeded. Slaves throughout the Americas, though they never reproduced their own num-

---

[26] "Slavery and Emancipation in Two Societies," *Social and Economic Studies*, III (1954), 239–90.

bers, were born by the millions into slavery. Newborn slaves were enculturated; it would be hard to apply that term to the immates of the concentration camps. Furthermore, it is not proved that this particular stereotype was or is applied in the United States only to the Negro people. In a footnote (p. 83), Elkins refers in another connection to "... the stereotypes of eastern and southern European immigrants that were held by certain classes in this country early in the twentieth century." For an amplification of the stereotypes and more perspective historically, the reviewer suggests a visit (in A.D. 1961) to New York's upper West Side, where the opinions of yesterday's immigrants from Europe may be collected on today's immigrants from Puerto Rico. The obverse of the "Sambo" stereotype is equally ugly and rather more frightening; it held for the Negro slaves as well; it holds for other peoples here as well today. But in spite of these strictures, the sudden juxtaposition of two such superficially unlike bodies of data as those on slavery and on the concentration camps is startling and illuminating. Elkins' own reservations (p. 104) are wise, but his contrast is justifiably daring all the same.

In arguing finally that the North American abolitionists were intransigent and outside the institutional framework, unlike their British opposite numbers, Elkins provides an idea of why the struggle was more bitter and unyielding here than in the case of Britain and her colonies. Two criticisms may be made. The position of the British abolitionists was neither uniform nor wholly conciliatory. Elkins fails to use or to evaluate, for instance, Eric Williams' excellent discussion of this.[27]

He omits as well what may be an important political consideration which is geographical at its roots. The United States alone, of all the great powers, had to fight for the abolition of slavery *within its own national territory*. That it did so—and that its people carry that fight forward to this day with bravery and honor—is admirable, but beside the point. The irreducible conflict, in the case of other nations, was fought by undermining mercantilism, pushing free trade, and shifting power to the industrial capitalists. As Williams indicates, this was accomplished within the metropolis, far from the colonies themselves. The American South, however, was integrated with United States institutions in a way that the British West Indies never were, and never could be, with the institutions of Great Britain. Surely the American struggle might have taken a different shape. But it is worth wondering what the tone of British abolitionism might have been like had like had Jamaica, as it was constituted in the eighteenth and nineteenth centuries, been Wales.

Slavery is gone now from this hemisphere. But the study of the "peculiar institution," as Kenneth Stampp calls it[28] goes on. For anthropologists, the task is nearly as fresh as it ever was. There are questions of Africanisms, and their perpetuation; of race relations; of the culture history of the plantation, and of the culture of the slave-holding countries and colonies. Meanwhile one central question can be asked again and again; how did these societies define man? Malinowski described slavery as

... the denial of all biological freedom except in the self-interest not of the organism but of its master. The slave is also deprived

---

[27] *Capitalism and Slavery*, 178–96.

[28] *The Peculiar Institution* (New York: Knopf, 1956).

of all satisfactions which culture guarantees to a man as the price paid for the trammels it imposes. The slave does not enjoy the protection of the law. His economic behavior is not determined by profits and advantages. He cannot mate according to his choice. He remains outside the law of parentage and kinship. Even his conscience is not his own."[29]

But Malinowski himself observes that, if this be slavery, in many instances the peculiar institution in question must have been something else indeed. This description comes closer, perhaps, to John V. Murra's personal correspondence definition of the real meaning of exploitation—the denial to certain individuals or groups of the conventionalized prerogatives of the human condition, as defined by the culture. It is worth noting that even recent attempts by European nations to define slavery for purposes of its elimination in African colonies and elsewhere have suffered from the difficulties of definition. Even the idea of "right of ownership" poses difficulties; Lord Lugard felt impelled to point out in 1933 that: "To an African the term 'right of ownership' might not convey the precise meaning intended, namely, that of a chattel without human rights."[30]

Glancing for the last time at the Latin American cases, one sees clearly that slavery meant different things to different societies, and at different times. The most important case, perhaps—carefully avoided by the reviewer up to here—is Brazil. In spite of Elkins' adjectival omission, the ". . . conservative, paternalistic, Catholic, quasi-medieval culture of . . . Portugal" created a slave-and-sugar empire in Brazil which *appears* capitalistic from the first. Yet most writers hold that the complete dehumanization of the Brazilian slaves was not realized. If so, we need to know how Brazil followed her unique path, why slaves there were not culturally "erased," even while the economic structure apparently had as its goals those which had led the British, Dutch, French, Americans, and finally, Spaniards, to trample on human rights with their plantations. After the arguments about economics and ideology are fully set forth, the cultural question does remain. What—*from the point of view of the culture*—is man? We still must "ask" the slave-owners and the slaves. Elkins makes the question clearer, helps us understand better what we should be asking.

---

[29] *Freedom and Civilization* (New York: Roy Publishers, 1947), p. 297.

[30] "Slavery in All Its Forms," *Africa*, VI (1933), 9.

MARVIN HARRIS

The Myth of the Friendly Master

Marvin Harris is Professor of Anthropology at Columbia University. He is the author of a work of anthropological theory, The Nature of Cultural Things (*1964*), *and of works on Brazil and Portuguese Africa. Professor Harris is a strong exponent of the economic determinist position in anthropology. The following selections are chapters six and seven of his book,* Patterns of Race in the Americas. *The first, "The Myth of the Friendly Master," is a critique of the Tannenbaum thesis while the second, "The Origin of the Descent Rule," presents an alternative thesis.*

The argument in the [my] previous chapters has been that differences in race relations within Latin America are at root a matter of the labor systems in which the respective subordinate and superordinate groups became enmeshed. I have already attempted to show how a number of cultural traits and institutions which were permitted to survive, or were deliberately encouraged under one system, were discouraged or suppressed in the other. It remains to be shown how the specific combination of features which characterize lowland race rela-

tions more narrowly construed can be accounted for by the same set of principles.

At present, probably the majority of American scholars who have found a moment to ponder the peculiar aspects of the Brazilian interracial "paradise" are devoted to an opposite belief. What could be more obvious than the inadequacy of a materialist explanation of the Brazilian pattern? How can plantation slavery be made to explain anything about the lack of interracial hostility in Brazil? Was it not a plantation system in the United States South which bred a condition contrary in every detail to that of Brazil?

The current vogue of opinion about this contrast derives in large measure from the work of Frank Tannenbaum, a

Reprinted from Marvin Harris, *Patterns of Race in America* (New York: Walker and Company, 1964); pp. 65–78, Copyright © 1964 by Walker and Company, a division of Publications Development Corporation.

noted United States historian, and Gilberto Freyre, Brazil's best known sociologist. The theories of these influential scholars overlap at many points. It is their contention that the laws, values, religious precepts, and personalities of the English colonists differed from those of the Iberian colonists. These initial psychological and ideological differences were sufficient to overcome whatever tendency the plantation system may have exerted toward parallel rather than divergent evolution.

Freyre's theories, originally proposed in his classic study of Brazilian plantation life, *Casa grande e senzala,* have remained virtually unchanged for over thirty years. What most impresses Freyre about Brazilian slavery is the alleged easy-going, humanized relations between master and slave, especially between master and female slave. Slaves, while subject to certain disabilities and although sometimes cruelly treated, frequently came to play an emotionally significant role in the intimate life of their white owners. A high rate of miscegenation was one of the hallmarks of this empathy between the races. The Portuguese not only took Negro and mulatto women as mistresses and concubines, but they sometimes spurned their white wives in order to enjoy the favors of duskier beauties. Behind these favorable omens, visible from the very first days of contact, was a fundamental fact of national character, namely, the Portuguese had no color prejudice. On the contrary, their long experience under Moorish tutelage is said to have prepared them to regard people of darker hue as equals, if not superiors:

The singular predisposition of the Portuguese to the hybrid, slave-exploiting colonization of the tropics is to be explained in large part by the ethnic or, better, the cul-tural past of a people existing indeterminately between Europe and Africa and belonging uncompromisingly to neither one nor the other of the two continents.[1]

Other colonizers were not as successful as the Portuguese because their libidos were more conservative. Especially poorly endowed sexually were the "Anglo-Saxon Protestants."

The truth is that in Brazil, contrary to what is to be observed in other American countries and in those parts of Africa that have been recently colonized by Europeans, the primitive culture—the Amerindian as well as the African—has not been isolated into hard, dry indigestible lumps . . . Neither did the social relations between the two races, the conquering and the indigenous one, ever reach that point of sharp antipathy or hatred, the grating sound of which reaches our ears from all the countries that have been colonized by Anglo-Saxon Protestants. The friction here (in Brazil) was smoothed by the lubricating oil of a deep-going miscegenation . . . .[2]

The next and fatal step in this line of reasoning is to assert that the special psychological equipment of the Portuguese, not only in Brazil but everywhere in "The World the Portuguese Created,"[3] yields hybrids and interracial harmony. In 1952, after a tour of Portuguese colonies as an honored guest of the Salazar government, Freyre declared that the Portuguese were surrounded in the Orient, America, and Africa with half-caste "luso-populations" and "a sympathy on the part of the native which contrasts with the veiled or open hatred directed toward the other Europeans."[4]

How Freyre could have been hood-

[1] Gilberto Freyre, *The Masters and the Slaves* (New York: Knopf, 1946), p. 4.
[2] *Ibid.,* pp. 181–82.
[3] Gilberto Freyre, *O Mundo que o português criou* (Rio de Janeiro: J. Olympio, 1940).
[4] Gilberto Freyre, *Um brasileiro em terras portuguêsas* (Lisbon: Ediçao Livros do Brasil, 1952), p. 39.

winked into finding resemblances between race relations in Angola and Mozambique and Brazil is hard to imagine. My own findings, based on a year of field work in Mozambique, have since been supported by the field and library research of James Duffy.[5] If any reasonable doubts remained about the falsity of Freyre's luso-tropical theory, tragic events in Angola should by now have swept them away. The fact is that the Portuguese are responsible for setting off the bloodiest of all of the recent engagements between whites and Negroes in Africa (including the Mau Mau). And the Portuguese, alone of all the former African colonial powers, now stand shoulder to shoulder with the citizens of that incorrigible citadel of white supremacy, the Republic of South Africa, baited and damned from Zanzibar to Lagos.

It is true that Portuguese *in Portugal* tend to be rather neutral on the subject of color differences, if they ever think about such things at all. But this datum can only be significant to those who believe that discrimination is caused by prejudice, when the true relationship is quite the opposite. When the innocent Portuguese emigrants get to Africa, they find that legally, economically, and socially, white men can take advantage of black men, and it doesn't take long for them to join in the act. Within a year after his arrival, the Portuguese learns that blacks are inferior to whites, that the Africans have to be kept in their place, and that they are indolent by nature and have to be forced to work. What we call prejudices are merely the rationalizations which we acquire in order to prove to ourselves that the human beings whom we harm are not worthy of better treatment.

Actually the whole issue of the alleged lack of racial or color prejudice among the Portuguese (and by extension among the Spanish as well) is totally irrelevant to the main question. If, as asserted, the Iberians initially lacked any color prejudice, what light does this shed upon the Brazilian and other Latin American lowland interracial systems? The distinguishing feature of these systems is not that whites have no color prejudices. On the contrary, color prejudice as we have seen is a conspicuous and regular feature in all plantation areas. The parts of the system which need explaining are the absence of a descent rule; the absence of distinct socially significant racial groups; and the ambiguity of racial identity. In Portuguese Africa none of these features are present. The state rules on who is a native and who is a white and the condition of being a native is hereditary:

Individuals of the Negro race or their descendants who were born or habitually reside in the said Provinces and who do not yet possess the learning and the social and individual habits presupposed for the integral application of the public and private law of Portuguese citizens are considered to be 'natives.'[6]

---

[5] Marvin Harris, *Portugal's African "Wards"* (New York: The American Committee on Africa, 1958); Marvin Harris, "Labour Emigration Among the Mozambique Thonga," *Africa*, XXIX, 50–66; James Duffy, *Portugal in Africa* (Cambridge, Mass.: Harvard University Press, 1962); and James Duffy, *Portugese Africa* (Cambridge, Mass.: Harvard University Press 1959). "Colonial authorities speak of Portugal's civilizing mission, but the realities of life for the Africans in the Colonies are grim. They are subject to an abusive contract labor system. . . . The standard of wages is among the lowest in Africa. . . . Social services for Africans are either minimal or nonexistent. *And, perhaps, most important of all, Africans have become the object of a growing racial prejudice created by the rapid influx of white settlers.*" James Duffy, "Portugal's Colonies in Africa," *Foreign Policy Bulletin* 40, pp. 89–96, italics added.

[6] Estatuto Indigena, May, 1954, quoted in Harris, "Labour Emigration . . .," p. 7.

As for miscegenation, the supposedly color-blind Portuguese libido had managed by 1950 to produce slightly more than 50,000 officially recognized mixed types in an African population of ten million after 400 years of contact.[7] This record should be compared with the product of the monochromatic libidos of the Dutch invaders of South Africa—in Freyre's terms Angle-Saxon Protestants to the hilt—a million and a half official hybrids (coloreds).[8] It is time that grown men stopped talking about racially prejudiced sexuality. In general, when human beings have the power, the opportunity, and the need, they will mate with members of the opposite sex regardless of color or the identity of grandfather. Whenever free breeding in a human population is restricted, it is because a larger system of social relations is menaced by such freedom.

This is one of the points about which Tannenbaum and Freyre disagree. Tannenbaum quite correctly observes that "the process of miscegenation was part of the system of slavery, and not just of Brazilian slavery. . . . The dynamics of race contact and sex interests were stronger than prejudice. . . . This same mingling of the races and classes occurred in the United States. The record is replete with the occurrence, in spite of law, doctrine, and belief. Every traveler in the South before the Civil War comments on the widespread miscegenation. . . ."[9] But it should also be

pointed out that there is no concrete evidence to indicate that the rank and file of English colonists were initially any more or less prejudiced than the Latins. It is true that the English colonists very early enacted laws intended to prevent marriage between white women and Negro men and between white men and Negro women. Far from indicating a heritage of anti-Negro prejudices, however, these laws confirm the presence of strong attraction between the males and females of both races. The need for legal restriction certainly suggests that miscegenation was not at all odious to many of the English colonists.

The idea of assigning differential statuses to white indentured servants and Negro workers was definitely not a significant part of the ideological baggage brought over by the earliest colonists, at least not to an extent demonstrably greater than among the Latin colonists. It is true, as Carl Degler has shown, that the differentiation between white indentured servants and Negro indentured servants had become conspicuous before the middle of the seventeenth century even though the legal formulation was not completed until the end of the century. But who would want to suggest that there was absolutely no prejudice against the Negroes immediately after contact? Ethnocentrism is a universal feature of intergroup relations and obviously both the English and the Iberians were prejudiced against foreigners, white and black. The facts of life in the New World were such, however, that Negroes, being the most defenseless of all the immigrant groups, were discriminated against and exploited more than any others. Thus the Negroes were not enslaved because the British colonists specifically despised dark-skinned people and regarded them alone as prop-

---

[7] Homer Jack, *Angola: Repression and Revolt in Portuguese Africa* (New York: American Committee on Africa, 1960), p. 7; and *Recenseamento Geral*, 1953, Provincia de Mocambique, p. xxxi.

[8] Absolom Vilakazi, "Race Relations in South Africa," in Andrew W. Lind, ed., *Race Relations in World Perspective*, (Honolulu: University of Hawaii Press, 1955), p. 313.

[9] Frank Tannenbaum, *Slave and Citizen* (New York: Knopf, 1947), pp. 121–23.

erly suited to slavery; the Negroes came to be the object of the virulent prejudices because they and they alone could be enslaved. Judging from the very nasty treatment suffered by white indentured servants, it was obviously not sentiment which prevented the Virginia planters from enslaving their fellow Englishmen. They undoubtedly would have done so had they been able to get away with it. But such a policy was out of the question as long as there was a King and a Parliament in England.

The absence of preconceived notions about what ought to be the treatment of enslaved peoples forms a central theme in Tannenbaum's explanation of United States race relations. According to Tannenbaum, since the English had gotten rid of slavery long before the Discovery, they had no body of laws or traditions which regulated and humanized the slave status. Why this legal lacuna should have been significant for the course run by slavery in the United States is quite obscure. Even Degler, who accepts the Freyre-Tannenbaum approach, points out that it was "possible for almost any kind of status to be worked out."[10] One might reasonably

conclude that the first settlers were not overly concerned with race differences, and that they might have remained that way (as many Englishmen have) had they not been brought into contact with Negroes under conditions wholly dictated by the implacable demands of a noxious and "peculiar" institution.

Let us turn now to the main substance of Tannenbaum's theory. Tannenbaum correctly believes that the critical difference between race relations in the United States and in Latin America resides in the physical and psychological (he says "moral") separation of the Negro from the rest of society. "In spite of his adaptability, his willingness, and his competence, in spite of his complete identification with the *mores* of the United States, he is excluded and denied. . . ." Also, quite correctly, Tannenbaum stresses the critical role of the free Negro and mulatto in Latin America. Manumission appears to have been much more common, and the position of the freed man was much more secure than elsewhere. Free Negroes and mulattoes quickly came to outnumber the slaves. However, according to Tannenbaum, this phenomenon came about because

---

[10] Carl Degler, "Slavery and the Genesis of American Race Prejudice," *Comparative Studies in Society and History*, II, 49–66. This article is attack on Handlin and Handlin's (1950) theory that the differentiation between Negro and white indentured servants developed gradually during the seventeenth century and that initially there was little specifically anti-Negro discrimination or prejudice. Degler contends that "the status of the Negro in the English colonies was worked out within a framework of discrimination; that from the outset, as far as the available evidence tells us, the Negro was treated as an inferior to the white man, servant or free." Degler suffers from the illusion that early examples of discriminatory treatment of Negroes in the English Colonies are relevant to the Tannenbaum (-Freyre) explanation of Latin American race relations. Somehow or other Degler has received the impression that in Latin America there was was not an equally early display of discrimina-

tion. But of course, in both cases, slavery was reserved for Negroes, Indians, and half-castes. Neither English nor Iberian whites were ever enslaved in the New World; surely this is an instance of discriminatory treatment. Degler explicitly accepts the Tannenbaum (-Freyre) point of view, despite the fact that his article really amounts to a denial of the significance of ideological and psychological factors in the explanation of race relations. The early *de facto* enslavement of Negroes, even when there was no body of law sanctioning slavery, is certainly a rather negative comment on Tannenbaum's use of law as evidence of behavior. To conclude that slavery ". . . was molded by the early colonists' discrimination against the outlander" is to confirm that prejudice followed discrimination, whereas it is essential for the Tannenbaum (-Freyre) point of view that the causality be reversed.

the slave was endowed with "a moral personality before emancipation . . . which . . . made the transition from slavery to freedom easy and his incorporation into the free community natural."[11] The Negro and mulatto were never sharply cut off from the rest of society because the Latin slave was never cut off from the rest of humanity. This was because slavery in southern Europe and Latin America was embedded in a legal, ethical, moral, and religious matrix which conspired to preserve the slave's individual integrity as the possessor of an immortal human soul. The "definition" of the slave as merely an unfortunate human being, primarily according to state and canonical code, is given most weight:

For if one thing stands out clearly from the study of slavery, it is that the definition of man as a moral being proved the most important influence both in the treatment of the slave and in the final abolition of slavery.[12]

Note that it is not merely being claimed that there was a critical difference between Latin American and United States race relations during and after slavery, but that the very institution of slavery itself was one thing in the United States and the British West Indies and another thing in Latin America:

There were briefly speaking, three slave systems in the Western Hemisphere. The British, American, Dutch, and Danish were at one extreme, and the Spanish and Portuguese at the other. In between these two fell the French. . . . If one were forced to arrange these systems of slavery in order of severity, the Dutch, would seem to stand as the harshest, the Portuguese as the mildest, and the French in between. . . .[13]

The contention that the condition of the average slave in the English colonies was worse than that of the average slave in the Latin colonies obscures the main task which confronts us, which is to explain why the treatment of the free mulatto and free Negro were and are so different. To try to explain why the slaves were treated better in Latin America than in the United States is a waste of time, for there is no conceivable way in which we can now be certain that they were indeed treated better in one place than the other. It is true that a large number of travelers can be cited, especially from the nineteenth century, who were convinced that the slaves were happier under Spanish and Portuguese masters than under United States masters. But there was plenty of dissenting opinion. Tannenbaum makes no provision for the fact that the English planters had what we would today call a very bad press, since thousands of intellectuals among their own countrymen were in the vanguard of the abolitionist movement. The West Indian and Southern planters, of course, were in total disagreement with those who preferred slavery under foreign masters. Actually all of the distinctions between the Anglo-American and Latin slave systems which Tannenbaum proposes were already the subject of debate at the beginning of the eighteenth century between Anglo-American abolitionists and Anglo-American planters. For example, in 1827, the Jamaican planter Alexander Barclay responded to the English critics of his island's slave system as follows:

According to Mr. Stephen [author of *Slavery of the British West India Colonies*] there exists among his countrymen in the West Indies, an universal feeling of hatred and contempt of the Negroes. . . . It is by this assumed hatred and contempt, that he strives to give probability to the most incredible

---

[11] Tannenbaum, op. cit., pp. 42, 100.

[12] *Ibid.*, p. vii.

[13] *Ibid.*, note p. 65.

charges of cruelty and oppression; and indeed, in many cases, this alleged feeling of aversion and abhorrence on the part of the whites, is the sole ground for supposing that the charges should be made, and the sole proof of them. Such things must have happened, because the colonists hate the Negroes. Now, I most solemnly affirm, not only that I am unconscious of any such surely unnatural feelings having place in my own breast, but that I have never seen proof of its existence in the breasts of others.[14]

All slave-owners of whatever nationality always seem to have been convinced that "their" slaves were the happiest of earthly beings. Barclay claims that the Jamaican slaves celebrated the cane harvest with an interracial dance:

In the evening, they assemble in their master's or manager's house, and, as a matter of course, take possession of the largest room, bringing with them a fiddle and tambourine. Here all authority and all distinction of color ceases; black and white, overseer and bookkeeper, mingle together in the dance.[15]

At Christmas time the same thing happens. The slaves

... proceed to the neighboring plantation villages, and always visit the master's or manager's house, into which they enter without ceremony, and where they are joined by the white people in a dance.[16]

Concludes Barclay:

All is life and joy, and certainly it is one of the most pleasing sights that can be imagined.[17]

In the United States, equally rapturous descriptions of the slave's lot were a conspicuous part of the ideological war between North and South. Many

planters felt that their slaves were better off than the mass of Northern whites, and Southern poets did not hesitate to cap their comparisons of free and slave labor with panegyrics

... on the happy life of the slave, with all his needs provided, working happily in the fields by day, enjoying the warm society of his family in the cabin at night, idling through life in "the summer shade, the winter sun," and without fear of the poorhouse at its close ... until we finally find the slave "luxuriating" in a "lotus-bearing paradise."[18]

If one were so inclined by lack of an understanding of the nature of sociological evidence, it would not be difficult to paint a picture in which the position of the Anglo-American slave system was promoted from last to first place. Freyre himself provides enough material on cruelty in the Brazilian plantations to fill at least a corner in a chamber of horrors:

And how, in truth, are the hearts of us Brazilians to acquire the social virtues if from the moment we open our eyes we see about us the cruel distinction between master and slave, and behold the former, at the slightest provocation or sometimes out of mere whim, mercilessly rending the flesh of our own kind with lashes?[19]

There are not two or three but many instances of the cruelties of the ladies of the big house toward their helpless blacks. There are tales of sinhámoças who had the eyes of pretty mucamas gouged out and then had them served to their husband for dessert, in a jelly-dish, floating in blood that was still fresh. ... There were others who kicked out the teeth of their women slaves with their boots, or who had their breasts cut off, their nails drawn, or their faces and ears burned.[20]

---

[14] Alexander Barclay, *A Practical View of the Present State of Slavery in the West Indies* (London: Smith, Elder & Co., 1827), pp. xi-xii.

[15] *Ibid.*, p. 10.

[16] *Ibid.*, p. 11.

[17] *Ibid.*

---

[18] Bernard Mandel, *Labor: Slave and Free* (New York: Associated Authors, 1955), p. 99.

[19] Gilberto Freyre, *The Masters and the Slaves*, p. 392, quoting Lopes Gomes.

[20] *Ibid.*, p. 351.

Another Brazilian observer, Arthur Ramos, goes even further:

During the period of slavery, suppression and punishment prevented almost any spontaneous activity. . . . The number of instruments of torture employed was numerous and profoundly odious. . . . There was the *tronco*, of wood or of iron, an instrument which held the slave fast at the ankles and in the grip of which he was often kept for days on end; the *libambo* which gripped the unfortunate victim fast at the neck; the *algemas* and the *anjinhos*, which held the hands tightly, crushing the thumbs. . . . Some plantation owners of more perverted inclinations used the so-called *novenas* and *trezenas*. . . . The Negroes tied face down on the ground, were beaten with the rawhide whip on from nine to thirteen consecutive nights. . . .[21]

The testimony of the travelers, poets, planters, abolitionists, and scholars in this matter, however, is worthless. Better to dispute the number of angels on a pinhead than to argue that one country's slavery is superior to another's. The slaves, wherever they were, didn't like it; they killed themselves and they killed their masters; over and over again they risked being torn apart by hounds and the most despicable tortures in order to escape the life to which they were condemned. It is a well known fact that Brazil was second to none in the number of its fugitive slaves and its slave revolts. In the seventeenth century one successful group held out in the famous *quilombo* of Palmares for 67 years and in the nineteenth century scarcely a year went by without an actual or intended revolt.[22]

In a recent book, the historian Stanley M. Elkins attempts to save Tannenbaum's theory by admitting that slavery in the United States (at least by 1850) "in a 'physical' sense was in general, probably, quite mild" and that there were very "severe" sides to the Spanish and Portuguese systems.[23] Elkins assures us, however, that even if slavery had been milder here than anywhere else in the Western Hemisphere, "it would still be missing the point to make the comparison in terms of physical comfort. In one case we would be dealing with cruelty of man to man, and, in the other, with the care, maintenance, and indulgence of men toward creatures who were legally and morally *not* men—not in the sense that Christendom had traditionally defined man's nature."[24] It is devoutly to be hoped that Elkins shall never be able to test his exquisite sense of equity by experiencing first thirty lashes dealt out by someone who calls him a black man and then a second thirty from someone who calls him a black devil. But if there be such talents as Elkins' among us, we had better take a closer look at the proposition that the Negro was regarded as a human being by the Latin colonists but not by the Anglo-Saxons. The principal source of evidence for this resides in the law codes by which the respective slave systems were theoretically regulated. Admittedly, these codes do show a considerable difference of legal opinion as to the definition of a slave. The Spanish and Portuguese codes were essentially continuations of medieval regulations stretching back ultimately to Roman law. The British and American colonial codes were the original creations of the New World planter class, developed first in the West Indies (Barbados) and

---

[21] Arthur Ramos, *The Negro in Brazil* (Washington: Associated Publishers, 1939), pp. 34–35.
[22] *Ibid.*, 43 ff.

[23] Stanley M. Elkins, *Slavery: A Problem in American Institutional and Intellectual Life* (Chicago: University of Chicago Press, 1959), p. 78.
[24] *Ibid.*

then copied throughout the South.[25] Although the Constitution of the United States said that slaves were persons, state laws said they were chattels—mere property. "Slave-holders, legislators, and judges were forever trying to make property out of them . . . They simply did not regard them as human beings."[26] On the other hand, Spanish and Portuguese slave laws did, as Tannenbaum claims, specifically preserve the human identity of the slave: "The distinction between slavery and freedom is a product of accident and misfortune, and the free man might have been a slave."[27] From this there flowed a number of rights, of which Fernando Ortiz identifies four as most significant: (1) the right to marry freely; (2) the right to seek out another master if any were too severe; (3) the right of owning property; and (4) the right to buy freedom.[28] Tannenbaum shows how all of the U.S. slave states denied these rights. He goes further and shows how the U.S. slaves were virtually left without legal remedy for harms committed upon them, and he emphasizes the casual fines which protected the life of a slave under the early laws,[29] and the total lack of legal recognition given to the slave's affinal or consanguine family. Indeed, for every favorable section in the Spanish law, both Elkins and Tannenbaum readily find an unfavorable section in the Anglo-Saxon codes.

What the laws of the Spanish and Portuguese kings had to do with the attitudes and values of the Spanish and Portuguese planters, however, baffles one's imagination. The Crown could publish all the laws it wanted, but in the lowlands, sugar was king. If there were any Portuguese or Spanish planters who were aware of their legal obligations toward the slaves, it would require systematic misreading of colonialism, past and present, to suppose that these laws psychologically represented anything more than the flatus of a pack of ill-informed Colonel Blimps who didn't even know what a proper cane field looked like. Ortiz leaves no room for doubt in the case of Cuba. Yes, the slave had legal rights, "But these rights were not viable . . . if they contrast with the barbaric laws of the French and above all, of the English colonies, it was no less certain that all of these rights were illusory, especially in earlier times. . . ." Sanctity of the family? "Man and wife were permanently separated, sold in separate places, and separated from their children."[30] "How many times was a son sold by his father!" and "Pregnant or nursing slaves were sold with or without their actual or future offspring."[31] Protection of the law? "The sugar and coffee plantations were in fact feudal domains where the only authority recognized was that of the master. . . . Could the Negroes hope in these circumstances to change masters? The rawhide would quiet their voices. . . ." Rights to property? "From what I have said in relation to the work of the rural slave, to speak of his right to hold property and to buy freedom, is futile. . . ." "But I repeat, the plantation slave was treated like a beast, like a being

---

[25] Dwight Lowell Dumond, *Antislavery* (Ann Arbor, Mich.: University of Michigan Press, 1961), p. 8.

[26] *Ibid.*, p. 251.

[27] Frank Tannenbaum, op. cit., p. 46.

[28] Fernando Ortiz, *Los negros esclavos* (Havana: Revista bimestre cubana, 1916), p. 303.

[29] Actually, quite severe laws regulating punishment of the slaves were eventually passed by the slave states. [Cf. Kenneth Stampp, *The Peculiar Institution* (New York: Knopf, 1956), pp. 217-21.]

[30] Ortiz, op. cit., pp. 303-4.

[31] *Ibid.*, p. 173.

to whom human character was denied. . . ."[32]

Tannenbaum makes much of the fact that there was no set of ancient slave laws to which the Anglo-Saxon planters or the slaves could turn for guidance. He prominently displays the meager penalties attached to murder of slaves as examples of their subhuman status in the eyes of the Anglo-Saxon colonists. But Ortiz informs us that "it was not until 1842 that there was any specific legal regulation of the form of punishment which a Cuban master could give his slave."[33] Actually it turns out that "the state did not concern itself with the limitation of the arbitrary power of the master in relation to the punishment of his slave until after the abolition of slavery [1880]."[34]

In Brazil, as everywhere in the colonial world, law and reality bore an equally small resemblance to each other. Stanley Stein's recent historical study of slavery in the county of Vassouras during the last century yields a picture almost totally at variance with that drawn by Gilberto Freyre for the earlier plantations. The Vassouras planters went about their business, methodically buying, working, beating, and selling their slaves, in whatever fashion yielded the most coffee with the least expense. The master's will was supreme. "It was difficult to apply legal restraints to the planter's use of the lash."[35]

Typical is an eyewitness account of a beating told by an ex-slave. On order from the master, two drivers bound and beat a slave while the slave folk stood in line, free folk watching from further back. The slave died that night and his corpse, dumped into a wicker basket, was borne by night to the slave cemetery of the plantation and dropped into a hastily dug grave. *"Slaves could not complain to the police, only another fazendeiro* [master] *could do that,"* explained the eyewitness.[36] [Italics are mine.]

If Stein's picture of nineteenth-century Vassouras is accurate—and it is the most carefully documented study of its kind in existence—then the following recent pronouncement from Charles Boxer will have to be accepted minus the time restriction:

The common belief that the Brazilian was an exceptionally kind master is applicable only to the nineteenth century under the Empire, and it is contradicted for the colonial period by the testimony of numerous reliable eyewitnesses from Vieira to Vilhena, to say nothing of the official correspondence between the colonial authorities and the Crown.[37]

Of special interest in Boxer's refutation of the myth of the friendly master is the evidence which shows that Brazilian planters and miners did not accept the legal decisions which awarded human souls and human personalities to the slaves. The Brazilian slave-owners were convinced that Negroes were descended from Cain, black and "therefore not people like ourselves." Making due allowance for exceptions and the special circumstances of household slaves, Boxer concludes that "it remains true that by and large colonial Brazil was indeed a 'hell for blacks.' "[38]

---

[32] *Ibid.*, pp. 303–4.

[33] *Ibid.*, p. 265.

[34] *Ibid.*, p. 267.

[35] Stanley Stein, *Vassouras* (Cambridge, Mass.: Harvard University Press, 1957), p. 135.

[36] *Ibid.*, p. 136.

[37] Charles Boxer, *The Golden Age of Brazil* (Berkeley, Calif.: University of California Press, 1962), p. 173.

[38] Charles Boxer, *Race Relations in the Portugese Colonial Empire, 1415–1825* (Oxford, Eng.: Clarendon Press, 1963), p. 114.

MARVIN HARRIS

The Origin of the Descent Rule

See the headnote on page 38 for bibliographical information on Marvin Harris.

At one point, and one point only, is there a demonstrable correlation between the laws and behavior, the ideal and the actual, in Tannenbaum's theory: the Spanish and Portuguese codes ideally drew no distinction between the ex-slave and the citizen, and actual behavior followed suit. The large hybrid populations of Latin America were not discriminated against *solely* because they were descended from slaves; it is definitely verifiable that all hybrids were not and are not forced back into a sharply separated Negro group by application of a rule of descent. This was true during slavery and it was true after slavery. With abolition, because a continuous color spectrum of free men had already existed for at

Reprinted from Marvin Harris, *Patterns of Race in America* (New York: Walker and Company, 1964); pp. 79–94, Copyright © 1964 by Walker and Company, a division of Publications Development Corporation.

least 200 years, ex-slaves and descendants of slaves were not pitted against whites in the bitter struggle which marks the career of our own Jim Crow.

However, to argue that it was the Spanish and Portuguese slave codes and slave traditions which gave rise to these real and substantial differences in the treatment of the free Negro and mulatto is to miss the essential point about the evolution of the New World plantation systems. If traditional laws and values were alone necessary to get the planters to manumit their slaves, and treat free colored people like human beings, the precedents among the English colonists were surely greater than among the Latins.

If anything, the laws and traditions of England conspired to make its colonists abhor anything that smacked of slavery. And so it was in England that in 1705 Chief Justice Holt could say, "As soon as a Negro comes into

England he becomes free."[1] Let it not be forgotten that five of the original thirteen states—New Hampshire, Massachusetts, Connecticut, Rhode Island, and Pennsylvania, plus the independent state of Vermont—began programs of complete emancipation before the federal Constitutional Convention met in 1787. Partial antislavery measures were enacted by New York in 1788, and total emancipation in 1799, while New Jersey began to pass antislavery legislation in 1786.[2] Furthermore, all of the original states which abolished slavery lived up to the declared principles of the Declaration of Independence and the Constitution to a remarkable degree in their treatment of emancipated slaves. "They were citizens of their respective states the same as were Negroes who were free at the time of independence."[3]

There were no restrictions prior to 1800 upon Negroes voting in any state which had abolished slavery. They were voting at that time and continued to vote without interruption in New Hampshire, Vermont, Rhode Island, and the two slave states of New York and New Jersey.

It was only later that Connecticut (1814) and Pennsylvania (1837) got around to imposing restrictions. Although the slave codes of New York, New Jersey, and Pennsylvania had forbidden slaves to testify in court cases involving white persons, these laws were never applied to free Negroes, and "there were no such laws in New England. . . . Nor were there any distinctions whatever in criminal law, judicial procedure, and punishments." In all of the Northern states, therefore, Negroes were citizens "by enjoyment of full political equality, by lack of any statements to the contrary in any constitution or law, by complete absence of legal distinction based on color, and by specific legal and constitutional declaration. . . ."[4]

We see, therefore, that if past laws and values had a significant role to play in the treatment of Negroes and mulattoes, the hounding persecution of the free Negroes and mulattoes should never have occurred in the English colonies. For contrary to the oft-repeated assertion that there was no matrix of English law or tradition into which the slave could fit, it is quite obvious that very specific laws and traditions existed to guide the Anglo-Saxon colonists. These laws and traditions held that all men had natural rights, that the Negroes were men and that slaves ought to become citizens. That the Constitution asserts "all men are created equal" is not some monstrous hypocrisy perpetrated by the founding fathers. It was an expression of a general Northern and enlightened Southern belief that slavery was an institution which was incompatible with the laws and traditions of civilized Englishmen. That the American versions of these laws were later subverted by court decisions and that the Constitution's guarantee of freedom and equality became a grim joke is surely ample testimony to the futility of trying to understand sociocultural evolution in terms of such factors.

Understanding of the differences in the status of free "nonwhites" in the plantation world can only emerge when one forthrightly inquires why a system which blurred the distinction between Negro and white was materially advantageous to one set of planters, while it was the opposite to another. One can

---

[1] Dwight Lowell Dumond, *Antislavery* (Ann Arbor, Mich.: University of Michigan Press, 1961), p. 5.

[2] *Ibid.*, p. 16ff.

[3] *Ibid.*, p. 120.

[4] *Ibid.*, p. 123.

be certain that if it had been materially disadvantageous to the Latin colonists, it would never have been tolerated— Romans, *Siete Partidas* and the Catholic Church notwithstanding. For one thing is clear, the slavocracy in both the Latin and Anglo-Saxon colonies held the whip hand not only over the slaves but over the agents of civil and ecclesiastical authority. To make second-class citizens out of all descendants of slaves was surely no greater task, given sufficient material reason, than to make slaves out of men and brutes out of slaves.

Although the slave plantation per se was remarkably similar in its effects regardless of the cultural background of the slaves or slave-owners,[5] the natural, demographic, and institutional environment with which slavery articulated and interacted was by no means

---

[5] Compare these two observations about the effects of slavery on children in the United States and Brazil: "The whole commerce between master and slave is a perpetual exercise of the most boisterous passions, the most unremitting despotism on the one part, and degrading submissions on the other. Our children see this, and learn to imitate it. . . . The parent storms, the child looks on, catches the lineaments of wrath, puts on the same airs in the circle of smaller slaves, gives loose to the worst of passions, and thus nursed, educated, and daily exercised in tyranny, cannot but be stamped by it with odious peculiarities." (Thomas Jefferson, quoted in *ibid.*, pp. 28–29.) "And what are the sons of these sluggards like? . . . The inhumanities and the cruelties that they practice from early years upon the wretched slaves render them all but insensible to the sufferings of their neighbors. . . . No sooner do we acquire intelligence than we observe, on the one hand, the lack of delicacy, shamelessness, dissoluteness, and disorderly conduct of the slaves, and on the other hand the harsh treatment, the thrashings, the blows that these unfortunates receive almost every day from our elders. . . . And what is the inevitable result of all this, if not to render us coarse, headstrong, and full of pride?" (Lopes Gomes, quoted in Gilberto Freyre, *The Masters and the Slaves* (New York: Knopf, 1956), p. 392.)

uniform. It is the obligation of all those who wish to explain the difference between United States and Latin American race relations to examine these material conditions first, before concluding that it was the mystique of the Portuguese or Spanish soul that made the difference.

The first important consideration is demographic. Latin America and the United States experienced totally different patterns of settlement. When Spain and Portugal began their occupation of the New World, they were harassed by severe domestic manpower shortages, which made it extremely difficult for them to find colonists for their far-flung empires. Furthermore, in the New World the conditions under which such colonists were to settle were themselves antithetical to large-scale emigration. In the highlands a dense aboriginal population was already utilizing most of the arable land under the tutelage of the *encomenderos* and *hacendados*. In the lowlands large-scale emigration, supposing there had been a sufficient number of potential settlers, was obstructed by the monopolization of the best coastal lands by the slave-owning sugar planters. Only a handful of Portuguese migrated to Brazil during the sixteenth century. In the seventeenth century, a deliberate policy of *restricting* emigration to Brazil was pursued, out of fear that Portugal was being depopulated. Cried the Jesuit father Antonio Vieira, "Where are our men? Upon every alarm in Alentejo it is necessary to take students from the university, tradesmen from their shops, laborers from the plough!"[6]

The migrations of Englishmen and Britishers to the New World followed an

---

[6] Quoted in Bailey Wallys Diffie, *Latin American Civilization: Colonial Period* (Harrisburg, Penn.: Telegraph Press, 1945), p. 660.

entirely different rhythm. Although the movement began almost a century later, it quickly achieved a magnitude that was to have no parallel in Latin America until the end of the nineteenth century. Between 1509 and 1790 only 150,000 people emigrated from Spain to the entire New World, but between 1600 and 1700, 500,000 English and Britishers moved to the North American territories.

The reason for this accelerated rate of migration is not hard to find:

As opposed to Spain and Portugal, harassed by a permanent manpower scarcity when starting to occupy the Western Hemisphere, seventeenth-century England had an abundant population surplus, owing to the far-reaching changes affecting the country's agriculture since the previous century.[7]

The changes in question were the enclosures by which much of England's farming population was being forced off the land in order to make way for sheep-raising (in turn stimulated by the manufacture of woolen cloth). The depletion of England's own natural resources, especially its forests, made it convenient to consider establishing overseas companies to produce commodities which were becoming increasingly more difficult to produce in England: potash, timber, pitch, tar, resin, iron, and copper. It was to produce these commodities that Jamestown was founded in 1607.

The staple and certain Commodities we have are Soap-ashes, pitch, tar, dyes of sundry sorts and rich values, timber for all uses, fishing for sturgeon . . . making of glass and iron, and no improbable hope of richer mines.[8]

Manufactures of this sort, plus subsistence agriculture, proved to be the mainstay of the more northerly colonies and were later to establish the United States, at least in the North, as an important industrial power. From Maryland on south, however, the colonists quickly switched to tobacco-growing as their basic commercial activity. Whether agriculture or manufacturing was the principal concern of a given colony, labor, as always, was the main problem. There were plenty of Englishmen eager to settle in the New World but the price of the Atlantic passage was high. The system developed to overcome this obstacle was indentured servitude, whereby the price of passage was advanced, to be worked off, usually in five to eight years, after which the immigrant would be free to do as he might choose. Despite the high mortality rate of the early indentured servants, tens of thousands of English men and women bought passage to the New World in this fashion. The great lure of it was that once a man had worked off his debt, there was a chance to buy land at prices which were unthinkably low in comparison with those of England.

For almost one hundred years, white indentured servants were the principal source of manpower in the Anglo-Saxon colonies. Black slave manpower was a relatively late introduction. The case of Virginia would seem to be the most important and most instructive. In 1624, there were only 22 Negroes in Virginia (at a time when several thousand a year were already pouring into Recife and Bahia). In 1640, they had not increased to more than 150. Nine years later, when Virginia was inhabited by 15,000 whites, there were still only 300 Negroes. It was not until 1670 that Negroes reached 5 per cent of

[7] Celso Furtado, *Formaçao econômica do Brasil* (Rio de Janeiro: Editôra Fundo de Cultura, 1959), p. 21.

[8] Thomas J. Wertenbaker, *The Planters of Colonial Virginia* (New York: Russell & Russell, 1959), p. 15, quoting the Virginia Council in 1608.

the population.[9] After 1680 slaves began to arrive in increasing numbers, yet it was not until the second quarter of the eighteenth century that they exceeded 25 per cent of the population.

In 1715 the population of all the colonies with the exception of South Carolina was overwhelmingly composed of a white yeomanry, ex-indentured servants and wage earners.

POPULATION OF THE COLONIES, 1715

	White	Negro
New Hampshire	9,500	150
Massachusetts	94,000	2,000
Rhode Island	8,500	500
Connecticut	46,000	1,500
New York	27,000	4,000
New Jersey	21,000	1,500
Pennsylvania-Delaware	43,000	2,500
Maryland	40,700	9,500
Virginia	72,000	23,000
North Carolina	7,500	3,700
South Carolina	6,250	10,500

Against a total white population of 375,000, there were less than 60,000 slaves in all of the colonies. If we consider the four Southern colonies— Maryland, Virginia, North Carolina, and South Carolina—the ratio was still almost 3 to 1 in favor of the whites.[10]

At about the same time, the total population of Brazil is estimated to have been 300,000, of whom only 100,000 were of European origin.[11] In other words, the ratio of whites to nonwhites was the exact opposite of what it was in the United States. A century

later (1819) is Brazil, this ratio in favor of nonwhites had climbed even higher, for out of an estimated total of 3,618,000 Brazilians, only 834,000 or less than 20 per cent were white.[12] At approximately the same time in the United States (1820), 7,866,797, or more than 80 per cent of the people, out of a total population of 9,638,453 were whites. Although the Negro population was at this time overwhelmingly concentrated in the South, Negroes at no point constituted more than 38 per cent of the population of the Southern states.[13] The high point was reached in 1840; thereafter, the proportion declined steadily until by 1940 it had fallen below 25 per cent in the South and below 10 per cent for the country as a whole.

Clearly, one of the reasons why the colonial population of Brazil shows such a preponderance of nonwhites during colonial times is that a large part of the population increase resulted not from in-migration but from miscegenation and the natural increase of the European-Negroid-Amerindian crosses. Thus, in 1819, there were almost as many mestizos, free and slave, as there were whites, and by 1870, there were more "mixed bloods" than whites. This situation reversed itself toward the end of the nineteenth century after the first great wave of European immigrants had begun to flood São Paulo and the Brazilian South. According to the 1890 census, there were 6,302,198 whites, 4,638,495 mixed types, and 2,097,426 Negroes.[14] This "whitening" trend has continued until the present

[9] Ibid., p. 124.

[10] Dumond, op. cit., p. 374, from the Board of Trade. Georgia, which had barely emerged from Spanish control at the time, was very sparsely populated. However, in 1761 there were an estimated 6,100 whites to fewer than 3,570 Negroes. (Cecil Greg, History of Agriculture in the Southern United States to 1860, vol. I (New York: Peter Smith, 1941), 100–101.)

[11] Furtado, op. cit., n. 81.

[12] Manoel Cardozo, "Slavery in Brazil as Described by Americans: 1822–1888," The Americas, XVII, 247.

[13] E. Franklin Frazier, The Negro in the United States (New York: Macmillan, 1949), p. 176.

[14] Fernando Henrique Cardozo and Octávio Ianni, Côr e mobilidade social em Florianópolis (São Paulo: Companhia Editôra Nacional [Brasiliana v. 307], 1960), p. 247.

day, when whites number about 62 per cent of the population, mixed types 27 per cent, and Negroes 11 per cent.[15] These figures, of course, should be read with an understanding that many persons classed as "whites" are actually "mixed" in conformity with what has previously been said about the inherent ambiguity of racial classification in Brazil.

There is no doubt that the number of Brazilians of color who were free was always greater than the number of free Negroes in the United States, absolutely and in proportion to the number of slaves. But the disparity may not have been as great as many people believe. Thus in 1819, when there were anywhere from 1,500,000 to 2 million slaves in Brazil, there were about 585,000 free men of color (not counting Indians),[16] while in the United States in 1820, 1,538,000 slaves were matched by 233,634 free Negroes.[17] Conservatively, therefore, one might claim that in Brazil there were only about twice as many free Negroes in proportion to slaves as in the United States. This fact permits us to place the claims for a higher rate of manumission in Brazil in proper perspective and leads us directly to the most important question about the demographic patterns under consideration. The number of free people of color in nineteenth-century Brazil is not at all startling in relationship to the number of *slaves*. What is amazing from the North American point of view is the number of free people of color in relationship to the number of *whites*.

Manumission may have been somewhat more frequent in Brazil than in the United States, but not so much more frequent that one can use it with any certainty as an indication that slavery in Brazil was a milder institution than it was in the United States. It should be borne in mind that the higher ratio of free coloreds to slaves in Brazil might to some extent represent a greater eagerness on the part of Brazilian masters to rid themselves of the care and support of aged and infirm charges. Since we know nothing about the age distribution of the free Brazilian colored population in comparison with that of the United States free colored population, it is obvious that less importance than is customary should be attached to the ratio of free to slave colored in Brazil.

But the ratio of whites to free colored is indeed astonishing, especially if one admits that many of the "whites" quite probably had nonwhite grandparents. The central question, therefore, is, why did the Brazilian whites permit themselves to become outnumbered by free half-castes? Several factors, none of them related to alleged special features of the Portuguese national character, readily present themselves.

In the first instance, given the chronic labor shortage in sixteenth-century Portugal and the small number of people who migrated to Brazil, the white slave-owners had no choice but to create a class of free half-castes. The reason for this is not that there was a shortage of white women, nor that Portuguese men were fatally attracted to dark females. These hoary sex fantasies explain nothing, since there is no reason why the sexual exploitation of Amerindian and Negro females had necessarily to lead to a *free* class of hybrids. The most probable explanation is that the whites had no choice in the matter. They were compelled to create an intermediate free group of

---

[15] Instituto Brasileiro de Geografia e Estatística (IBGE), *Contribuições pàra o estudo da demografia do Brasil*, IBGE, Consêlho Nacional de Estatística, 1961, p. 169.

[16] Manoel Cardozo, op. cit., p. 247.

[17] Frazier, op. cit., pp. 39, 62.

half-castes to stand between them and the slaves because there were certain essential economic and military functions for which slave labor was useless, and for which no whites were available. One of these functions was that of clearing the Indians from the sugar coast; another was the capture of Indian slaves; a third was the overseeing of Negro slaves; and a fourth was the tracking down of fugitives. The half-caste nature of most of the Indian-fighters and slave-catchers is an indubitable fact of Brazilian history. Indian-Portuguese *mamelucos* were called upon to defend Bahia and other cities against the Indians, and the hordes of people who were constantly engaged in destroying the *quilombos*, including Palmares, were also half-castes.[18] There was little help from the armed forces of the Crown:

The land owners had to defend themselves. They were obliged to organize militarily. Within each sugar plantation, in every large estate, in the solitude of every cattle ranch, under the command of the *senhor*, there lived for this reason, a small perfectly organized army.

This rabble of *mestizos* . . . provided the fighting corps charged with the defense of the estates. Out of them came the *morenos*, the *cafusos*, the *mulatos*, the *carijos*, the *mamelucos* . . . to guarantee the safety of the master's mills, plantations, and herds.[19]

A second great interstice filled by free half-castes was the cattle industry. The sugar plantations required for the mills and for the hauling of wood and cane, one ox and one horse per slave. These animals could not be raised in

the sugar zone, where they were a menace to the unfenced cane fields and where the land was too valuable to be used for pasturage. As a matter of fact, a royal decree of 1701 prohibited cattle raising within 10 leagues of the coast.[20] The cattle industry developed first in the semiarid portions of the state of Bahia and rapidly fanned out in all directions into the interior. Open-range mounted cowboys, for obvious reasons, cannot be slaves; nor would any self-respecting Portuguese immigrant waste his time rounding up doggies in the middle of a parched wilderness. The *vaqueiros* were a motley crew:

. . . they were recruited from among Indians and mestizos as well as among fugitives from the coastal centers: escaped criminals, fugitive slaves, adventurers of every type.[21]

The people who bring them [the cattle] are whites, *mulatos*, and Negroes and also Indians. . . .[22]

The foundation of cattle ranches . . . opened new possibilities in the interior . . . to these new *sesmarias* . . . there flowed the . . . free mestizo population of every sort.[23]

Although the Brazilian economist Celso Furtado estimates that only 13,000 people were supported by stock-raising in its initial phases, the capacity of both the human and the animal population to expand rapidly in response to negative economic trends on the coast is given great emphasis.[24] It is also at least a reasonable hypothesis that half-castes were used to

---

[18] Jaime Cortesão and Pedro Calmón, *Brasil* (Barcelona: Salvat Editores, 1956), p. 476: F. J. Oliviera Vianna, *Evolución del pueblo Brasileño* (Buenos Aires: Imprenta Mercatali, 1937), p. 86; and Bailey Wallys Diffie, *Latin American Civilization: Colonial Period* (Harrisburg, Penn.: The Telegraph Press, 1945), pp. 668–73.

[19] Oliviera Vianna, op. cit., p. 84.

[20] R. Simonsen, *História econômica do Brasil*, vol. I (São Paulo: Companhia Editôra Nacional, 1937), p. 228.

[21] Caio Prado Júnior, *História econômica do Brasil*, 6th ed. (São Paulo:), Editôra Brasiliense, 1961), p. 45.

[22] Simonsen, op. cit., p. 237, quoting Antonil.

[23] *Ibid.*, p. 232.

[24] Celso Furtado, *The Economic Growth of Brazil, A Survey From Colonial to Modern Times*, tr. Ricardo W. deAguiar and Eric Charles Drysdale (Berkeley, Calif.: University of California Press, 1963), pp. 63–71.

help supplement the colony's supply of basic food crops. That there was a perennial shortage of food in the colonial cities and on the sugar plantations is well established. Says Freyre, about the state of alimentation during colonial times: "Bad upon the plantations and very bad in the cities—not only bad, but scarce."[25] It is known that in the West Indies the concentration on sugar was so great that much of their subsistence food requirements had to be met by imports from New England.[26] At least in times of high sugar prices it seems probable that the Brazilian plantations suffered the same fate:

The profitability of the sugar business was inducive to specialization, and it is not surprising ... that the entrepreneurs avoided diverting production factors into secondary activities, at least at times when the prospects of the sugar market seemed favorable. At such times even the production of food for the sustenance of the slaves was anti-economic. ...[27]

Who then were the food growers of colonial Brazil? Who supplied Bahia, Recife, and Rio with food? Although documentary proof is lacking, it would be most surprising if the bulk of the small farmer class did not consist of aged and infirm manumitted slaves, and favorite Negro concubines who with their mulatto offspring had been set up with a bit of marginal land. There was no one to object in Brazil, if after eight years of lash-driven labor, a broken slave was set free and permitted to squat on some fringe of the plantation.

All those interstitial types of military and economic activities which in Brazil could only be initially filled by half-caste free men were performed in the United States by the Southern yeomanry. Because the influx of Africans and the appearance of mulattoes in the United States occurred only *after* a large, intermediate class of whites had already been established, there was in effect no place for the freed slave, be he mulatto or Negro, to go.

It would be wrong, however, to create the impression that the Southern yeomanry, from whence sprang the "rednecks," "crackers," and hillbillies, were capable of intimidating the lords of the Southern plantations. The brutal treatment suffered by the small white farmers as they were driven back to the hills or into the swamps and pine barrens should suffice to set the record straight. If the slave in the South came less and less frequently to be manumitted and if the freedmen were deprived of effective citizenship, and if mulattoes were forced back into the Negro group by the descent rule, it was not because of the sentimental affinity which Southern gentlemen felt for their own "kind." To be sure, there was an intense feeling of racial solidarity among the whites, but nothing could be more in error than to suppose that the racial camaraderie of planter and yeoman was merely the adumbration of some biopsychological tendency on the part of racially similar people to stick together and hate people who are different. Race prejudice once again explains nothing; such an explanation is precisely what the planters and yeomen came to agree upon, and what the rest of America has been sold for the last 150 years. There were alternate explanations, but these the American people has never permitted itself to learn.

The most remarkable of all the phenomena connected with the "peculiar institution" in the United States is the failure of the nonslave-holding yeo-

[25] Freyre, op. cit., p. 57.
[26] Furtado, *The Economic Growth of Brazil* ... , p. 28.
[27] *Ibid.*, p. 59.

manry and poor whites who constituted three-fourths of all Southerners to destroy the plantation class.[28] These whites were as surely and as permanently the victims of the slave system as were the free half-castes and Negroes and the slaves themselves. Their entire standard of living was depressed by the presence of the slaves. Artisans, farmers, and mechanics all found themselves in competition with the kind of labor force it is impossible to undersell—people who work for no wages at all! In 1860, the average annual wage among the textile workers in New England was $205; in the South, it was $145. "Even in industries that employed no slaves, the threat to employ them was always there, nonetheless."[29] The relationship between the precarious condition of the Southern white yeomen and mechanics and the slave system was known and avidly discussed by many planters, reformers, and abolitionists. Some of the planters were perfectly willing to see the poor whites depressed to the level of the slaves, in the conviction that the ruling oligarchy was blessed with a divine mandate to rule over the "mudsills"—"the greasy mechanics, filthy operatives, small-fisted farmers. . . ." The slave-holders, "born to command and trained to ride their saddled underlings, assumed the usual aristocratic disdain for the 'lower order' whether Negro or white. . . ."[30] A South Carolina member of the House of Representatives overtly expressed what was probably a general feeling among

the planters: "If laborers ever obtain the political power of a country, it is in fact in a state of revolution, which must end in substantially transferring property to themselves . . . unless those who have it shall appeal to the sword and a standing army to protect it."[31] Another Southern spokesman did not hesitate to admit that the Southern government was based on excluding "all of the lowest and most degraded classes . . . whether slaves or free, white or black."[32] Why this opinion of them did not penetrate the minds of the majority of the poor whites, we shall see in a moment. However, there were thousands of individuals and even organized groups of Southern yeomen and mechanics who understood that they as much as the Negroes were suffering the effects of slavery. Some of them were able to put the story together with breathtaking insight:

When a journeyman printer *underworks* the usual rates he is considered an enemy to the balance of the fraternity, and is called a *"rat."* Now the slave-holders have *ratted* us with the 180,000 slaves till forbearance longer on our part has become criminal. They have *ratted* us till we are unable to support ourselves with the ordinary comfort of a laborer's life. They have *ratted* us out of the social circle. They have *ratted* us out of the means of making our own schools. . . . They have *ratted* us out of the press. They have *ratted* us out of the legislature. . . . Come, if we are not worse than brutish beasts, let us but speak the word, and slavery shall die![33]

But slavery did not succumb at the hands of those who could most easily have killed it, and who, it would seem, had every reason to want it dead. Instead, the Southern yeomanry followed

---

[28] "Nearly three-fourths of all free Southerners had no connection with slavery through either family ties or direct ownership. The 'typical' Southerner was not only a small farmer but also a nonslave-holder." (Kenneth Stampp, *The Peculiar Institution* [New York: Knopf, 1956], p. 30.)

[29] *Ibid.*, p. 426.

[30] Bernard Mandel, *Labor: Slave and Free* (New York, Associated Authors, 1955), p. 38.

[31] *Ibid.*, p. 40, quoting F. W. Pichins.

[32] *Ibid.*, quoting Edmund Ruffin.

[33] *Ibid.*, p. 50, quoting Cassius Marcellus Clay.

the planters into a war and bled themselves white in defense of the "property"
which was the cause of all their sorrow.
Why? Were they so loyal to the owners
of the slaves because the measure of
their hatred for dark skin and curly
hair was so great? They fought because
they were prejudiced, but it is no
ordinary prejudice that leads a man to
kill another over his looks.

It is not surprising that a Negro
abolitionist, Frederick Douglass, an ex-
slave himself, came so close to the
answer, which many Americans, including scholars of high repute, cannot
face:

> The slave-holders, with a craftiness pecu-
> liar to themselves, by encouraging the
> enmity of the the poor, laboring white man
> against the blacks, succeeded in making
> the said white man almost as much a slave
> as the black man himself. The difference
> between the white slave, and the black
> slave, is this: the latter belongs to *one*
> slave-holder, and the former belongs to *all*
> the slave-holders, collectively. The white
> slave has taken from him by indirection,
> what the black slave has taken from him,
> directly, and without ceremony. Both are
> plundered, and by the same plunderers.
> The slave is robbed by his master of all his
> earnings above what is required for his
> bare physical necessities; and the white man
> is robbed by the slave system, of the just
> results of his labor, because he is flung into
> competition with a class of laborers who
> work without wages. . . . At present the
> slave-holders blind them to this competi-
> tion by keeping alive their prejudices
> against the slaves, as *men*—not against them
> *as slaves*. They appeal to their pride, often
> denounce emancipation, as tending to
> place the white working man, on an equal-
> ity with negroes, and, by this means, they
> succeed in drawing off the minds of the poor
> whites from the real fact, that, by the rich
> slave master, they are already regarded as
> but a single remove from equality with
> the slave.[34]

---

[34] *Ibid.*, p. 59.

This account of the origin of the
Southern race mania betrays an under-
standable tendency to exaggerate both
the diabolism of the masters and the
stupidity of the poor whites. It does not
suffice to account for the equally virulent anti-Negro sentiments in the North
as expressed by the Northern mobs
which burned Pennsylvania Hall, destroyed the abolitionist presses, burned
down a Negro orphan asylum in New
York, and rioted against Negroes in almost every major Northern city during
the Civil War. It does not explain why
the Civil War was begun ostensibly to
"save the Union" and why the Emancipation Proclamation could only be
sold to the country as a military
measure designed to throw additional
manpower against the enemy.[35] The
fact is, the Southern planters held a
trump. To the abolitionists who warned
both the Northern and Southern lower-
class farmers and laborers that slavery
would eventually drag them all down
together, the planters countered that
slavery was the only thing that was
keeping 4 million African laborers
from *immediately* taking the lands,
houses, and jobs which white men
enjoyed. The unleashing of 4 million
ex-slaves on the wage market was indeed a nightmare calculated to terrify
the poor whites of both regions.

The guiding principle of the slavocracy was
divide et impera. Its basic policy followed two
lines, the first of which was to convince the
white laborers that they had a material
interest in the preservation of the chattel

---

[35] Lincoln regarded the Thirteenth Amendment as a military measure worth a million
soldiers. Lorraine Williams, "Northern Intellectual Reaction to the Policy of Emancipation," *The Journal of Negro History*, XLVI
(1961), 187. Charles Wesley ("The Civil War
and the Negro-American," *The Journal of
Negro History*, XLVII (1962), 77–96) views the
confusion over the cause of the Civil War as
part of the continuing battle for Negro rights.

system. They were constantly told that, by consigning the hard, menial, and low-paid tasks to slaves, the white workers were led to constitute a labor aristocracy which held the best and most dignified jobs, and that the latter were lucrative only because they were supported by the super-profits wrung from the unpaid labor of slaves. Unless abolitionism was "met and repelled" ... the whites would have to take over the menial jobs and the emancipated slaves would be able to compete with them in every branch of industry.[36]

White laborers, both North and South, believed that emancipation was a plot of Northern capital to lower wages and enlarge its labor pool. Insistent propaganda pounded this line across; anti-slavery men were called "Midas-eared Mammonites" who wanted to bring Southern slaves into the North to "compete with and assist in reducing the wages of the white laborer."[37] First-hand experience with the use of slaves in the South and of free Negroes in the North to break strikes made this story quite believable. And indeed, minus the allegation of complicity between abolitionists and capitalists, there was more than a grain of truth in it.[38]

One more point needs to be made before the freed United States Negro and mulatto are properly located in relationship to the immense economic and political forces which were building race relations in their country as they swept the North and South toward civil war. One gains the distinct impression that fear of slave uprisings in the United States was far more pervasive than it was in Brazil, considering the relatively large number of armed whites who con-

fronted the defenseless, brutalized, and brainwashed slaves. However, this fear was not based on miscalculation of the enemy. For unlike the case in Brazil, the enemy was not merely the slave, but an organized, vocal, persistent, and steadily increasing group of skilled abolitionists who from the very day this country was founded dedicated their lives to the destruction of the slave power. Although Brazil was not entirely devoid of abolitionist sentiment early in the nineteenth century, the scope and intensity of antislavery agitation cannot be compared with the furor in the United States. A congressional investigating committee in 1838 was told that there were 1,400 antislavery societies in the United States with a membership of between 112,000 and 150,000.[39] In Brazil, the lucky slave fled to a *quilombo*, where cut off from all contact with the rest of the world, the best he could hope for was that the dogs would not find him. In the United States, however, the whole North was a vast *quilombo* in which not only were there escaped slaves but free men of all colors, actively and openly campaigning to bring an end to the thralldom of the whip. The constant patrolling of Southern roads, the fierce punishments for runaways, the laws discouraging manumission, the lumping of free mulattoes with free Negroes, their harassment and persecution, and the refusal to permit either of them to reside in some of the slave-holding states, were all part and parcel of the same problem. One wonders what effect it would have had in Brazil, if the larger and more powerful part of the country had been officially dedicated to the

---

[36] Mandel, op. cit., p. 57.

[37] Dumond, op. cit., p. 352, quoting Henry Field James.

[38] Cf. Norris Preyes, "The Historian, the Slave, and the Ante-Bellum Textile Industry," *Journal of Negro History*, XLVI (1961), 67–82, description of Negro textile workers.

---

[39] *Ibid.*, p. 258; according to Edgar J. Mc-Manus ("Antislavery Legislation in New York," *Journal of Negro History*, XLVI (1961), 207–16), "Practically every American leader during the Revolution favored some plan of emancipation."

proposition that slavery ought to be abolished, and if in every major city in that region freed Negroes and mulattoes had preached and plotted the overthrow of the system. In a sense, the Civil War did not begin in 1860, but in 1776. From the moment this country came into existence the issue of Negro rights was caught in a thousand conflicting currents and countercurrents. Under these circumstances, it hardly seems reasonable to conclude that it is our "Anglo-Saxon Protestant heritage" which is at fault. Indeed there are so many more palpable things at which to point, that I hope I will be forgiven for mentioning only the few which seem to me most important.

DAVID BRION DAVIS

The Comparative Approach to
American History: Slavery

David Brion Davis is Ernest I. White Professor of History at Cornell University. He is the author of Homicide in American Fiction, 1798–1860 *(1957). The first of the two Davis selections is from a recent book edited by C. Vann Woodward,* The Comparative Approach to American History. The Problem of Slavery in Western Culture, *from which the other selection is taken, is the first volume of a projected multivolume study of the antislavery movement in Britain and the United States. It was awarded the 1967 Pulitzer prize for general nonfiction and was a leading contender for the National Book Award in history and biography (1967).*

Of all American institutions, Negro slavery has probably been the one most frequently compared with historical antecedents and foreign counterparts, and with the least benefit to systematic knowledge. Quite understandably, modern scholars have been so impressed by the long submission and degradation of Southern Negroes, as well as by the extraordinary prevalence of racial prejudice in the United States, that they have often pictured American slavery as a system of unique and un-

mitigated severity that stands in marked contrast to other forms of servitude. Yet Thomas Jefferson could confidently assert that in Augustan Rome the condition of slaves was "much more deplorable than that of the blacks on the continent of America," and list barbarities and cruelties which were commonplace in Rome but presumably unknown in Virginia. Apologists for American slavery were always fond of comparing the mildness of their own institution, supposedly evidenced by a rapidly increasing Negro population, with the harshness of slavery in the West Indies or ancient Rome, where a constant supply of fresh captives made up

Chapter 9 (pp. 121–33) in *The Comparative Approach to American History* edited by C. Vann Woodward, © 1968 by C. Vann Woodward, Basic Books, Inc., Publishers, New York.

for an appalling mortality. Yet abolitionists were always inclined to argue that the slave system of their own country or empire was the worst in history. Foreign travelers were not only subject to nationalistic prejudice but tended to rank various slave systems on the basis of fortuitous impressions or the biased accounts of hospitable planters. When we recognize how often comparisons have been influenced by ulterior motives and have been directed to the fruitless question "Which nation's slavery was the worst?" we might conclude that the subject can most profitably be studied in geographical isolation.

Yet American slavery was a product of the African slave trade, which was itself an integral part of both European commercial expansion and New World colonization. Most of the components of the slave-trading and plantation systems were developed in the thirteenth and fourteenth centuries by Italian merchants who purchased Circassians, Tartars, and Georgians at commercial bases on the Black Sea and then transported them to markets in Egypt, Italy, and Spain. As early as 1300 the enterprising Italians were even working Negro slaves on sugar plantations in Cyprus. In the fifteenth century, when the Portuguese adopted similar practices in trading with West Africa, Negro slaves displaced the Moors and Russians as the lowest element in the labor force of Spain. Negroes were shipped to Hispaniola as early as 1502; and as the Spanish colonists gradually turned to the cultivation of sugar, the rising demand for labor became an enormous stimulus to the Portuguese African trade. By the seventeenth century the Atlantic slave trade had become a vast international enterprise as the Dutch, British, French, Danes, Swedes, and even Brandenburgers established forts

and markets along the West African coast. On both sides of the Atlantic there was close contact between merchants, seamen, and planters of various nationalities. In addition to competing and fighting with one another, they borrowed techniques and customs, cooperated in smuggling, and gathered to buy slaves at such entrepôts as Curaçao. If the British planters of Barbados looked to Brazil as a model, Barbados itself provided the impulse for settling Carolina. There was, then, a high degree of institutional continuity which linked the European maritime powers in a common venture. A trade which involved six major nations and lasted for three centuries, which transported some 10 to 15 million Africans to the New World, and which became a central part of international rivalry and the struggle for empire, cannot be considered as a mere chapter in the history of North America.

The unpleasant truth is that there could hardly have been successful colonization of the New World without Negro slaves, since there was no alternative source of labor to meet the needs required by the cultivation of sugar, rice, tobacco, and cotton, and since even the more diversified colonies were long dependent economically on the markets and earnings of the staple-producing regions. It must be emphasized that this common dependence on Negro slavery was never universally recognized or welcomed. From the first Spanish in Hispaniola to the British in Barbados and Virginia, colonists were slow and hesitant in committing themselves to a labor force of foreign captives. Among the frequent dreams of New World Utopias and second Edens, no one envisioned a model society of several thousand free Europeans overseeing the life and labor of several hundred thousand Negro slaves. From the beginning, racial antipathy was reinforced by the much stronger emotion of fear; and the dread of insurrection and racial war would always balance the desire for quick wealth through a reckless increase in slaves.

Nonetheless, from sixteenth-century Mexico to eighteenth-century Jamaica and South Carolina, colonial administrators were unable to maintain a reassuring ratio between white immigrants and Negro slaves. In regions where tropical or semitropical staples could be cultivated, it became clear that investment in slave labor was the key to expanded production and spectacular profit. The Negro slave played an indispensable role in the conquest and settlement of Latin America and in the clearing and cultivation of virgin land from Trinidad to the lower Mississippi Valley and Texas. And as the possession of slaves became itself a symbol of affluence, prestige, and power, the demand for Negroes spread to urban and temperate zones. Important leaders in New England and French Canada seriously argued that only Negro slaves could meet the labor needs of their colonies. From 1732 to 1754 Negro slaves constituted more than 35 per cent of the immigrants entering New York City; by mid-century they were owned by about one-tenth of the householders of the province and accounted for 15 per cent of the total population. Meanwhile, the slave trade and American Negro slavery were sanctioned by treaties and the law of nations, by the acts and edicts of kings and parliaments, by the Spanish Council of the Indies and the great trading companies of England, Holland, and France, by the Catholic Church and the major Protestant denominations. All the colonies of the New World legalized the institution, and many competed with one another for a supply of labor that

was never equal to the demand. For more than three centuries the Negro slave was deeply involved in imperial wars, revolutions, and wars of independence. Insofar as the Western Hemisphere has a common history, it must center on a common experience with Negro slavery.

But did slavery mean the same thing to the various colonists of the New World? The fact that Dutch slave-traders imitated the Portuguese and that a Dutch ship brought the first Negroes to Virginia did not mean that a Negro's status would be the same in Virginia as in Brazil. In England, unlike Italy and the Iberian Peninsula, true slavery disappeared by the thirteenth century. On the other hand, English jurists perpetuated the legal concept of unlimited servitude, and English judges recognized the validity of enslaving and selling infidels. We still have much to learn about the character of servitude in the sixteenth century and the later evolution of slave status in the British, Dutch, and French colonies. In making future comparative studies it would be well to keep in mind two points which should prevent hasty generalizations. First, in many societies the slave has only gradually been differentiated from other kinds of unfree workers, and his status, rights, and obligations have been defined in practice before receiving legal recognition. Second, although the actual condition of slaves has varied greatly even within a single society, there has been a remarkable persistence and uniformity in the legal concept of the slave. Since this last point has often been disregarded in comparative approaches to American slavery, we shall elaborate on it here.

The status of slavery has always been surrounded with certain ambiguities that seem related to the institution's origins. To be enslaved as a result of capture in war or punishment for crime implied total subordination to coercive authority. Yet bondage for debt or as the result of self-sale suggested merely a reciprocal exchange of labor and obedience for sustenance and protection. When a boundwoman's offspring were claimed by her owner on the same basis as the natural increase of livestock, the status was assimilated to that of movable property. In societies where slaves have largely been recruited from the native poor and have performed no specialized economic function, as in ancient China, Egypt, and the Near East, the elements of reciprocal rights and obligations has taken precedence over the elements of punishment and ownership. Nevertheless, the slave was legally defined as a thing not only in the Southern United States but in ancient Egypt, Babylonia, Greece, and Rome. And the Roman conception of the slave as at once a person and a piece of movable property prevailed in medieval France, Italy, and Spain; it was extended to Latin America and was incorporated in the *Code Noir* for the French colonies; and it reappeared in the laws and judicial decisions of British North America. A Virginia court merely affirmed the ancient Latin concept of chattel slavery when it ruled that "Slaves are not only property, but they are rational beings, and entitled to the humanity of the Court, when it can be exercised without invading the rights of property." And when an American master claimed the offspring of his female slaves or asserted his right to move, sell, trade, bequest, or give away his chattel property, he added nothing to a legal notion of slavery that had persisted in Europe for more than two thousand years.

The definition of the slave as chattel property implied a condition of right-lessness on the part of the slave. In neither Europe nor the Americas could a slave testify in court against a free person, institute a court action in his own behalf, make a legally binding will or contract, or own property. There were, to be sure, minor exceptions and variations. Slaves were sometimes allowed to testify in certain civil cases or give evidence against a master accused of treason. In North America at various times Negro bondsmen were permitted to plead benefit of clergy and to give evidence in capital cases involving other slaves. As in Rome and Latin America, they were accorded limited rights over personal property, including horses and cattle, and might act as a master's legal agent, though never with the freedom and complex prerogatives of the Roman slave. But what stands out above the exceptions and variations is the fact that from pre-Christian laws to the slave codes of the New World the bondsman had no civil capacities and was considered only as an extension of his master's legal personality. Even in Puritan Massachusetts slaves were, in the words of Cotton Mather, who was simply echoing Aristotle, "the *Animate, Separate, Active Instruments* of other men."

One of the few significant differences in the legal status of slaves was that bondsmen were denied legal marriage in ancient Rome and in Protestant America, whereas slave marriages were recognized in Carthage, Hellenistic Greece, and in Catholic Europe and America. Largely to prevent the sin of fornication, Catholic theologians even ruled that a slave might marry against his master's will. Yet according to St. Thomas Aquinas, slavery was an "impediment" to marriage, comparable to impotence, and a slave's first obligation must be to his master, not his spouse. If a master had a moral duty to try to preserve the integrity of slave families, he still had a legal claim to all slave children, and might of necessity divide husband from wife or children from parents. Since there is evidence that Latin American masters often did little to encourage or respect slave marriages, and that North American masters often recognized such marriages and tried to keep families intact, one may suspect that actual differences were more the result of individual personality and economic pressure than of legal and moral rights. The main point is that in no society have slaves had a legal claim to their wives and children.

Religious conversion has always complicated the question of a slave's status. The Muslims and ancient Hebrews drew a sharp distinction between enslaving infidels and temporarily holding servants of their own faith who had been deprived of freedom by economic necessity. Although the first Church Fathers ruled unmistakably that baptism should have no effect on the temporal status of slaves, medieval Christians showed an increasing reluctance to enslave their fellow Christians and came to think of perpetual bondage as a punishment suitable only for infidels. But the authorities who condemned the sale of Christians and yet preached slaving crusades against the infidels were ultimately faced with the problem of the baptized infidel. In 1366 the priors of Florence explained that it was valid to buy or sell slaves who had been baptized so long as they had originally come "from the land and race of the infidels." This was, in effect, the same test later applied in Virginia and other North American colonies. Baptism was to have no effect on a slave's status unless he had been a Christian in his native country. And if the Catholic colonists felt a much greater obligation

to have their slaves baptized, North American laws encouraged conversion and recognized that the Negro had a soul that might be redeemed. After a century of inaction, the Protestant churches slowly began their work of spreading religion among the slaves, and by the mid-nineteenth century the proportion of converted Negroes was probably as large in parts of the United States as in Brazil. It is doubtful, however, whether the mass of slaves in any country ever enjoyed a meaningful religious life.

There was little that was distinctive in the police regulations and penal laws restricting the lives of North American slaves. Throughout the ages, and in virtually all parts of the Western Hemisphere, slaves were prohibited from carrying arms, traveling at night or without permission, and acting with disrespect toward a freeman. Fairly typical was a law of 1785 for Spanish Santo Domingo which ordered one hundred lashes and two years in jail for any Negro who raised his hand against a white man. The penalties for such crimes as theft and assault were everywhere more severe for slaves than for others. During the eighteenth century there was a tendency in most New World colonies to abandon the most sanguinary punishments, such as mutilation, dismemberment, and burning at the stake. Harsh restrictions and terrifying punishments persisted longest in the West Indies, where the disproportion of Negroes to whites was the greatest. But even in the West Indies the long-term trend was toward more humane punishment and an extension of the slave's legal protections.

It is misleading to say that Anglo-American law never recognized the Negro slave as a human personality whose rights to life, food, and shelter were protected by law. There was ample precedent for the 1846 ruling of a Kentucky judge that "A slave is not in the condition of a horse. . . . He is made after the image of the Creator. He has mental capacities, and an immortal principle in his nature. . . . The law . . . cannot extinguish his high born nature, nor deprive him of many rights which are inherent in man." Although a master might kill his slave with impunity in the ancient Near East, the Roman Republic, Saxon England, and under certain circumstances in the Iberian Peninsula and Latin America, and although in much of British America the murder of a slave was thought to merit only a modest fine, by the early nineteenth century the slave states of North America had put the killing or maiming of a Negro bondsman on the same level of criminality as the killing or maiming of a white man. In both the British Caribbean and the Southern states, courts sometimes held that slaves were protected by common law against such crimes as manslaughter or unprovoked battery. Georgia and North Carolina both held that slaves had a right to trial by jury, and North Carolina went so far as to recognize a slave's right to resist unprovoked attack. Of course it was one thing for American states to threaten punishment for cruelty to slaves, and to make masters legally obligated to give their bondsmen adequate food and shelter and to provide for their care in sickness and old age, and it was another matter to enforce such laws when Negroes were barred from testifying against white men. Nevertheless, one can plausibly argue that in terms of legal protections and physical welfare American slaves by the 1850's were as favorably treated as any bondsmen in history.

Yet one of the paradoxes of American slavery was that the laws protecting the physical welfare of slaves were accompanied by the severest restrictions on manumission. This brings us to the most important distinction between the legal status of slaves in British and Latin America. It should be stressed that taxes and other restrictions on manumission were common in antiquity, particularly in Rome, and that freedom suffered from prejudice and legal disabilities even when the stigma of slavish origin was not associated with race. There were discriminatory freedmen's laws, for example, in medieval Spain and Italy, and in Latin America as well. But only in the Southern United States did legislators try to bar every route to emancipation and deprive masters of their traditional right to free individual slaves. It is true that thousands of American slaves were manumitted by their owners, many after buying their freedom in installments, as was far more common in Latin America. It is also true that in some areas of Latin America a slave had no more realistic chance of becoming free than did his brother in Mississippi. Nevertheless, one may conclude that slavery in North America was distinctive in its efforts to build ever higher barriers against manumission. And there is evidence that this had less to do with slavery as such than with social attitudes toward racial integration.

Although the questions are of compelling importance, we cannot begin to determine whether slavery was a source of racial prejudice or prejudice a source of slavery, nor can we explain why prejudice became more dominant in the United States than in other parts of the New World. One may briefly state the principal facts that are relevant to a comparative study of slavery. Without denying the significance of racial difference as an aggravation to American bondage, we may note that throughout history slaves have been said to be naturally inferior, lazy, cunning, thievish, lascivious, fawning, deceitful, and incapable of life's higher thoughts and emotions. When not differentiated by race, they have often been physically marked off by shaven heads, brands, tattoos, and collars. There is unmistakable evidence of racial prejudice in Italy and the Iberian Peninsula, where colored slaves generally suffered from various indignities and disabilities. In Latin America Negro bondsmen were long denied the privileges and protections of Indian workers. Nonetheless, while Latin America was by no means immune from racial prejudice, even against freemen of mixed blood, there was a gradual acceptance of racial intermixture and a willingness to accept each stage of dilution as a step toward whiteness. In the British colonies, although the first Negroes had an ill-defined status and worked side by side with white servants, there was never any tolerance of racial blending. White fathers seldom acknowledged their colored offspring, and a mulatto or quadroon was still legally classed as a Negro. These differences may have been related to religion, sexual mores, social stratification, or the proportion of white women in a colonial population. But whatever the reason, prejudice against Negroes seems to have grown in the United States with the advance of popular democracy. It can be argued that this had less to do with slavery than with the status of the free Negro in an unusually mobile and unstratified white society. In other words, differences in slave systems may not account for the fact that while the Negro in the United States today has far more economic and educational opportunities than the Negro in Latin America, he also suffers from more overt discrimination from whites who feel superior but are unsure of their own status.

By focusing thus far on the legal status of slaves, we have given an oversimplified picture of institutional homogeneity. In actuality, of course, American slavery took a great variety of forms that were largely the result of economic pressures and such derivative factors as the nature of employment, the number of slaves owned by a typical master, and the proportion of slaves in a given society. Thus we correctly categorize North American slavery as plantation and staple-crop slavery, but tend to forget that in 1820 Negro bondsmen constituted 20 per cent of the population of Southern cities and that in 1860 there were a half million slaves working in factories, on railroad construction, as stevedores, as lumberjacks, on steamboats, and in numerous other jobs unconnected with agriculture. As in ancient Athens and Rome, and as in Latin America, slaves in the Southern states were employed as valets, waiters, cooks, nurses, craftsmen, and prostitutes. In spite of these well-known facts, most comparisons of slavery in British and Latin America have assumed that the institutions were virtually monolithic. We still lack comparative studies of the domestic servant, the slave artisan, the rented worker, and the slave in manufacturing establishments.

It has been said that the latifundia of southern Italy and Sicily provided an ancient precedent for the gang labor, the rationalized system of production, and the absentee ownership of the Caribbean plantation. But one must be careful not to lump all plantation agriculture in an undifferentiated class. Since the production of sugar, for example, was a long and continuous process that could be ruined by a delay in cutting, milling, boiling, or curing, the rhythm of plantation life was probably much the same in parts of Brazil as in Jamaica and Louisiana. The cultivation of sugar and rice required heavy capital investment, and in the West Indies and South Carolina led to slave gangs of several hundred being divided for specialized tasks under constant surveillance. Slavery in colonial South Carolina, though less characterized by absentee ownership, had more in common with slavery in the West Indies than either had with the institution in Virginia and Maryland. By 1765 South Carolina's 40,000 whites were outnumbered by 90,000 slaves; eight years later Jamaica's 16,000 whites kept uneasy watch over 200,000 slaves. In neither society could a field slave be in close or frequent contact with white men. In Virginia, on the other hand, the proportion of Negroes and whites was roughly equal, and the typical tobacco plantation employed less than twenty slaves. Unlike any of the previously mentioned staples, cotton did not require elaborate stages of preparation and processing, and could be profitably grown on small-scale farms. It was thus not uncommon for a cotton farmer to own less than ten slaves and even to work beside them in the field. Even by 1860, after a long period of rising slave prices, nearly one-half of the Southern slave-holders owned less than five Negroes apiece; 72 per cent owned less than ten apiece and held approximately one-quarter of the entire number of American slaves.

Compared with the plantation agriculture of the West Indies and Brazil, the striking features of the American South were the wide dispersal of slave ownership and the relatively small units of production scattered over immense areas. This may have led to a greater variation and flexibility in the relationship between master and slaves, although we still lack comparative research on such vital questions as labor management, the social roles and subculture of Negroes, and the relation of plantation life to social structure. It seems plausible that if American Negroes sometimes benefited by a close relationship with white families, they were also denied the sense of massive solidarity that was probably essential for revolt. In the West Indies slaves not only had the opportunity to plan and organize revolts, but they were seldom tied by the close bonds of loyalty that led so many North American slaves to divulge plots before they were hardly formed.

This is not to suggest that North American slaves were less oppressed than those of other times and regions, but only that there were different forms of oppression. As comparative studies move ahead toward finer distinctions and a typology of slave systems, it is likely that less attention will be paid to legal status than to stages of economic development. It would be absurd to claim that all slave economies must pass through a pre-set cycle of boom and depression. Nevertheless, regardless of cultural differences and other variables, there are striking examples throughout the Americas of a pattern which began with an unmitigated drive for quick profit, a rapid expansion in slaves and land under cultivation, and a subsequent overproduction of staples. Whenever slaves were worked under boom conditions, as in the West Indies in the mid-eighteenth century and the Brazilian coffee plantations in the nineteenth, the institution was one of grinding attrition. A more relaxed paternalism tended to appear when prices had fallen, when there was little incentive to maximize production, and when planters in longer-settled regions looked to social and cultural distinctions to differentiate themselves from new generations of hard-driving speculators. Thus in the mid-nineteenth century there is evidence that in such states as Virginia and Maryland a more easy-going, paternalistic pattern of slavery was emerging, not unlike that of the depleted sugar plantations of Brazil. In Maryland and Delaware there was even a rapid decline in the proportion of slaves to freedmen, though this was partly a result of interstate migration. At the same time there was a heavy drain of slaves toward the expanding cotton areas of the Southwest, where the price of labor kept rising and slaves became more concentrated in the hands of a relatively few planters.

The question of stages of economic development is related to the much larger question of the place of slavery in the evolution of industrial capitalism. And here, though historians have long acknowledged the dependence of the world's cotton textile industry on the slave systems of North and South America, there is an astonishing lack of systematic and comparative analysis. The whole complex relationship between capitalism and slavery is still in the realm of suggestive speculation. Scholars still debate whether slavery was profitable and whether the forms it took in America can be termed capitalistic. We do not yet fully understand why so many areas where slavery flourished were stultified by soil depletion and a lack of capital formation, by an absence of internal markets, of urbanization, and of technological innovation. And finally, if we are really to comprehend the significance of slavery and the burdens it has entailed, comparative history must explain the great challenge posed to the institution by an emerging urban, bureaucratic, and capitalistic civilization, which led to a bitter conflict between England and her Caribbean colonies, to a sharp struggle between the Brazilian coastal cities and the interior valleys, and to an epic contest between the North and South in the United States.

DAVID BRION DAVIS

A Comparison of
British America
and Latin America

See the headnote on page 60 for bibliographical information. In the following selection Davis begins with a question about abolitionism. To answer that question, he discusses the nature of different slave societies in the hemisphere and the significance of the differences among them.

Was antislavery, then, a direct out-growth of slavery itself? We have maintained that the concept of man as a material possession has always led to contradictions in law and custom. In the ancient world these contradictions did not give rise to abolitionism; but in the historical development of American slavery there were deep strains that made the institution a source of dis-sonance and discontent. Even men whose interests were closely tied to the system expressed occasional misgivings over mounting debts and economic

From David Brion Davis, *The Problem of Slavery in Western Culture* (Ithaca, N. Y.: Cornell University Press, 1966), pp. 223–43. Copyright © 1966 by Cornell University. Used by permission of Cornell University Press.

decay, the rising proportion of Negroes to whites, the haunting threat of insurrection, the failure to infuse masters and slaves with a spirit of Christian love, and the growing discrepancy between American servitude and European ideals of liberty. It remains to be asked whether the evolution of colonial laws and customs provided a basis for believing that the worst evils of slavery could be gradually eliminated through wise legislation, or for concluding that slavery by its very nature was beyond reform.

Such a question poses many problems. As a result of differences in economy, social, and political institutions, and the ratio of Negroes to whites, the actual status and condition of colonial slaves varied considerably from one region to another. Yet no slave colony had a monopoly on either kindness or cruelty. Slave codes were often enacted with a view to quieting local fears or appeasing a church or government. Travelers were sometimes biased or quick to generalize from a few fleeting impressions. Since we still seriously lack a thorough comparative study of Negro slavery in the various colonies, we must be content with fragmentary evidence and with extremely tentative conclusions. There would seem to be some basis, however, for questioning two assumptions which have been widely accepted by modern historians.

The first is that Negro slavery in the British colonies and Southern United States was of a nearly uniform severity, the slave being legally deprived of all rights of person, property, and family, and subjected to the will of his owner and the police power of the state, which barred his way to education, free movement, or emancipation. The second assumption is that the French, and especially the Spanish and Portuguese, were far more liberal in their treatment of slaves, whom they considered as human beings who had merely lost a portion of their external freedom. Untainted by racial prejudice and free from the pressures of a fluid, capitalistic economy, these easygoing colonists are supposed to have protected the human rights of the slave and to have facilitated his manumission. Some historians have simply held that slavery in North America was much harsher than that in Latin America, but Stanley M. Elkins has argued more persuasively that the great contrast was not in the bondsman's physical well-being but in the recognition of his basic humanity.[1] As

[1] Stanley M. Elkins, *Slavery: A Problem in American Institutional and Intellectual Life* (Chicago,

a methodological device, this distinction has obvious merit, since a master might look upon his slaves as subhuman animals and still provide them with comfortable maintenance. On the other hand, it would be unrealistic to draw too sharp a line between moral status and physical treatment. It is difficult to see how a society could have much respect for the value of slaves as human personalities if it sanctioned their torture and mutilation, the selling of their small children, the unmitigated exploitation of their labor, and the drastic shortening of their lives through overwork and inadequate nourishment. While a few isolated instances of sadistic cruelty would reveal little about the legal or moral status of slaves, we should not exclude physical treatment when it is part of a pattern of systematic oppression which is fully sanctioned by the laws and customs of a society. We shall find, however, that there is other evidence than physical treatment for challenging the assumption that Latin

1959), pp. 27–80. It is not my purpose to question all of Elkins' highly imaginative insights, or to attempt to prove that differences in religion, economy, and social structure had no bearing on the institution of Negro slavery. My aim is simply to show that the importance of such national and cultural differences has been exaggerated, and that all American slaveholding colonies shared certain central assumptions and problems. I do not believe that the modern historian can escape what Elkins terms the moral "coercions" of the great nineteenth-century controversies by portraying both American slavery and antislavery as the pathological results of "the dynamics of unopposed capitalism." It should be noted that Elkins borrowed much of his conceptual framework from Frank Tannenbaum's enormously influential *Slave and Citizen: The Negro in the Americas* (New York, 1947). Though Tannenbaum was one of the first historians to emphasize the importance of Negro slavery in the over-all development of the Americas, it seems to me that his comparison of Latin and Anglo-American slavery suffers from three basic weaknesses. First, he assumes

Americans were more sensitive than Anglo-Americans to the essential humanity of their slaves.

This assumption has important implications for a history of antislavery thought. If servitude under the Spanish and Portuguese was generally mild and humane, and if the institution itself tended to promote a gradual achievement of freedom, then we should not be surprised by the fact that antislavery agitation began in Britain and British America. The peculiar severities of British colonial slavery would appear to have arisen from local economic or social conditions, and we should have reason to suspect that antislavery movements were a direct response to an unprecedented evil. And while the extremes of both slavery and antislavery could be explained by the absence of a stable social structure, we could conclude that the Anglo-American reformer might well have looked to Latin America for a rational model. By gradually imposing the institutional protec-

tions of Latin American slavery on the formless and unregulated slavery of the north, he might have removed the evils from a necessary system of labor. But if the contrast between slavery in the various American colonies was not so clear-cut as has generally been supposed, we are left with a different set of implications. It would be likely that the appearance of antislavery agitation was less a direct response to a unique evil than a result of particular cultural and religious developments in the English-speaking world. And if both the evils of slavery and the attempts to ameliorate them were fairly pervasive throughout the Americas, we should look more skeptically at programs for slow and gradual reform. We should expect to find general emancipation often associated with revolutions and civil wars, as was the case in Saint Domingue, the United States, and several of the Spanish colonies, or with political upheaval and the fall of a government, as in Brazil.[2]

---

that North American law, unlike that of Latin America, refused to recognize the slave as a moral personality. But this is an error, as we shall see. Second, he ignores the fact that the "classical" view of slavery, as embodied in Latin culture, drew as much from Plato and Aristotle as from Cicero and Seneca. Nineteenth-century Brazilian reformers, such as José Bonifácio, found it necessary to counter their opponents' use of classical authorities by arguing that Greeks and Romans had been ignorant of divine religion, and that, in any event, slavery in antiquity had not been so severe as that in Brazil, where racial and cultural differences deprived the bondsman of opportunities for equality (José Bonifácio de Andrada e Silva, *Memoir Addressed to the General, Constituent and Legislative Assembly of the Empire of Brazil* . . . [tr. by William Walton, London, 1826], pp. 20–22). As in Roman and North American law, the slave in Latin America was conceived at once as a chattel or instrument, and as a man with a soul. Third, Tannenbaum seems to think of Negro slavery in Latin America as a relatively unchanging institution, and assumes that certain humane laws of the late eighteenth and nine-

teenth centuries were typical of bondage in all Latin America throughout its long history. Even more questionable is his assumption that the admirable laws of European governments were obeyed by colonial slave-holders. For a thoughtful discussion of the Tannenbaum-Elkins thesis, see Sidney Mintz's long review of Elkins' book in *American Anthropologist*, LXIII (June, 1961), 579–87. An article which appeared after this chapter was written, and which presents a similar thesis, is Arnold A. Sio, "Interpretations of Slavery: The Slave Status in the Americas," *Comparative Studies in Society and History*, VII (April, 1965), 289–308.

[2] The violence of the American Civil War has led some historians to assume that other nations abolished Negro slavery without bitter conflict. Yet even in Brazil, where Dom Pedro II strove consciously to avoid the bloody course taken by the United States, there was a radical abolitionist movement, an underground railroad, and sectional cleavage; the stormy conflict played an important part in bringing the downfall of the monarchy (see especially, Percy A. Martin, "Slavery and Abolition in Brazil," *Hispanic American Historical Review*, XIII [May,

A word of explanation is in order regarding the chronological range of selected examples and illustrations. If we are to judge the influence of traditional Catholic culture, the crucial period in Latin American slavery is the early colonial era, before the full impact of the Enlightenment, the American and French Revolutions, and the wars of independence. But when we test the assumption that slavery in the British colonies and Southern United States was of a monolithic character, unmitigated by any recognition of the Negro's rights of personality, it is appropriate to select examples from the nineteenth century, when laws and customs had hardened to form a self-contained system of values and precedents. If some of the ameliorative elements we usually associate with Latin American slavery were common in North America, even at a time when bondage had grown more formalized and severe, then we should have less reason to suppose that the basic evils of the institution could have been eliminated by mere palliative reforms.

By the late eighteenth century most travelers agreed that in Brazil and the Spanish colonies the condition of slaves was considerably better than in British America.[3] Any comparison must consider Negro slavery as a system of forced labor, of social organization, and of class and racial discipline. Numerous accounts from the late eighteenth and nineteenth centuries tell us that the Latin American slave enjoyed frequent hours of leisure and was seldom subjected to the factory-like regimentation that characterized the capitalistic plantations of the north; that he faced no legal bars to marriage, education, or eventual freedom; that he was legally protected from cruelty and oppression, and was not stigmatized on account of his race. This relative felicity has quite plausibly been attributed to a culture that de-emphasized the pursuit of private profit, to the Catholic Church's insistence on the slave's right to marry and worship, and to what Gilberto Freyre has termed the "miscibility" of the Portuguese, which submerged sensitivity to racial difference in a frank acceptance of sexual desire.[4]

No doubt there is much truth in even the idyllic picture of the Brazilian "Big House," where slaves and freemen

1933], 151–96). British planters in the Caribbean frequently threatened secession, and finally submitted to the superior force of the British government only because they were too weak, economically and politically, to resist. They might have acted differently, as did the planters of Saint Domingue during the French Revolution, if Britain had moved to abolish slavery at the time of their greatest power.

[3] Sir Harry Johnston, The Negro in the New World (New York, 1910), pp. 42–47, 87–94; Henry Koster, Travels in Brazil (London, 1816), pp. 385–86, 390, 444; Mary M. Williams, "The Treatment of Negro Slaves in the Brazilian Empire; a Comparison with the United States," Journal of Negro History, XV

(1930), 313–36; Donald Pierson, Negroes in Brazil (Chicago, 1942), pp. 45–46; H. B. Alexander, "Brazilian and United States Slavery Compared," Journal of Negro History, VII (1922), 349–64; Gilberto Freyre, The Masters and the Slaves: A Study in the Development of Brazilian Civilization, tr. by Samuel Putnam (New York, 1946), pp. 7–11, 40–41, 369ff and passim; Tannenbaum, Slave and Citizen, pp. 56, 100–105. An occasional traveler, such as Alexander Marjoribanks, observed that if Brazilian slaves were as well treated as those in the United States, there would have been no need to rely so heavily on the African trade as an answer to slave mortality (Travels in South and North America [London, 1853], p. 60). Freyre, Johnston, and Pierson have balanced a generally favorable picture of Latin American slavery with references to extreme cruelty and suffering.

[4] Gilberto Freyre, Masters and Slaves, pp. 7–11, and passim. But Freyre also maintains that the sexual relations of masters and slaves were authoritarian in character, and often led to sadistic cruelty.

pray and loaf together, and where masters shrug their shoulders at account books and prefer to frolic with slave girls in shaded hammocks. But we should not forget that West Indian and North American planters were fond of idealizing their own "Big Houses" as patriarchal manors, of portraying their Negroes as carefree and indolent, and of proudly displaying humane slave laws which they knew to be unenforceable. Their propaganda, which was supported by travelers' accounts and which long seemed persuasive to many Northerners and Englishmen, has largely been discredited by numerous critical studies based on a wealth of surviving evidence. Many of the records of Brazilian slavery were destroyed in the 1890's, in a fit of abolitionist enthusiasm, and the subject has never received the careful scrutiny it deserves.[5] Only in recent years have such historians as Octávio Ianni, Fernando Henrique Cardoso, Jaime Jaramillo Uribe, and C. R. Boxer begun to challenge the stereotyped images of mild servitude and racial harmony.

There is little reason to doubt that slavery in Latin America, compared with that in North America, was less subject to the pressures of competitive capitalism and was closer to a system of patriarchal rights and semifeudalistic services. But after granting this, we must recognize the inadequacy of thinking in terms of idealized models of patriarchal and capitalistic societies. Presumably, an exploitive, capitalistic form of servitude could not exist within a patriarchal society. The lord of a manor, unlike the entrepreneur who might play the role of lord of a manor, would be incapable of treating men as mere units of labor in a speculative enterprise. But neither would he think of exploring

[5] Arthur Ramos, *The Negro in Brazil*, tr. by Richard Pattee (Washington, 1951), pp. 19–20.

new lands, discovering gold mines, or developing new plantations for the production of sugar and coffee. It is perhaps significant that accounts of Latin American slavery often picture the relaxed life on sugar plantations after their decline in economic importance, and ignore conditions that prevailed during the Brazilian sugar boom of the seventeenth century, the mining boom of the early eighteenth century, and the coffee boom of the nineteenth century. Similarly, Southern apologists tended to overlook the human effects of high-pressure agriculture in the Southwest, and focus their attention on the easygoing and semipatriarchal societies of tidewater Maryland and Virginia. Eugene D. Genovese has recently suggested that while the North American slave system was stimulated and exploited by the capitalist world market, it retained many precapitalistic features, such as a lack of innovation, restricted markets, and low productivity of labor, and actually gravitated toward an uneconomical paternalism that was basically antithetical to capitalistic values.

Although a particular instance of oppression or well-being can always be dismissed as an exception, it is important to know what range of variation a system permitted. If an exploitive, capitalistic form of servitude was at times common in Brazil and Spanish America, and if North Americans conformed at times to a paternalistic model and openly acknowledged the humanity of their slaves, it may be that differences between slavery in Latin America and the United States were no greater than regional or temporal differences within the countries themselves. And such a conclusion would lead us to suspect that Negro bondage was a single phenomenon, or *Gestalt*, whose variations were less significant than underlying patterns of unity.

Simon Gray, a Natchez river boatman, provides us with an example of the flexibility of the North American slave system. During the 1850's, most Southern states tightened their laws and to all appearances erected an impassable barrier between the worlds of slave and freeman. But the intent of legislators was often offset by powerful forces of economic interest and personality. Simon Gray was an intelligent slave whose superior abilities were recognized by both his master and the lumber company which hired his services. In the 1850's this lowly slave became the captain of a flatboat on the Mississippi, supervising and paying wages to a crew that included white men. In defiance of law, Gray was permitted to carry firearms, to travel freely on his own, to build and run sawmills, and to conduct commercial transactions as his company's agent. Entrusted with large sums of money for business purposes, Gray also drew a regular salary, rented a house where his family lived in privacy, and took a vacation to Hot Springs, Arkansas, when his health declined. Although there is evidence that in Southern industry and commerce such privileges were not as uncommon as has been assumed, we may be sure that Simon Gray was a very exceptional slave.[6] He might well have been less exceptional in Cuba or Brazil. The essential point, however, is that regardless of restrictive laws, the Southern slave system had room for a few Simon Grays. The flatboat captain could not have acted as he did if the society had demanded a rigorous enforcement of the law.

By the time Simon Gray was beginning to enjoy relative freedom, Portugal

and Brazil were the only civilized nations that openly resisted attempts to suppress the African slave trade. It has been estimated that by 1853 Britain had paid Portugal some £2,850,965 in bribes intended to stop a commerce whose horrors had multiplied as a result of efforts to escape detection and capture. But despite British bribes and seizures, the trade continued, and was countenanced by the society which has been most praised for its humane treatment of slaves. One of the boats captured by the British, in 1842, was a tiny vessel of eighteen tons, whose crew consisted of six Portuguese. Between decks, in a space only eighteen inches high, they had intended to stow 250 African children of about seven years of age.[7] Suspicion of Britain's motives probably prevented more outspoken attacks on a trade that outraged most of the civilized world. But the fact remains that Brazilian society not only permitted the slave trade to continue for nearly half a century after it had been outlawed by Britain and the United States, but provided a flourishing market for Negroes fresh from Africa. During the 1830's Brazil imported more than 400,000 slaves; in the single year of 1848 the nation absorbed some 60,000 more. That the

---

[6] John H. Moore, "Simon Gray, Riverman: A Slave Who Was Almost Free," *Mississippi Valley Historical Review*, XLIX (Dec., 1962), 472–84.

[7] Christopher Lloyd, *The Navy and the Slave Trade; the Suppression of the African Slave Trade in the Nineteenth Century* (London, 1949), pp. 34, 45. The United States showed laxness in suppressing the African trade, and American ships and capital helped to supply slaves to the chief nineteenth-century markets, Cuba and Brazil. But this laxness was quite a different thing from the open approval of the slave trade by Brazilians. And a recent study which takes a more favorable view of American attempts to suppress the slave trade points out that between 1837 and 1862 American ships captured at least 107 slavers (Peter Duignan and Clarence Clendenen, *The United States and the African Slave Trade, 1619–1862* [n.p. (Stanford University), 1963], p. 54).

reception of these newcomers was not so humane as might be imagined is suggested by a law of 1869, six years after Lincoln's Emancipation Proclamation, which forbade the separate sale of husband and wife, or of children under fifteen. Not long before, even children under ten had been separated from their parents and sent to the coffee plantations of the south.[8]

These examples are intended only to illustrate the range of variation that could occur in any slave society, and hence the difficulties in comparing the relative severity of slave systems. Barbados and Jamaica were notorious for their harsh laws and regimentation, but occasional proprietors like Josiah Steele or Matthew Lewis succeeded in creating model plantations where Negroes were accorded most of the privileges of white servants. John Stedman, who provided Europe with ghastly pictures of the cruelty of Dutch masters in Surinam, also maintained that humanity and gentleness coexisted with the worst barbarity. The well-being of any group of slaves was subject to many variables. It seems certain that the few Negroes in eighteenth-century Québec lived a freer and richer life than hundreds of thousands of slaves in nineteenth-century Brazil and Cuba, despite the fact that the latter were technically guarded by certain legal protections, and the former were defined as chattels completely subject to their owners' authority. Islands like

Dominica and Saint Lucia, which were disorganized by war and a transfer from one nation to another, had few social resources for restraining the unscrupulous master or curbing slave resistance. In the newly developed lands of captured or ceded colonies, such as Berbice, Demerara, Trinidad, and Louisiana, there were few effective checks on the speculative planter bent on reaping maximum profit in the shortest possible time. And whereas the North American slave frequently lived in a land of peace and plentiful food, his West Indian brother was the first to feel the pinch of famine when war cut off essential supplies, or when his master was burdened by debt and declining profits. On the small tobacco farms of colonial Virginia and Maryland the physical condition of slaves was surely better than in the mines of Minas Gerais or on the great plantations of Bahia, where a Capuchin missionary was told in 1682 that a Negro who endured for seven years was considered to have lived very long.[9]

North American planters were fond

---

[8] Octávio Tarquinio de Sousa, *História dos fundadores do Império do Brasil* (Rio de Janeiro, 1957–58), IX, 74; Stanley J. Stein, *Vassouras: A Brazilian Coffee County, 1850–1900* (Cambridge, Mass., 1957), p. 20; Williams, "Treatment of Negro Slaves in the Brazilian Empire," p. 325. Not only did laws protecting the unity of slave families come surprisingly late, but they were for the most part unenforceable. See Stein, *Vassouras*, pp. 155–59; Martin, "Slavery and Abolition in Brazil," *passim*.

[9] Lowell Joseph Ragatz, *The Fall of the Planter Class in the British Caribbean, 1763–1833* (New York, 1928), pp. 66–67, 70–71; John Gabriel Stedman, *Narrative of Five Years' Expedition, Against the Revolted Negroes of Surinam* . . . (London, 1796), I, 201–7; Marcel Trudel, *L'Esclavage au Canada français; histoire et conditions de l'esclavage* (Québec, 1960), pp. 160–92, 232–56; C. R. Boxer, *The Golden Age of Brazil, 1695–1750: Growing Pains of a Colonial Society* (Berkeley, 1962), p. 174; *Acts of the Assembly, Passed in the Charibbee Leeward Islands from 1690, to 1730* (London, 1732), *passim;* W. L. Burn, *Emancipation and Apprenticeship in the British West Indies* (London, 1937), pp. 64–70. Jean F. Dauxion-Lavaysse, who had traveled widely in the Spanish, French, and British colonies, said that the slaves on Sir William Young's model plantation at Saint Vincent were treated better than any he had seen (*A Statistical, Commercial, and Political Description of Venezuela, Trinidad, Margarita, and Tobago,* [tr. by E. Blaquière (London, 1820)], p. 390).

of comparing the fertility of their own slaves with the high mortality and low birth rate of those in the West Indies and Latin America, and of concluding that theirs was the milder and more humane system. Such reasoning failed to take account of the low proportion of female slaves in the West Indies, the communicable diseases transmitted by the African trade, and the high incidence of tetanus and other maladies that were particularly lethal to infants in the Caribbean. No doubt differences in sanitation and nutrition, rather than in physical treatment, explain the fact that while Brazil and the United States each entered the nineteenth century with about a million slaves, and subsequent importations into Brazil were three times greater than those into the United States, by the Civil War there were nearly four million slaves in the United States and only one and one-half million in Brazil.[10] But after all such allowances are made, it still seems probable that planters in Brazil and the West Indies, who were totally dependent on fresh supplies of labor from Africa, were less sensitive than North Americans to the value of hu-

man life. When a slave's life expectancy was a few years at most, and when each slave could easily be replaced, there was little incentive to improve conditions or limit hours of work. According to both C. R. Boxer and Celso Furtado, Brazilian sugar planters took a short-term view of their labor needs, and accepted the axiom, which spread to the British Caribbean, that it was good economy to work one's slaves to death and then purchase more. In colonial Brazil, Jesuit priests felt it necessary to admonish overseers not to kick pregnant women in the stomach or beat them with clubs, since this brought a considerable loss in slave property.[11]

But what of the benevolent laws of Latin America which allowed a slave to marry, to seek relief from a cruel master, and even to purchase his own freedom? It must be confessed that on this crucial subject historians have been overly quick to believe what travelers passed on from conversations with slave-holders, and to make glowing generalizations on the basis of one-sided evidence.

Much has been made of the fact that the Spanish model law, *Las Siete Partidas*, recognized freedom as man's natural state, and granted the slave certain legal protections. But the argument loses some of its point when we learn that the same principles were ac-

[10] Gaston Martin, *Histoire de l'esclavage dans les colonies françaises* (Paris, 1948), pp. 124–35; Ragatz, *Fall of Planter Class*, pp. 34–35; Frank W. Pitman, "Slavery on British West India Plantations in the Eighteenth Century," *Journal of Negro History*, XI (Oct., 1962), 610–17; Celso Furtado, *The Economic Growth of Brazil; a Survey from Colonial to Modern Times* (Berkeley, 1963), pp. 127–28. There is a certain irony in the fact that proslavery Southerners like Thomas R. R. Cobb accepted the conventional antislavery view of the West Indies. In contrast with the cruelty, impersonality, and despotism of the islands, North American masters and slaves worked side by side in clearing forests, building new homes, and hunting game; consequently, there developed a sense of cooperation and mutual sympathy which was unknown in the Caribbean, or so Cobb claimed in his *Inquiry into the Law of Negro Slavery* (Savannah, 1858), pp. clvii–clix.

[11] Furtado, *Economic Growth of Brazil*, p. 51, n. 129; C. R. Boxer, *Race Relations in the Portuguese Colonial Empire, 1415–1825* (Oxford, 1963), p. 101; Boxer, *Golden Age of Brazil*, pp. 7–9; Maurilio de Gouveia, *História da escravidão* (Rio de Janeiro, 1955), p. 68. In 1823 José Bonifácio noted that while Brazil had been importing some 40,000 slaves a year, the increase in the total slave population was hardly perceptible. Like British and North American reformers of a generation earlier, he was confident that the abolition of the trade would force masters to take better care of their human property (*Memoir Addressed to the General, Constituent and Legislative Assembly*, pp. 26–28).

cepted in North American law, and that *Las Siete Partidas* not only made the person and possessions of the bondsman totally subject to his master's will, but even gave owners the right to kill their slaves in certain circumstances.[12] Some of the early Spanish and Portuguese legislation protecting Indians has erroneously been thought to have extended to Negroes as well. In actuality, the first laws pertaining to Negroes in such colonies as Chile, Panama, and New Granada were designed to prohibit them from carrying arms, from moving about at night, and above all, from fraternizing with Indians.[13] It is true that in the late seventeenth and early eighteenth centuries the Portuguese crown issued edicts intended to prevent the gross mistreatment of Negro slaves. But as C. R. Boxer has pointed out, Brazilian law was a chaotic tangle

of Manueline and Filipine codes, encrusted by numerous decrees which often contradicted one another, and which were interpreted by lawyers and magistrates notorious for their dishonesty. Even if this had not been true, slaves were dispersed over immense areas where there were few towns and where justice was administered by local magnates whose power lay in land and slaves. It is not surprising that in one of the few recorded cases of the Portuguese crown intervening to investigate the torture of a slave, nothing was done to the accused owner. This revisionist view receives support from Jaime Jaramillo Uribe's conclusion that the judicial system of New Granada was so ineffective that even the reform legislation of the late eighteenth century did little to change the oppressive life of Negro slaves.[14]

In theory, of course, the Portuguese or Spanish slave possessed an immortal soul that entitled him to respect as a human personality. But though perfunctorily baptized in Angola or on the Guinea coast, he was appraised and sold like any merchandise upon his arrival in America. Often slaves were herded in mass, stark naked, into large warehouses where they were examined and marketed like animals. As late as the mid-nineteenth century the spread of disease among newly arrived Negroes who were crowded into the warehouses of Rio de Janeiro brought widespread fears of epidemic. The Spanish, who

---

[12] *Las Siete Partidas de Rey don Alfonso el Sabio* ... (Madrid, 1807), III, 117–28. Even Elsa V. Goveia exaggerates the liberality of Spanish law, although she rightly emphasizes the importance of an authoritarian government in checking the worst inclinations of slave-holding colonists. In the British West Indies, where the colonists long had a relatively free hand in framing their own laws, slaves were for a time deprived of virtually any legal protection. But given the loopholes and ambiguities in the Spanish law, one suspects that any difference in actual protection was more a result of differences in administrative machinery than in legal traditions (see Goveia, "The West Indian Slave Laws of the Eighteenth Century," *Revista de ciencias sociales*, IV [Mar., 1960], 75–105).
[13] Rollando Mellafe, *La introducción de la esclavitud negra en Chile: tráfico y rutas* (Santiago de Chile, 1959), pp. 76–82; Richard Konetzke (ed.), *Colección de documentos para la historia de la formación social de Hispanoamérica, 1493–1810* (Madrid, 1962), II, 280, 427–28; Magnus Mörner, "Los esfuerzos realizados por la Corona para separar negrese indies en Hispano-américa durante el siglo XVI" (unpublished paper); Jaime Jaramillo Uribe, "Esclavos y señores en la sociedad colombiana del siglo XVIII," *Anuario colombiano de historia social y de la cultura*, I (Bogotá, 1963), 5, 21.

[14] Boxer, *Race Relations in Portugese Colonial Empire*, p. 103; Gouveia, *História da escravidão*, p. 69; Boxer, *Golden Age of Brazil*, pp. 7, 138–39, 306–7; Uribe, "Esclavos y señores en la sociedad colombiana," pp. 22–25. In 1710 the king of Spain, hearing of the extremely cruel treatment of slaves in Peru and New Spain, issued orders allowing the governors to intervene and sell slaves who had been abused to kinder masters (Konetzke [ed.], *Colección de documentos*, III, pt. 1, 113–14).

ordinarily sold horses and cows individually, purchased Negroes in lots, or *piezas de Indias*, which were sorted according to age and size. There is abundant evidence that Brazilians were little troubled by the separation of Negro families; in the 1850's coffee planters in the rich Parahyba Valley thought nothing of selling their own illegitimate children to passing traders. Despite protests from priests and governors, it was also common practice for Brazilians to purchase attractive girls who could profitably be let out as prostitutes.[15]

In Brazil, as in other slave societies, there were apparently authentic reports of bondsmen being boiled alive, roasted in furnaces, or subjected to other fiendish punishments. More significant than such extreme cases of sadism is the evidence that planters who were successful and were accepted as social leaders equipped their estates with the chambers and instruments of torture; that it was common custom to punish a recalcitrant slave with *novenas*, which meant that he would be tied down and flogged for nine to thirteen consecutive nights, his cuts sometimes being teased with a razor and rubbed with salt and urine. In the mid-eighteenth century, Manuel Ribeiro Rocha attacked the Brazilian "rural theology" which allowed masters to welcome their new slaves with a vicious whipping, to work them in the fields without rest, and to inflict one hundred or more lashes without cause. A century later planters in the Parahyba Valley taught their sons that Negroes were not true men but inferior beings who could only be controlled by continued punishment; and some of the clergy maintained that Africans were the condemned sons of Cain. This widespread conviction of racial inferiority justified a regime of hatred and brutality in which the slave had no right of appeal and even fatal beatings went unpunished.[16]

Obviously much depended on regional differences in economy and social tradition. The recent studies of the extreme southern provinces of Brazil by Octávio Ianni and Fernando Cardoso reveal a picture of harsh chattel slavery and racial prejudice which stands in marked contrast to the familiar images of benign servitude in the north. During the last third of the eighteenth century the southern states developed a capitalistic economy which was initially stimulated by the export of wheat but which came to rely heavily on the production of jerked beef. Whether engaged in agriculture, stock-raising, or the processing of meat or leather, the slave-holding capitalists were bent on maximizing production for commercial profit. Because the economy rested on slave labor and because physical labor was largely associated with the African race, Negroes and mulattoes were regarded as mere instruments of production, wholly lacking in human personality. According to Ianni, the slave was a totally alienated being; able to express himself only through the intermediary of his owner, he was under the complete dominion of a master class which rigidly controlled his movements

[15] Boxer, *Golden Age of Brazil*, pp. 2–7, 138, 165; Robert Southey, *History of Brazil* (London, 1817–22), II, 644, 674–75; Georges Scelle, *La traite négrière aux Indes de Castille: contrats et traités d'assiento* (Paris, 1906), I, 504–5; Stein, *Vassouras*, pp. 64, 156–59.

[16] Boxer, *Golden Age of Brazil*, pp. 8–9, 45–47; Williams, "Treatment of Negro Slaves in the Brazilian Empire," p. 326; Ramos, *Negro in Brazil*, pp. 34–36; Koster, *Travels in Brazil*, pp. 429, 444–55; Boxer, *Race Relations in Portuguese Colonial Empire*, pp. 27, 101, 112; Tarquinio de Sousa, *História dos fundadores do Império do Brasil*, IX, 70; Stein, *Vassouras*, pp. 132–39.

and held power over his life and death. Though kind and paternalistic masters were to be found in Paraná, Santa Catarina, and Rio Grande do Sul, as elsewhere in the Americas, the overriding fact is that the ideology and judicial framework of southern Brazil were geared to the maintenance of an exploitive system of labor, to the preservation of public security, and to the perpetuation of power in the hands of a white ruling caste. At every point the Negro was forced to shape his behavior in accordance with the actions and expectations of the white man.[17]

Conditions were undoubtedly better in the cities, where protective laws were more often enforced and where Negroes had at least a chance of acquiring money that could purchase freedom. But in colonial Cartagena, Negro slaves were subject to the most repressive police regulations, and to punishments which ranged from death to the cutting off of hands, ears, or the penis. In Mariana the city councilors demanded in 1755 that the right to purchase freedom be withdrawn and that slaves who tried to escape be crippled for life. While both proposals aroused the indignation of the viceroy at Bahia, they indicate the state of mind of a master class which, in Minas Gerais, posted the heads of fugitive slaves along the roadsides. And men who accepted such brutality as a necessary part of life could not always be expected to abandon their fields or shut down their sugar mills on 35 religious holidays, in addi-

tion to 52 Sundays.[18] It was not an idyllic, semifeudal servitude that made colonial Brazil widely known as "the hell for Negroes," and as a place where their lives would be "nasty, brutish, and short"; or that drove countless bondsmen to suicide or revolt, and reduced others to a state of psychic shock, of flat apathy and depression, which was common enough in Brazil to acquire the special name of *banzo*.[19]

---

[17] Octávio Ianni, *As metamorfoses do escravo* (São Paulo, 1962), pp. 82, 134–49, 282–85; Fernando Henrique Cardoso, *Capitalismo e escravidão no Brasil meridional* (São Paulo, 1962), pp. 35–81, 133–67, 310–13; Cardoso and Ianni, *Côr e mobilidade social em Florianópolis: aspectos das relações entre negros e brancos numa comunidade do Brasil meridional* (São Paulo, 1960), pp. 125–35.

[18] Southey, *History of Brazil*, III, 780–84; Uribe, "Esclavos y señores en la sociedad colombiana," pp. 21–23; Boxer, *Golden Age of Brazil*, pp. 171–72. According to Boxer, in Brazil's "Golden Age" slaves on sugar plantations were worked around the clock when the mills were grinding cane, and some planters successfully evaded the rules against work on Sundays and religious holidays (*Golden Age of Brazil*, p. 7). In the nineteenth century, slaves worked on Sundays and saints' days in the Parahyba Valley (Stein, *Vassouras*, p. 75). Obviously there was more incentive to observe such rules when there were fewer pressures to maximize production. But the laws of many British colonies prohibited Sunday work and provided for religious holidays. Edward Long claimed that Jamaican slaves enjoyed about 86 days of leisure a year, counting Sundays and Saturday afternoons. The Jamaican slave code of 1816 prohibited Sunday work and ruled that at least 26 extra days a year should be given to slaves to cultivate their own gardens. There is evidence, however, that these regulations were disregarded, especially during crop time ([Edward Long], *The History of Jamaica; or, General Survey of the Antient and Modern State of that Island* . . . [London, 1774], II, 491; *Slave Law of Jamaica: with Proceedings and Documents Relative Thereto* [London, 1828], pp. 2, 63–65, 145–58; Burn, *Emancipation and Apprenticeship*, pp. 44–45).

[19] Boxer, *Golden Age of Brazil*, pp. 7–9; Boxer, *Race Relations in Portuguese Colonial Empire*, p. 101; Stein, *Vassouras*, pp. 139–41; Pierson, *Negroes in Brazil*, pp. 3–7; Ramos, *Negro in Brazil*, p. 36. It is interesting to note that, according to Elkins, slavery in the United States was so severe and absolute that it molded the Negro's character into a submissive, childlike "Sambo," whose traits resembled those of the victims of Nazi concentration camps. Elkins could find no "Sambos" in Latin America, and concludes that the character type was unique to the United

In the second half of the eighteenth century Spain and Portugal, like Britain and France, became intensely concerned with the reform of imperial administration. Severe losses in the Seven Years' War forced Spain to reexamine her colonial policy and to consider the best means for increasing the labor force, especially in Cuba. Ideas derived in part from the French Enlightenment encouraged statesmen to centralize administration, draft vast systems of law, and experiment with plans for social and economic progress. In Portugal, the Marquis de Pombal initiated colonial reforms that included a tightening of administration and the enactment of laws for the protection of slaves and the greater equalization of races. It is important to note, however, that Pombal's legislation affirming the civil rights of Indian and Asiatic subjects did not, in the words of C. R. Boxer, extend "in anything like the same measure to persons of Negro blood." And even in Asia there was such racial prejudice among the Portuguese that colonists long resisted the decrees, though they dreaded Pombal's dictatorial methods and usually carried out his orders without delay.[20]

Inspired by French ideals and administrative techniques, Charles III of Spain also supported a series of enlightened reforms that were intended to increase the force of reason and humanity in the Spanish Empire. Since Spain intended to stock Cuba with prodigious numbers of new slaves, and since the existing laws were a confused patchwork of ancient statutes and ordinances, it was obviously essential to follow the example of Colbert, and construct a code that would ensure a profitable use of labor without wholly subverting the cardinal precepts of religion and morality. Because the *Real Cédula* was drafted in 1789 and bore the influence of the Enlightenment as well as of Spanish-Catholic tradition, it was an improvement over the *Code Noir* of 1685. Most notably, it included provisions for registering and keeping records of slaves, and machinery for securing

---

States (*Slavery*, pp. 81–139). Without debating the merits of this intriguing thesis, we should point out that one source of "Sambo," which Elkins ignores, can be found in eighteenth-century English literature. In Chapter Fifteen we shall consider how this fictional stereotype suited the tastes of a sentimental age. In actuality, ship captains and planters of various nationalities agreed that when Negroes were subjected to the harshest treatment, their usual responses were revolt, suicide, flight, or a sullen withdrawal and mental depression. The state which the Portuguese described as *banzo* was clearly the result of severe shock which altered the entire personality.

[20] Raúl Carrancá y Trujillo, "El estatuto jurídico de los esclavos en las postrimerías de la colonización española," in *Revista de historia de América* (México, D.F.), No. 3 (Sept., 1938), 28–33; Agostinho Marques Perdigão Malheiro,

A escravidão no Brasil; ensaio historico-juridico-social (Rio de Janeiro, 1866–67), part iii, pp. 32, 89–129; James Ferguson King, "The Evolution of the Free Slave Trade Principle in Spanish Colonial Administration," *Hispanic American Historical Review*, XXII (Feb., 1942), 34–56; Boxer, *Race Relations in Portuguese Colonial Empire*, pp. 73–74, 98–100. In 1761 Portugal prohibited the introduction of Negro slaves and ruled that all slaves brought to Portugal, the Azores, or Madeira would be emancipated. This law has sometimes been interpreted as humanitarian in motive and has been credited with having abolished slavery in metropolitan Portugal. According to Charles Verlinden, however, slavery remained legal in Portugal, and such legislation was an answer to the protests of free laborers against slave competition. A law of 1773 which provided for the emancipation of imported slaves also prohibited the importation of free colored laborers from Brazil, and in some ways resembled a French law of 1777 excluding all Negroes (see José Antonio Saco, *Historia de la esclavitud desde los tiempos mas remotos hasta nuestros dias* [2nd ed., Habana, 1936–45], III, 345; Charles Verlinden, *L'Esclavage dans l'Europe médiévale; tome premier: Péninsule Ibérique, France* [Bruges, 1955], p. 839; Boxer, *Race Relations in Portuguese Colonial Empire*, p. 100).

information and punishing masters who denied their slaves adequate food or religious instruction. In 1784 a royal edict had also prohibited the branding of Negroes, a protection which had been given to Indians long before. But in spite of laws and traditions in the Spanish colonies that permitted slaves to buy their own freedom, the *Real Cédula* was silent on the subject of manumission. And it not only ruled that every slave was to work from dawn to dusk, but made clear that his employment should be confined to agriculture alone.[21] There are many indications, moreover, that Spanish planters paid little attention to the law. Certainly the Negro slaves who revolted in Venezuela in 1795 did not think their grievances could be expressed through appeals to kindly priests and judges.[22] Without minimizing the importance of the *Real Cédula* as an advance in humane legislation, one may observe that by 1789 there were far more enlightened proposals being discussed in Britain, France, and the United States, and that even British and American slave-holders were suggesting reforms that went beyond the Spanish law.

Furthermore, to round out one's picture of Spanish attitudes toward slavery it is well to look at other colonial slave codes, such as the one written for Santo Domingo in 1785, which claimed to be in accordance with a recent royal ordinance. The chief purposes of this detailed code were to reinvigorate a declining economy, to prevent insurrection, to put an end to the growing

idleness, pride, and thievery of Negroes, and to preserve a clear-cut division between the white race and "las clases ínfimas." Since slaves were regarded as indispensable instruments for the public welfare, their owners were obliged to provide adequate food and clothing. Yet slaves were incapable of acting in their own behalf in court, and could acquire no property except for the benefit and by the permission of their masters. All Negroes, whether slave or free, were barred from public and religious elementary schools; their movements and employment were placed under the strictest regulations; they were required at all times to be submissive and respectful to all white persons, and to treat each one like a master. Any Negro or mulatto who contradicted a white man, or who spoke in a loud or haughty voice, was to be severely whipped. The penalties increased for raising a hand against a white person, but diminished in accordance with the lightness of the offender's skin. The stigma of slavish origin extended even to occupation and dress: Negroes were not to deprive white men of jobs by working in artisan trades, nor were they to wear fine clothes, gold, or precious jewels.[23]

There is evidence that, beginning in the late eighteenth century, Negro bondage became milder and better regulated in certain parts of Latin America. In such areas as New Granada the very survival of the institution was jeopardized by the revolutionary example of Saint Domingue, the outbreak of rebellions and continuing raids by fugitive *cimarrons*, the uncer-

[21] The text of the *Real Cédula* is in Carrancá, "Estatuto jurídico de los esclavos," pp. 51–59; for a detailed discussion of the law, see pp. 34–49.

[22] Uribe, "Esclavos y señores en la sociedad colombiana," pp. 22–35, 42ff; Federico Brito Figueroa, *Las insurrecciónes de los esclavos negros en la sociedad colonial Venezolana* (Caracas, 1901), pp. xii–xiii, 15–17, 41–42.

[23] Konetzke (ed.), *Colección de documentos*, III, 553–73. If a Negro raised his hand against a white man, the penalty was one hundred lashes and two years in jail. In the next chapter we shall discuss the parts of this code pertaining to manumissions.

tainty of the African trade in the face of war and British humanitarianism, and the unsettling effects of war on markets and credit. The tumultuous period from the French Revolution to the Spanish American wars for independence brought abrupt changes in economic and political interests which often favored the Negro slave. But even Cuba, which had a long tradition of encouraging manumissions, was the scene of gross cruelty and heavy slave mortality through much of the nineteenth century; and critics of the regime, like the reformer José Antonio Saco, were either silenced or banished from the island.[24]

In 1823, when the British government pledged itself to the amelioration and eventual eradication of colonial slavery, José Bonifácio de Andrada hoped to persuade his fellow Brazilians that the success of their independence and new constitution depended on making a similar commitment. Although Portugal, he charged, was guilty of the initial sin, "we tyrannize over our slaves and reduce them to the state of brutish animals, and they, in return, initiate us in their immorality and teach us all their vices." Calling on Brazil to follow the lead of Wilberforce and Buxton, José Bonifácio's words approached the violence of a Garrison: "Riches, and more riches, do our pseudo-statesmen cry out, and their call is re-echoed by the buyers and sel-

lers of human flesh, by our ecclesiastical blood hounds, by our magistrates." His proposals included the abolition of the African trade, the creation of special councils for the protection of bondsmen, the encouragement of marriage and religious instruction, and the transfer to a new master of any slave who could prove he had been the victim of cruelty or injustice. While we have been told that these moderate provisions were always characteristic of Brazilian slavery, they received no hearing after the General Constituent Assembly was dissolved and José Bonifácio was arrested and banished. His proposal that the sale of slaves be registered so that a price could be fixed for the eventual purchase of freedom was not guaranteed by statute until 1871, although judges in some areas often enforced such a rule.[25]

In conclusion, it would appear that the image of the warmly human Big House must be balanced by a counterimage of the brutal society of the coffee barons, who even in the 1870's and 1880's governed a world in which there were no gradations between slavery and freedom. In their deep-rooted racial prejudice, their military-like

---

[24] Uribe, "Esclavos y señores en la sociedad colombiana," pp. 21–25, 42–51; Figueroa, *Las insurrecciónes de los esclavos negros*, pp. 41–42; Goveia, "West Indian Slave Laws," p. 79; Friedrich Heinrich Alexander von Humboldt, *The Island of Cuba*, tr. J. S. Thrasher (New York, 1856), pp. 211–28, and *passim;* Hubert H. S. Aimes, "Coartación: A Spanish Institution for the Advancement of Slaves into Freedom," *Yale Review*, XVII (Feb., 1909), 421; Augustin Cochin, *The Results of Slavery*, tr. Mary L. Booth (Boston, 1863), pp. 159–85.

[25] José Bonifácio de Andrada, *Memoir Addressed to the General, Constituent and Legislative Assembly*, pp. 14–23, 38–53; José Bonifácio de Andrada, *O patriarcha da independencia* (São Paulo, 1939), pp. 288–316; Tarquinio de Sousa, *História dos fundadores do Império do Brasil*, I, 129–30, 247–49; IX, 71–72. The English translator of José Bonifácio's address wrote a preface presenting a more favorable view of Brazilian slavery; but this was in line with British antislavery doctrine, which held that British slavery was much worse than that in either Latin America or the United States. José Bonifácio, on the other hand, said his reforms had been drawn from Danish, Spanish, and Mosaic legislation, and clearly thought Brazil was lagging behind the more enlightened nations. He was particularly harsh on the clergy, whom he accused of oppressing slaves for profit and sexual gratification.

discipline, their bitter resistance to any restrictions on a slave-owner's will, their constant fear of insurrection, and their hostility toward meaningful religious instruction of their Negroes, these planters were hardly superior to their brothers in Mississippi. Even with the approach of inevitable emancipation, they made no effort to prepare their slaves for freedom. It was in the face of this "slave-power" that the Brazilian abolitionists resorted to the familiar demands for "immediate" and "unconditional" emancipation, and modeled themselves on the champions of British and American reform. Joaquim Nabuco, the great leader of the Brazilian antislavery movement, adopted the pen name of "Garrison."[26]

---

[26] Stein, *Vassouras*, pp. 67, 132–45, 155–60, 196–99, 290; Ianni, *As metamorfoses do escravo*, pp. 144–49; Cardoso, *Capitalismo e escravidão no Brasil meridional*, pp. 133–67; Carolina Nabuco, *The Life of Joaquim Nabuco*, tr. and ed. Ronald Hilton (Stanford, 1950), pp. 108–13. One complex question which we cannot begin to consider is whether the survival of African cultural patterns in Brazil was the result of a less rigorous system of slavery. It seems possible that this persistence of culture was partly a product of heavy slave mortality and a continuing reliance on the African trade. By 1850 most slaves in the United States were removed by many generations from their African origins; this was certainly not the case in Brazil.

With the exception of legal barriers to manumission, the salient traits of North American slavery were to be found among the Spanish and Portuguese. Notwithstanding variations within every colony as a result of environment, economic conditions, social institutions, and the personality of owners, the Negro was everywhere a mobile and transferable possession whose labor and well-being were controlled by another man. Any comparison of slavery in North and South America should take account of the fact that Brazil alone had an area and variety comparable to all British America, and that the privileged artisans, porters, and domestic servants of colonial Brazilian cities can be compared only with their counterparts in New York and Philadelphia. Similarly, conditions in nineteenth-century Alabama and Mississippi must be held against those in the interior coffee-growing areas of south-central Brazil. Given the lack of detailed statistical information, we can only conclude that the subject is too complex and the evidence too contradictory for us to assume that the treatment of slaves was substantially better in Latin America than in the British colonies, taken as a whole.

II

Comparative Viewpoints Applied

The selections in Part Two fall into four categories, more or less arbitrarily constructed: Wider Perspectives, Institutional and Economic Forces, Race, and Special Problems (i.e., slave revolts and treatment). Other arrangements are possible, but this one corresponds roughly to the main lines along which work has been proceeding.

The first category, Wider Perspectives, links the hemispheric developments to changes elsewhere and in earlier times—to Africa before and during the period of European penetration and to the slave regimes of the ancient world. A. Norman Klein's contribution, which appears in print for the first time, demonstrates how vastly different indigenous African "slavery" was from the kind of slavery imposed in the New World. The second selection, by Arnold A. Sio, a sociologist, reassesses the status of the slave in several American systems in the light of the experience of the ancient world. This article, together with Davis's *Problem of Slavery* and M. I. Finley's extraordinary review of that book (see Part Three of this volume), should reawaken the old interest in the comparison of ancient and modern slavery.

The second category, Institutional and Economic Forces, brings the debate, outlined in Part One, into sharp focus, as only the application of general viewpoints to specific problems can. Elsa V. Goveia surveys the legal codes of the West Indies and thereby takes up a critical stance toward some of the ideas contained in the Tannenbaum-Elkins approach. Herbert Klein, on the other hand, contrasts the role of the Catholic Church in Cuban slave society with that of the Anglican in North American and vigorously defends Tannenbaum and Elkins. The comment by Miss Goveia on Klein's article constitutes a direct confrontation with the opposing point of view. Finally, Mintz's study of Puerto Rico and Jamaica takes up the question of the relative importance of economic and institutional factors by discussing the shifts in labor conditions.

The literature on race relations is vast and growing and is only partially congruent with the literature on slavery. We have selected two articles, both of which deal with Anglo-Saxon societies. If this procedure seems strange, we should explain that virtually every selection in this volume touches the race question as a whole and that the selections in Part Three, which review the debates, all have much to say on Iberian developments. The special usefulness of these two essays by Harry Hoetink and Winthrop D. Jordan is that they attempt to control for nationality and cultural inheritance (the Tannenbaum-Elkins variable) and therefore to test for the effects of economy, geography, and material conditions generally.

Finally, under Special Problems, we present Genovese's exploration of the methodological aspect of the problem of treatment, which suggests ways in which it can be defined and analyzed, and H. Orlando Patterson's analysis of slave revolts. The Patterson essay appears, at first glance, to be concerned only with Jamaica, but it actually analyzes the Jamaican revolts in an implicit hemispheric context. It appeared about the same time as two other comparative analyses—Monica Schuler's paper, "The Ethnic Slave Rebellions in the West Indies during the 18th Century," which should be published soon and Genovese's "The Legacy of Slavery and the Roots of Black Nationalism," *Studies on the Left*, 1966—but represents the fullest comparative study produced to date.

WIDER PERSPECTIVES

A. NORMAN KLEIN

West African Unfree Labor
Before and After the Rise of
the Atlantic Slave Trade

A. Norman Klein is Associate Professor of Anthropology at Sir George Williams University, Montreal. He is currently completing a study of state formation in West Africa before and during the establishment of European hegemony. This essay, which will be part of that larger study, was prepared especially for this collection.

THE PROBLEM

Any examination of forms of social servitude in precolonial West Africa must address itself to two questions. First, in what ways were the unfree statuses in West African societies similar to, and different from, "slavery" and "serfdom" as we know them from Western societies? Put positively, how did the forms of West African social servitude or "social oppression" function within the context of particular West African cultures? Secondly, what relationships, if any, can we posit between developments in West African systems of social stratification, political economy, and over-all cultural milieu

and the establishment of the European Powers on the coast from the fifteenth century? Specifically, how were the consequences of slave trade internalized by the African cultures affected?

Our notions of "slave society" have grown from and been colored by the models of classical antiquity and the antebellum South. The term "slavery" has itself come to imply a class structure within a particular type of political economy, and even special formulations of social outlook and political ideology. It tends to conjure up images of a culture whose organization of political authority is, in some way, dependent on the productivity of chattel labor, and whose rulers are recruited from a group of masters who are owners of their producer-subjects. "Slavery" tends, therefore, to define the existence of a slave-owning class whose income and political authority is derived from ownership of *all* the factors of production and a social system whose political and economic organization could not be maintained without the existence of a population of human chattel.

Such conditions were simply not characteristic or dominant in either of the inland Guinea Forest kingdoms, Ashanti and Dahomey, which we associate with the Gold and Slave Coasts, respectively, from the seventeenth through the nineteenth centuries. The defining characteristic of slave society, its class structure, was never a determining feature in the development of Ashanti or Dahoman state societies. Its appearance remained at most, only incipient and embryonic. Despite the large number of human beings these societies marketed as commodities to the Euro-American powers, their political and economic organization never came to depend on the productivity of slave labor; nor may we speak, in any meaningful sense, of a slave-owning class as a significant feature of their internal development.

BACKGROUND OF THE GUINEA FOREST KINGDOMS

Both Ashanti and Dahomey began state formation more than 150 years after the European powers had begun establishing themselves on the Guinea Coast. Among the Akan-speaking peoples, it was only "the importation of firearms from the coast," toward the end of the seventeenth century, which made possible a combination of matriclan segments that had come under the leadership of Osei Tutu resulting in

the formation of the Ashanti Confederacy. When the kingdom of Dahomey appeared on the coast in 1727 it was barely a century old.

In other words, both Ashanti and Dahomey inaugurated their careers as "state" societies with a direct and immediate economic dependence on the European powers. The guns and powder necessary for the maintenance of state armies waging almost continuous warfare and slave-raiding had to come from overseas, or at least across the Sahara. Meanwhile, evidence from the period before the emergence of these kingdoms points to a village-culture, prestate level of organization of relatively small, self-sufficient territorial units, linked to one another by ethnic and linguistic ties as well as descent-group organization. There is no indication of any large-scale military-political enterprise in the prehistory of the area before the appearance of Ashanti and Dahomey. Both kingdoms established their inland capitals during the period of intensifying slave-trading on the coast. Moreover, in spite of Kumasi and Abomey no real urban economy evolved in the area. Both capitals functioned primarily as bureaucratic, administrative centers. Their slave-produce and commodity markets notwithstanding, none of the urban clusters of Ashanti or Dahomey began to fulfill Max Weber's definition: "Economically defined, the city is a settlement the inhabitants of which live primarily off trade and commerce rather than agriculture."[1] Rural life dominated the economies of Ashanti and Dahomey. This, in the context of precolonial West African culture means subsistence economy. The underdevelopment of urban economy, in spite of all the variety and complexity

---

[1] Max Weber, *The City* (Glencoe, Ill.: The Free Press, 1958), p. 66.

of West African markets,[2] braked the potential growth of markets for goods produced by unfree labor, which—as in the cases of Mesopotamia and the Classical World—might have triggered and accelerated the emergence of a genuine slave society. The scale of Guinea Forest exchange economy during the precolonial period never rose above the level of demand for product-from-free-citizen labor, and, since its productive economic base and loci of demand were overseas, the trade in slaves and gold impeded rather than helped the development of the internal West African exchange economy.

The data from Ashanti clearly indicate some of the social, economic, and political barriers to the kind of development which might have given rise to a class of slave-owners, and similar conditions may generally be said to have been operative in Dahomey. The redistributive political characteristic of Ashanti state economy contributed to its inability to concentrate—or even regularly control and coordinate—economic surpluses that might otherwise have been more fruitfully accumulated. The political structure of the Ashanti Confederacy held back any evolution of a real *oikos* economy[3] built up around the lavish expenditures of royal and noble households. There was no extravagance on the part of the Ashanti royal family on anywhere near the scale sufficient to provide a continuous demand for the commodities from production by a large force of unfree labor. Nor was there any Ashanti (or Dahoman) administrative bureaucracy of the sort that could generate any effective demand into the countryside. The nonstate sector of Ashanti and

Dahoman exchange economy remained at the familial and local level and was characterized by the networks of primitive, prestate circulation and exchange: householding and reciprocity. The very low level of development of exchange economy is reflected in the absence of professional merchants in Ashanti (and likely in Dahomey as well). Moreover, though warfare was an ever-present if irregular source of profit, it was, at the same time, disruptive to economic growth. While putting wealth in the hands of some men, it depleted the state economy as a whole. War and slave-raiding devoured the economic and social organization of the countryside, moved villages and scattered whole populations, leaving nothing to fill the organizational and demographic vacuum it created.

FORMS OF SOCIAL SERVITUDE IN THE ASHANTI STATE

Still more inhibiting to the growth of a slave-owning class of Ashanti freemen than the general conditions of state and local economy were the particular functions and structure of social servitude in Ashanti culture. The Ashanti distinguished three statuses of social servitude, which they perceived as successive gradations between citizen-freeman and *Akyere* (those unfortunates whose capital punishment was held over until required by the executioner at the funeral sacrifices of a dignitary):

1. *Odonko:* "foreign-born slave"
2. *Awowa:* "pawn"
3. *Akoa pa:* "pawn-become-slave"

In spite of the Ashanti conception of these statuses of servitude as steps or degrees of sociopolitical freedom, their economic functions within that society were quite different.

---

[2] See, for example, P. Bohanan and G. Dalton, *Markets in Africa* (Evanston, Ill.: Northwestern University Press, 1962).

[3] Max Weber, loc. cit.

Odonko: In spite of his salability as a commodity on the slave markets, and his legal and social inferiority in Ashanti society, the foreign-born slave was indistinguishable from a freeman so far as his relation to the land and the product of his own labor was concerned. An *odonko* was given land by his master which he held in usufruct, the same as any lineage member. He held as inalienable personal property the product of his own labor and initiative. He could accumulate more wealth and concomitant prestige than his master. This condition of Ashanti law of property, giving the *odonko*—equally with freemen—ownership of his own economic outputs, thwarted the growth of an Ashanti slave-owning class at the very outset. There was no mechanism in Ashanti society for any group of slave-owners to liberate themselves from preoccupation with the mundane problem of subsistence production in favor of intellectual and other noneconomic activities. They could not take away, still less market, what belonged to their "slaves," or their slaves' children, who were, for that matter, practically freemen.

The primary function of *odonko* "slavery" in Ashanti was not in production but as a social status. The *odonko's* great liability stems from his having no connection to any of the descent groups that channeled so many of the activities, rights, and obligations of native-born members of the Ashanti closed-corporate community. Having no lineage membership, hence corporate protection, he was an isolated "solitary creature" who could be depersonalized and treated as a commodity. His isolation was an effective barrier to the organization of the *odonko* into a social class. The small scale of Ashanti economic enterprise never brought together large groups of slaves who worked and lived in a coordinated economic activity. There was, moreover, no mechanism for economic accumulation from *odonko* labor, but society did provide for the assimilation of the *odonko* into the domestic group *by marriage with an Ashanti free citizen.* These circumstances combined with the absence of any socially organized group of Ashanti slave-owners with separate vested interests and incentives from the rest of Ashanti freemen, sealed off any possibility for the development of the class structure of slave society.

Nothing bears this out more than the drama of the ritual execution of slaves at funerals. Entire villages were made to provide sacrificial victims when they were needed. Imagine a Roman or American slave-owner thus liquidating his labor force! The social values, economic incentives, and political ideology of social servitude in Ashanti culture are so different from those of latifundia Rome or the plantation South as to demand an altogether different terminology and analysis.

Awowa: The pawn is the second status of social servitude in Ashanti. It resulted from the individual or corporate indebtedness of a lineage segment, one of whose members was "leased" to the creditor. It has been called "debt slavery." Unlike the *odonko,* a stated fraction (usually one-half), of the *awowa*-pawn's economic outputs belonged to his lessee-creditor as interest on the debt. The lessee-creditor, *awowa*-debtor relation is contractual, and terminated on repayment of the original sum owed, unlike the master-*odonko* relation which is consummated by war and the slave market, and usually interminable during the lifetime of the *odonko*-slave. The appropriation, as his own personal property, of an extracted surplus product from his pawn by the lessee-creditor, constitutes a special kind of income derivation in Ashanti society. In contrast to the master-*odonko* relation, the emergence of pawnage in Ashanti signals the development of two distinct income strata: one enriched, the other deprived of a stated fraction of the productivity of the latter. The *awowa* is still afforded the protection of his rights by the lineage segment which gave him in pawn, so that we may speak of him or her as semidetached, in contrast to the completely isolated position of the *odonko*-slave.

There are elements in the lessee-creditor—*awowa*-pawn relation which reflect the internalized consequences within Ashanti society of the market mechanism inherent in the economic relationship of the Ashanti state to the European powers. Pawnage offers another sort of evidence, albeit indirect, of the internalization by African societies—the practice spread far beyond Ashanti and Dahomey—of the conditions of new Euro-African economic relations. In the first place, Ashanti economy was, on the whole, a premarket structure. That is, together with the redistributive aspects of exchange in the state economy the links of kinship and village reciprocity were those characteristic of collective tribal food-sharing and pooling rather than market conditions. When in the midst of such a primitive system of exchange we find evidence of an intrusive market mechanism at work, its genesis requires analysis. Pawnage in Ashanti provides such evidence. First, there is the risk-bearing function of the lessee-creditor who contracts for his *awowa*-pawn's liabilities and debts while in pawnage, as well as his gains. This risk-bearing is an anomalous and novel economic role in such a society as precolonial Ashanti. More striking, however, is the fact that the order of priorities for pawnage within the kin group is determined

strictly by conditions of supply and demand rather than those of descent and marriage.[4] In fact, "mother" was pawned before "slave" in a matrilineal social organization! Such incongruous market niches within the core of a premarket social economy are indicative of the transformations underway within Ashanti state society as it underwent adaptions to the new conditions of statehood and undertook serious commercial and political relations with European powers.

Akoa pa, the final unfree status in precolonial Ashanti society consisted of those who were genuinely in a state of servitude—real slaves. This status of servitude resulted from either a lack of desire or inability of the lineage segment to redeem its pawned kinsmen by raising the capital of its debt. The unfortunate individual was sold outright to the lessee-creditor, who now became a real master. *Akoa pa* status completely severed all connections to lineage and confederacy. His person, like that of any *odonko* became the marketable property of his master. The transition from *awowa* to *akoa pa* completely voided any individual's social and political birthright. Not only is a fraction of *akoa pa*'s income syphoned off by his or her master, but their children inherited *akoa pa* status as well. The Ashanti "pawn-become-slave" begins to resemble the condition of the Roman or American Negro slave. His lessee-creditor has become a master for life and in perpetuity.

These three forms of Ashanti social servitude were structured by different socioeconomic mechanisms than those of a slave society. Most important, the unfree wives of Ashanti freemen allowed a concentration of wealth and potestal-

---

[4] I shall develop this point, which requires considerable amplification, in another essay—A. N. Klein.

ity within a *man's* household for as long as three generations and thereby cut off the matrilineal descent group from a portion of its collective income and authority. These household groupings, with their male heads, and unfree wives, represent an organization running counter to the dominant matricentral values of Ashanti society. They were probably foci for "investment" of new income from slave and other trading activities by the groups of "rich men" described by Bosman in the early eighteenth century. It is clear, however, that by no later than the third generation the offspring from such unions were completely assimilated into traditional Ashanti social organization as *de jure* and *de facto* freemen. This is nowhere better demonstrated than by a fact of Ashanti law which makes it a punishable offense to accuse someone of having descended from a matriclan segment with a slave ancestress.

The social structure embedded in the principle of matrilineal descent remained remarkably stable yet flexible during the entire period of Ashanti state formation and the slave trade. The statuses of servitude which were themselves, in large measure, a consequence of the appearance of a new and potentially dominating political economy on the Guinea Coast were assimilated into the matrilineal nexus of Ashanti society. This was achieved primarily through the *social* mechanism of marriage within the framework of matrilineal descent group organization. Simply stated, the collective incentive structure of the matrilineage was to increase its membership to augment its numbers. That "recruits" to these lineages were often the captives of war and slave raids, or their descendants, had little structural consequence so far as the over-all, large-scale organization of Ashanti descent groups was concerned. Parallel

social and economic conditions of assimilation of unfree statuses into Dahoman society appear also to have been at work.

CONCLUSION

Ashanti and Dahomey were not the only type of state-formation in evidence in West Africa during the precolonial period. I need only mention two other forms, each of which is significantly different from and independent of the Guinea Forest developments to require detailed analysis if we are to formulate meaningful general statements on comparative "slaver" in West African societies. First, there were the great Islamic states which spread through the Western Sudan to Northern Nigeria; next there were the slave-trading "city-state" or "town-state" developments, as at Calabar in the Niger Delta. Since a fundamental feature of the political economy of state-formation involves the generation of mechanisms for the accumulation of state surpluses which supply the economic substance for the political machinery of state power—the maintenance of new organizations of political authority—the comparative analysis of forms of social servitude or nonfreedom ought, in the case of precolonial West Africa, go hand in hand with the study of the evolution of the state societies of the area. Since, furthermore, a significant amount of West African state-formation took place after European "contact" and during the period of an intensifying slave-trade, the entire problem has an international dimension which deserves further study.

It should by now be obvious, for even this brief, schematic account of developments in the precolonial Guinea Forest, that such notions as that Africans who were shipped to the New

World merely traded one master for another are inconsistent with the evidence. Whatever the forms of social servitude in precolonial West African societies (including those on the African-operated slave plantations of Benin and the Niger Delta), they are different in form, and, in large measure, *generated by*, the plantation economy of the Americas. All the evidence points to a massive and varied response to the political economy of slavery from the outside—at first, on a very small scale from Islamic States to the North, followed by the export of large populations of slave labor by the Euro-American powers on the coast. To say that the Guinea Forest kingdoms became an agency for collecting and marketing slaves is to define an aspect of their function in an international market relation in which they were instrumental in mobilizing the labor which made possible the great capital accumulation in Western Europe and North America; to assert that West Africa's states merely exported a social relation of slavery into a New World context—that men came from Africa already conditioned to plantation slavery—is to turn the evidence inside out. Such logic reflects more of the ideology of its purveyor than it does any African reality. It is, in fact, no more and no less than another of those *post hoc* rationales which we Americans seem compelled to produce in order to justify the most blatant inhumanities of our past.

BIBLIOGRAPHY

The materials on Ashanti and Dahomey are taken from the sources listed below. A recommended starting point for further study of Ashanti history and social organization is the work of Rattray, Fortes, and Wilks. The corpus of Rattray's work on Ashanti represents a thoroughgoing ethnographic compendium by an observer with many years' experience among these people. His field records of their oral tradition and his intimate knowledge of their law and culture provide one of the most complete files on any of West Africa's peoples. Meyer Fortes is an outstanding social anthropologist who specializes in problems of the domestic cycle, kinship, and marriage. His papers provide the most detailed information on Ashanti social organization. Ivor Wilks is a historian whose recent work in the Ghanian archives has begun to clear up our picture of the changing organization of the Ashanti state. He has given us the first detailed picture of some African influences during the formative period of Ashanti state-building (1957, 1961), and the internal centralization, differentiation, and social structure of a rapidly changing Ashanti political organization during the precolonial period.

Ashanti

Basehart, Harry W., "Ashanti," in David M. Schneider and Kathleen Gough, eds., *Matrilineal Kinship* (Berkeley and Los Angeles, 1961), pp. 270–97.

Bosman, W., *A New and Accurate Description of Guinea, etc.* (London, 1705).

Busia, K.A., *The Position of the Chief in the Modern Political System of Ashanti* (London, 1952).

Fortes, M., *The Ashanti Social Survey: A Preliminary Report, Human Problems in British Central Africa*, VI (1948).

———, "Time and Social Structure: An Ashanti Case Study," in Meyer Fortes, ed., *Social Structure* (Oxford, 1949), pp. 54–58.

———, "Kinship and Marriage Among the Ashanti," in A. R. Radcliffe-Brown and C. D. Forde, eds., *African Systems of Kinship and Marriage* (London, 1949), pp. 252–84.

———, R. W. Steele, and P. Ady, "Ashanti Survey, 1945–46: An Experiment in Social Research," *Geographical Journal*, CX, 4–6.

Rattray, R. S., *Ashanti* (London, 1923).

———, *Religion and Art in Ashanti* (Oxford, 1927).

———, *Ashanti Law and Constitution* (London, 1929).

Wilks, I., "The Rise of the Akwamu Empire, 1650–1710, *Transactions of the Historical Society of Ghana*, III (1957).

———, *The Northern Factor in Ashanti History* (Accra, 1961).

———, "The Position of Muslims in Metropolitan Ashanti in the Early 19th Century," in I. M. Lewis, ed., *The Influence of Islam in Tropical Africa* (Cambridge, 1966).

———, "Aspects of Bureaucratization in Ashanti in the Nineteenth Century," *Journal of African History*, VII (1966).

———, "Ashanti Government," in D. Forde and P. M. Kaberry, eds., *West African Kingdoms in the Nineteenth Century* (Oxford, 1967).

Thorough, detailed accounts of Dahomey are more scarce than of Ashanti. Nevertheless, the works of Herskovits, and recent analyses—primarily of economic aspects of the Dahoman Kingdom—by Rosemary Arnold and Karl Polanyi pose some interesting questions on the exchange economy of West African states. Unfortunately, in the absence of such fine scale reportage of social organization as Rattray and Fortes produced for Ashanti, the historical reconstruction of precolonial Dahoman political economy must remain much more speculative and tentative for the present.

Dahomey

Arnold, Rosemary, "A Port of Trade: Whydan on the Guinea Coast," and "Separation of Trade and Market: Great Market of Wyndah," in Karl Polanyi, Conrad M. Arensberg, and Harry W. Pearson, eds., *Trade and Market in the Early Empires* (Glencoe, Ill., 1957).

Herskovits, Melville, *Dahomey, an Ancient West African Kingdom*, 2 vols. (New York, 1938).

Lombard, J., "The Kingdom of Dahomey," in D. Forde and P. M. Kaberry, eds., *West African Kingdoms in the Nineteenth Century* (Oxford, 1967). This is the best summary of Dahoman political organization available.

Polanyi, Karl, *Dahomey and the Slave Trade* (Seattle, 1966).

The "city-state" or "town-state" developments of the Niger Delta represent a unique and fascinating moment in African history. Here there appeared a quite different—predominantly mercantile, as well as sociopolitical response to slave trade—development from the state formations of the Guinea Forest. The reader is referred to:

Dike, K. O., *Trade and Politics in the Niger Delta* (Oxford, 1956).

Forde, D., *Efik Traders of Old Calabar* (London, 1956).

Jones, G. I., *The Trading States of the Oil Rivers* (Oxford, 1963).

For an introduction to the Sudanic states and the questions posed by Islam in West Africa, see:

Smith, M. G., *Government in Zazzau* (Oxford, 1960). This is a comprehensive monograph on the political organization of an Islamic West African State.

Trimingham, J. S., *Islam in West Africa* (Cambridge, 1959).

ARNOLD A. SIO

Interpretations of Slavery:
The Slave Status in the Americas

Arnold A. Sio is Chairman of the Department of Sociology-Anthropology at Colgate University. He is currently working on "Slavery and Personality: Problems in Method and Theory" for a volume, The Negro in the Americas, to be published in 1969, and on a book, The Slave Systems of the Americas.

Recent interpretations of slavery in the United States suggest that we may be entering a new phase of scholarship on slavery as new approaches and categories are introduced by historians, and as anthropologists and sociologists again take up the study of an institution that was of such concern to their nineteenth-century predecessors.

As an assessment of these interpretations, the concern of this essay is with those aspects of the legal status of the slave which appear as problematic or neglected. The purpose is to reformulate, refocus, and clarify rather than to introduce an alternative interpretation or to present new materials.[1]

Although the scholarship on slavery has tended to shift away from the strong moral bias as well as the categories of analysis carried over for so long from the proslavery and antislavery debates, those aspects of the slavery system traditionally at issue also constitute the problematic aspects in the more recent interpretations. These are the legal status of the slave, the relations of masters and slaves, and the relationship

[1] The author wishes to acknowledge his obligations to M. I. Finley, John Hope Franklin, Robert Freedman, and Richard Robbins, among others, who have read and criticized this paper, and to the Research Council of Colgate University for a generous research grant.

Reprinted, by permission of the Editors, from Comparative Studies in Society and History, vol. VII, no. 3 (1965), pp. 289–308.

between these two facets of the institution.[2]

I

The concept of slavery covers a considerable variety of social phenomena, but it is generally thought of as the practice of bringing strangers into a society for use in economic production and legally defining them in terms of the category of property. The complete subordination of the slave to the will of the master is regarded as a main defining feature of the institution.

Subordination implies and is an aspect of authority. Authority is the socially recognized right to direct, control, or manage some or all of the affairs of a person or group or thing. In this sense there is an overlap between property as a bundle of rights over things and the authority which is invested in some persons over others as their slaves, with the result that such types of authority are treated as property at law.[3]

Slavery involves the "legal assimilation of interpersonal rights to the norm of property rights over things."[4]

This definition of the legal status of the slave has been taken in many studies as a basis for an interpretation solely in terms of the property component in the status.[5] Thus although the interpretations of slavery in the United States to be discussed in this essay involve both the historical and comparative methods and an emphasis on

economic as well as ideological forces, they arrive at a similar conception of the legal status of the slave as property. This conception obscures significant differences between the property and racial components in the status, and circumvents critical evidence pertaining to the personal component in the status.[6]

In this essay an attempt is made to distinguish between the property and racial components in the status of the antebellum slave through a comparison with Roman slavery where the status involved a property but not a racial component. This is followed by a consideration of the evidence for a personal component in the definition of the slave status in the United States. The essay concludes with some re-examination of the status of the slave in Latin America in terms of the three components.

The interpretations of Frank Tannenbaum[7] and Stanley Elkins[8] exem-

---

[2] See Stanley Elkins, *Slavery* (Chicago, 1959), Chap. I; Kenneth Stampp, "The Historian and Southern Negro Slavery," *American Historical Review*, LVII (April, 1952), 613–24; Richard Hofstadter, "U. B. Phillips and the Plantation Legend," *Journal of Negro History*, XXIX (April, 1944), 109–25.

[3] M. G. Smith, "Slavery and Emancipation in Two Societies," *Social and Economic Studies*, III, Nos. 3 and 4 (1954), 245–46.

[4] *Ibid.*, p. 246.

[5] The classic account is H. J. Nieboer, *Slavery as an Industrial System* (Rotterdam, 1910).

[6] Wilbert Moore, "Slave Law and the Social Structure," *Journal of Negro History*, XXVI (April, 1941), 171–202.

[7] *Slave and Citizen* (New York, 1947).

[8] *Slavery*, Chap. 2. This discussion is limited to his treatment of the legal status of the slave. Elkins proposes an alternative to the established approach to slavery in the United States which, taking its stance from the debates over slavery, has been concerned mainly with the rightness or wrongness of the institution considered in terms of categories pertaining to the health and welfare of the slaves. The historical study of slavery has alternated over the years between a proslavery and an antislavery position, but the purpose and the categories of analysis have remained unchanged. The result has been a continuing confusion of the historical study of slavery with moral judgments about slavery. Elkins proposes discarding this approach and adopting instead the method of comparison as followed by Tannenbaum. Slavery as an evil is taken for granted. Elkins' treatment of slavery as analogous to the concentration camp in its effects on Negro personality is discussed in Earle E. Thorpe, "Chattel Slavery and Concentration Camps," *The Negro History Bulletin*, XXV (May, 1962), 171–76.

plify the shift away from the moral approach to the institution of slavery and the introduction of new methods and categories. The treatment in both is comparative. Why did slavery in the United States differ in form and consequences from the kind of servitude developed in the Latin American colonies of Spain and Portugal? According to Tannenbaum, there were at least three traditions or historical forces in Latin America which prevented the definition of the slave there solely as property; namely, the continuance of the Roman law of slavery as it came down through the Justinian Code, the influence of the Catholic Church, and the long familiarity of the Iberians with Moors and Negroes.[9] Tannenbaum puts his emphasis on whether, "The law accepted the doctrine of the moral personality of the slave and made possible the gradual achievement of freedom implicit in such a doctrine" and on a universalistic religion, i.e. Catholicism, in preventing the definition of the slave solely as property.[10] In the United States slavery developed in a legal and moral setting in which the doctrine of the moral personality of the slave did not affect the definition of his status in the society. "Legally he was a chattel under the law, and in practice an animal to be bred for market."[11]

In comparing North American and Latin American slavery, Elkins adds to Tannenbaum's earlier treatment. The legal status of the slave in "the liberal, Protestant, secularized, capitalist culture of America" is contrasted with that of the slave in "the conservative, paternalistic, Catholic, quasimedieval culture of Spain and Portugal and their New World colonies."[12] Elkins con-

cludes that in the absence of such restraining institutions in the United States the search for private gain and profit was unlimited, and the law of slavery developed in such a way as to eliminate the slightest hindrance to the authority of the slave-holder over his slaves. The legal status of the slave developed exclusively in terms of property as the result of the demands of an emerging capitalism. Slavery in the United States was "a system conceived and evolved exclusively on the grounds of property."[13]

For Elkins and Tannenbaum the definitive feature of the legal status of the antebellum slave was the centrality of the property component. The rights of personality were suppressed by the law, and the legal subordination of the slave to the authority of the master in the areas of parentage and kinship, property and other private rights, and police and disciplinary power over the slave was developed to such an extent as to make slavery in the United States a unique system.[14] The entire institution became integrated around the definition of the slave as property.

Kenneth Stampp's *The Peculiar Institution*[15] has been viewed as one of the most important and provocative contributions since Ulrich B. Phillips' *American Negro Slavery*.[16] Although it is organized essentially in terms of the categories used by Phillips and other earlier students of slavery, Stampp's study exceeds the earlier work in comprehensiveness, in presenting the response of the slave to the institution, and in its use of the available scientific

---

[9] Tannenbaum, pp. 43–65.
[10] *Ibid.*, p. 8.
[11] *Ibid.*, p. 82.
[12] Elkins, p. 37.

[13] *Ibid.*, p. 55.
[14] *Ibid.*, p. 52. These categories are taken from Elkins, but they are also used by Stampp and Tannenbaum in describing the status of the slave.
[15] (New York, 1957).
[16] (New York, 1918).

evidence regarding race. In contrast to Elkins and Tannenbaum, Stampp takes up the social organization of slavery as well as its legal structure. His interpretation of the legal status of the slave is mainly in terms of economic values, and stresses the property component as do Elkins and Tannenbaum.[17] Unlike Elkins and Tannenbaum, however, he finds that the status also contained a personal element, which made for a certain degree of ambiguity in the status.[18]

In these interpretations, the initial status of the Negro is taken as having been neither that of a slave nor that of a member of a racial group against which discrimination was practiced. The status of the Negro as a slave and his status as a member of a racial minority apparently developed concurrently, since there was no tradition of slavery or of racial discrimination in the colonies to inform the initial status of the Negro. The causal connection implied between slavery and racial discrimination is a widely held conception and needs to be reconsidered in the light of recent historical investigation and comparative evidence.

Much more difficult to grasp is the effect of racial discrimination on the definition of the slave status. Elkins refers to "the most implacable race-consciousness yet observed in virtually any society" as affecting the definition of the status, but the stress on economic values in his interpretation obscures any distinction that may have been intended between the property and racial components in the status.[19] Similarly, although Stampp refers to the fact "that chattel slavery, the caste system, and color prejudice" were a part of

custom and law by the eighteenth century, no clear distinction is made between those features of the status which are to be attributed to the definition of the slave as property and those which are the consequence of racial discrimination.[20]

Tannenbaum is clearly concerned with the consequences of racial discrimination for the legal status of the Negro as slave and as freedman. He stresses the fact that slavery in the United States meant Negro slavery. In contrast to Latin America, slavery in the antebellum South involved "caste," "by law of nature," or "innate inferiority."[21] Slavery systems can be distinguished in terms of the ease and availability of manumission and the status of the freedman, as these indicate whether or not the law denied the moral personality of the slave.[22] In the United States the conception of the slave as a racial inferior led to severe restrictions on manumission and to a low status for free Negroes. At the same time, however, it is readily apparent from Tannenbaum's comparison with slavery in Latin America that in his view the conception of the antebellum Negro as innately inferior affected all the legal categories defining his status: the extent of the assimilation of his rights to property in law as well as manumission and the status of the freedman.[23] Racial discrimination accentuated the legal definition of the slave as property.

The slave as property is taken as the primary or exclusive component in these interpretations of the legal status of the slave in the United States. For Elkins and Stampp this is the conse-

---

[17] Stampp, Chap. 5.
[18] Ibid., pp. 192–93.
[19] Elkins, p. 61.

[20] Stampp, p. 23.
[21] Tannenbaum, pp. 55–56.
[22] Ibid., p. 69. See also William L. Westermann, The Slave Systems of Greek and Roman Antiquity (Philadelphia, 1955), p. 154.
[23] Tannenbaum, p. 69.

quence mainly of economic forces, while for Tannenbaum ideological forces are basic. The focus on the definition of the slave as property results in a tendency to fuse the property and racial components, and in a failure to consider the evidence bearing on the personal component in the legal status.

II

While the assimilation to property in law of the rights of slaves was common to slavery in classical antiquity and the United States, slavery in ancient society "was a type unfamiliar to Europeans and Americans of the last two centuries. It had no color line. (Therefore, *pace* Aristotles, it had no single and clearly defined race or slave caste.)"[24] Moreover, the law of slavery in ancient society did not deny the moral personality of the slave as, according to Roman law, the institution of slavery was of the *Ius Gentium* but at the same time contrary to the *Ius Naturale*, for all men were equal under natural law.[25] A comparison with slavery in Rome where slaves were defined as property in law but did not constitute a separate caste in the society, and where the legal suppression of the personality of the slave, as expressed in the attitude toward manumission and the status of the freedman, did not occur, thus provides a method for distinguishing between the

property and the racial components in the definition of the legal status. Since the categories of marriage and the family, property and other rights, and police and disciplinary powers over slaves are used by Elkins, Tannenbaum, and Stampp in describing the status of the slave as property in the United States, these will guide the comparison with Rome.[26]

As to marriage and the family in the antebellum South, marriages between slaves had no legal standing. "The relation between slaves is essentially different from that of man and wife, joined in lawful wedlock . . . with slaves it may be dissolved at the pleasure of either party, or by the sale of one or both, depending on the caprice or necessity of the owners."[27] The denial of legal marriage meant, in conjunction with the rule that the child follow the condition of the mother, that the offspring of slaves had no legal father, whether the father was slave or free. The duration of the union between slaves depended on the interests of the master or those of the slaves. The union was subject at any time to being dissolved by the sale of one or both of the slaves. The children of these "contubernial relationships," as they were termed, had no legal protection against separation from their parents. In the law there was no such thing as fornication or adultery among slaves. A slave

---

[24] William L. Westermann, "Slavery and Elements of Freedom in Ancient Greece," *Bulletin of the Polish Institute of Arts and Sciences in America*, I (Jan., 1943), 346. See also M. I. Finley, "Between Slavery and Freedom," *Comparative Studies in Society and History*, VI (Apr., 1964), 246.

[25] Westermann, *The Slave Systems*, pp. 57, 80; W. W. Buckland, *The Roman Law of Slavery* (Cambridge, 1906), p. 1. The consequent ambiguity in the status of the slave as property and as a person in ancient society is discussed at a later point.

[26] Materials for the description of the legal status of the antebellum slave are standard and taken from Elkins, Chap. 2; Stampp, Chap. 5; Tannenbaum, p. 69ff; and Helen T. Catterall, *Judicial Cases Concerning Slavery and the Negro* (Washington, 1926). Those for the Roman Republic are taken from the standard work by Buckland; R. H. Barrow, *Historical Introduction to the Study of Roman Law* (Cambridge, 1932); and Rudolph Sohm, *The Institutes* (Oxford, 1907).

[27] *Howard v. Howard*, 6 Jones N.C. 235 (December, 1858). Catterall, II, p. 221.

could not be charged with adultery, and a male slave had no legal recourse against another slave, free Negro, or white person for intercourse with his "wife." Nor could the slave present this abuse as evidence in his defense in a criminal charge of assault and battery, or murder.

Roman slaves were also legally incapable of marriage. Any union between slaves or between slaves and free persons was differentiated as *contubernium* as opposed to *conubium*. A marriage was terminated if either party became enslaved. Infidelity between slaves could not be adultery. Although a slave could be guilty of adultery with a married free woman, it was not possible for an enslaved female to commit the offense, or for it to be committed with her. The inheritance of slavery followed the rule that the child follow the status of the mother, whatever the position of the father. A child born of a free father and a slave mother was a slave and the property of the owner, while the child of a slave father and a free mother inherited the free status of the mother. The children of slaves were the property of the owner of the mother, and, since the economic use of slaves during the Republic was at the discretion of the master, slaves were bought and sold without regard for their families. "There was nothing to prevent the legacy of a single slave away from his connections."[28]

According to the legal codes of the antebellum South, a slave "was unable to acquire title to property by purchase, gift, or devise."[29] A slave might not make a will, and he could not, by will, inherit anything. Slaves were not to hire themselves out, locate their own employment, establish their own resi-

dence, or make contracts for any purpose including, of course, marriage. A slave "can do nothing, possess nothing, nor acquire anything but what must belong to his master."[30] He could engage in financial transactions, but only as his master's agent. A slave could not be a party to a suit, except indirectly, when a free person represented him in a suit for freedom. Slaves might only be witnesses in court in cases involving slaves or free Negroes. When the testimony of a slave was allowed, he was not put under oath as a responsible person. Teaching slaves to read and write was prohibited, and instruction in religion was also subject to legal restrictions.

"Of the slave's civil position," in Rome, "it may be said that he had none."[31] A slave could not make a contract, he could be neither creditor nor debtor, he could not make a will, and if he became free, a will made in slavery was void. Slaves could in no way be concerned in civil proceedings which had to be made in the name of the master. A judgment against a slave was null and void and the pact of a slave was likewise void.

As to his participation in commerce, "his capacity here is almost purely derivative, and the texts speak of him as unqualified in nearly every branch of law."[32] Although the Roman slave could acquire possessions for the master, "the will of the slave and, in fact, his mental faculties in general, operate, in principle, where they operate at all, for the benefit of the master."[33] Legally the slave did not have possessory rights in the property acquired by him or granted to him. The *peculium* assigned to

---

[28] Buckland, p. 77.
[29] Stampp, p. 197.

[30] The Civil Code of Louisiana quoted in John C. Hurd, *The Law of Freedom and Bondage in the United States* (Boston, 1858), II, p. 160.
[31] Buckland, p. 82.
[32] *Ibid.*, p. 82.
[33] *Ibid.*, p. 82.

him by the master, to which the slave might add by investment, earnings, gift, interest, produce, or wages existed by the authority of the master and was subject to partial or total recall at the slave-owner's wish. The *peculium* was not alienable by the slave any more than other property. The *peculium* did not change the legal position of the slave. He was still a slave. No legal process which was closed to a slave without *peculium* was available to him if he had one. The *peculium* did not go with the slave upon manumission unless expressly given by the master.

Slaves were legally incapable of prosecution as accusers either on their own behalf or on behalf of others. As a general rule the evidence of slaves was not admissible in court, and when it was taken it was taken by torture, for it could not be received in any other form from slaves. Slaves were excluded from giving testimony on behalf of their masters.

The slave codes of the South supported the "full dominion" of the master in matters of policy and discipline. The slave's relationship with his master was expected to be one of complete subordination. Generally, homicide was the major crime that could be committed against an enslaved individual. The owner of a slave, however, could not be indicted for assault and battery on his own slave. "The power of the master must be absolute to render the submission of the slave perfect."[34] Furthermore, the master was not held responsible for the death of a slave as a consequence of "moderate correction," for "it cannot be presumed that prepensed malice (which alone makes murder felony) should induce any man to destroy his own estate."[35] The master

was to recover damages caused by an assault or homicide against his slave.

During the Roman Republic there was no legal limitation on the power of the slave-owner: "his rights were unrestricted."[36] "Except in cases of revolt which endangered the government the Roman state left the problem of the discipline and punishment of slaves to their masters."[37] Sohm writes that as against his master, "a slave had no legal rights whatsoever."[38] In dealing with the offenses of slaves the owner's powers of punishment included corporal punishment, confinement in chains, confinement in the ergasulum, banishment from Rome and Italy, and the death penalty. Slaves, as possessions of value, were protected from mistreatment by persons other than their masters. In case of injury done to a slave "the master had cause of action for damages against the perpetrator."[39] If a slave was enticed into escaping or forcibly removed the owner might resort to both criminal and civil action.

These comparisons suggest that, on the legal evidence which defines the authority of the master in the areas of parentage and kinship, property and other rights, and police and disciplinary power over slaves, there is nothing sufficiently distinctive to distinguish the legal status of the slave as property in the United States from that in Rome.

Arnold Toynbee refers to the "Negro slave immigrant" as having been "subject to the twofold penalization of racial discrimination and legal servitude."[40] A society may extensively assimilate to property in law the rights of slaves, as indeed many have, but yet

---

[34] *State v. Mann*, 2 Deveroux N.C., 263 (December, 1829). Catterall, II, p. 57.
[35] Virginia Act of 1669, Hurd, I, p. 232.

[36] Buckland, p. 36.
[37] Westermann, p. 75.
[38] Sohm, p. 166.
[39] Westermann, p. 83.
[40] Arnold J. Toynbee, *A Study of History* (Oxford, 1934), II, p. 218.

not restrict the status of slavery to members of a particular group for whom slavery is defined as natural, inevitable, and permanent as occurred in the United States. This was the introduction of caste into the status of the antebellum Negro, slave or free.[41] The Negro as slave occupied both a slave status and a caste status.[42] He was subject to disabilities in addition to those connected with the legal categorization of him as property, and these disabilities continued to define his status as a freedman. Caste law as well as slave law governed the status of the Negro.

The restriction of slavery to the Negro rested on the legal principle that it was a status properly belonging to the Negro as an innately (racially) inferior being. If slavery was a status attaching to a racial inferior, then it was inherit-

able even where one parent was white. Intermarriage between Negro slaves and whites was prohibited. Racial inferiority, legalized inheritance, and endogamy were related to another principle; namely, that slavery was the presumptive status of every Negro or person of color. The slave status was to follow naturally and inevitably from Negro ancestry.[43]

Although the slave and caste statuses were coextensive for the preponderant majority of antebellum Negroes, there were free Negroes in the North and South who, however, continued to be members of the lower caste. Caste was inclusive of the slave and free status. Thus the rule that the child follow the condition of the mother made slaves of the majority of Negroes and members of the lower caste of all Negroes. Negroes, slave or free, were legally prohibited from intermarrying with members of the dominant group. All members of the lower caste were presumed to be slaves unless they could establish that they should be legally free. There was a definite strain in the legal structure to establish slavery and caste as coextensive for all Negroes. The status of the free Negro is evidence of this strain. Although legally no longer an object of property rights, he was legally and socially a member of a lower caste and as such his life chances, whether he lived in the North or South, were held within narrow limits.[44]

Slavery in Republican Rome was not restricted to any particular group who ought properly to occupy the legal

---

[41] There has been considerable disagreement as to whether the term "caste" is applicable to the American case. It has been insisted that it should be limited to India. The present writer agrees with Everett Hughes who writes: "If we grant it, we will simply have to find some other term for the kind of social category into which one is assigned at birth and from which he cannot escape by action of his own: and to distinguish such social categories from classes or ranked groups, from which it is possible, though sometimes difficult, to rise." Everett C. Hughes and H. MacGill Hughes, *Where Peoples Meet* (Glencoe, 1952), p. 111. Berreman has recently defined the term as to be useful cross-culturally. He defines a caste system "as a *hierarchy of endogamous divisions in which membership is hereditary and permanent*. Here hierarchy includes inequality both in status and in access to goods and services. Interdependence of the subdivisions, restricted contracts among them, occupational specialization, and/or a degree of cultural distinctiveness might be added as criteria, although they appear to be correlates rather than defining characteristics." Gerald D. Berreman, "Caste in India and the United States," *American Journal of Sociology*, LXVI (Sept., 1960), 120–21, cf. Louis Dumont, "Caste, Racism, and 'Stratification,' Reflections of a Social Anthropologist," *Contributions to Indian Sociology*, V (Oct., 1961), 20–43.

[42] Moore, pp. 177–79.

[43] *Ibid.*, 184–88. See also Winthrop D. Jordan, "American Chiaroscuro: The Status and Definition of Mulattoes in the British Colonies," *William and Mary Quarterly*, XIX, No. 2 (April, 1962), 183–200.

[44] John Hope Franklin, *The Free Negro in North Carolina* (Chapel Hill, 1943); Leon F. Litwack, *North of Slavery* (Chicago, 1961).

status of slaves. The legal restrictions on intermarriage of slave and free, on manumission, and on the status of freedmen, though at times severe, were not the consequence of a conception of the slave or former slave as innately inferior. Those who were enslaved in Rome did not constitute a caste in the society for whom the proper and permanent status was conceived to be slavery.[45]

It is not surprising that the highly perceptive Alexis de Tocqueville should have noticed this essential difference between slavery in antiquity and the United States. However, observing that discrimination against the Negro persisted in those parts of the United States where slavery had been abolished, he concluded that slavery must have given "birth" to "prejudice."[46] A causal relationship between slavery and racial discrimination is also implied in the interpretations under discussion.

Setting aside the conventional question as to "why slavery produced discrimination?" Carl Degler has separated the two elements, and, still treating the question historically, asks rather "which appeared first, slavery or discrimination?" His main argument is that from the beginning "the Negro was treated as an inferior to the white man, servant or free."[47] Caste or elements of caste antedated slavery, and as the legal status evolved "it reflected

and included as a part of its essence, this same discrimination the white man had practiced against the Negro" from the outset in New England as well as the South.[48]

The colonists of the early seventeenth century not only were well aware of the distinction between indentured servitude and slavery, but they had ample opportunity to acquire the prejudicial attitudes and discriminatory practices against Negroes through the slave trade and from Providence, Bermuda, Barbados, Jamaica, and the Spanish and Portuguese colonies.[49] Moreover, there was the inferior status ascribed to the non-Caucasian Indians and even their enslavement almost from the beginning of English settlement.

The evidence summarized by Degler indicates that Negroes were being set aside as a separate group because of their race before the legal status of slavery became fully crystallized in the late seventeenth century. There was legislation (1) preventing interracial marriages and sexual union; (2) declaring that the status of the offspring of a white man and a Negro would follow that of the mother; and (3) establishing civil and legal disabilities applying to Negroes either free or in servitude.[50] As to the situation of the Negro in the North, "from the earliest years a lowly differentiated status, if not slavery itself, was reserved and recognized for the Negro—and the Indian, it might be added."[51] Degler concludes that "long before slavery or black labor became an important part of the Southern

---

[45] Westermann, p. 15, 23.

[46] Alexis de Tocqueville, *Democracy in America* (New York, 1948), I, pp. 358–60.

[47] Carl N. Degler, "Slavery and the Genesis of American Race Prejudice," *Comparative Studies in Society and History*, II (Oct., 1959), 52. Cf. Oscar and Mary F. Handlin, "Origins of the Southern Labor System," *William and Mary Quarterly*, 3rd. Ser., VI (April, 1950), 199–222; Winthrop D. Jordan, "Modern Tensions and the Origins of American Slavery," *Journal of Southern History*, XXVII (Feb., 1962), 18–33.

[48] Degler, p. 52.

[49] *Ibid.*, pp. 53–56. See also Winthrop D. Jordan, "The Influence of the West Indies on the Origin of New England Slavery," *William and Mary Quarterly*, XVIII (April, 1961), 243–50.

[50] *Ibid.*, pp. 56–62. See also Moore, pp. 177–86.

[51] Degler, p. 62.

economy, a special and inferior status had been worked out for the Negroes. . . . It was a demand for labor which dragged the Negro to American shores, but the status he acquired cannot be explained by reference to that economic motive."[52]

Turning now to the personal component in the status of the antebellum slave, it is apparent that a conception of a legal relationship between persons or groups of persons is implied in the definition of slaves as a caste in the society. As we have seen, the antebellum slave was not uniformly regarded in the law as a person. There were certain situations and relationships, however, in which he was not regarded solely as property.

Kingsley Davis has observed that "slavery is extremely interesting precisely because it does attempt to fit human beings into the category of objects of property rights. . . . Always the slave is given some rights, and these rights interfere with the attempt to deal with him solely as property."[53] Westermann found this to be a "constant paradox" in Greek and Roman antiquity, and "inherent in the very nature of the institution." "Theoretically," the slave was a chattel and subject only to the laws pertaining to private property, and in "actuality" he was "also a human being and subject to protective legislation affecting human individuals."[54] Isaac Mendelsohn refers to "the highly contradictory situation" in the slavery systems of the ancient Near East "in which on the one hand, the slave was considered as possessing qualities of a human being, while on the other hand, he was . . . regarded as

a thing."[55] Under the law in Greek, Roman, and Near Eastern society the slave had an ambiguous status: he was both an object of property rights and a rudimentary legal person.

As to the personal component in the status of the slave in the United States, Elkins argues that as a consequence of the requirements of capitalistic agriculture "to operate efficiently and profitably," through the rational employment of slaves as economic instruments, any ambiguity in the legal status of the slave as property could not be tolerated.[56] Any rights of personality that remained to the Negro at the end of the seventeenth century had been suppressed by the middle of the eighteenth.[57] However they may differ as to causation, Elkins and Tannenbaum are in agreement that the status of the slave was determinate as property. For Tannenbaum the "element of human personality" had been lost in the definition of the slave in the United States.[58] Stampp, on the other hand, found a "dual character" in the legal codes. The legal authorities "were caught in a dilemma whenever they found that the slave's status as property was incompatible with this status as a person."[59] In a much earlier and very careful treatment of the personal component, Moore found that initially the question as to whether a slave was a person or a piece of property was involved in the difficult issue as to the status of the slave after conversion and baptism. Allowing the slave the privilege of salvation implied a recognition of him as a Christian person, and, by implication, as a legal personality. The idea that

---

[52] *Ibid.*, p. 62. Jordan, *The Influence of the West Indies*, pp. 243–44, 250.

[53] *Human Society* (New York, 1949), p. 456.

[54] Westermann, p. 1.

[55] *Slavery in the Near East* (New York, 1949), p. 64.

[56] Elkins, p. 49, 53.

[57] *Ibid.*, p. 42.

[58] Tannenbaum, p. 97.

[59] Stampp, pp. 192–93.

conversion and baptism altered the status of the slave as property was not easily changed, and the settling of the difficulty in favor of continued enslavement does not appear to have finally disposed of the matter.[60] "The persistence of this indeterminacy arising out of religious status," concludes Moore, "must be regarded as at least one source of the continued legislative and judicial declarations of the personality of the slave, despite other definitions and implications to the contrary."[61]

There are three aspects to be considered in taking up the matter of the doubtful status of the slave before the law. The most obvious, of course, is that the dual quality is inherent in the status itself. Slaves are conscious beings defined as economic property. On the one hand, the definition of the legal status conceives of them as objects of economic value. On the other hand, the slave as an item of economic value also remains a social object. The values he possesses as a conscious being can be utilized by the master, namely, his body, his skill, and his knowledge. The definition of the slave as a physical object overlaps that of the slave as a social object, since only social objects can perform and have intentions. The value of a slave as property resides in his being a person, but his value as a person rests in his status being defined as property.[62]

The second aspect involves the recognition in the law not only of the humanity of the slave, but also that he may be the subject of rights of his own. In this connection, Stampp has noted

a significant juxtaposition of two clauses in the legal code of Alabama in 1853. The first defines the status of the slave as property and establishes the owner's rights to the slave's "time, labor, and services," as well as the slave's obligation to comply with the lawful demands of the master. The second contains the personal element and states the master's obligation to be humane to his slaves and to provide them with adequate food, clothing, and with care during illness and old age.[63] Similarly a Kentucky court ruled in one case that "a slave by our code, is not a person, but (negotium) a thing," while in another case in the same state the court considered "slaves as property, yet recognizes their personal existence, and to a qualified extent, their natural right."[64]

Cases clearly affirming that the slave was a person were also numerous during the antebellum period. One judgment in Tennessee held:

A slave is not in the condition of a horse . . . he is made after the image of the Creator. He has mental capacities, and an immortal principle in his nature . . . the laws . . . cannot extenguish his high born nature, nor deprive him of many rights which are inherent in man.[65]

That the slave as an object of property rights was protected by law and by remedies the law provided whereby an owner could recover damages done to his property has already been discussed. A slave was also entitled in his own right to protection from malicious in-

---

[60] Moore, pp. 195–96.

[61] *Ibid.*, p. 196. See also Charles Sellers, "The Travail of Slavery," in Charles Sellers, ed., *The Southerner as American* (Chapel Hill, 1960), pp. 40–71.

[62] Talcott Parsons and Neil J. Smelser, *Economy and Society* (Glencoe, 1956), p. 12.

[63] Stampp, pp. 192–93. The following discussion is not intended to be comprehensive. For a detailed treatment of the definition of the slave as a person see Moore, pp. 191–202.

[64] *Jarman v. Patterson*, 7 T.B. Mon. Ky 644 (December, 1828). Catterall, I, p. 311. See also *Catherine Bodine's Will*, 4 Dana Ky 476 (Oct., 1836). *Ibid.*, I, pp. 334–35.

[65] *Kennedy v. Williams*, 7 Humphreys Tenn. (Sept., 1846). *Ibid.*, II, p. 530.

jury to his life and limb. The courts ruled that manslaughter against a slave "exists by common law: because it is the unlawful killing of a human being,"[66] that a slave is "a reasonable creature in being, in whose homicide either a white person or a slave may commit the crime of murder or manslaughter;"[67] and that "Negroes are under the protection of the laws, and have personal rights, and cannot be considered on a footing only with domestic animals."[68] The justification of the legal principle that a crime could be committed against an enslaved individual tended to shift, and in many cases revealed the ambivalence between the conception of the slave as property, and as a person. In a judgment acknowledging that an indictment for an assault upon a slave could be made, a Louisiana court ruled that "slaves are treated in our law as property, and, also, as persons . . . ."[69] As stated earlier, however, generally homicide was the major crime that could be committed against a slave, and the owner of a slave could not be indicted for assault and battery on his slaves.

Many of the laws also implied that a slave was a legal person in that he was capable of committing crimes and could be held to trial. Cases involving slave crimes were very numerous and frequently they turned on the conception of the slave as a person. In the judgment of a Georgia court in 1854:

. . . it is not true that slaves are only chattels, . . . and therefore, it is not true that it is not possible for them to be prisoners . . .

the Penal Code . . . has them in contemplation . . . in the first division . . . as persons capable of committing crimes; and as a . . . consequence . . . as capable of becoming prisoners.[70]

Another court held that a white man could be indicted and convicted as an accessory to a murder commited by a slave. The judgment stated that "Negroes are under the protection of the laws, and have personal rights . . . . They have wills of their own—capacities to commit crimes; and are responsible for offenses against society."[71]

Again, however, there were limits on the extent to which the personality of the slave was recognized, and in defining these limits the courts frequently expressed the indeterminate character of the status:

Because they are rational *human beings*, they are capable of committing crimes; and, in reference to acts which are crimes, are regarded as *persons*. Because they are *slaves*, they are . . . incapable of performing civil acts; and in reference to all such, they are *things;* not persons.[72]

That slaves were held to some of the responsibilities usually expected of persons in society and few of the privileges is further illustrated by the fact that slaves were persons who could abscond and commit capital crimes, but if killed or maimed in capture or put to death by law, the slave-owner was reimbursed for the loss of his property.

The third aspect pertains to the cases of manumission by will, deed, and legislative action; the instances of successful suits for freedom; and the cases of self-purchase—all of which implied

---

[66] *Fields v. State*, I Yerger Tenn. 156 (Jan., 1829). *Ibid.*, II, p. 494.

[67] *Hudson v. State*, 34 Ala. 253 (June, 1859). *Ibid.*, III, p. 233.

[68] *State v. Cynthia Simmons and Laurence Kitchen*, I Brevard S.C. 6 (Fall, 1794). *Ibid.*, II, p. 277.

[69] *State v. Davis*, 14 La. An. 678 (July, 1859). *Ibid.*, III, p. 674.

[70] *Baker v. State*, 15 Ga. 498 (July, 1854). *Ibid.*, III, p. 35.

[71] *State v. Cynthia Simmons and Laurence Kitchen*, I Brevard S.C. 6 (Fall, 1794). *Ibid.*, II, p. 277.

[72] *Creswell's Executor v. Walker*, 37 Ala. 229 (January, 1861). *Ibid.*, III, p. 247.

evaluation of the slave as a person with some legal capacity:

They may be emancipated by their owners; and must, of course, have a right to seek and enjoy the protection of the law in the establishment of all deeds, or wills, or other legal documents of emancipation; and so far, they must be considered as natural persons, entitled to some legal rights, whenever their owners shall have declared ... they ... be free; and to this extent the general reason of policy which disables slaves as persons, and subjects them to the general reason of mere brute property, does not apply.[73]

Moreover, the presence of free Negroes in the population from the beginning; manumission; suits for freedom; and self-purchase indicated that slavery did not follow naturally and inevitably from Negro ancestry. The intrusion of the values of liberty and individual achievement into the legal structure meant that race and slavery were not coextensive for all Negroes. The law sanctioned the possibility of slaves legitimately aspiring to and attaining in attenuated form the culture goals of the enslaving group having to do with freedom and individual achievement. The status of the free Negro was real and symbolic evidence of the indeterminacy resulting from the attainment of goals that were presumably denied to Negroes and applicable only to whites.[74]

III

In the interpretations of Elkins, Tannenbaum, and Stampp much has been

[73] *Catherine Bodine's Will*, 4 Dana Ky 476 (October, 1836). *Ibid.*, I, pp. 334–35.
[74] Wilbert Moore and Robin Williams, "Stratification in the Ante-bellum South," *American Sociological Review*, VII (June, 1942), 343–51. Cf. Douglas Hall, "Slaves and Slavery in the British West Indies," *Social and Economic Studies*, II, No. 4 (December, 1962), 305–18.

made of the legal status of the slave as property and the extent to which the rights of slaves were assimilated to property in law. As the preceding discussion has indicated, in the United States where slaves were conceived of as innately inferior they constituted a caste in the society and their rights were extensively assimilated to property in law. In Republican Rome where slaves were not conceived of as innately inferior to the enslaving group and did not form a separate caste an equally extensive assimilation of their rights to property occurred. In contrast to the United States, manumission was easily available to the Roman slave, and the freedman could look forward to assimilation into Roman society.

Although the slave status in Rome was not justified in terms of the innate inferiority of the slave, the assimilation of ownership in slaves to property was comparable to that in the United States. Roman law respected the moral personality of the slave, as reflected in the rules governing manumission and the status of the freed slave, but this did not prevent the assimilation of his rights to property in law.

In so far as the legal categorization of the slave as property is concerned we are dealing with a common social form in Rome and the United States. Caste produced the contrast between the legal structures of the two systems of slavery. The consequence of racial discrimination for the legal structure of antebellum slavery was the creation of a hereditary, endogamous, and permanent group of individuals in the status of slaves who, moreover, continued as members of a lower caste in the society after freedom. Although the conception of the slave as innately (racially) inferior to the enslaving group had important consequences for manumission and for the status of freedmen, as Tannenbaum has indicated, the comparison with Rome suggests that it did not accentuate the assimilation of ownership in slaves to property. Racial discrimination does not appear to have affected the legal status of the slave as property.

Now slavery in Rome was not a single social phenomenon historically. Not until the first two centuries of the Empire did significant changes occur in the authority of the master over the rights of slaves. "In their ultimate legal formulation the changes found expression in the Codes of Theodosius and Justinian."[75] Up to that time, although Roman law respected the moral integrity of the slave, the subordination of the slave to the authority of the master was comparable to that in the United States. The slave law that came down through the Justinian Code to influence the Iberian law of slavery, later to be transferred to Latin America, contained not only the doctrine of the moral personality of the slave, but also embodied those changes in later Roman law which had "loosened the strict controls by which the slave element had formerly been bound to the will of the master group."[76]

According to the interpretations of slavery in Latin America by Tannenbaum and Elkins, it was this body of law in conjunction with certain traditions and institutional arrangements that functioned to protect the slaves both from an extensive assimilation to property in law and from a caste status. Some reference will be made in the concluding portion of this essay to the need for a revision of this interpretation on the basis of more recent research.

Considerable variation occurs among slavery systems in the extent to which the slave is assimilated to property in law. Variations in this component are generally taken to be related to "the level of technical development and the accompanying institutional apparatus, including the economic system."[77] Where slavery was a domestic system, as in China and the Near East, the assimilation of the slave to property in law was less extensive than in Rome and the United States where slavery was an industrial system.[78]

The property component in the status of the antebellum slave was undoubtedly related to economic values and the labor needs of an emerging capitalism, as Elkins and Stampp have emphasized, but the entire status cannot be derived from the operation of economic values. On the one hand, the extensive assimilation to property in law of the Roman slave did not generate a conception of him as innately inferior and create a caste of slaves and freedmen. On the other hand, the absence of certain institutions and traditions embodying values respecting the moral personality of the slave does not account for the conception of the Negro as inherently inferior and for caste. If these were absent, then the assimilation of ownership in slaves to property in law must have caused racial discrimination and caste. The historical evidence indicates rather that discrimination against the Negro occurred before the slave status was fully defined and before

---

[75] Westermann, p. 140.
[76] *Ibid.*, p. 140.

[77] Sidney W. Mintz, Review of *Slavery* by Stanley Elkins, *American Anthropologist*, LXIII (June, 1961), 580.
[78] G. Martin Wilbur, *Slavery in China During the Former Han Dynasty* (Chicago, 1943), p. 243; Mendelsohn, pp. 121–22.

Negro labor became pivotal to the economic system.[79]

In the conception of the legal status of the slave as determinate in terms of property the slave has neither a juridical nor a moral personality. The values of the dominant group in the United States that had a bearing on the law of slavery were, on the one hand, those which legitimatized slavery and the rigid system of stratification, and on the other hand, those values pertaining to freedom and individual dignity and worth. Although there was no complex of laws, traditions, and institutions pertaining to the institution of slavery as such that embodied these latter values, a significant element in the general value system of the South was an ethical valuation of the individual. The legal evidence indicates that these extralegal values of the society were expressed in the legal definition and conception of slavery. The law of slavery shows the existence of an ethical norm, however vague and rudimentary, attaching value to the individual.[80]

The interpretation of the legal status of the slave primarily or wholly in terms of property has implications as well for the conception of the pattern of relations between masters and slaves. In discussing the connection between the legal structure and the master-slave relationship, David Potter has observed that "the human relationship within this legal context was complex and multiple." The relation between masters and slaves had "two faces—a paternalistic manorial one and an exploitative commercial one."[81]

In the interpretations of Tannenbaum, Elkins, and Stampp there is a close correspondence between the legal structure and the pattern of the master-slave relationship. Since, according to these writers, the slave status was governed by instrumental and economic values and not affected by the religious and ethical convictions of the dominant group attaching value to the individual, there was nothing to impede the rational use of slaves as economic instruments. The exploitative commercial pattern was expected to be followed in organizing the relations of masters and slaves. It was normatively and numerically the predominant pattern in the South.

Given this conception of the connection between the legal structure and the relations of masters and slaves, the paternalistic manorial pattern can only

---

[79] That the essential features of a caste status for the Negro may have preceded the full development of the slave status does not alter the widely accepted proposition that the initial status of the Negro was not that of a slave but rather that of an indentured servant or free man. Some aspects of caste appear to have developed later than others, but the main defining features were fixed early and before the complete development of the status of slavery. Racial segregation, although obviously foreshadowed in the status of the free Negro, did not appear as a part of the caste system until the late nineteenth and early twentieth centuries. The system of restricted contacts between Negroes and whites, clearly based on the long-standing assumption of the innate inferiority of the Negro, was simply the latest feature of caste to develop. See C. Vann Woodward, *The Strange Career of Jim Crow* (New York, 1957).

[80] Moore, pp. 201–2. For another discussion of the alternative value systems and the resulting conflicts within Southern society and within individuals see Sellers, pp. 51–67. A similar ambiguity existed in connection with slavery in ancient society. In Roman law "slavery is the

only case in which, in the extant sources . . . , a conflict is declared to exist between the *Ius Gentium* and the *Ius Naturale*." Buckland, p. 1. "No society," writes Finley, "can carry such a conflict within it, around so important a set of beliefs and institutions, without the stresses erupting in some fashion, no matter how remote and extended the lines and connections may be from the original stimulus." M. I. Finley, "Was Greek Civilization Based on Slave Labour?" in M. I. Finley, ed., *Slavery in Classical Antiquity* (Cambridge, 1960), p. 162.

[81] David M. Potter, Review of *The Peculiar Institution* by Kenneth Stampp, *Yale Review*, XLVI (Winter, 1957), 260–61.

be interpreted as a deviation from the expected and approved pattern of the master-slave relationship. It is not interpreted as an equally recognized and approved mode of organizing and managing the relations of masters and slaves, but rather as the result of fortuitous circumstances. It is attributed to the smallness of the plantation or to the "personal factor."[82] According to this interpretation there was nothing in the law to sanction the paternalistic manorial pattern, while the commercial exploitative pattern was clearly compatible with the instrumental use of slaves as sanctioned in the definition of the slave as an object of property rights. Yet, the paternalistic manorial pattern was widespread in the South as an accepted and approved mode of organizing the master-slave relationship and represented, as did the personal component in the legal status, the intrusion of the valuation of the individual into a categorized relationship.[83]

---

[82] Elkins, pp. 137–38.

[83] The pattern of the master-slave relationships continues to be one of the most problematic and debated aspects of antebellum slavery. The exploitative commercial pattern tends to be taken as the predominant pattern and in accordance with the normative prescriptions of antebellum society, while the paternalistic manorial pattern is generally treated as the result of the intrusion of non-normative factors, and usually attributed to smallness of size. However, Franklin has pointed out that the bulk of the slaves were on small plantations. If so, then the paternalistic manorial pattern must have been exceedingly widespread. On the other hand, it has also been suggested that this pattern was to be found on the larger holdings. Phillips had this conception of the master-slave relationship on large plantations. It seems likely that both patterns were normative; that is, accepted and approved ways of organizing the master-slave relationship. If this was the case, then further investigation must be directed at ascertaining the determinants of these patterns on the concrete level. Size would be one among several determinants. See John Hope Franklin, *From Slavery to Freedom* (New York, 1952), pp. 185–86. Needless to say, the pattern of the

IV

Since the contrast with slavery in Latin America is central to the interpretations of slavery in the United States by Tannenbaum and Elkins, some reference may be made to the more recent studies of slavery and race relations in Latin America and the implications for a comparison with North America. The results of these studies appear to be consistent with those of this essay.

In connection with the interpretations of slavery in Latin America by Elkins and Tannenbaum, Mintz questions whether slavery in Latin America can be treated as a single phenomenon historically.[83a] He points out that once slavery became a part of the industrial plantation system in Cuba and Puerto Rico, for example, an extensive assimilation to property in law of the rights of slaves occurred in spite of an institutional framework protecting the moral personality of the slave. Slavery in Cuba "dehumanized the slave as viciously as had Jamaican or North America slavery."[84] Much the same thing happened in Puerto Rico. Between 1803 and 1873 repressive laws were passed "more and more limiting the slaves' legal, social, economic status."[85] In

---

master-slave relationship is significant for the impact of slavery upon the personality of the Negro. If the paternalistic manorial pattern was widely institutionalized in the antebellum South, then a very significant number of Negro slaves were able to escape the tendency for the system to absorb the personality. Cf. Elkins, pp. 137–38.

[83a] Useful summaries are to be found in Juan Comas, "Recent Research on Race Relations—Latin America," *International Social Science Journal*, XIII, No. 2 (1961), 271–99; Oracy Nogueira, "Skin Color and Social Class," *Plantation Systems of the New World* (Washington, 1959), pp. 164–83; Roger Bastide, "Race Relations in Brazil," *International Social Science Bulletin*, IX, No. 4 (1957), 495–512.

[84] Mintz, p. 581.

[85] *Ibid.*, p. 583, See also O. A. Sherrard, *Freedom from Fear* (London, 1959), p. 75.

connection with slavery on the sugar plantations and in the mines of Portuguese Brazil, C. R. Boxer writes that the widely accepted "belief that the Brazilian was an exceptionally kind master is applicable only to nineteenth-century slavery under the Empire" and not to the colonial period.[86] At the same time, however, "one of the few redeeming features in the life of slaves . . . was the possibility of their buying or being given their freedom at some time, a contingency which was much rarer in the French and English American colonies."[87]

As to the racial component in the slave status, investigations of race relations in Brazil, where most of the work has been done, indicate that during the colonial period slavery also involved a caste system between whites and Negro slaves, "based on white supremacy and the institutionalized inferiority of colored slaves."[88] Concubinage was widely practiced, but intermarriage was rare, "as the system demanded the separation of the two castes and the clearcut distinction of superiors and inferiors."[89] Colonial legislation discriminated against the free Negroes who "were often coupled with enslaved Negroes in the laws."[90] They were prevented from acquiring possessions or participating in activities in the society "which might tend to place them on a

level with whites."[91] Mulattoes who attained positions of importance in Brazil "did so in spite of the official and social prejudices which existed against them throughout the whole of the colonial period."[92]

It is readily apparent from these studies that a much greater similarity existed between slavery in the United States and Latin America than heretofore suspected. The status of slaves in Latin America, as well as in Rome and the United States, indicates that whether or not the law respected the moral personality of the slave, an extensive assimilation of his rights to property in law occurred under slavery as an industrial system. Moreover, contrary to the widely held conception, racial discrimination was present in Latin America and had the consequence of creating a duality in the status of the slave as property and as a member of a racial caste.[93] These elements were apparently combined to some extent with a respect for the moral personality of the slave in the law.

Further comparative study of slavery in the United States and Latin America will enable us to delineate more precisely the differences and similarities in the property, racial, and personal components of the slave status in these societies. We may also expect such study to reveal, as this essay has attempted to do, that economic and ideological forces were not mutually exclusive in their consequences for the legal structure of slavery.

---

[86] *The Golden Age of Brazil* (Berkeley, 1961), p. 173. Gilberto Freyre's *The Masters and the Slaves* (New York, 1946), on which much of the existing conception of slavery in Brazil is based, wrote mainly about domestic slaves.

[87] Boxer, p. 177.

[88] Harley Ross Hammond, "Race, Social Mobility and Politics in Brazil," *Race*, IV, No. 2 (1962), p. 477. See Charles Wagley, "From Caste to Class in North Brazil", in Charles Wagley (ed.), *Race and Class in Rural Brazil* (New York, 1963), pp. 142–156.

[89] *Ibid.*, p. 4.

[90] Boxer, p. 17.

[91] *Ibid.*, p. 17.

[92] *Ibid.*, p. 17.

[93] Nogueira, pp. 167–76, has attempted to distinguish race prejudice in Brazil from that in the United States. With reference to the origin of race prejudice in Brazil, James. G. Leyburn, in his discussion of Nogueira's paper, questions whether it was slavery which produced prejudice. *Ibid.*, p. 181.

INSTITUTIONAL AND ECONOMIC FORCES

ELSA V. GOVEIA

The West Indian Slave Laws
of the Eighteenth Century

Elsa V. Goveia is Professor of West Indian History at the University of the West Indies, Jamaica. She is the author of Slave Society in the British Leeward Islands at the End of the 18th Century (*1965*) *and a recognized authority on West Indian history.*

The West Indian slave laws of the eighteenth century mirror the society that created them. They reflect the political traditions of the European colonizers and the political necessities of a way of life based upon plantation slavery.

The foundation of these laws was laid in the earliest days of colonization; and the body of slave laws existing in the eighteenth century included a substantial proportion of laws made at an earlier time. The thirteenth-century code of laws, known as the *Siete Partidas*, was from the beginning incorpo-

Reprinted from Elsa V. Goveia, "The West Indian Slave Laws of the Eighteenth Century," *Revista de Ciencias Sociales*, IV, No. 1 (March, 1960), 75–105, by permission of the *Revista de Ciencias Sociales*.

rated in the common law of the Spanish colonies and provided a series of principles for the government of slaves.[1] The great slave code of the French West Indies, which came to be called the *Code Noir*, was promulgated during the seventeenth century. The early slave laws of the British colonies, though they were not codified in this way, were generally retained as part of the slave law of the islands during the eighteenth century; and even when these laws were repealed in detail, a continu-

[1] Samuel P. Scott, C. S. Lobingier, and John Vance, eds., *Las Siete Partidas* (New York, 1931) is an English translation of the code, based upon the 1843–44 edition of the text of the original printed editions by Gregorio López (Salamanca; 1st. Ed., 1555; 2nd Ed., 1565–98).

ity of principle can be traced. The early laws were elaborated. Their emphasis changed with changes in the life of the islands. But the structure of the eighteenth-century slave laws rested upon older laws and was molded by forces, early at work in the islands, which had shaped not only the law but also the society of these slave colonies.

Both in the creation and in the maintenance of the slave laws, opinion was a factor of great significance. Law is not the original basis of slavery in the West India colonies, though slave laws were essential for the continued existence of slavery as an institution. Before the slave laws could be made, it was necessary for the opinion to be accepted that persons could be made slaves and held as slaves. To keep the slave laws in being, it was necessary for this opinion to persist. Without this, the legal structure would have been impossible. Spain's role in establishing slavery as part of the pattern of European colonization in the West Indies is thus of primary importance. Of equal importance, is the influence exerted by developments within the West Indies in sustaining the legal structure, first introduced by the Spaniards, and, to a greater or lesser extent, transforming its content.

Slavery was an accepted part of Spanish law at the time of the discovery. It was legal to hold slaves, and it was accepted in law that slavery was transmitted by birth, through the mother to her children. This was the core of the system of enslavement transferred from Spain to the West Indies.[2] But in Spain, at this time, slavery was a relatively insignificant and declining institution, and by no

means the dominant force that it was to become in the West Indies. The early and vigorous growth of plantations and slavery in the Spanish West Indies, though it was sharply checked, revealed the dynamic, expansive force of slavery in the new environment. With the growth of the French and English plantation colonies, slavery came to provide the economic and social framework of a whole society. Both the institution and the society were radically transformed.

In the Spanish colonies, the decline of the plantation system, after its first phase of rapid growth, created a situation still different from that of Spain, but different also from the classic pattern of plantation slavery to be found elsewhere in the West Indies. The Spanish slave laws were less completely adapted to the will of the slave-owning "planter" than was the case elsewhere, during the eighteenth century. In addition, the strong conservatism of the Spanish crown and government made possible the retention of some of the fundamental concepts borrowed originally from the slave laws of Spain.

These concepts are very clearly expressed in the *Siete Partidas*, in which may be found what is chronologically the earliest legal view of the slave and slavery in the history of the West Indian slave laws. In the *Siete Partidas*, the slave is considered as part of the "familia," and the distinction between slaves and serfs is not clear-cut. The term "servitude," which may cover the unfree condition of both, is defined, as is the concept of liberty, which is its opposite. According to the *Siete Partidas*: "Servitude is an agreement and regulation which people established in ancient times, by means of which men who were originally free became slaves and were subjected to the authority of others contrary to natural reason." (Partida

---

[2] See C. Verlinden, *L'Esclavage dans l'Europe médievale* (Vol. I, *Péninsule Ibérique-France*) (Brugges, 1955).

IV, Tít. XXI, Ley i.) Slavery is defined as "something which men naturally abhor and . . . not only does a slave live in servitude, but also any one who has not free power to leave the place where he resides." (Partida VII, Tít. XXXIV, Reg. ii.) Logically then, liberty is "the power which every man has by nature to do what he wishes, except where the force of law or *fuero* (privilege) prevent him." The preamble to the section on liberty states: "All creatures in the world naturally love and desire liberty, and much more do men, who have intelligence superior to that of others." (Part. IV, Tít. XXII.)

Deriving from these premises, the principle of the Spanish slave law was, on the whole, a principle friendly to the protection of the slave and to his claims of freedom. For the *Partidas* envisaged the slave as a "persona" and not as "mere property." The master was regarded as having duties toward his slaves, as well as rights over them: "A master has complete authority over his slave to dispose of him as he pleases. Nevertheless, he should not kill or wound him, although he may give cause for it, except by order of the judge of the district, nor should he strike him in a way contrary to natural reason, or put him to death by starvation." (Part. IV, Tít. XXI.) In the *Partidas*, slavery is undoubtedly accepted as legal. It is not accepted as good. Liberty is the good which the law strives to serve: "it is a rule of law that all judges should aid liberty, for the reason that it is a friend of nature, because not only men, but all animals love it." (Partida IV, Tít. XXXIV, Reg. i.)

The liberality of these principles relating to slaves cannot be denied, though it may be doubted whether they were ever fully enforced even in Spain. In the *Partidas*, it is clear that slavery is looked upon as a misfortune, from the consequences of which slaves should be protected as far as possible, because they are men, and because man is a noble animal not meant for servitude. The growth of enslavement in the West Indies undermined and even reversed this view; and many later apologists of slavery attempted to prove that enslavement is not an evil but a good. The myth of "inevitable progress" has prevented for long an appreciation of the fact that humaneness predates humanitarianism. The truth is that this "medieval" slave code was probably the most humane in its principles ever to be introduced in the West Indies. It appears to have been the one section of the West India slave law in which was made the unequivocal assertion that liberty is the natural and proper condition of man.

The case of the *Siete Partidas* illustrates that, within the general agreement that slavery could legally exist, a considerable latitude of opinion about the institution itself was possible. The slave laws of the Spanish West Indies tended positively to favor the good treatment of slaves and their individual emancipation. From the beginning, under the provisions of the *Siete Partidas*, the slave was legally protected in life and limb. As the celebrated jurist Solórzano pointed out, the slave was, in law, entitled to the protection and intervention of the law on his behalf, and the master could actually lose his property in the slave as a result of proved maltreatment of him.[3] Failure to subsist the slave adequately was, from the standpoint of the law, a serious abuse. So was the infliction upon the slave of inordinate work. In addition, slaves might be compulsorily manumitted for specific kinds

---

[3] Juan de Solórzano, *Politica indiana* (5 vols., Madrid and Buenos Aires, 1930), Vol. I, Lib. 2, c. 4, n. 34 and c. 7, n. 77.

of abuse—for example, in the case of women slaves, for violation or prostitution of the slave by her owner.[4] Under the Spanish slave laws codified in 1680, *audiencias* were instructed to hear cases of slaves who claimed to be free, and to see that justice was done to them.[5] When slaves of mixed blood were to be sold, it was provided that their Spanish fathers, if willing, should be allowed to buy them so that they might become free.[6] Orders were also given that peaceful settlements of free Negroes were not to be molested, and, throughout the eighteenth century, Puerto Rico followed the practice of giving asylum to fugitive slaves from non-Spanish islands, with very little variation from the principle that, once they had embraced the Roman Catholic religion, they were not to be returned.[7]

Custom, as well as law, appears to have favored the growth of the free colored group. By the custom of *coartación*, slaves by degrees bought themselves free from the ownership of their masters.[8] When the customary institution was incorporated in the slave laws, it had to be made clear that the master retained his property in the slave undiminished until the last payment was made. The law, which was more severe than custom had been, acknowledged a

right in the master to claim all the *coartado's* time if he wished.[9]

Customary *coartación* was widespread in the Spanish islands in the eighteenth century, and it was probably of great importance in increasing the numbers of freed men in these territories at the time. One estimate of Cuban population in 1774, which Friedlaender apparently considers not too wide of the mark, gives a total of 171,620, of whom 96,440 were whites, 30,847 were free colored, and only 44,333 were slaves.[10] Figures for Puerto Rico, which was even slower than Cuba in turning to sugar and the great plantation, are equally interesting. As late as 1827, Puerto Rico was still a country with a predominantly free and even predominantly white population, though here the margin of difference between whites and nonwhites was less than in Cuba of 1774.

The spirit of the Spanish slave laws, which was relatively liberal, undoubtedly influenced the form of these societies, in particular by aiding the growth of the free colored group. In turn, the less rigid and less slave-centered societies of these islands enabled the liberality of the Spanish law to survive and to exercise its influence upon them. When the change-over to sugar and the great plantation came in real earnest, the processes consequent on this change-over had to be worked out in a social environment different from that of other islands which had suffered transformation during the seventeenth and early eighteenth centuries. Despite the brutalities of the nineteenth century, slavery in the Spanish islands was, on the whole, milder than was the case elsewhere in the West Indies.

---

[4] *Ibid.*, Vol. I, Lib. 2, c. 7, n. 13 and Vol. II, Lib. 3, c. 17, n. 23.

[5] *Recopilación de leyes de las Indias* (3 vols., Madrid, 1943), Vol. II, Lib. 7, tít. 5, ley 8.

[6] *Ibid.*, ley 6.

[7] *Ibid.*, ley 19. See also Luis M. Díaz Soler, *Historia de la esclavitud negra en Puerto Rico* (Madrid, 1953), p. 235; Fernando Ortiz, *Los negros esclavos, estudio sociológico y de derecho público* (Havana, 1916), p. 351; Arturo Morales Carrión, *Puerto Rico and the Non-Hispanic Caribbean* (Río Piedras, 1952).

[8] On *coartación* see H. H. S. Aimes, "Coartación," *Yale Review* (Feb., 1909), 412–31; Díaz Soler, *op. cit.*, especially chap. X; Ortiz, *op. cit.*, especially chap. XVII.

[9] Aimes, *loc. cit.*, pp. 424–25.

[10] H. E. Friedlaender, *Historia economica de Cuba* (Havana, 1944), p. 84.

Nevertheless, this is a contrast which can be overemphasized. As Ortiz points out in his illuminating study *Los negros esclavos*, the attitude of the Cuban upper class throughout its history has not been so far different from that of the slave-owners of other islands as the difference in their slave laws might suggest. The relative despotism of the Spanish government acted as a check on the local oligarchies, which did not necessarily share the view of slavery expressed in the *Siete Partidas*. In fact Ortiz suggests that, if the task of making slave laws had been placed as firmly in the hands of these men as it was in the hands of a slave-owning ruling class in the British islands, there might not be so much to choose between Spanish and English slave laws.[11] Certainly, when this class became strong enough in Cuba to resist official policy successfully, one of its earliest successes was the defeat of the humane Slave Code of 1789, in which the Spanish government had attempted to provide for the amelioration of conditions among a growing slave population. Certainly also, it is generally agreed that the increase in the numbers of slaves in Cuba, which accompanied the expansion of the sugar industry there, brought a marked and general deterioration in their treatment. As Cuba became a sugar colony, its slave conditions more approximately resembled those of the other sugar colonies.[12]

What is more, even in the period of relatively mild treatment of slaves in the Spanish colonies, enacted law and practice were not one and the same thing.[13] The custom of *coartación*, which

existed before it was recognized in law, serves to illustrate a case where custom was in advance of the law from the point of view of the slaves. In other cases, the law was decidedly more humane than was custom. The existence of the slave laws of the *Siete Partidas*, and of later enactments, did not prevent the existence of numbers of slaves who were underfed, overworked, and badly treated.

Lastly, though this is by no means of least importance, the humane regulations do not tell the whole story of the enacted slave law in the Spanish colonies. In addition to the structure of protective regulations already described, there existed other and different laws governing slaves and free colored, and these show the direct influence of the necessities of the slave system which depended in part upon force for its maintenance. In his discussion of the Cuban slave laws, Ortiz has pointed out how much the Spanish and local governments were concerned with the problem of slavery as a problem of public order. He shows that in the evolution of the slave laws, as in the restrictions on the slave trade in the Spanish colonies, political considerations were often of great weight. The slave laws very clearly reflect this concern.[14]

In the Code of 1680,[15] for example, the police regulations governing slaves already outnumber all others, and there were also several restrictions on the free colored. (Vol. II, Lib. 7, Tít. 5.) All of these were based upon the determination to preserve public order. It was provided, for instance, that Negroes were subject to a curfew in cities; and the magistrates were enjoined to try them for any disturbances

[11] Ortiz, *op. cit.*, pp. 335–44.
[12] *Ibid.*, passim. See also H. H. S. Aimes, *A History of Slavery in Cuba, 1511–1865* (New York, 1907).
[13] For an illustration see Javier Malagón, *Un documento del siglo XVIII para la historia de la esclavitud en las Antillas* (Havana, 1956).

[14] Ortiz, *op. cit.*, pp. 342 ff.
[15] *Recopilación, op. cit.*

which they might commit. (Leyes 12, 13.) No Negro, whether slave or free, and no person of Negro descent, except in special cases, was to be permitted to carry arms. (Leyes 14–18.) There were several regulations for the policing of runaway slaves. (Leyes 20–25.) One provided for their protection by forbidding that they should be mutilated in punishment. (Ley 24.) But it is fair to say that this was exceptional. Most of the provisions were made with an eye to the control and suppression of the runaways as a threat to public order. Finally, there were regulations for preventing, defeating, and punishing the risings of slaves, and for the summary arrest of any Negro found wandering or engaged in similar suspicious activities. (Ley 26.)

As for the free colored, they were supposed to live under the supervision of a patron, even though free; and, by a special law, they were forbidden to wear gold, silk, cloaks, or other kinds of clothing considered unsuitable to their station in society. (Leyes 3, 28.) From the first too, the Spanish government tried to prevent race mixture in its colonies between Spaniards, Indians, and Negroes, whether slave or free. (Ley 5.) In this, it was, of course, generally unsuccessful.

Among the provisions made to secure public order in Cuba during the seventeenth century, Ortiz lists laws prohibiting the sale of wine to slaves, regulations governing the work of hired slaves, the perennial restrictions against the bearing of arms by slaves, and provisions for the pursuit of runaways and their punishment. These, rather than purely protective measures, continued most to occupy the active attention of the authorities until the ameliorative codification of 1789.

This code included provisions regulating the work and recreation of slaves, their housing and medical care, their maintenance in old age, their marriages and similar subjects, their punishments, and their formal protection in law. Besides providing for the protection of slaves, the code of 1789 made provision for the detection and punishment of abuses by the colonists in the management of slaves. Unlike the police regulations, this code ran into strong opposition from the colonists, especially in Cuba, where the resistance was so determined that the government was forced virtually to withdraw the new code in 1791.[16]

There was in Puerto Rico a comparative neglect of those regulations which affected the activities of the master, while the laws penalizing the criminal actions of slaves were far more effectively enforced.[17] The intention behind protective regulations could thus be defeated, and the law was given an emphasis in practice which does not emerge to the same extent in its enactment. Even in these relatively liberal slave islands, therefore, it can be seen that slavery presented a minimum requirement of rigor, which pressed upon the slave because of his status, and because of the necessity to maintain it.

In the British islands, during the eighteenth century, the marks left by the slave system upon the law are less ambiguous. This is not only because the plantation system had here taken a very firm hold, but also because of the nature of the British political tradition. England, which was earlier freed of slavery and even of serfdom than was Spain, had no *Siete Partidas* to transfer to her West India colonies when they were acquired, even though these colonies quickly adopted the slave sys-

---

[16] Ortiz, *op. cit.*, Ch. XX.
[17] Díaz Soler, *op. cit.*, pp. 192–93.

tem brought to the West Indies by the Spaniards. The English government never, until the nineteenth century, showed so careful and sustained an interest in the subject of slave regulations as did the government of Spain from earliest times. Most important of all, perhaps, traditions of representative government determined that the slave laws of the British colonies were made directly by a slave-owning ruling class. These laws were, therefore, an immediate reflection of what the slave-owner conceived to be the necessities of the slave system.

It has often been said that the greater freedom incorporated in the British constitutional system helped to breed respect for the property of the subject, as well as for his liberty. This may be part of the explanation of the legal convention which, in the British slave colonies, left the power of the master over his property, the slave, virtually unlimited, even in some cases as to life and limb. For this convention to apply, however, it had to be made clear that the slave was property and subject to police regulations. In fact, the experience of the British colonies makes it particularly clear that police regulations lay at the very heart of the slave system and that, without them, the system became impossible to maintain.

This was the moral of Somersett's case decided by the Chief Justice, Lord Mansfield, in 1771–72, and also of the case of the slave Grace decided by Lord Stowell in 1827.[18] Given police regulations, the English law in the West Indies worked against the slave, because he was there mere property or something very near it. In the absence

of such regulations, the slave had to be regarded as an ordinary man; and, in this context, the respect for liberty of the subject, which was also a part of the English legal tradition, worked in his favor. Somersett's case illustrates the operation of the principle of liberty of the subject. There was no law against slavery in England. But the absence of a law providing sanctions for slavery enabled Somersett to win his freedom by refusing any longer to be held as a slave. The case of the slave Grace shows the potency of police provisions in maintaining the slave system. For on returning voluntarily to Antigua, she lost the temporary freedom gained by a visit to England.

English respect for the liberty of the subject was thus restricted by the erection of a slave system, and had to be so restricted to keep the slave system in being. Under the English slave system in the West Indies, the slave was not regarded as a subject, but as a property; and when the English humanitarians attempted to take the view that he was a subject, they were advocating an innovation which only slowly gained acceptance in the controversies over amelioration and emancipation.

The basic conception of the English law in relation to the slave was not, as with the Spaniards, that he was an inferior kind of subject. It was rather that he was a special kind of property. First of all, he was merchandise when bought and sold in the course of the slave trade. Once acquired by a planter, the slave became private property— regarded in part as a chattel, in part as real property. As a chattel, for instance, he could be sold up for debts if other movable assets were exhausted. But in other cases, he was subject to the laws of inheritance of real estate. He could be entailed, was subject to the widow's

---

[18] H. T. Catterall, *Judicial Cases Concerning American Slavery and the Negro* (5 Vols., Washington, 1926–36), Vol. I, pp. 1–8, 14–18, 34–37.

right of dower, and could be mortgaged.[19]

These aspects of the law appeared both in the law of the West Indies and in the law of England. Under both, trading in slaves was a recognized and legal activity. Under both, there were provisions for regulating the mortgage of slaves and obliging their sale as chattels in cases of debt.[20] The point is worth stressing. The idea of slaves as property was as firmly accepted in the law of England as it was in that of the colonies; and it was not for lack of this provision that Somersett had to be freed. It was the lack of the superstructure raised on this basis—in the form of police law governing slaves—which made it impossible for Somersett to be held in slavery by force in England. Before and after the Somersett case, slaves were taken to and from England, as the case of the slave Grace shows; and, so long as they did not refuse to serve, as Somersett did, it may be said that they remained property and did not become subjects in fact, though in theory this change was supposed to take place on their arrival in England.

In the West Indies, they were slaves because the superstructure, lacking in England, was there available. By the eighteenth century, it was elaborate and, generally speaking, comprehensive. On the basic idea of the slave as property, a whole system of laws was

built up. Some concerned the disposal of the slave as property, others governed the actions of slaves as an aspect of public order. Some gave slaves a species of legal protection. But, up to the time when organized humanitarian agitation began in the 1780's, the protective enactments were relatively few and sometimes rather ambiguous. Police regulations occupied the most ample proportion of the attention of the British West India legislators.

Some of the regulations made are clearly related to the conception that the slave was property, but even those border on the idea of police. Thus, owners whose slaves suffered the judicial penalty of death were usually compensated for the loss. Obviously, this was because their property in the slave was recognized. But the intention was also to reduce the temptation of owners to conceal criminal slaves from justice. Again, persons who employed or hired the slaves of others without proper consent were guilty of a form of trespass, which was subject to both civil and criminal proceedings. Taking the slaves of another by violence was robbery. To carry off a slave from the provisions safeguarded the slave as private property. They also penalized those aiding runaways, either by enabling them to support themselves away from the master or by aiding their flight directly. They are part of a whole series of laws which penalized all persons, whether slave or free, who sheltered or otherwise assisted the runaway slave.[21]

Every island passed laws for the pursuit, capture, suppression, and punishment of runaway slaves; and these laws were usually severe. Similar

---

[19] A good summary of the basic provisions of the British West Indian slave law during the eighteenth century is given in Reeves' "General View of the Principles on which this System of Laws Appears to have been Originally Founded" in House of Commons Accounts and Papers, Vol. XXVI (1789), No. 646a, Part III. See the section dealing with "Slaves Considered as Property."

[20] Statute 5 Geo. II, c. 7, and Statute 13 Geo. III, c. 14. For a West Indian example see Laws of Jamaica (2 vols., St. Jago de la Vega, 1792), Vol. II, 23 Geo. III, c. 14.

[21] See for example Laws of the Island of Antigua (4 vols., London, 1805), Vol. I, no. 130 (1702), no. 176 (1723).

police regulations were made in islands other than those of the British. Slaves were not to wander abroad without written passes, they were not to have firearms or to assemble together in numbers. Usually they were forbidden to beat drums and blow horns, since these were means of communication which might be used to help runaways.[22] All such activites were dangerous, too, as means of concerting uprisings—another reason for the existence of these laws. Not all of them were enforced at all times with equal rigor. Slave dances, feasts, and drumming were often allowed; and even the pass laws were not always strictly observed. The laws remained in force however, and they were used when necessary to prevent or to control emergencies.

The function served by the laws may be illustrated by a comparison. In Barbados, under an early law of the seventeenth century, it was provided that if a Negro slave died under punishment by his master and no malice was proved, the master killing his own slave was to pay a fine of £15. If the slave belonged to another master, the fine to be paid was £25, and an additional payment of double the slave's value was to be made to compensate his owner.[23] This law was made notorious by abolitionist criticism. It is one of the worst of its type, but its singularity lay rather in the lowness of its fines than in its principle. It was a brutal law, but its brutality flowed in well defined, socially accepted channels. This is why a struggle was necessary to achieve a change of principle. Few islands in the British West Indies, until the later eighteenth century, showed any willingness to recognize that the willful killing of a slave was an act of homicide or murder. It was usually regarded in theory, though not always in practice, as a criminal offense. But generally it was a criminal offense of a lesser order, to which it was not felt necessary to attach so heavy a penalty as that of death.

By contrast, heavy penalties were attached to the commission of a crime, the gravity of which depended entirely on its social context. For striking or insulting a white, slaves were subject to the penalties of whipping, mutilation, or death; and usually the law provided that if the white was in any way hurt or if the blow drew blood, then the more severe punishments should be inflicted.[24] Even free persons of color were often made liable to similar punishments for similar offenses against whites—and this meant all whites, from the great planter to the poor white, and white indenture servant.[25] The contrast in treatment of the crime of killing a slave and the crime of striking or abusing a white is due in each case to the social significance attached to the crime.

Yet the slave was a special kind of property, as these laws attest. For to kill even one's own slave maliciously was penalized, though not usually as much as the killing either of the slave of another or of a free man. The law with regard to the striking or wounding of whites also had to envisage the slave as something more than a "thing." The dilemma was that he was not "mere

---

[22] Reeves, "General View," loc. cit.

[23] Ibid., section on "Punishment by Masters." See Act no. 82 (1688) in Acts Passed in the Island of Barbados (1643–1762) (London, 1764); a ms. copy is in C. O. 30/5, P. R. O. London.

[24] For examples, see the Virgin Islands slave act (1783) in C. O. 152/67, the St. Kitts Act no. 2 (1711) "for the better government of Negroes and other slaves" in C. O. 240/4, and the St. Vincent Act (July 11, 1767) in C. O. 262/1, P. R. O. London.

[25] See the Antigua Act no. 130 (1702) and the Virgin Islands Slave Act (1783).

property," as the law wished to suppose him, but a creature possessing volition, and the capacity for resistance which must be checked, indeed crushed, if the society were to survive. Obviously, the slaves were also regarded as a special kind of property in the laws governing them as runaways, and punishing them as conspirators or rebels. If the slave had been truly a thing in fact, as well as in the fiction of the law, such legislation would not have been necessary. Because he was a person, he posed a problem of public order, which the police regulation tended to cover. The law was forced to allow the slave some kind of "persona" for the purpose of dealing with him under this aspect of his activity as a special kind of property.

In the earlier British slave laws, and even up to the beginning of the humanitarian controversy, the dominant tendency was to recognize the slave as a "persona" in a sphere far more limited than that allowed him in either Spanish or French slave law. Early English slave law almost totally neglects the slave as a subject for religious instruction, as a member of a family, or as a member of society possessing some rights, however inferior. Insofar as the slave is allowed personality before the law, he is regarded chiefly, almost solely, as a potential criminal.

This is true of the police regulations governing the movements of slaves. It is true of the regulations to restrain and punish thefts by slaves, which were numerous. It is true even of the regulations governing the economic activities of slaves, in which may be traced a constant preoccupation with the problems of running away and theft, as well as a desire to limit the economic competition of slaves with whites.

The humanitarians, in their criticism of the West India slave laws, attacked this limited legal concept of the slave, and, in the course of their long struggle with the West Indians, substantial changes were made in the laws by the island legislatures. In particular, attempts were made, during the controversies over amelioration, to define the duties of masters towards their slaves, and the degree of protection to which slaves were entitled in law. During this phase, the status of the slave as a "persona," in the eyes of the law, was significantly broadened. But this development came relatively late, and was, to a considerable extent, due to the pressure built up by the humanitarian critics of the West Indies.

Before the beginning of the humanitarian assault, the British West India slave laws included relatively few protective clauses, and even these often seem to rest on an ambiguous view of the slave. Indeed, it is misleading to regard many of these regulations as providing anything comparable to the "positive protection" sought for in later laws. There was, for instance, a Montserrat regulation of 1693, which provided that one acre of provisions should be cultivated for every eight slaves belonging to a plantation. But this is only one clause of an extremely severe act intended to punish thefts by slaves, and especially thefts of provisions. The act was concerned with a problem of public order, rather than with any idea of the rights of slaves to sufficient food in return for their services.[26]

Provisions for holidays to be given to slaves at particular times reflect similar police problems. In these laws, fines were often imposed on those who gave more, as well as those who gave less, than the prescribed holidays, and this practice only gradually came to be

---

[26] Montserrat Act no. 36 (1693).

modified later in the eighteenth century.[27]

Laws to prevent old and disabled slaves from being abandoned by their masters have a similar ambiguity. For wandering and destitute slaves always constituted a serious problem of public order; and local authorities usually refused to have them become a burden on poor relief. The most obvious expedient was, therefore, to insist upon the master's obligation to keep even useless slaves, rather than have this burden thrown on the public.[28] Here, for once, the idea that the slave was private property operated against, rather than in favor of, the master's will. The result of this insistence upon the private responsibility of the master was not always favorable to the slave however. For it led to severe laws providing life-sentences of hard labor for destitute slaves whose masters could not be found, and to an unwillingness on the part of the legislators to permit even the manumission of able-bodied slaves unless the public was indemnified beforehand against the possibility that the new freedman might become destitute. During the second half of the eighteenth century, in particular, several laws were passed, imposing a tax for this purpose upon manumissions.[29] Even where the object was not directly to check the growth in numbers of the free population, the effect was certainly to make the achievement of manumission more difficult, because more costly.

In the British West India slave laws in force during the eighteenth century, there were, of course, some unambiguous protective clauses. But some of these carry little weight in comparison with the other kinds of regulation. For example, Barbados in 1668 had provided that slaves should be given clothing once a year, specifying drawers and caps for men, and petticoats and caps for women. The penalty for failure to comply with this law was 5 shillings per slave.[30] In the newer colonies of the eighteenth century, for instance, St. Vincent and Dominica, heavier fines were imposed, but the amount of clothing provided as a compulsory allowance was still either small or inadequately defined in the law.[31] Even under the consolidated slave law passed at Jamaica in 1781, where the penalty of £50 was inflicted for neglect, the allowances to be made to slaves were stated without proper definition.[32] It can hardly be doubted that such weaknesses must have lessened the effectiveness of these protective laws.

Other more considerable regulations for the protection of slaves were also instituted. But their comparatively small number indicates that they were exceptional. It has already been noticed that the wilful killing of slaves was not generally considered to be murder, but was nevertheless judged to be a criminal offense of some gravity. Jamaica, from relatively early days, went a step further than the other islands by providing under an act of 1696 that anyone found guilty of a second offense of willingly, wantonly, or "bloodymindedly" killing a Negro or slave, should be convicted of murder. The first offense was declared a felony, and, as this was found to be an insufficient deterrent, an

---

[27] Compare Antigua Act no. 176 (1723) and Antigua Act no. 390 (1778) in *Laws . . . of Antigua, op. cit.,* Vol. I.

[28] Virgin Islands Slave Act (1783).

[29] See Reeves, "General View," *loc. cit.,* section "Of Manumissions."

[30] Barbados Act no. 82 (1688).

[31] St. Vincent Act (July 11, 1767), in C. O. 262/1, P. R. O. London.

[32] 22 Geo. III, c. 17, in *Laws* (Spanish Town, Jamaica), Lib. 8, I. R. O.

additional punishment of imprisonment was provided in 1751.[33]

There were also laws penalizing the
dismemberment or mutilation of slaves,
by fine or imprisonment or both. The
range of fines ran from a minimum fine
of £20, provided at Antigua in 1723, to
the much heavier fine of £500, provided by the St. Kitts legislature sixty
years later.[34] But such provisions were
by no means ubiquitous, and in many
of the islands it remained true that, as
one report of 1788 states: "Very little
Measure appears to have been assigned
by any general laws, to the Authority
of the Master in punishing Slaves."[35]
In particular, the regulation of lesser
punishments by law was very generally
neglected, and the partial nature of
such legislation is illustrated by the
fact that a St. Vincent law which provided against mutilation of slaves also
contained a clause inflicting a £10 fine
on persons taking off iron collars and
similar instruments of punishment
from slaves, without the consent of the
master.

When the controversy over abolition
of the slave trade drew attention to
the inadequacy of statutory protection
offered slaves in the matter of punishment and maltreatment, defenders of
the West India interest had recourse to
the argument that common law protection was available, where statutory
protection was lacking.[36] Insofar as
this was clearly true, however, it affected the slave as a piece of property

rather than as a person. The master
had the right to bring suit for damages
against anyone harming his slave, even
where there was no statutory provision
for this. Indeed, acts which added a criminal penalty for such offenses generally made specific reference to this civil
right. The more dubious part of the case
concerns not this right, but the right of
slaves to personal protection, without
the intervention of the owner, or against
the owner or his representatives.[37] A
thorough search of judicial records
throughout the British islands at this
time would be necessary to determine
whether, before the matter became a
contentious one, cases against owners
and their representatives were normally, or even occasionally, brought to the
common law courts in any of the islands.

The evidence already available does
not suggest that the personal protection
of slaves under the common law was
very effective. As late as 1823, when
Fortunatus Dwarris, as a member of
the legal commission to the West
Indies, investigated this matter, he was
forced to report a "want of remedy"
for slaves at common law in Barbados,
and a conflict of opinion on the subject
there and throughout the British islands.[38] Dwarris wished to have the
situation clarified and recommended
that

it might be advantageous, that in the
Windward as well as in the Leeward

---

[33] Jamaica Acts 8 Wm. III, c. 2, and 24 Geo.
II, c. 17, in *Laws* (Spanish Town Jamaica), Lib.
4, I. R. O.

[34] Antigua Act. no. 176 (1723); St. Kitts Act
(1783) in C. O. 152/66, P. R. O. London.

[35] Reeves. "General View," *loc. cit.*

[36] For instance, evidence given by James
Tobin before a Select Committee of the House
of Commons (1790), printed in House of Commons Accounts and Papers, Vol. XXIX (1790),
no. 695/5, esp. pp. 272–73.

[37] This view of the case is put by Drewry
Ottley, Chief Justice of St. Vincent, in his
evidence, reported in House of Commons
Accounts and Papers, Vol. XXIV (1790–91),
no. 476, pp. 158 ff.

[38] F. Dwarris, "Substance of the Three
Reports of the Commissioners of Enquiry into
the Administration of Civil and Criminal
Justice in the West Indies," extracted from the
Parliamentary Papers (London, 1827), pp. 113
ff., 431 ff.

Islands, the common law of England should be declared to be the "certain rule for all descriptions of persons being subjects of His Majesty, and to obviate all doubts real or pretended upon this head, it might be recited and set forth explicitly in such declaratory law, that all African, or Creole slaves admitted within the King's allegiance, are, and shall at all times be taken and held to be, entitled to the protection, and subject to the penalties, of the common law; and to this, the slave code carefully compiled would properly be supplemental."[39]

Yet he doubted that even when this had been done, the common law would protect the slave from other than scandalous abuse.[40]

Dwarris' report, and his doubts, reflect an uncertainty as to the degree of protection offered under the common law. At St. Kitts, in 1786, a jury trying a case of maltreatment involving a slave also questioned whether "immoderate correction of a slave by the Master be a Crime indictable."[41] On this occasion, the judge decided that it was. But, what the attorney-general of Dominica said in 1823 of the whole question of common law protection is true here too: "the rule upon this subject is so vague, and so little understood in the colonies, that decisions founded upon it will be often contradictory."[42]

Even graver doubts about the application of the common law to slaves were current in the West Indies, and these may have sprung from an unwillingness to recognize the slave as having personal status in law. In 1823, Dwarris reported many assertions made by the judge and crown law officer of St. Kitts to the

effect that "the justices have no jurisdiction over slaves except what is expressly given them by Colonial Acts." It was not their duty, or even their right, to hear and deal with the complaints of slaves.[43]

The existence of this belief in the West Indies underlines the contrast, already noted in the discussion of Somersett's case and of the case of the slave Grace, between the situation of the slave in England and in the West Indies. Somersett's freedom was due to the common law, the slavery of Grace was secured by enacted law. In the West Indies, the slave was a "thing" rather than a person, a "property" rather than a subject. The same conception, which led to inadequate protection of slaves under enacted law, explains the uncertainty regarding their protection under the common law. The legal nullity of the slave's personality, except when he was to be controlled or punished, was the greatest obstacle to his adequate personal protection.

The law of evidence with regard to slaves reveals both the nullity and the anomaly of the conception of the slave as property. Any free man could give evidence against or for a slave. But during the eighteenth century, the evidence of slaves was not admitted for or against free persons in the British islands. Nevertheless, at the discretion of the courts, the evidence of slaves was admitted for or against other slaves. Thus the legal disability of the slave reinforced his inferior position. Still exposed to detection for his own crimes, he was deprived of protection against the crimes of all but his fellow slaves. He had no legal redress against those very abuses of power to which his inferior position already exposed him.

The existence of special forms of trial

---

[39] *Ibid.*, p. 433.
[40] *Ibid.*, pp. 114–16.
[41] House of Commons Accounts and Papers, Vol. XXVI (1789), no. 646a, pt. 3 (St. Kitts), appendix A.
[42] Dwarris, *loc. cit.*, p. 432.

[43] *Ibid.*, pp. 431ff., 113ff.

for slaves in the British islands, as well as the limited validity of their evidence, served to mark them off from the rest of the body politic. In many cases, they were placed under the summary jurisdiction of judges, acting without a jury, for the trial even of capital crimes.[44] When a solemn form of trial was provided, as for instance in Montserrat, where capital cases were tried by the Governor in Council, the form of trial still differed from that given to free men.[45] The Barbados legislature put the matter succinctly in 1688, when it provided a solemn court for capital cases but omitted the usual jury of twelve men, on the ground that the accused "being Brutish Slaves, deserve not, from the Baseness of their condition, to be tried by the legal trial of twelve men of their Peers, or Neighbourhood, which truly neither can be rightly done, as the Subjects of England are."[46]

Every aspect of the slave law of the British islands reveals the fundamental political concern with the subordination and control of slaves. This emphasis was characteristic right up to the beginning of the abolitionist struggle and beyond. In 1784, when their first cautious ameliorated slave code, the Act of 1781, expired, the members of the Jamaican legislature were apparently too busy to bring in a new improved slave law. But this did not prevent them from passing an act providing for parties to hunt runaway slaves, nor from reviving the very severe laws under which thefts and destruction of horses and cattle by slaves were visited with the punishment of death.[47] It seems fair to conclude not only that

these were less controversial than improvements in the slave laws, but also that they were regarded as being more urgently necessary than, for instance, the new provisions against mutilation and dismemberment of slaves which lapsed when the Act of 1781 did.

It was not that the West Indians were always disinclined to serve the cause of humanity, but simply that they considered the cause of self-preservation infinitely more important. The primary function of the British West India slave laws was either directly or indirectly repressive. For, as Bryan Edwards, who was himself a planter and a slave-owner, put it: "In countries where slavery is established, the leading principle on which the government is supported is fear: or a sense of that absolute coercive necessity which, leaving no choice of action, supercedes all questions of right. It is vain to deny that such actually is, and necessarily must be, the case in all countries where slavery is allowed."[48]

The French West Indies, unlike the British islands, had, after 1685, a slave code drawn up by the metropolitan government as the basis of their slave laws.[49] However, the contrast between these groups of islands, with regard to their slave laws, was not as great as that between the Spanish and British islands. The *Siete Partidas* was a code of Spanish laws, containing provisions relating to slaves. The *Partidas* came into existence long before the creation of a West Indian empire. They were not framed to deal with the circumstances of the West Indies, though they were incorporated into the law of the

---

[44] Antigua Act no. 130 (1702).

[45] Reeves, "General View," *loc. cit.*

[46] Barbados Act no. 82 (1688).

[47] 25 Geo. III, c. 23 and 22, in *Laws of Jamaica, op. cit.*, Vol. II.

[48] Bryan Edwards, *History of the British Colonies in the West Indies* (3 vols., London, 1801), Vol. III, p. 36.

[49] See the definitive text of the *Code Noir* of 1685 in L. Peytraud, *L'Esclavage aux Antilles Françaises avant 1789* (Paris, 1897), pp. 158–66.

Spanish colonies there. But the *Code Noir*, though drawn up in France, was never intended to be a code of French laws. Like the laws of the British islands, the *Code Noir* of the French West Indies was made with West Indian conditions firmly in mind, and for the purpose of dealing with problems already posed by the existence and acceptance of slavery in the West Indian colonies. The *Code Noir* bears some resemblance to the *Siete Partidas* because both were influenced, to some extent, by the concepts of Roman and canon law. Nevertheless, it more fundamentally resembles the slave laws of the British West Indies by reason of its intention and function.

The fact that the *Code Noir* was a metropolitan code is, nevertheless, important. Even in the early 1680's, the French monarchical government was less limited than that of England, a difference reflected in the government of the French and English colonies. In the English colonies, the crown's legislative power was incorporated in the structure of a representative legislature, including council and assembly. In the French colonies, the crown retained more autonomous powers of legislation. The laws of the French colonies were made by the royal government in France, by the royal officials in the West Indies, and by the local councils. The *Code Noir* is described as a metropolitan code, because it was made by the exercise of the legislative power of the royal government in France.

However, the *Code*, although made in France, was based upon earlier local laws and was prepared in consultation with the local authorities in the West Indies. Even after promulgation, it was revised to meet strong local criticisms on some points. Long before the *Code Noir* was prepared, local authorities had concerned themselves with the prob-

lems of religious conformity, with the regulation of the status and conduct of slaves, with the necessity for public security, and with the protection to be given to slaves as property and as persons. These were the matters which also occupied the framers of the *Code Noir;* and a few examples will show the similarities between the earlier laws and the later *Code.*

As early as 1638, it was provided that Protestants should not be allowed to own slaves in the islands; and, by later laws, made by representatives of the crown in the West Indies, provisions were added for the punishment of blasphemers, and the regulation of Jews and non-Catholics, and also to encourage the Christianization of slaves.[50] Undoubtedly, the crown may be regarded as having special interests in religious conformity; and it is hardly surprising that the *Code Noir*, which was promulgated in the same year that saw the Revocation of the Edict of Nantes, should have given great prominence and emphasis to the provisions enforcing religious conformity. But the regulations of the crown in this matter already had precedents in the accepted local law, and did not arouse much local opposition. On the one subject—the abolition of Negro markets on Sundays and holidays—where local opinion showed itself immediately hostile to the provisions of the crown for enforcing religious observance, the crown quickly gave way.[51] In the matter of religious conformity, the predilec-

[50] France, Archives Nationales. Colonies F3 247, p. 63 (Martinique), règlement of Sept. 1, 1638; F3 221, pp. 477–80 (Guadeloupe), ordonnance of Sept. 14, 1672. Louis Elie Moreau de St.-Méry, *Loix et constitutions des colonies françaises de l'Amérique sous le vent* (6 vols., Paris, 1784–90), Vol. I, pp. 117–22 (règlement of June 19, 1664).

[51] *Ibid.*, Vol. I, pp. 447–48 (arrêt of Oct. 13, 1686).

tions of the crown enjoyed the general support of a large body of local opinion.

As for regulations concerned more directly with the slaves, a good many may be cited which occur in the earlier laws and recur in some form in the *Code Noir*. They illustrate that, before the *Code Noir* was instituted, the French colonies already possessed a fairly comprehensive series of slave laws, and that the *Code Noir* really may be regarded as an extended codification of these laws.

Some of these laws were made by officials and some by the Council; and perhaps it is significant that the Council appears to have concerned itself mainly with police laws. It is notable, however, that the Council, as a court, heard cases arising from the cruelty of masters to their slaves, and already, before 1685, had made judgments punishing cruelty.[52] The point is probably significant of a contrast in attitudes in the British and French islands arising from a contrast in their political traditions.

In British law, the tendency was to limit the sphere of interference of the crown, and to foster, in particular, a respect for the rights of private property. In France and in its colonies, because the power of the crown was less limited, its sphere of interference, even with private property, was commonly accepted to be much wider. The slave, by being private property, did not cease to be in his person a matter of public concern; and public interference in the management of slaves was more taken for granted at this stage of development in the French West Indies than it was in the British islands at the same time. With the continued growth of slavery in the French West Indies, and with the

related development of a feeling of white solidarity in those colonies, two very important changes of sentiment with regard to slaves made themselves felt. Public concern for their welfare declined rapidly, and public acceptance of interference between the master and his property became less and less certain.

An analysis of the content of the *Code Noir* reveals the same concern for public order which marks the slave laws of the British West Indies. But the *Code Noir* was, nevertheless, based on a wider conception of the slave as a "persona" and on a different conception of the elements of public order. The contents of the code may be placed under a number of heads. Provisions regarding religious conformity are laid down in the earlier clauses; provisions governing the status of slaves and their political control follow. The protection of slaves is then provided for, after which their civil disabilities are carefully listed. These disabilities arose, of course, from the legal view that the slave was property, though as in the British law, he had to be admitted to be a peculiar kind of property. The element of political control over slaves, which was inseparable from their regulation as property, appears clearly in the section of the code which deals with the slave as property, as it does in the slave laws elsewhere. In this section, however, the police regulations are accompanied by protective regulations; and, in fact, these two categories make up a large part of the code. Lastly, there are clauses providing for the manumission of slaves and for the regulation of the status of freedmen. Underlying these provisions is the assumption that all groups in the community are subject to the will and direction of the state.

A short summary of the more important clauses of the code shows this

---

[52] *Ibid.*, Vol. I, p. 203 (arrêt of Oct. 20, 1670). Arch. Nat. Cols. F3 247, pp. 825–26 (Martinique), arrêt of May 10, 1671.

assumption in operation. Under the provisions of the code, Jews were to be expelled from the colonies, and Protestants were subjected to religious and civil disabilities—such as incapacity for legal marriage by their own rites. The object was to secure public conformity of all, and not even the slaves were excluded. They were to be baptized and instructed as Catholics; and their overseers could be of no other religious persuasion. They were to observe Sundays, and the holidays of the church, to be married, and if baptized, buried in holy ground. The concubinage of free men with slaves was penalized, except in those cases where the irregular union was converted into marriage. (Cls. 1–11.) Under this section, conformity to the state religion is the duty enforced on all.

The regulations concerning slavery provided that children should take the status of the mother in all cases. (Cls. 12, 13.) The slave mother being property, the slave child was property. This property was to be kept in a state of subordination by the usual means. Slaves were forbidden to carry arms or other weapons, to assemble together, to engage in certain kinds of trade, to strike the master or mistress or to use violence against free persons. Penalties were provided for those slaves who were guilty of thefts, and for those slaves who were guilty of running away. Finally, it was expressly provided that slaves could be criminally prosecuted, without involving the master if he was not responsible for the crime. (Cls. 15–21, 33–38.) As in the British law, therefore, the slave was subject to coercion; and was treated as being personally responsible to the state before the law.

He was also viewed as, to some extent, a person in a state of dependence. As such, the master who owned him was obliged to give him fixed allowances of food and clothing, to care for old and disabled slaves, to avoid concubinage with his slaves, and to leave them free to observe the rules of the church. His property in the slaves was regarded as conferring on him the right to punish them by whipping, or by putting them in irons. But he was expressly prohibited from torturing or mutilating them; and a master killing a slave was to be prosecuted as a criminal, and penalized "according to the atrocity of the circumstances." The clergy were enjoined not to marry slaves without the master's consent, but also not to constrain slaves to marry if they were unwilling to do so. Under the law, families were not to be broken up when slaves were sold; and those slaves between the ages of 14 and 60 who were employed in sugar—or indigo—works and plantations were attached to the soil and could not be sold except with the estate. Slaves not falling within these categories were, however, regarded as chattels. (Cls. 9–11, 22–25, 27, 42, 43, 47–54.)

As a piece of property, rather than a person, the slave was incapable of legally possessing property or of legally making contracts, and he was, of course, incapable of holding any public office or acting legally as a responsible agent. The code declared that slaves could not legally be parties to a trial, though they themselves were subject to criminal prosecution. Masters received compensation for their loss when criminal slaves were executed. But they were also liable to make good losses caused by their slaves. (Cls. 28, 30–32, 37, 40.)

All these clauses with regard to the protection and disabilities of the slave assumed that the master, in return for public recognition of the dependency of the slave, accepted certain conditions of obligation laid down by the state. His property in the slave was held subject to these obligations, and could be forfeited as a result of failure to observe the limitations on his authority, imposed by the state as a condition of its support. Under the British slave laws, where the disabilities arising from the slave's dependency were the same, the conditions of this dependency, as they affected the master, were less carefully defined. In both British and French slave law, the inferior position of the slave was accepted. But in the British slave law, the state showed far greater unwillingness to interpose in the relations between masters and slaves.

The inferior position of the slave, though it was recognized in the French slave laws, was not directly reflected in the forms of trial provided for slaves under the *Code Noir*. The slave was to be tried before the ordinary judges, and he had the right of appealing his case to the Council—"the process to be carried on with the same formalities as in the case of free persons." (Cl. 32.) In 1711, however, the slave's right of appealing against his sentence was restricted to capital cases and sentences of hamstringing.[53] This was one of the symptoms of the change which gradually transformed the French West Indian slave code. But, at the time of the promulgation of the *Code Noir*, concern for the protection of the slave in law was still strong. Clause 30 of that code, which provided that slave evidence was inadmissible except against slaves, was immediately protested by the Martinique Council, on the grounds that this would result in an impunity for many crimes committed against slaves. As a result of this protest, the crown, in 1686, amended the code so as to allow the admission of evidence by slaves, in

the absence of evidence by whites, in all cases except against their own masters.[54]

Even here, at one of the most touchy points in the whole slave system, the *Code Noir* provided for the protection of the slave in law, by enabling him, under clause 26, to make complaints to the crown's *procureur-général* against his master in cases where the master failed to give him subsistence, or treated him cruelly. The attorney-general was thus given a status as protector of slaves which compensated, to some extent, for the unwillingness to admit slave evidence against masters. In keeping with this relative liberality, manumissions were made easy for all masters who had attained their legal majority; and, once freed, the former slave was to be treated as a freeborn subject of the king, entitled to the same rights as other subjects, so long as he lived in obedience to the law and performed the duties of the subject—with this difference only that he was expected to give due respect to his former master, the source of his freedom. (Cls. 26, 55–59.)

In one respect, the provisions of the *Code Noir* regarding manumissions were restrictive. Until the promulgation of the code, it was customary for children of mixed blood to be freed during their teens.[55] But the crown, in its desire to secure religious conformity, was most anxious to discourage concubinage; and therefore, it provided that the illegitimate offspring and their mothers could never be free, except by the marriage of the parents. (Cl. 9.) But in this matter, the will of the crown was at variance

[53] Moreau de St.-Méry, *op. cit.*, Vol. II, pp. 241, 242–43 (letter and ordonnance of April 20, 1711).

[54] *Ibid.*, Vol. I, pp. 447–48 (arrêt of Oct. 13, 1686).

[55] See R. P. DuTertre, *Histoire générale des Antilles habitées par les françois* (3 vols., Paris, 1667–71), Vol. II, pp. 511–13; H. A. Wyndham, *The Atlantic and Slavery* (Oxford, 1935), pp. 256–57.

with the will of the local society, and was defeated. Masters continued to engage in irregular sexual unions with their slaves and continued to free their offspring. In the end, the crown itself expressly withdrew from its former position, in the belief that the mulattoes, being sworn enemies of the Negroes, might safely be freed.[56]

While the special provisions against manumission of mulattoes fell into disuse, the general provisions for manumission became more difficult. Early in the eighteenth century, the royal representatives in the colonies made it a rule that their written permission was necessary to validate all manumissions of slaves.[57] In 1713, this rule was confirmed by the crown, and it continued to be enforced during the century.[58] Instead of encouraging manumissions, the crown and its officers in the colonies showed a constant determination to control the accession of slaves to freedom. Even in France, where it was an accepted axiom of law that slaves became free on entering the realm, the crown proved willing to protect West Indian property by altering the law so as to nullify this usage.[59] The crown and its officers also allowed the wide privileges, originally granted to freedmen under the Code Noir, to be gradually contracted, and joined with the councils in multiplying laws against them and

in subjecting them to increasing disabilities.[60]

This series of changes in the laws reflects the process by which the law was adapted to fit in with the development of society in the French colonies. In framing the Code Noir, the metropolitan government had shown itself generally disposed to follow local practice and to respect local opinion, even though, as in the case of the mulattoes, it occasionally rejected local customs. Unlike the Spanish government which, for long, showed a tendency to limit the increase of slaves in its colonies, the government in France was early committed to a policy of increasing slave numbers and even, though somewhat more reluctantly, to encouraging the growth of large plantations. In line with mercantile thought, it regarded these as the means of acquiring wealth and power from its West India possessions. Slavery must be maintained if these benefits were to be secured and enjoyed.

In his monumental study of French West Indian slavery, Peytraud supports the view that Colbert, who was largely responsible for preparing the Code Noir, was moved to protect the slaves by commercial, rather than humane, considerations.[61] Material considerations, a concern for public security, and a strengthening of race prejudice later produced a much greater hardening in the attitude of the crown and its officials towards the Negroes. The crown's desire for order, which had led to the regulation of masters as well as of slaves under the Code Noir, led on to a certain tolerance of the abuses committed by masters against their slaves.

In 1713, the crown expressed great indignation on learning that masters

---

[56] Moreau de St.-Méry, op. cit., Vol. III, pp. 453–54 (letter of March 29, 1735).

[57] Ibid., Vol. II, pp. 272–73 (ordonnance of Aug. 15, 1711). Arch. Nat. Cols. F³ 222, pp. 189–90.

[58] Moreau de St.-Méry, op cit., Vol. II, pp. 398–99 (ordonnance of Oct. 24, 1713). Wyndham, op. cit., pp. 256–57. An instance of a later law regulating manumissions is found in Arch. Nat. Cols. F³ 233 (Guadeloupe), ordonnance of March 3, 1789.

[59] Arch. Nat. Cols. F³ 249, p. 818 (Martinique). Moreau de St.-Méry, op. cit., Vol. II, pp. 525–28.

[60] Wyndham, op. cit., pp. 256ff.

[61] Peytraud, op. cit., pp. 150–57.

were torturing their slaves barbarously.[62] In 1742, disapproval was also expressed, this time concerning a case in which a slave had been killed.[63] But the crown was now rather more concerned with the need for maintaining subordination among the Negroes. In the following year, the crown declared that "while the Slaves should be maintained and favorably treated by their Masters, the necessary precautions should also be taken to contain them within the bounds of their duty, and to prevent all that might be feared from them."[64]

The humaneness of the *Code Noir* itself can be overstated. The allowances of food and clothing fixed in the code were small. In the matter of punishments, the code prohibited the private infliction of torture and mutilation, but did not prevent their use by judicial authorities. Slaves could still be tortured in official investigations, and judges were left free to sentence slaves to be burnt alive, to be broken on the wheel (a favorite punishment), to be dismembered, to be branded, or to be crippled by hamstringing—a penalty expressly provided for runaways under the code.[65] Masters maltreating or killing slaves were liable to prosecution, and there are records of cases having been brought against them, although no master appears to have suffered the death penalty for killing a slave. By contrast, atrocious sentences were usually passed on slaves guilty of killing whites; and even for the crime

of raising a hand against one of the children of his mistress, a slave was sentenced to have his hand cut off and to be hanged.[66] The attorney general, who was appointed as guardian of slaves under the *Code Noir*, was far oftener engaged in prosecuting slaves, or in complaining of abuses by them, than in presenting the abuses committed against them. Like his employer, the crown, he was preoccupied with the task of securing public order.

A glance through the very numerous police regulations, passed with the object of enforcing or of supplementing the police clauses in the *Code Noir*, shows that many of these were initiated by a complaint on the part of the *procureur-général*, citing incipient or actual disorders. Thus, at the beginning of the eighteenth century, the Council of Léogane passed laws forbidding slaves to carry arms, or to assemble together, and providing for a hunt of runaways. At Le Cap, a pass-system was enforced; and the attention of masters was again called to the prohibitions against slaves carrying arms. Later, the council at Port-au-Prince penalized those selling arms and ammunition to slaves without the master's written authority.[67]

The attorney-general also occupied himself with the suppression of thefts by slaves and with the restrictions on their trading. In 1710, complaint was made that the clauses of the *Code Noir* regulating trade by slaves were not being properly enforced. In the same year, the council at Petit-Goâve, on advice from

---

[62] *Ibid.*, p. 326.

[63] Arch. Nat. Cols. F³ 225, p. 777 (Guadeloupe), letter of May 17, 1742.

[64] Moreau de St.-Méry, *op. cit.*, Vol. III, pp. 727–29 (déclaration of Feb. 1, 1743); pp. 500–502, (jugement of Nov. 11, 1691); Vol. II, p. 103 (arrêt of Aug. 1, 1707).

[65] For examples see *ibid.*, Vol. V., p. 805 (arrêt of Dec. 11, 1777); Vol. I, Arch. Nat. Cols. F³ 221, pp. 925–28 (Guadeloupe), arrêt of March 4, 1698. Also, *Code Noir*, Cl. 38

[66] Moreau de St. Méry, *op. cit.*, Vol. V, p. 744 (arrêt of Nov. 20, 1776); Vol. IV, p. 136 (arrêt of Nov. 5, 1753).

[67] *Ibid.*, Vol. II, pp. 25–27 (arrêt of March 16, 1705), p. 117 (arrêt of May 9, 1708), pp. 568–69 (ordonnance of July 1, 1717); Vol. III, pp. 177–78 (arrêts of July 2 and 8, 1726); Vol. V, pp. 97–98 (arrêt of March 9, 1767).

the crown attorney, forbade gold-and silver-smiths to buy anything from slaves without express permission. Neglect of the rules against trading with slaves in the staple crops at Guadeloupe was similarly brought to the attention of the council there during the eighteenth century.[68]

Even in performing those duties which might be regarded as protective, the *procureur-général* showed a tendency to consider the public interest rather than the slave. Thus, one source of unfailing annoyance was the practice adopted by masters in giving their slaves Saturday or some other day of the week to work for themselves, instead of giving an allowance. This was presented as an abuse, not only because it might lead to thefts of provisions by slaves, or to want among those who paid no attention to their cultivations, but also because the gain made by industrious slaves as a result of this practice "has made them so proud that they can scarcely be recognized for what they are."[69] The laws for the planting of provisions by estates, constantly reiterated and constantly neglected, were not motivated only by the desire to protect the slaves.[70] Similarly, though the attorney-general complained when colonists had their slaves beaten in the streets, the disorder caused in the towns by this practice was obviously important in calling forth an objection to it.[7.1]

The crown, the royal officials, and the councils did not need much urging to concern themselves with police regulations in any case. These made up the large majority of the laws passed after the *Code Noir* was instituted. The subjects of these laws are, generally speaking, those to which attention has already been drawn in discussing the complaints made by the crown's attorney—the control of runaways, the general subordination of slaves and the need to prevent them from concerting risings, the prevention and detection of thefts, and the limiting of their economic opportunities, as well as of their physical mobility. The laws emphasized their dependence, because it was an element of social stability, directly related to their subordination. The regulations occasionally made, enforcing the allowances fixed under the *Code Noir*, have to be seen in this context.

In 1712, the crown returned to its insistence that slaves should not be privately tortured, and the cases brought against masters from time to time for cruelty to slaves were a reminder that the principle of governmental supervision was not forgotten.[72] But the crown would have needed to maintain a much closer watch than it did, if it had meant to enforce those protective clauses which were included in the *Code Noir*. Religious instruction, at first so much insisted on, was neglected or prevented by the colonists, and their attitudes were in turn defeated by government officials like Fénelon, who had come to believe that: "The safety of the Whites, less numerous than the slaves, surrounded by them on their estates, and almost completely at their mercy, demands that the slaves be kept in the most profound ignorance."[73]

---

[68] *Ibid.*, Vol. II, pp. 208, 213 (arrêts of Sept. 1 and Oct. 6, 1710). Arch. Nat. Cols. F³ 223, pp. 717–23 (Guadeloupe), arrêt of Sept. 6, 1725; F³ 225, pp. 139–45, arrêt of Nov. 8, 1735.

[69] Arch. Nat. Cols. F³ 226, pp. 269–82 (Guadeloupe), arrêt of July 9, 1746.

[70] Moreau de St.-Méry, *op. cit.*, Vol. IV, pp. 401–3 (ordonnance of Aug. 19, 1761).

[71] *Ibid.*, Vol. IV, p. 566 (ordonnance of March 24, 1763).

[72] Arch. Nat. Cols. B. 34, ordonnance of Dec. 30, 1712.

[73] Peytraud, *op. cit.*, pp. 193–94.

Pierre Regis Desalles, himself a colonist, writing in the second half of the eighteenth century, admitted that regulations favoring the marriage of slaves, and providing fixed allowances of food and clothing for them, were generally neglected. The laws against concubinage were notoriously ineffective. Abuse against slaves went undetected because "No one cares to inform on his neighbor; and it is so dangerous to let Negroes make complaints against their masters."[74]

All evidence points to one conclusion. As they were actually administered during the eighteenth century, the French slave laws differed far less from their English counterparts than might be imagined. The enforcement of the *Code Noir* during this period, in fact, shows a well-defined emphasis markedly similar to that already noticed in the British slave laws before the period of amelioration. Thus the provisions safeguarding the slave as "persona" were either laxly enforced or neglected. His religious instruction, his protection against ill-treatment, his right to food, clothing, and care, provided for in the law, depended in practice far more on the will of the master than on enacted regulations. The law tended to become more and more a dead letter in these matters. Changes in the law made his manumission less easy, and deprived him, when free, of equality with other free men. Thus, the benefits which the law had originally conferred upon the slave and the freedman were either lost or reduced in their value by practice or by legislative change. Meanwhile, the part of the law which was provided for his control and submission continued in vigor—as the activities of the crown's attorney serve to make abundantly

clear. As in the British islands, so in practice in the French, police laws were the heart of the slave code. They were not neglected because the continuance of slavery depended upon them, and was understood to depend upon them. The law actually and continuously enforced was here, as in the Spanish colonies, different from the law as enacted. As Peytraud says: "Reality is sometimes far from corresponding to legal prescriptions."[75]

The will to bring about a correspondence was also much weaker than it had been. In 1771, the crown issued official instructions which show this change at work:

It is only by leaving to the masters a power that is nearly absolute, that it will be possible to keep so large a number of men in that state of submission which is made necessary to their numerical superiority over the whites. If some masters abuse their power, they must be reproved in secret, so that the slaves may always be kept in the belief that the master can do no wrong in his dealing with them.[76]

That the feeling of white solidarity had grown even stronger in the colonies is indicated by the well-known case involving the coffee-planter, Le Jeune, who was alleged to have killed four slaves and to have severely burnt two others, in the course of torturing them. Heavy pressure was brought to bear upon the governor; and the judges, afraid to go against local opinion, dismissed the case. The Council also refused to see Le Jeune punished, and he suffered no legal penalty whatever for his crimes.[77]

The Le Jeune case occurred in 1788, about four years after the crown had made several new provisions for the

---

[74] Adrien Desalles, *Histoire générale des Antilles* (Paris, 1847), III, pp. 291ff.

[75] Peytraud, *op. cit.*, p. 150.
[76] Pierre de Vaissière, *St. Domingue (1629–1789)* (Paris, 1909), p. 181.
[77] *Ibid.*, pp. 186–89.

protection of slaves in its act "concerning Attorneys and Managers of Estates situated in the Leeward Islands." This order which was intended to correct abuses at St. Domingue, where the Le Jeune case occurred, contained clauses limiting the working hours of slaves and fixing their holidays, and also allowing them to cultivate small plots of land for their own profit, besides compelling proprietors to plant provisions and to make allowances of food and clothing to their slaves. Provision was also made for the care of pregnant women and the sick, and for encouraging child-bearing. The protection against physical maltreatment given the slaves under the *Code Noir* was renewed, and a limitation was placed on the number of lashes which a master might give his slave.[78] These last clauses did not prevent Le Jeune's escape, and it is difficult to believe that the rest of the code can have been much more effective. Peytraud appears to be justified in his conclusion that "the material condition of the Negroes did not cease to be miserable. As for their legal condition, so for their moral education, the advances achieved were very small. The facts cry aloud the condemnation of slavery, which reduced so many human beings to being scarcely more than beasts of burden."[79]

The rule of force inherent in slavery produced comparable results in the Spanish, British, and French colonies in the West Indies, though variations were introduced by the degree of their dependence on slavery and by differences in their political traditions. The experience of the Dutch and Danish colonies supports this conclusion. Westergaard, in his study of the Danish

islands, has said that the slave laws, which were made by the local government, "became more severe as the ratio of negro to white population increased." He cites repressive measures against runaways, who were specially aided by the nearness of the islands to Puerto Rico, and against thefts and the trading carried on by slaves without the permission of their owners.[80] In particular, he refers to the very severe ordinance of 1733, which, in his opinion, precipitated the serious slave rebellion of that year at St. John's. This ordinance provided such punishments for the crimes of slaves as pinching and branding with hot irons, dismemberment, hanging, and flogging. It was a police law, entirely concerned with the prevention of revolts and conspiracies, the control of runaways, thefts, and slave assemblies. It forbade the carrying of weapons by slaves, and punished severely any Negro found guilty of raising his hand against a white. These were the elements which attracted most attention in the government of slaves. Other laws protected the master's property in the slave, and masters were indemnified for their losses when their slaves were judicially punished.[81] There was also supposed to be official supervision of the punishment of slaves, but, generally speaking, their protection was left to custom rather than law. The Company, which governed the islands, was more interested in the slaves as objects of trade and sources of manual labor for the production of wealth, than as persons. Here as elsewhere, they were subject to public repression and private tyranny.

The Danish West Indies under Company rule were at once entrepôts and

---

[78] Arch. Nat. Cols. F³ 233, pp. 231–35 (Guadeloupe), ordonnance of Dec. 17, 1784.

[79] Peytraud, *op. cit.*, p. 241.

[80] W. Westergaard, *The Danish West Indies under Company Rule (1671–1754)* (New York, 1917), pp. 158ff.

[81] *Ibid.*, pp. 162ff.

plantation colonies. The Dutch also held both plantation colonies and trading colonies in the region; but these were geographically separate. In the main trading centers, Curaçao and St. Eustatius, and in the other small islands held by the Dutch, planting was of almost negligible importance. They lived by trade. The Guiana colonies, by contrast, developed a planting economy.

Throughout these Dutch colonies, the slaves were considered in law as things rather than as persons.[82] But the difference in the economic functions of the two types of colonies was reflected in a difference of slave conditions within them, despite their common basic law. The slaves in the Guiana colonies were subject to very harsh conditions of enslavement. The resident slave populations of the trading colonies—as distinct from the slave cargoes merely brought to be sold through these ports—generally enjoyed more humane treatment. In the Guianas, also, the slave laws, especially those for the control of runaways, were extremely severe in comparison with the laws of the islands. The influence of the plantation economy on slavery is thus again demonstrated.

In many of its aspects, the Dutch slave law resembled the slave law of the French West Indies—a resemblance due no doubt to their common origins in Roman law. Under the Dutch law, slaves could be bought and sold as chattels, and slave status was transmitted by birth through the mother. Plantation slaves were attached to the soil, and could only be sold with the estate. The dependency of the slave on his

master was held to imply an obligation on the master to feed, clothe, and otherwise care for his slave; and a degree of protection was, in principle, made available to the slave through the fiscal of each colony. For a time, also, the Dutch West India Company showed some interest in the religious instruction of slaves, and made provisions to prevent their masters from forcing them to work on Sundays.

But the divorce of law and practice was as characteristic of the Dutch as of the other colonies in the West Indies. In general, the Dutch Company, like the Danish, regarded the slaves primarily as objects of profit; and the settlers in the Dutch colonies took a similar view. The police regulations, which were numerous and often severe, were constantly invoked. Extralegal and illegal punishments were privately inflicted on slaves, especially in the Guiana colonies, where the existence of bands of runaway slaves in the hinterland encouraged a brutal stringency in estate discipline. Fear of the Bush Negro threat increased also the repressive tendencies of public policy. Inhuman punishments were inflicted on slaves, not merely by masters privately and illegally, but also by the judicial authorities acting under the law.

As in the French colonies, a conflict arose between the principle of repression and that of protection; and, on the whole, it was repression that triumphed.

Scandalous mistreatment of slaves by plantation-managers and others, acting on their own authority, was more than once punished by banishment or otherwise; but the persons responsible for the punishment were themselves slave-holders and this was reflected in the kind of punishment inflicted. The slave laws, which were revised from time to time, also failed to achieve the end in view. Those who administered them were all slave-holders. At the beginning of the nineteenth

---

[82] The discussion of the Dutch West Indian slave law is based upon the article "Slavernij" in *Encyclopaedie van Nederlandsch West Indie* (Hague, 1914–17), pp. 637ff.

century, there was humane treatment of the slaves because of the abolition of the slave trade, but long after that time very crude punishments were apparently still in existence and the slaves were looked upon as a sort of cattle.[83]

---

[83] *Ibid.*, p. 640.

Both in their content and in their enforcement, the West India slave laws follow a remarkably consistent pattern, imposed by the function of the law in maintaining the stability of those forms of social organization on which rested the whole life of the West India colonies during the eighteenth century.

HERBERT S. KLEIN

Anglicanism, Catholicism,
and the Negro Slave*

Herbert S. Klein is Assistant Professor of Latin American History at the University of Chicago. He is the author of Slavery in the Americas: A Comparative Study of Cuba and Virginia *(1967) and is presently working on a study of Brazilian slave society.*

I

In recent years, American scholars have begun to search for the uniqueness of the American institution of Negro slavery, by contrasting it with the experience of the other colonizing nations of Europe in the New World. Even as far back as the seventeenth century, a sharp difference in slave institutions was noted between English, French, and Spanish possessions, yet few historians until recently have attempted to analyze the causes and consequences of these distinctions.

Beginning with the work by Frank Tannenbaum,[1] which was expanded by Stanley Elkins,[2] such a preliminary comparative study has been undertaken. Concentrating on the vast structure of the law, these two scholars have relied essentially on a comparative legal analysis. Critics have challenged their generalizations on the grounds that there exists a great distinction between the model of the law and the reality of practice, while recently the very distinctness of the legal structure has been questioned.[3]

Reprinted, by permission of the Editors, from *Comparative Studies in Society and History*, vol. VIII, no. 3 (April 1966), pp. 295–327.

* Research for this article was made possible by a grant from the Social Science Research Council.

[1] Frank Tannenbaum, *Slave and Citizen, the Negro in the Americas* (New York: Knopf, 1947).
[2] Stanley M. Elkins, *Slavery, A Problem in American Institutional and Intellectual Life* (Chicago: University of Chicago Press, 1959).
[3] Arnold A. Sio, "Interpretations of Slavery: The Slave Status in the Americas," *CSSH*, VII, No. 3 (April, 1965), 289–308.

But while subjecting these pioneer attempts to internal textual criticism, few have attempted to challenge their conclusions and generalizations by empirical investigation. The aim of this paper is to take such an approach, by subjecting to detailed analysis the slave systems of two colonial powers in the New World. It studies the operation of one crucial aspect of the slave system, the relationship between infidel Negro and Christian Church, in two highly representative colonies, those of Cuba and Virginia.

The problem of dealing with non-Christian African Negro slaves was one of the most difficult tasks faced by the churches of the New World in the colonial period. Whether of the Roman Catholic or Protestant denomination, each metropolitan church suddenly found its colonial parishes flooded with human beings held in bondage and ignorant of the doctrines of Christianity. For each church the question of the validity of that bondage had to be dealt with, and for each the human and Christian nature of the African Negro had to be determined. While the problem might be ignored in the first hours of establishing a functioning church among the white colonists, and dealing with the problem of the evangelization of the American Indians, these questions had to be eventually resolved before a Christian kingdom could be established on the shores of the New World.

How the two metropolitan churches dealt with the African Negro slaves would be determined by a host of considerations, from the question of organizational differences, to the problem of religious climate. Whatever the cause, however, the patterns of dealing with these slaves, which they both evolved, would have a profound impact on the life of the bondsmen. For especially in the Pre-Enlightenment world, when religious thought and action completely pervaded the life of Colonial America, the attitudes and actions of the church did much to create and define the moral, legal, social, and even economic position of the Negro, slave and free, within colonial society.

II

Within colonial Latin American society the Spanish Catholic Church was the prime arbiter in the social and to a considerable extent in the intellectual life of all men. Not only did it define the moral basis of society and determine the limits of its intellectual world view, but it also sanctified and legalized the most basic human relationships. While this was the traditional role of the Church in Catholic Europe, and especially within Spain, the Church in the New World also faced the unique task of dealing with non-European peoples and defining their place within traditional social patterns.

Acutely aware of this problem from the first days of the conquest, the Church conceived of its primary function in the New World as an evangelical one. Putting aside its harsh and negative role as defender of the faith, which dominated its European attitudes against the other "peoples of the book," it adopted a positive role of sympathetic conversion of virgin peoples to the true faith.[4]

---

[4] The evangelizing mission of the Catholic Church in the New World was in fact a truly novel and powerful departure from previous experience. While the wars of *reconquista* against the Moors had brought the expansion of the faith, this had been through means of the fire and sword. Only in rare instances were attempts made to convert Mohammedans and Jews to Christianity peacefully, and thus despite the

While the thrust of this missionary activity was directed toward the American Indians,[5] the evangelical Catholic Church of the New World also intimately concerned itself with the other great religiously primitive peoples, the African Negro slaves. From the beginning of slave importation, in fact, the Church took up the position that the African Negroes were to be considered part of the New World Church, on much the same level as the untutored Amerindians. And while the Church was often forced to concede colonists prior claims for the labor of these black and brown races, it never relinquished its position as the guardian of the moral, religious, and even social life of the untutored Indian and Negro races within its New World domain.

This dominant role of the Church in the life of the Negro slaves is well illustrated in the history of the Cuban Church. Because of the virtual extinction of the precontact Indians on the island and the subsequent dominance of the slave population, the Cuban Church was forced to give its undivided attention to its Negro communicants, almost from the first years of colonization. Eventually becoming the most heavily populated Negro colony in Spanish America, Cuba, more than any other area, tended to set the pattern of Church-slave relations.

In defining its attitude toward the African slave, the Cuban clergy was of course governed by the ideas which had evolved on the institution of slavery and on African Negroes both in the contemporary mores of Iberians and in the decrees of the Metropolitan Church. In both sets of standards there had been built up in the Iberian peninsula an historic pattern which preceded the creation of the modern Spanish state. The sub-Saharan Negro as well as the North African peoples had had intimate contact with the population of Spain from recorded times to the sixteenth century. Especially important in the armies and slave populations of the Spanish Moslem states, the Iberian peoples had long accepted the individuality, personality, and coequality of the Negro. In fact, large numbers of Negroes mixed freely in slavery under the Moslem and Christian states, with Iberian Christians, Eastern European Slavs, and other Mediterranean peoples.[6]

religious overtones of the centuries-long *reconquista*, the whole concept of evangelization was practically nonexistent. Even when the opening up of virgin territories suddenly brought this great movement to life within Spanish Catholic circles, it was an entirely unique phenomenon, with no parallel in Europe. Thus while the New World church was pacifically preaching a gentle Christ to the Indians, the peninsular church during these same three centuries of colonial rule, waged an unrelenting war against Jews, Moors, *mudejares, moriscos, conversos,* judaizers, Lutherans, and Calvinists. Intolerant defender of the faith at home, it proved to be unusually tolerant, patient, and intelligently assimilationist in its encounters with the New World pagans. As one scholar concluded, "Militant Spain guarded its religious purity in the metropolitan territory with the sword, and turned itself into a missionary at the service of the same faith in the New World." Antonio Ybot León, *La iglesia y los eclesiasticos españoles en la empresa de indias,* 2 vols. (Barcelona: Salvat Editores, 1954–1963), I, 347–50.

[5] See, e.g., Robert Ricard, *La "conquête spirituelle" du Mexique* (Paris: Institut d'ethnologie, 1933).

[6] On the role of the African Negro in medieval Spain, see E. Lévi-Provençal, *Histoire de l'espagne musulmane,* 3 vols. (Paris: G.-P. Maisonneuve, 1950–1953), III, 72, 74–75, 177–78, 208ff.; Charles Verlinden, *L'esclavage dans l'europe médiévale, péninsule ibérique—France* (Bruges: "De Tempel," 1955), pp. 225–26, 358–62; José Antonio Saco, *Historia de la esclavitud desde los tiempos mas remotos hasta nuestra dias,* 3 vols. (Barcelona: Jaime Jepus, 1875–77), II, 140–41. African Negro slaves were still a known and recognized element within Iberia's small slave population right up to the opening up of the modern slave trade with West Africa by Portugal in the fifteenth century. *Ibid.,* III, 36; Elizabeth Donnan, *Documents Illustrative of the History of the Slave Trade to America,* 4 vols. (Washington: Carnegie Institution of Washington, 1930–1935), I, 1.

Since North African Berbers blended into mulatto and black sub-Saharan Negroes, there was no reason for the white Iberians to conceive of these Africans as anything but normal human beings. As for their position under the slave systems developed by the Christian kingdoms of the North, they were treated as coequal to all other non-Christian peoples, with the same obligations, duties, and even rights. For those in the Castilian region, this meant that they were under the modified Roman slave laws elaborated in *Las Siete Partidas* of Alfonso X, a thirteenth-century codification of existing Castilian law and custom, which was the fountainhead for the slave code later to be applied to the New World.

The most fundamental aspect of the slave sections of *Las Siete Partidas* was the initial proposition that the institution of slavery was against natural reason.[7] It declared that "slavery is the most evil and the most despicable thing which can be found among men, because man, who is the most noble, and free creature, among all the creatures that God made, is placed in the power of another . . . ."[8] While recognizing it as an institution of long standing and custom which had to be continued, the code considered it a necessary evil rather than a positive good; thus the slave was to be guaranteed every possible right which he held as a member of the human community, with modification of these rights only where absolutely necessary.

From this position, it followed that the basic legal personality of the slave was to be preserved as much as possible. While the slave was forced to relinquish his natural primary right to liberty, he was guaranteed his other rights to personal security and even the right to property. From the point of view of the Church, his secondary or social rights were even more important. Thus the slave was guaranteed the right of full Christian communion, and through the sanctity of the Church, the right to marriage and parenthood.

To guarantee the sanctity of these sacraments, the Catholic Church, according to these thirteenth-century codes, was made responsible for their fulfillment even in the face of opposition from masters. Thus the Church itself had to pay compensation to masters if slaves married outside their own master's household, so that the couples could be united.[9] It also had to guarantee that no families that were legally bound together could be separated, especially through sale overseas.[10] Finally, the Church was used by the state to encourage the process of manumission as much as possible.[11]

With the opening up of the New World to African slavery, the Castilians transferred these historic codes to the overseas "kingdoms" with little change, adding to them only as local conditions warranted. In the first years, this meant dealing with the background of the African immigrants. When raw blacks (*bozales*) were heavily imported directly from Africa after the granting of the *asientos*, it was suddenly discovered that many of these religiously "primitive" peoples were in fact practicing Moslems. Having as its major aim the religious purity of the Indies, especially in regard to its old enemy, the Crown quickly suppressed all such importations, and thenceforth only "primitive" *bozales* were allowed to enter, and they, like the Indians, fell into the same tutorial status as regards the

---

[7] *Las siete partidas del rey Alfonso el sabio, cotejadas con varios codices antiguos, por la Real Academia de Historia*, 3 vols. (Madrid: Imprenta Real, 1807), III, 117, Partida IV, titulo xxi, ley 1.

[8] *Ibid.*, 30, Partida IV, titulo v, introducción.

[9] *Ibid.*, 31–32, Partida IV, titulo v, ley 2.

[10] *Ibid.*, ley 1.

[11] Among the numerous laws on manumission see *ibid.*, 121–22, Partida IV, titulo xxii, ley 1.

Church.[12] While this meant exclusion of Indians and Negroes from the priesthood for this period, it also meant that they were exempt from the jurisdiction of the Inquistion.

Although the majority of the Catholic Church both in Spain and the New World had early and successfully attacked the legality and practice of enslaving the Indians,[13] only a few exceptional clerics contested the right to Negro slavery.[14] For the Negro was not

originally a subject of the Crown of Castile and his enslavement had occurred prior to his entrance into the Spanish realms. This left the clerics no legal grounds and less moral will for denying the practice, since it was initiated, according to the thinking of the day, by the heathens themselves. But while the Church never officially opposed the institution of Negro slavery, it deliberately interfered in the direct relationship between master and slave on the grounds that both were communants in the Church and that nothing must challenge this primary Christian right to salvation and the sacraments.

This responsibility of the Church to care for its Negro communicants, as well as to guarantee that no subject of the Crown was not a practicing Christian, was specifically laid on the New World clergy by the Crown itself. In the very opening book of the *Leyes de Indias*, the famous compilation of colonial legislation, the Crown demanded that the Church take especial care in dealing with Negro slaves. It stated that:

We order and command to all those persons who have Slaves, Negroes, and Mulattoes, that they send them to the Church or Monastery at the hour which the Prelate has designated,[15] and there the Christian Doctrine be taught to them; and the Archbishops and Bishops of our Indies have very particular care for their conversion and endoctrination, in order that they live Christianly, and they give to it the same order and care that is prepared and entrusted by the laws of this Book for the

---

[12] Fernando Ortiz, *Hampa afro-cubana: los negros esclavos, estudio sociologico y de derecho público* (La Habana: Revista Bimestre Cubana, 1916), p. 343 n; also José Antonio Saco, *Historia de la esclavitud de la raza africana en el nuevo mundo y en especial en los paises americo-hispanos*, 2 vols. (Barcelona: Jaime Jepus, 1879), I, 69.

[13] Silvio Zavala, *La filosofía política en la conquista de América* (Mexico: Fondo de Cultura Economica, 1947), chap. iv. For the ending of Indian slavery in Cuba, see Irene Aloha Wright, *The Early History of Cuba, 1492–1586* (New York: Macmillan, 1916), pp. 229, 232.

[14] Las Casas, who had stood at first for the introduction of Negro slaves, later held that the Negroes were unjustly enslaved, "for the same reasoning," he claimed, "applies to them as to the Indians." Alonso de Montufar, archbishop of Mexico, in 1560 questioned the enslavement of the Negroes, while Fray Tomas de Mercado in his work *Tratos y contractos de mercaderes* (1569) attacked the right of procuring and enslaving Negroes in Africa itself. Bartolome de Albornoz in his *Arte de contratos* (1573) approved of the slave trade in Moors from Berber, Tripoli, and Cyrenaica, but rejected entirely the trade in Negroes from Ethiopia and the Portuguese traffic in it. Perhaps the most outstanding figures in the evangelical mission to the African Negro slave in the New World were two seventeenth-century friars: Pedro Claver, who worked among the Negro slaves arriving at Cartagena, for which he was later canonized, and the American Jesuit, Alonso de Sandoval who wrote the famous evangelical tract, *De instaurada aethiopum salute* (1627). Silvio Zavala, *New Viewpoints on the Spanish Colonization of America* (Philadelphia: University of Pennsylvania Press, 1943), p. 65; Zavala, "Relaciones historicas entre indios y negros en Iberoamerica," *Revista de las Indias*, XXVIII, No. 88 (1946), 55–65; Saco, *Historia de la esclavitud de la raza africana*, I, 252–55; Rafael Altamira, *Historia de España y de la civilización española*, 5 vols. (Barcelona: Juan Gili, 1900–1930), III, 242.

[15] "We order that in each one of the towns of Christians a determined hour each day, be designated by the prelate in which all the Indians, Negroes, and Mulattoes, free as well as slave, that there are within the towns, are brought together to hear the Christian Doctrine." This same law also provided a similar arrangement for those who worked and lived in the countryside. *Recopilación de leyes de los reynos de las Indias*, 3 vols. (Madrid: D. Joaquin Ibara, 1791), I, 4–5, Libro I, titulo i, ley 12.

Conversion and Endoctrination of the Indians; so that they be instructed in our Holy Roman Catholic Faith, living in the service of God our Master.[16]

Nor was the Church itself slow in meeting these demands, and in its earliest colonial synods it dealt long and extensively with the problems of its Negro members. Given the close tie which existed between civil and canonical law, the legislation issuing from these synods became an essential part of the Cuban slave legislation.[17]

The first of these colonial Church synods to meet in the Caribbean was the Dominican provincial synod which met early in the seventeenth century on the island of Española. Held under the auspices of the Archbishopric of Española, which included all of the West Indies, Cuba, Florida, and Venezuela,[18] this first Caribbean Church synod spent a good part of its time considering the problem of its Negro communicants. With strong royal representation, in the person of the Governor and President of the Audiencia of Santo Domingo,[19] the leading bishops and clerics prepared, after much discussion, a series of laws and ordinances known as *sanctiones*.[20] Because of royal representation and support, these Latin codes were later translated into Spanish and became the official civil code within the *audiencia*, as well as being canonical law for the ecclesiastical province.[21]

One of the very earliest of these *sanctiones* of the Provincial Dominican Council and the first dealing with the Negro concerned the very basic task of determining if the Negro had been properly admitted into the church:

Since we learn from a certain experienced leader that Negroes have been transported from Africa and brought from other parts to these Indies without benefit of baptism, so if at some time it is claimed that these were besprinkled with holy water by traders when they are put ashore by us it is recommended that they be questioned concerning their baptism: that is, if they have received the water of baptism before they left from Africa, or on the sea, or in any other place or whether they did not receive it at all? ... Also one may question them whether at the time they received the baptism they had obtained any knowledge, however imperfect, concerning the performance of this sacrament which was conferred upon them, ... and also whether they willingly received this holy water at the time it was offered to them. If however, any of these conditions are found to be lacking in their baptism, they must be baptized anew.[22]

In the next section it was stated that redoing the baptism was essential if there were any doubts, because to the Negro "it is thus shown that the privilege of the sacrament is given to them, and the Negroes know themselves to be baptized equal to the others."[23] It followed that no cleric of the province could "confer baptism upon Negro adults unless they have been imbued first with the Christian doctrine,"[24] which education was to be undertaken as soon as they entered the province, by a priest specifically designated for this task.[25] If Negroes refused to be baptized, they were given two to three months "during which the fear of the doctrine must be found." At the end of this time the cleric "may administer baptism to them, provided they are, one and all, sorry for their transgressions, they display the sign of this sorrow, and

---

[16] *Ibid.*, 5, Libro I, titulo i, ley 13.

[17] Ortiz, *op. cit.*, p. 348.

[18] Ybot León, *op. cit.*, II, 55.

[19] Fr. Cipriano de Utrera, "El Concilio Dominicano de 1622, con una introdución historica," *Boletín eclesiastico de la arquidiócesis de Santo Domingo* (1938–1939), pp. 8–9.

[20] The original Latin ordinances, or *Sanctiones Concilii Dominicani*, are reprinted in *ibid.*, pp. 23–81.

[21] *Ibid.*, pp. 10–11.

[22] *Sanctiones Concilii Dominicani*, Sessio Secunda, Caput I, Sectio vii.

[23] Sessio Secunda, Caput I, Sectio vii.

[24] Sessio Secunda, Caput I, Sectio ix.

[25] Sessio Secunda, Caput I, Sectio x.

they realize the power of the sacrament of baptism."[26]

As for the sacrament of confirmation, it was demanded that the "priest even warns the master of Negroes to place before these same ones the means and the place to receive this divine sacrament, but if they do otherwise they may be punished with a judgment."[27] In the sacrament of marriage, it was required that at Negro weddings (as in the case of Indian ones) two special benedictions be given instead of the usual one, to impress them with the importance of this sacrament.[28] In the case of an unbaptized Negro contracting marriage with someone already baptized, it was required that a new agreement be made and the marriage ceremony be repeated. And this was to be done as soon as possible, "so that the benefits of marriage may be rightfully enjoyed."[29]

Negroes were not to be granted absolution until they had overcome their ignorance and inexperience and had finally accepted the faith.[30] It was also provided that every qualified confessor could hear the confessions of Negroes.[31] Again, with the administration of extreme unction as with all other sacraments, it was demanded that the Negro be taught its meaning and accept its significance before it could be administered to him.[32]

It was required by these *sanctiones* that Negroes who lived at great distances from the churches and worked in the country should hear mass at least at six festive holy days per year. If the master was not willing to allow his slaves to hear mass at least these six times, then the prelate was to see to his legal chastisement.[33] The Church council also demanded that "no master of Negroes may put slaves to any servile work on the festive days, nor may he hire others; under the penalty of ten silver pounds for the first transgression, for the second he will truly be implicated with excommunication."[34] For the Negroes on these days were to be taught by the priest "so that they may learn the articles of faith and reap the harvest of sacraments."[35]

Largely supporting the declarations and ordinances of the Dominican Provincial Synod of 1622, and also providing further clarifications of the rights of Christian Negroes, were the *Constituciones* published by the Church synod which met for the Cuban diocese in June of 1680. Constitución IV repeated a proviso that had become an essential part of the imperial slave code, that is, that all slaves be instructed in the Roman Catholic faith and be baptized within a year of their admittance into the Indies.[36]

It also provided that *bozales* could not be married by a priest until both parties were baptized.[37] In attempting to deal with this problem, the Diocesan Synod was forced to take into account the African background of the slave and to adjust the Catholic atmosphere

---

[26] Sessio Secunda, Caput I, Sectio ix.
[27] Sessio Secunda, Caput II, Sectio iii.
[28] Sessio Secunda, Caput IV, Sectio iii.
[29] Sessio Secunda, Caput IV, Sectio vii.
[30] Sessio Secunda, Caput V, Sectio i.
[31] Sessio Secunda, Caput V, Sectio vi.
[32] Sessio Secunda, Caput VII, Sectio iv.

[33] Sessio Tertia, Caput I, Sectio iv.
[34] Sessio Tertia, Caput I, Sectio v.
[35] Sessio Quarta, Caput VII, Sectio ii.
[36] Fernando Ortiz, *Hampa afro-cubana: los negros brujos* (Madrid: Librería de Fernando Fe, 1906), p. 304. This same command was also contained in the very first chapter of the 1789 Slave Code, see "Real Cédula de Su Magestad sobre la educación, trato y ocupaciones de los esclavos en todos sus dominios de Indias...," reprinted in *Revista de Historia de America*, No. 3 (September, 1938), pp. 50–51.
[37] Constitución III, quoted in F. Ortiz, *Los Negros Esclavos...*, p. 348.

to the matrimonial situation brought by the slave from his native land. "Because there come many Indians . . . and Negro *bozales*, married in their infidelity: we order that wanting to live together in this bishopric, after being baptized, their marriage be ratified *in facie ecclesiae* [in the sight of the Church]." If either partner refused the faith, he or she was given up to seven months and six warnings to be baptized. If after this time elapsed they still refused baptism they could not continue their marital relations. And "if any of the said infidels come married with many wives" he was required to be baptized and married to the first one with whom "according to their custom and rites" he had contracted marriage. If the first one could not be so ascertained, then the male could marry the one he desired. And it was also required that if he was married within the direct parental line (mother, sister, etc.), his marriage was declared invalid and the couple had to separate before baptism was administered.[38]

The Diocesan Synod also attempted to eradicate a continuing problem, that of unscrupulous masters who, for either personal reasons or those of economic expediency, tried to prevent their slaves from marrying or refused to honor these marriages. Thus Constitución V established that "marriage should be free" and ordered that:

no master prohibit his slaves against marriage, nor impede those who cohabit in it, because we have experienced that many masters with little fear of God and with serious damage to their consciences, proscribe that their slaves not marry or impede their cohabitation with their married partners, with feigned pretexts; . . .

In this same law, masters were prohibited from taking their slaves outside

of Havana to sell them unless they took husband and wife together. Constitución VI added that masters could not sell their slaves overseas or in remote parts, in order to impede marital cohabitation. If this was done, then the slaves sold in this manner should be brought back with the master paying the expense.[39]

The local Church did all in its power to carry out the intent of the metropolitan slave codes, and to guarantee to their Negro communicants their full rights. They met in powerful synods to deal with local conditions and the unique backgrounds of their particular colored congregants, and always legislated in favor of the fullest freedom and rights that were permissible. While the upper clergy dealt with these problems in law, the lower clergy, especially at the parish level, effectively carried this law into practice.

This correlation between law and practice is abundantly supported by the local parish statistics available on the administration of the sacraments. What these materials indicate is that the slave and free colored population had the same percentage and absolute figures of baptism as the white population. According to the census of 1827, for example, when whites represented 44% and the slaves 41% of the total population,[40] each group respectively had 12,938 and 12,729 baptisms performed on the island in that year.[41]

Not only were slaves and free colored fully admitted into the Church, but they also heavily participated in all the

---

[38] *Ibid.*, pp. 349–50.

[39] *Ibid.*, p. 349.

[40] Ramón de la Sagra, *Historia economico-política y estadística de la isla de Cuba* (Habana: Imprenta de las viudas de Arazoza y Soler, 1831), pp. 7–8.

[41] *Ibid.*, p. 20. The free colored, who made up 15% of the total population in 1827, had 4,826 baptisms.

sacraments, and most importantly in that of marriage as well. Thus, for example, in the four years from 1752 to 1755, the Rector of the Cathedral Church at Santiago de Cuba reported 55 slave marriages to 75 free white marriages in his parish.[42] At this time the entire urban population of Santiago de Cuba consisted of 6,525 whites, and 5,765 slaves,[43] which means that the slave marriages in that period represented one out of 105 slaves in the city, and the free whites one out of 96.3. In short, despite the sharp differences in education, social status, and wealth, the slave marriage rate was very close to that of the free white rate. This is all the more extraordinary a figure, given the fact that a large portion of the adult population, of all colors and social conditions, lived in free unions because of the high cost of clerical ceremonies.

This same pattern is repeated in the local parish of Santo Tomas, also in the jurisdiction of the Santiago de Cuba Church. In the parish census for 1824 there were listed 794 married whites, 855 free colored married persons, and 855 married slaves. This breaks down into a percentage of 44% for the whites, 42% for the free colored and 29% for the slaves of the adult population, that is, of persons seventeen or older.[44] On the one hand these figures reveal the great extent of illegal unions among adults of all races, but they also seriously underrate the slave marriages. For the general statistics of the entire island consistently reveal that the free colored marriage rate was considerably

below that of the colored slaves.

Thus, in 1827 there were listed a total of 1,868 white marriages, 1,381 slave marriages and only 385 free colored marriages. The ratios in the total population figures for that year come to one marriage performed for 166 white persons, for 207 colored slaves and 236 free mulattoes, the worst being one out of 347 free Negroes.[45] The reason for the high slave marriage rate as contrasted to the free colored population appears to be the fact that the slave population was accountable to a master, and through him to the local church, and was therefore far more under the influence of the local parish priest.

Another remarkable factor is the large number of legal marriages between free and slave persons. Of the 702 colored marriages on record in six selected parishes of Havana between 1825 and 1829, 278 were between slaves, 293 between free persons and 131 involved a slave and a free person.[46]

All of these baptismal and marriage statistics reinforce the fact that civil and canonical law was the very essence of actual practice, and that the Negro slave enjoyed coequal status with his masters before the sacraments of the Church. That the Church was so effective in carrying law into practice and constantly guaranteeing these rights, is also due to the extraordinarily large number of priests on the island. In the census of 1778, exclusive of nuns, there were listed 1,063 practicing clergy in Cuba. This meant that for the island's total population of 179,484, there was one priest for every 168 persons, a figure

---

[42] Archivo General de Indias [hereafter cited as AGI], Sevilla, Audiencia de Santo Domingo, legajo 516, no. 30, June 14, 1758.

[43] Sagra, *op. cit.*, p. 3.

[44] AGI, Santo Domingo, leg. 223, February 15, 1824.

[45] Sagra, *op. cit.*, pp. 20, 24. In France at this time, the figure was one married couple for each 134 persons. *Ibid.*, p. 24 n.

[46] *Ibid.*, p. 65.

not even approached in any country in the Americas today.[47]

Aside from its direct role in the sacraments and the carrying out of Catholic education, the Church also encouraged manumission by impressing on masters that it was a meritorious act in the eyes of God. On his special Saint's day, or in honor of a marriage, a birth, or a recovery from a severe illness, a master would give thanks to God by freeing some of his slaves. The Crown greatly encouraged these procedures by making it possible to manumit a slave by simple declaration of the master in a church before the local priest.[48]

That the work of the clergy in providing a moral climate conducive to manumission was successful can also be seen in the statistics. From the early days of slave importation, a large free colored class began to appear in Cuba, largely as a result of voluntary manumission by their masters. By the 1560's the free colored population on the island was numerous enough to elect its own *aguacil*, or constable, in Havana,[49] and by the end of this century they had already fielded one full company of free colored militia of around 100 men.[50] By the end of the next century the free Negro community was able to

sponsor a full battalion of some 800 men,[51] and by the census of 1774 the island listed 30,847 free colored, as opposed to 43,333 Negro slaves, making the free colored some 41% of the total black population on the island.[52] In fact, from this first census, until the era of mass illegal importations of African slaves after 1820, the percentage of freedmen to slaves never fell below 36%. Even at its lowest ebb, in 1841, the free colored class still numbered 152,838, 26% of the total colored population. When this mass illegal trade was finally halted in the late 1850's, the temporary disequilibrium was overcome; by 1861 the free colored accounted for 39% of the total colored or 213,167 free persons as against 339,872 slaves.[53]

The Church was not only the most important factor in encouraging and maintaining the impetus to voluntary manumission, which accounts for the majority of freedmen, it also encouraged *coartación*. Most fully developed in Cuba, *coartación* was the system whereby a slave had the right to purchase his freedom from his master. The slave was granted the right to appear in court at any time to have his price fixed and to begin to pay his purchase price in agreed installments after the initial down payment, usually a minimum sum of 50 pesos, or something like 1/4 of his value. Once a slave became *coartado* he had a whole range of rights including the right to change masters if he could find a purchaser for his remaining price, and to buy his

---

[47] For the 1778 census breakdown, see AGI, Indiferente General, leg. 1527, December 31, 1778. For a clerical census of the Americas in 1959, see Donald S. Castro, *et al.*, *Statistical Abstract of Latin America, 1963* (U.C.L.A., Center of Latin American Studies, 1964), p. 22. The lowest figure for any contemporary Latin American country was Chile, with one priest for every 2,750 Catholics. The United States figure in 1965 is 1 priest to 778 practicing Catholics. *The Official Catholic Directory, 1965*, General Summary, pp. 1–2.

[48] Tannenbaum, *op. cit.*, pp. 53ff.

[49] Saco, *Historia de la esclavitud de la raza africana*, I, 221.

[50] For the history of the first company of *pardos libres* (free mulattoes) of Havana, see AGI, Santo Domingo, leg. 418, no. 7, 1714.

[51] AGI, Santo Domingo, leg. 419, no. 8, 1715.

[52] Sagra, *op. cit.*, p. 3.

[53] The figures for the census from 1774–1827 can be found in *ibid.*, pp. 3–6; and for those for the census from 1841–61 are calculated by Julio J. Le Riverend Brusone, in Ramiro Guerra y Sanchez, *et al.*, *Historia de la nación cubana*, 10 vols. (La Habana: Editorial Historia de la Nación Cubana, 1950), IV, 170.

freedom as soon as he was able. Because of the expense and labor involved, it was only the exceptionally able artisan and urban slave who most benefitted from the system, though it was open to rural plantation slaves as well, and it has been estimated that about 4,000 per year took advantage of it.[54]

Throughout the whole practice of *coartación* the Church played a vital role, for it was the prime guarantor of the free time and labor of the Negro outside his master's jurisdiction. To obtain funds, the Negro slave was permitted by custom and the Church to work for himself in his own private truck garden, or *conuco*, on all holy days and Sundays. Income from these *conucos* was also exempted from tithe payments. This was a very unusual privilege in colonial society, where the *diezmos*, or tithes, were the most universal form of production and property taxes.[55] Finally in seeking a reliable third party to hold his savings toward the initial down payment, and also to help him present his legal case, the Negro slave often relied on the local parish priest.[56]

Although the clergy did not interfere with the actual functioning of the slave regime, they could be critical of it. The Bishop of Santiago de Cuba in the late seventeenth century bitterly complained that the masters were not properly clothing their slaves, so that the latter were often embarrassed to come

to Church. He warned the masters that they were under obligation to provide the slaves with decent clothing, and not force them to provide for themselves.

The clergy also criticized the Negroes, especially on matters of laxity in church attendance and disinterest in learning their doctrine. This same Bishop who concerned himself over the poor dress of his Negro communicants, also was rather shocked at the indifference of some of the slaves to Church service. He charged that many were not attending mass on holidays and Sundays, before they began to work on their own properties, and that others were not seriously learning their lessons. In both situations he wanted the civil authorities to intervene, and in the latter case even proposed that instead of the present gentle method of instruction, the local clergy should adopt "the method by which the clerical teachers of New Spain and Peru teach their Indians," that is by using the whip on them in front of their fellow communicants if they forgot their lessons.[57]

This stern attitude was the exception rather than the rule, most clergy dealing gently with their Negro churchgoers. One who attempted to mold custom to the Church, and who largely succeeded, was Bishop Pedro Agustin Morel de Santa Cruz, in the middle of the eighteenth century. When he took up residence he found that there were 21 Negro clubs, or *cabildos*, in Havana where Negroes of both sexes gathered on holidays and Sundays to drink, dance "in extremely torrid and provocative dances" and commit other excesses too sinful to mention. Many told the Bishop that it was better to leave these *cabildos* alone, for they provided

---

[54] For a complete discussion of this system, see Herbert H. S. Aimes, "Coartación: A Spanish Institution for the Advancement of Slaves into Freedmen," *Yale Review*, XVII (February, 1909), 412–31; and Ortiz, *Los negros esclavos*, pp. 313ff.

[55] AGI, Santo Domingo, leg. 152, ramo 2, no. 39, September 24, 1680.

[56] Such for example was the experience of the parish priest of the copper mining town of Santiago del Cobre in the seventeenth century with his 500 free and slave Negro communicants. AGI, Santo Domingo, leg. 417, no. 15, December, 1709.

[57] AGI, Santo Domingo, leg. 151, ramo 2, no. 22, February 22, 1682.

a reasonable outlet for the slaves and freedmen without causing undue harm. But, he declared, "not being satisfied with similar scruples, I attempted the gentle method of going by turns to each of the *cabildos*, to administer the sacrament of confirmation, and praying the Holy Rosary with those of that organization (*gremio*), before an Image of Our Lady which I carried with me. Concluding this act, I left the image in their houses, charging them to continue with their worship and devotion. . . ." He then named a specific clergyman to each of the *cabildos* to go to them on Sundays and holidays to teach them Christian doctrine. He also placed each *cabildo* in charge of a particular Virgin that it was to venerate under the direction of a clergyman. This unusual and enthusiastic bishop went so far as to propose that his clergymen should learn the various African languages spoken by the slaves so that they might teach them better.[58]

Although this step was never taken, there is no question of the successful syncretization of Catholicism with the African folk religions brought to Cuba by the Negro slaves. Bishop Morel de Santa Cruz's action was only one link in a long chain of effort to construct a *cofradía* (or religious brotherhood) system by the Church. This was so successful that the African *cofradías* came to play a vital role in the social life of both slaves and freedmen, with their own saints and special functions in various holy marches and carnivals. Usually organized along lines of regional African origins, their members coming from the same *nación*, or geographic location, these were both religious and benevolent associations. They were not only normal *cofradías* tied to the local church

and carrying saintly images in religious processions, but cooperated with the *cabildos* in other activities. Throughout the year the *cabildo* acted as a mutual relief association, the chief of the *cabildo* aiding his subordinates if they were sick; their general funds were also used to pay burial expenses and sometimes to free old and invalided slaves. They also maintained *cabildo* houses as general meeting-places for the members of the *cofradía*, available to them at all times. Finally, the *cabildos* were recognized as legitimate political agents for the slaves and freedmen in dealing with the local authorities, thus providing outlets for political organization and leadership.

The African *cabildo* was not peculiar to Cuba, but existed throughout the Spanish and Portuguese Indies wherever Negroes were congregated. It had its origins in medieval Seville, whose Negro *cofradías* and *cabildos* were active and fully recognized from as far back as the fourteenth century. As early as 1573, the Havana municipal government ordered that all the Negroes of the city turn out for the Corpus Christi processions, "the same as they assisted in the famous one of Seville." In the great religious processions, the Negro *cabildos* in fact played an increasingly important part. Though outright African fetishes were quickly prohibited from display, the local saints and virgins were so entwined with African mythology and even costume that these displays often tended to perpetuate pre-New World patterns and beliefs.[59]

The most important religious processional for these organizations was the famous Christmas festival of the Day

---

[58] AGI, Santo Domingo, leg. 515, no. 51, 1755.

[59] An excellent study of these *cabildos* is Fernando Ortiz, "Los cabildos afro-cubanos," *Revista Bimestre Cubana*, XVI (1921), 5–39.

of the Kings. This day was recognized throughout the island as a special day for the Negro *cabildos* and *cofradías* and almost unlimited license was permitted by the white authorities in the great dances, drinkings, and ceremonies. For the Negroes, both slave and free, it was the crowning event in their year, and provided an unparalleled opportunity for individual and community expression for the entire Negro population. Thus, between religious processions, annual *dia de reyes* celebrations and the daily conduct of their *cofradías* and *cabildos* the Negro masses were provided by the Church with a vast and crucial outlet for social expression and community development.[60]

While proving a rich fabric of social existence for the masses under the canopy of the Church, the Cuban clergy also aided the exceptionally able Negro to break through the rigid class-caste barriers of the white community through their control over the educational processes. Since, at the preuniversity level, education was exclusively in the hands of the church, primary and secondary education was available to the exceptional and upwardly mobile free Negro. Education was the only means by which a colored person could break through from the lower economic classes, at least to the learned professions, and possibly higher. For sons of prosperous colored artisans and successful colored militia officers, both mulattoes and Negroes, the open opportunity of the schools run by the secular and regular clergy was their avenue for mobility of their children.

For example, the mulatto, or *pardo*, Antonio Flores, a militia officer in Havana in the mid-eighteenth century, had a son who had graduated with highest distinctions from the courses of Theology and Grammar offered by the local Jesuit college of Havana. When his son's right to enter the University was challenged on the grounds of his color, Flores, in bitter though unsuccessful opposition, pointed out to the Council of the Indies the innumerable examples of free Negro and mulatto children who had attended local church and primary schools in preuniversity training courses.[61] And while the University consistently fought the entrance of colored persons into its ranks, the large number of petitions of colored persons to the Crown demanding the right to practice a profession to which they had already been trained, indicates that many succeeded in "passing" with little trouble, through the combination of light skins and the precollegiate training they had received from the clerical schools.[62] And even given denial of University admission to the majority of free colored, the very possession of a secondary *colegio* education in the days of mass illiteracy and nonprofessional university programs, was more than enough to break into the professional classes and the upper social levels. To read and write, at least, according to the Church, if not the colonial universities, was a right open to all, and a right which held out almost unlimited opportunities for the few who could achieve it.

Concerned for his social existence, his freedom, his family, and his soul, and even in a minority of cases for the training of his mind, the Church deeply and vitally committed itself to its

---

[60] Fernando Ortiz, "La fiesta afro-cubana del 'dia de reyes'," *Revista Bimestre Cubana*, XV (1920), 5–26.

[61] AGI, Santo Domingo, leg. 1455, no. 5, 1760.

[62] For example, see the petition of the mulatto Auditor of War of Cuba, who was a law graduate of the University, in AGI, Santo Domingo, leg. 2236, October 1, 1791.

guardian role with its Negro slave communicant. Because it effectively controlled an important part of their lives, the Church was unquestionably the primary intermediary agent between master and slave, and the only institution which daily claimed its rights, as opposed to the property rights of the masters.

Although the Church could not abolish the rigors of harsh plantation servitude, it could modify that life to the extent of guaranteeing minimal periods of rest and independence for the blacks. The Church could also guarantee a degree of self-expression for all slaves, which enabled them to escape the close confines of bondage in many ways and thus to validate their human personality and potential. Finally it could create the panoply of mores and attitudes which permitted the Negro to be treated as a coequal human being, and allowed him to fully merge into Cuban society when the harsh regime of slavery was destroyed.

III

Like Cuba, Virginia was settled by a dominant established church, in this case the Church of England. Both Spain and England at the times of colonization had a hierarchical metropolitan church which was closely tied to the royal government and was considered one of the major governing institutions of the realm. But while the counter-reformation Church of Spain was able to suppress all opposition to its religious authority, the Anglican Church found itself constantly struggling against Protestant dissenter groups who attempted to challenge its established authority. However, at the time of the initial planting of Virginia, the Crown and the Church were fully united and the Anglican Church was declared the

established church of the colony. As early as 1606, the Crown decreed that the Virginia Company ". . . should provide that the true word and service of God should be preached, planted and used, *according to the Rites and Doctrine of the Church of England.*"[63] In the first organization of the Company, there was even a bishop of the realm, John King of the London diocese, who was a leading member.[64] Through these actions, Anglicanism was guaranteed as the religion of the colonists, and from then until the end of the colonial period, the Church of England was overwhelmingly the state Church of Virginia, and its membership encompassed the majority of the population.

But while there was never any challenge to the religion of the metropolitan Church in Virginia, the Crown never established the leadership and organization whereby the established church could function in its accustomed manner in the colony. In sharp contrast to Cuba, where this problem was never raised, the Crown and the hierarchy made no attempt to fit the colony into the normal functioning of the Church. Whereas Cuba had its first bishop appointed in 1516 just five years after the conquest, neither the Archbishop of Canterbury nor the Crown saw fit to appoint a native bishop, nor even to place the colony within the jurisdiction of an insular diocese.

The Bishop of London, because of his connection with the Company, originally assisted in providing clergymen and some financial assistance to establishing the Virginia church, but this

---

[63] Quoted in Arthur Lyon Cross, *The Anglican Episcopate and the American Colonies* (Cambridge: Harvard University Press, 1924), p. 10.

[64] George Maclaren Brydon, *Virginia's Mother Church and the Political Conditions Under Which it Grew*, 2 vols. (Richmond: Virginia Historical Society, 1947–1952), I, 40–42.

tenuous connection was destroyed when the Company was dissolved by the Crown in 1624. While the Company provided land for church income, divided the colony up into parishes and encouraged the migration of clergy-men,[65] it made no effort to obtain the establishment of a native bishop, pri-marily because of the cost; nor was the Church or the Crown at this time the least bit interested in subsidizing such a venture, or even in considering it.

Because of this amazing and gross neglect, the colonists within a few short years had completely usurped hierar-chical authority and had transformed the centuries-old organization of Eng-lish church government. In traditional English ecclesiastical organization, the local landowner, or other outside body or institution, had the power to nomi-nate ministers for the local parish within their jurisdiction. This meant that the landowner or institution could present his own candidate for the local parish office to the Bishop for investiture. The Bishop then had the power to certify or reject the nominee, but once invested with his office, the clergyman served for life. The local parishioners had no say either in the nomination or investiture process, and had no recourse but to accept their minister on a life basis. The minister, in fact, was accountable only to the church, and only the Bishop could control him. What duties the local parishioners' vestry and church-warden performed were all determined by law and were subservient to the local clergymen.[66]

The Church hierarchy also had the task of guaranteeing religious unifor-mity, and had extensive civil-ecclesiasti-cal functions. Thus the Bishops could appoint special courts to try and condemn heretics; they had full juris-diction over marriages, the probating of wills, the collation to benefices, the appointment of notaries; and extensive rights over tithes and other ecclesiastical taxes.[67]

Without the hierarchic structure, however, most of these functions could not be maintained; and, in fact, rapid erosion soon wiped out the complete edifice of the church as it was known in England. Although the Company at first appeared to claim the right of nomination of clergymen to Virginia parishes, it seems not to have exercised that right, but simply sent out pre-ordained clergymen, which left open the question of their initiation into their parishes. With the dissolution of the Company, and the failure of English authorities to claim their rights, the local colonists absorbed all power. First the General Court of Virginia, consist-ing of the members of the upper house of the General Assembly, claimed that the right of nomination, or presentation, devolved on them from the Company. They also proceeded to absorb a host of other juridical, administrative, and even ecclesiastical matters which by tradition belonged to the Bishop. This meant that control over vital statistics, notaries, wills, etc., the establishment of parishes, the naming and defining of all ecclesiastical offices, the collection of tithes, the regulation of church conduct, and even the maintenance of purity of faith and dogma, was determined, not by the Bishop, canonical law courts, and ecclesiastical officials, as in Eng-land, but by the local General As-sembly of Virginia.[68]

While central authority now came to rest in a popular civil assembly, the local church came increasingly under

[65] Ibid., pp. 10–11.
[66] Ibid., pp. 42–44.

[67] Ibid., p. 67; Cross, op. cit., p. 2.
[68] Brydon, op. cit., I, 67–68; 86ff.

the power of the parishioners themselves, rather than the ministry. Developing new institutions and adopting
old practices to local conditions, the
colonists began to establish their own
distinctly unique form of Church
government, at whose center stood the
all-powerful locally elected board of
governing parishioners known as the
Vestry.

With the devolution to the General
Assembly of all matters pertaining to
the Church, the Assembly in turn gave
to each local parish vestry a multitude
of civil and ecclesiastical rights and
obligations, and made it the prime institution of a new type of established
church. As early as the 1620's the Assembly was providing that local churchwardens and leading members of the
parish should concern themselves with
the maintenance of the church. From
this simple maintenance task the evolv-
ing vestry organization quickly began
to assume ever greater powers. A reflection of this occurred in 1643, when, in
a formal legal enactment, the Assembly provided that each parish should
have a vestry, and "that the most sufficient and selected men be chosen and
joyned to the minister and churchwardens to be of that Vestrie." Among the
tasks enumerated for the Vestry, was
the crucial absorption of the right of
nomination. The 1643 Act declared
"that the vestrie of evrie parish . . . shall
henceforward have power, to elect and
make choyce of their ministers. . . ."[69]
The Vestry was to present the minister
candidate for their parish appointment
to the governor, not to a bishop, as in
England, and the governor then made
the formal induction and confirmation

of that minister to hold the given
office for life.[70]

While creation of the first vestries
seems to have been by appointment of
the General Court,[71] by the 1640's the
Assembly provided that the vestry was
to be organized on the basis of election
from among the parishioners. By the
time of the codification of the laws on
the Church by the General Assembly in
1662, it was provided:

That for the makeing and proportioning
the levyes and assessments for building and
repayring the churches, and chappells,
provision for the poore, maintenance of
the minister, and such other necessary *duties*
for the more orderly managing all parociall
affaires, *Be it enacted* that twelve of the most
able men of each parish be by the major
part of the *said* parish, *chosen* to be vestry-
men out of which number the minister and
vestry to make choice of two churchwardens
yearly, as *alsoe* in the case of death of any
vestry man, or his departure out of the
parish, that the said minister and vestry
make choice of another to supply his
roome. . . .[72]

By this act, which abolished the electoral system, the vestries in fact became
autocratic local bodies of the leading
planters, who exercised enormous control over social and economic conditions within the parish. After their
initial establishment, elections never
took place, and members usually held
their office till death or resignation.
When vacancies occurred, the vestry-
men themselves proceeded to choose
leading planters as members. So
oligarchic and powerful did these
vestries become, that one of the constant
themes of colonial Virginian history
was the popular, and continually un-
satisfied, demand for periodic elections

---

[69] William Waller Hening, *The Statutes at
Large, being a Collection of the Laws of Virginia*,
13 vols. (New York: R. and W. and G. Bartlow,
1823), I, 241–42.

[70] Brydon, *op. cit.*, I, 92.
[71] *Ibid.*, p. 93.
[72] Hening, *Statutes*, II, 44–45.

and the breakup of this autocratic control.[73]

Given this entrenched self-perpetuating planter leadership in control of the Church, the role of the transitory minister could be only a subordinate one at best. In complete contradiction to the entire organization of the Church of England, the Vestry refused to present their ministers for induction. Since induction by the Governor would guarantee the minister his parish for life, barring ill conduct, the Vestries simply refused to present their ministers, and by this means made the minister's position completely dependent on the goodwill of his leading parishioners. Though the royal governors had full power to force induction on the Vestries, not one governor in the entire history of the colony saw fit to exercise this right, out of fear of vestry power.[74]

This entire system was bitterly attacked by regular Church of England clergymen. The mid-seventeenth century clergymen, Morgan Godwyn, who served in Virginia and the British West Indies, scornfully called this arrangement a "probational tenure" system,[75] while the Bishops' representative in the colony, Commissary James Blair, at the end of the century, was badly disturbed by what he described as this "Custom of making annual Agreements with the Ministers, which they [i.e., the vestries] call by a Name coarse enough, viz. Hiring of the Ministers; so that they seldom present any ministers, that they may by that Means keep them

in more Subjection and Dependence."[76] In short, stated the commissary, "they are only in the nature of Chaplains," whose tenure of office was dependent on an annual agreement renewable at the option of a small body of men.[77] Thus any independence on the part of the clergymen was quickly suppressed by the planters, who by the very nature of their positions would naturally be the strongest representatives of the status quo in the community. As Godwyn noted, they "obstruct all designs for the good of those Churches, and to report all things already so well settled as not needing the least amendment or alteration."[78]

Because of these developments, the regular clergy of England by and large refused to come to Virginia. For as Blair lamented, "no good Ministers that were inform'd of it would come into the Country, and if they came ignorant of any such Custom, they quickly felt the Effects of it in the high Hand wherewith most Vestries manag'd their Power, and got out of the Country again as soon as they could."[79] A goodly portion of the practicing clergymen in Virginia, until well into the eighteenth century, were in fact deacons, or as Morgan Godwyn called them, "*Lay-Priests* of the *Vestries ordination.*"[80]

Even in his very vocation, the minister was challenged by the vestry. Thus

---

[73] One of the major reforms of Bacon's rebellion was the call for vestry elections every three years. Brydon, *op. cit.*, I, 97.

[74] Philip Alexander Bruce, *Institutional History of Virginia in the Seventeenth Century*, 2 vols. (New York, G. P. Putnam's Sons, 1910), I, 136–39.

[75] Morgan Godwyn, *The Negro's and Indians Advocate, Suing for their Admission into the Church* (London: J. D., 1680), p. 168.

[76] Henry Hartwell, James Blair, and Edward Chilton, *The Present State of Virginia*, 2d Ed. (Williamsburg: Colonial Williamsburg, Inc., 1940), p. 66.

[77] *Ibid.*, p. 67.

[78] Godwyn, *op. cit.*, Preface, p. i. According to Godwyn the Virginia colonists chafed at the cost of Church tithes, and quickly lost their interest in the Anglican creed, because, he charged, Virginians "for the most part do know no other *God* but *Money*, nor *Religion* but *Profit*."

[79] Hartwell, Blair, and Chilton, *loc. cit.*

[80] Godwyn, *op. cit.*, p. 170.

the Reverend Hugh Jones in 1724 warned that ". . . in several places the clerks [of the parish] are so ingenious or malicious, that they contrive to be liked as well or better than the minister, which created ill-will and disturbance, besides other harm."[81] Given the chance, he charged, they will usurp almost all of the clergymen's functions, even to the giving of sermons, and warned that they should have their functions carefully defined by law to prevent these abuses.

So all-embracing was parishioner influence and control, that the clergyman had to win popular endorsement, and constantly keep his congregation happy, which of course excluded all possibilities of independent thought or challenge to the given moral and social situation, for this was the sure road to ruin. This dependence was so pervasive, in fact, that often parishioners even went so far, in this era of nonconformity, as to question and modify standard Church dogma. Reverend Jones noted in his analysis of contemporary Virginia: "In several respects the clergy are obliged to omit or alter some minute parts of the liturgy, and deviate from the strict discipline and ceremonies of the Church; to avoid giving offense. . . ."[82]

While the mother church soon became deeply aware of the heterodoxy and complete breakdown of the established church in Virginia, it could do little to change the situation. Deeply involved in religious civil wars at home, it was not until after the Restoration that the Church of England could even begin to deal with the situation. It was only with the investiture of Henry Compton as Bishop of London, in 1675,

that the Church finally forced the crown to place the colony within a diocese. For a number of historical reasons, the Bishopric of London was chosen; however, traditions were so entrenched that this brought little real change. The Bishop made no attempt to oppose vestry control, or to retake possession of his normal ecclesiastical or civil functions, or even his right of investiture. His only concern was to maintain some kind of purity of dogma by guaranteeing minimal standards for clergymen. This he did by forcing the colonists to accept only accredited clergymen licensed by himself. Thus in the instruction to Governor Culpeper of Virginia, the Bishop had the Crown declare that "no Minister be prefrr'd by you to any Ecclesiastical Benefice in that our Colony *without a Certificate from the Lord Bp. of London, of his being conformable to the Doctrine of the Church of England.*"[83]

While the Bishop eventually succeeded in sending a representative to the colony, with the title of commissary, or vicar general, this clergyman could only exercise moderating influence, and had to persuade rather than enjoin acceptance of church rules.[84] The first commissar, James Blair (1689–1743) created much heat, but little concrete change,[85] and despite all attempts of several energetic London Bishops, the Vestries could not be forced to induct their ministers, leaving the majority of them to the arbitrary will of their congregations. Through the commissary rule of Blair and his successors, some positive results were attained with the problem of providing a regular ordained clergy for all the parishes, but in the end, the commissaries had little or

---

[81] Hugh Jones, *The Present State of Virginia*, 2d Ed. (Chapel Hill: University of North Carolina Press, 1956), p. 96.
[82] *Ibid.*, p. 98.

[83] Quoted in Cross, *op. cit.*, p. 26.
[84] *Ibid.*, pp. 3–4, 44.
[85] *Ibid.*, pp. 78–80.

no effect at reforming the general structure of the Virginia Church. When the metropolitan hierarchy realized this failure, it attempted to establish a resident Bishop for the American colonies. But this was a potentially powerful challenge to local authority, and colonial opposition was so constant and vehement against this idea that the matter was never carried to fruition, despite all the strenuous efforts made by mother church.[86]

Not only was the Church after the Restoration terribly concerned about the religion of the white colonists, but it also began to take an increasingly involved position on the status of the Negro and Indian heathens within England's American Empire. This concern with the plight of the Negro slave, especially, is heavily attested to by the growing movement for conversion, education, and even emancipation among the lower and upper clergy. This movement began as early as the end of the seventeenth century, and one of its first advocates was Morgan Godwyn, the angry clergyman, who served both in the British West Indies and the colony of Virginia, and whose *The Negro's and Indians Advocate* (1680) created a good deal of sentiment. This growing awareness of the complete lack of impact of the Church on the Negro slaves, in sharp contrast to the Catholic Church in the Spanish and French islands, as many Church of England men noted,[87] caused the Bishop of London to put pressure on the Crown.

In the royal instructions to Governor Culpeper of Virginia in 1681–1682, the Crown proposed that:

Ye shall endeavour to get a Law passed for the restraining of any inhuman severity which by ill masters or overseers may be used towards their Christian Servants or Slaves. And you are alsoe with the assistance of the Council and Assembly, to find out the best means to facilitate and encourage the conversion of Negroes to the Christian Religion, *wherein you are to leave a due* caution and regards to ye property of the Inhabitants and safety of the Colonies.[88]

The unusual restraint of this request indicates the royal government's recognition of the primacy of local law and custom over the humanitarian demands of the clergymen.

Nevertheless, the English hierarchy was becoming deeply concerned over the failure of the colonials to Christianize the Negro slaves. Finding that little could be accomplished directly through regular Church and governmental channels, despite the establishment relationship of the Church, the Bishops decided that the only alternative was a missionary society, completely financed from England. Thus in 1701, the hierarchy in England founded

---

[86] For the history of this struggle, see Cross, *loc. cit.*, and Carl Bridenbaugh, *Mitre and Sceptre, Transatlantic Faiths, Ideas, Personalities and Politics, 1689–1775* (New York: Oxford University Press, 1962).

[87] In his famous denunciation of West Indian Slavery, for example, the Reverend James Ramsay constantly contrasted the British to the French treatment of slaves. "In the French colonies," he declared, "the public pays an immediate attention to the treatment and instruction of slaves. The intendants [gov't administrative officers] are charged with their protection; proper missionaries are appointed for the purpose of training them up to a certain degree of religious knowledge; and ample estates and funds are allotted for their maintenance of these ecclesiastics." "The respect in which marriage is held, brings a farther advantage to French slaves. The ceremony is solemnized by the priest, and the tie continues for life. This gives them an attachment to their families . . . that is seldom seen among English slaves; where the connection between the sexes is arbitrary, and too frequently casual." Rev. James Ramsay, *An Essay on the Treatment of African Slaves in the British Sugar Colonies* (London: James Philipps, 1784), pp. 52, 54.

[88] *The Virginia Magazine of History and Biography*, XXVIII (1920), 43–44.

the famous Society for the Propagation of the Gospel in Foreign Parts.[89]

That one of the primary aims of the Society was conversion of the slaves was understood by the Bishops from the very beginning. Thus in the annual sermon given to the society in 1710, Bishop William Fleetwood bitterly attacked the refusal of the masters of slaves to permit their conversion to Christianity. He claimed the refusal to permit baptism and Christian education was:

A thing so common in all our *Plantations* abroad, that I have reason to doubt, whether there be any Exception of any People *of ours*, who cause their slaves to be Baptized. What do these people think of Christ? . . . That He who came from Heaven, to purchase to Himself a Church, with his own precious Blood, should sit contented, and behold with unconcern, those who profess themselves his Servants, excluding from its Gates those who would gladly enter if they might, and excercising no less Cruelty to their Souls (as far as they are able) than to their Bodies?

These People were made to be as Happy as themselves, and are as capable of being so; and however hard their Condition be in this World, with respect to their Captivity and Subjugation. . . . They were bought with the same Price, purchased with the same Blood of Christ, their common Saviour and Redeemer; and on order to all this, they were to have the Means of Salvation put into their Hands, they were to be instructed in the Faith of *Christ*, to have the Terms and Conditions fairly offered to them.

Not only did Bishop Fleetwood attack the very Christianity of the masters, but also considered that this was probably their greatest sin, for he declared, "no Man living can assign a better and more justifiable Cause, for God's withholding Mercy from a *Christian*, than that *Christian's* with-holding the Mercy of *Christianity* from an Unbeliever."[90] The radical Bishop even went so far as to attack slavery itself, holding, as Adam Smith was later to proclaim, that hired labor was a far superior system and thet slavery should be abolished. He attacked the ideas of colonists, which held that Christianity challenged the slave status, but instead of proclaiming the docility of slaves under Christian doctrine as some clerics did, he properly attacked the Christianity of the colonists who would refuse to treat fellow human beings with Christian brotherly love. Finally, he proposed that the Society take up the crucial task of Christianizing the infidels, Negroes and slaves, and that this example would have a powerful impact on the masters, who apparently are unimpressed by "the Example both of *French* and *Spaniards* . . . , who all along have brought their Slaves to Baptism."[91]

This call appears to have been heeded, for in the annual sermon of 1740, Bishop Secker pointed to the work of the Society in this special area. But the Bishop noted the vast difficulty still faced by the Church in this work as only a few had been converted and thousands yet remained outside the fold.

For it is not to be expected, that Masters, too commonly negligent of Christianity themselves, will take much Pains to teach it to their Slaves: whom even the better Part of them are in a great measure habituated to consider, as they do their Cattle, merely with a View to the Profit arising from them. Not a few therefore have openly

---

[89] H. P. Thompson, *Into All Lands, The History of the Society for the Propagation of the Gospel in Foreign Parts, 1701–1950* (London, S. P. C. K., 1951), chap. 1.

[90] This sermon is reprinted in its entirety in Frank J. Klingberg, *Anglican Humanitarianism in Colonial New York* (Philadelphia: Church Historical Society, 1940), pp. 203–4.

[91] *Ibid.*, p. 211.

opposed their Instruction, from an Imagination, now indeed proved and acknowledged to be groundless, that Baptism would entitle them to Freedom. . . . And some, it may be feared, have been averse to their becoming Christians, because, after that, no Pretence will remain for not treating them like Men.[92]

Both within and without the society, the upper clergy were beginning, by the middle of the eighteenth century, to put pressure on the colonies to change their local customs and laws on these subjects, and to create a new panoply of beliefs that would permit the Church to carry on the work of conversion in a positive atmosphere.

The Bishop of London in 1742 put great pressure on Commissary Blair to get the local government to support a school for Negroes, and to indicate to them his great zeal in converting Negroes to the Christian faith.[93] But incapable of even fully protecting standard dogma and church practice, Blair and his successors could accomplish little. As for the SPG, the demands on its resources were so great, that it concentrated its efforts on the British West Indies, where the bulk of the New World slaves resided, and on the colonies in which the Church was unestablished.[94]

This meant, in essence, that whatever the feelings of the hierarchy in England as to the desirability of conversion of the slaves to Christianity and their participation in the sacraments, this desire had little if any impact on New World conditions. The religious life of the slave remained wholly dependent upon the will of his master, and this was determined almost exclusively by local custom. With no clergymen

capable of opposing these assumptions and customs, the planters felt under no obligation to change their ways.

Unfortunately, custom was indifferent, if not openly hostile, to the conversion of Negro slaves. In the early years of the seventeenth century, there had existed the almost universal belief that conversion for the slave required his freedom, since Christians could not hold Christians in bondage. While the General Assembly eventually declared that this was not so,[95] the idea was hard to uproot, and persisted throughout the colonial period. Even when this factor was resolved or admitted by the reluctant master, there was still the key fear of education making the slaves intractable. As the Reverend Hugh Jones reported, he constantly tried to disprove this latter assumption among colonials. "As for baptizing Indians and Negroes," he said, "several of the people disapprove of it, because they say it often makes them proud, and not so good servants: But these, and such objections, are easily refuted, for Christianity encourages and orders them to become more humble and better servants, and not worse, then when they were heathens." He did agree with

[92] *Ibid.*, p. 217.
[93] *William and Mary Quarterly*, 1st Series, IX (1901), 225.
[94] Thompson, *op. cit.*, chap. 3.

[95] The Virginia legislature itself seriously accepted the thesis that Christianity was incompatible with slavery, and in its early definitions actually defined slaves as those who were not Christians. Thus in 1670 it enacted a statute which declared that "all servants not being christians imported into this country by shipping shalbe slaves for life." Henings, *Statutes*, II, 283. This was finally rectified in 1682 when the Assembly decreed that: "all servants except Turks and Moores . . . which shall be brought or imported into this country, either by sea or land, whether Negroes, . . . Mulattoes or Indians, who and whose parentage and native country are not christian, although afterwards, and before such their importation . . . they shall be converted to the christian faith; . . . shall be judged, deemed and taken to be slaves. . . ." *Ibid.*, 490–91.

general opinion, however, which held that Negro slaves should not be taught to read and write, since this "has been found to be dangerous upon several political accounts, especially self-preservation."[96]

While masters could be found who sponsored the baptism of their slaves, encouraged them to learn the catechism, and some who even read to them from the Bible, these were the exception rather than the rule. The pattern, in fact, was quite haphazard, and in the majority of cases conversion was never properly undertaken. This is well revealed in a survey of the colonial church of Virginia carried out in the early eighteenth century. In 1724 Commissary Blair sent out an extraordinarily revealing and exhaustive questionnaire to all the parishes of Virginia. Among the questions asked was: "Are there any Infidels, bond or free, within your Parish; and what means are used for their conversion?" The 29 clergymen who answered the inquiry give the overwhelming impression of only moderate clerical interest in the problem, and general planter indifference, if not hostility. As the Reverend George Robertson of Bristol Parish reported, "I have several times exhorted their Masters to send such of them as could speak English to Church to be catechised but they would not. Some masters instruct their Slaves at home and so bring them to baptism, but not many such."[97] The Reverend Henry Collings of St. Peter's Parish reported that of the Negro slaves in his parish "Some . . . are suffered by their respective masters to be baptized and to attend on divine service but others not."[98] The Reverend John Warden reported that in his parish "some masters will have their slaves baptised and others will not, by reason that they will not be surities for them in Baptism,"[99] while Alexander Forbes reported that in his parish the local Negro slaves "as soon as they are capable they are taught and baptised by the care of some Masters, but this is too much neglected by many."[100] The clergymen of Henrico and Southwark parishes respectively replied of the slaves in their parishes that "their Masters, do no more than let some of them now and then go to Church for their Conversion," and that "there are some of their Masters on whom I do prevail to have them baptised and taught, but not many."[101] The Reverend John Brunskill of Willmington Parish probably best summed up the problem when he concluded that:

The Negroes who are slaves to the whites cannot, I think, be said to be of any Religion for as there is no law of the Colony oblidging their Masters or Owners to instruct them in the principles of Christianity and so they are hardly to be persuaded by the Minister to take so much pains with them, by which means the poor creatures generally live and die without it.[102]

[96] Jones, *op. cit.*, p. 99.

[97] William Stevens Perry, ed., *Historical Collections Relating to the American Colonial Church*, 5 vols. (Hartford: Church Press Company, 1870–1878), I, 267.

[98] *Ibid.*, p. 269.

[99] *Ibid.*, p. 289.

[100] *Ibid.*, p. 295.

[101] *Ibid.*, pp. 304, 306.

[102] *Ibid.*, pp. 277–78. Interestingly, the few records which survive of slave education and conversion carried out by masters, come not from Church of England slave-owners, but from Presbyterians and Quakers. Thus Roberts Pleasants, one of the wealthiest planters of Virginia in the eighteenth century, and a Quaker, not only converted his slaves, but even educated and eventually freed them. Adair P. Archer, "The Quakers' Attitude towards the Revolution," *William and Mary Quarterly*, 2d Series, I (1921), 168. For his part, the Presbyterian planter Colonel James Gordon, in his journal in 1761 noted that "Several strange negroes come to Mr. Criswell [the local presby-

Even for the minority that were baptized, converted and taught the Christian religion, there were no positive rewards. No matter how Christian, no master allowed his slaves to be married. For if the sacrament of marriage was not to be made totally ridiculous, Negro slaves could not be admitted: it deprived human agencies of the right to separate the couple, and this was never accepted. Even when the best of masters died, the constant fluidity of fortunes meant that no slave community could remain intact beyond a few generations. Families were not sold together; to do so was uneconomic and therefore impractical. As the Virginia Baptist chronicler John Leland noted in 1790, "the marriage of slaves, is a subject not known in our code of laws. What promises soever they make, their masters may and do part at pleasure."[103]

As for the complex web of social organizations to which the Cuban slave had recourse this simply did not exist under the established church of Virginia. There were no fraternal brotherhoods, no great processionals and

special holidays, and absolutely no syncretization of Christian belief with folk religion of African origin. For the Negro slaves on the frontier of Virginia after 1740 there did exist the possibility of admission into the evangelical movement known as the "Great Awakening." From 1740 and especially after 1760 numbers of Methodist, Baptist, Presbyterian, and a host of other sect preachers began invading the frontier counties of Virginia above the Tidewater.[104] For these preachers, most of whom like Wesley himself were bitter opponents of slavery, welcomed the Negroes into the Church. Thus John Leland in his Virginia Chronicle of 1790 reported:

The poor slaves, under all their hardships, discover as great inclination for religion as the free-born do, when they engage in the service of God, they spare no pains. It is nothing strange for them to walk 20 miles on Sunday morning to meeting, and back again at night. They are remarkable for learning a tune soon, and have very melodious voices.

They cannot read, and therefore are more exposed to delusion than the whites are; but many of them give clear, rational accounts of a work of grace in their hearts, and evidence of the same by their lives. When religion is lively they are remarkable fond of meeting together, to sing, pray and exhort, and sometimes preach, and seem to be unwearied in the procession. They seem in general to put more confidence in their own colour, then they do in whites; when they attempt to preach, they seldom fail of being very zealous; their language is broken, but they understand each other, and the whites may gain their ideas. A few of them have undertaken to administer baptism, but it generally ends in confusion; they commonly are more noisy in time of preaching than the whites, and are more subject to bodily exercise, and if they meet

terian teacher] to be instructed, in which he takes great pains." *William and Mary Quarterly*, 1st Series, XI (1903), 223. Nevertheless, despite these and other efforts, the consensus of historical opinion is best summed up by Marcus W. Jernegan who declared that throughout the colonial period, "most of the slaves lived and died strangers to christianity" and that "with comparatively few exceptions the conversion of Negro slaves was not seriously undertaken by their masters. On the contrary many of them strenuously and persistently opposed the Church of England, and the Society for the Propagation of the Gospel in Foreign Parts. . . ." Marcus W. Jernegan, "Slavery and Conversion in the American Colonies," *American Historical Review*, XXI, no. 3 (April, 1916), 504; also see Jerome W. Jones, "The Established Virginia Church and the Conversion of Negroes and Indians, 1620–1760," *Journal of Negro History*, XLVI, no. 1 (January, 1961), 12–31.

[103] John Leland, *The Virginia Chronicle* (Norfolk: Prentis and Baxter, 1790), p. 8.

[104] *Ibid.*, pp. 21ff; also see Wesley M. Gewehr, *The Great Awakening in Virginia, 1740–1790* (Durham, N. C.: Duke University Press, 1930).

with any encouragement in these things, they grow extravagent.[105]

But these camp meetings and non-hierarchical churches were not open to the majority of Virginia Negroes, who lived in the predominantly Church of England areas. Nor were the masters too ready to permit them to go to revivalist gatherings. As Leland himself notes: ". . . many masters and overseers will whip and torture the poor creatures for going to meeting, even at night, when the labor of the day is done."[106] As fear of insurrection developed in the period after independence, such meetings became less and less common, public gatherings of more than a few slaves being prohibited.[107]

Not only was the Church incapable of undertaking a general conversion of the slaves, but it was also unable to promote manumission. Thus the common pattern of church-inspired individual planter manumission, which was accepted custom and practice in Cuba, was unknown in Protestant Virginia. Though the Methodists and Quakers early demanded that their members give up slave-trading and emancipate their slaves, and though several revolutionary leaders followed their enlightenment thought to its logical conclusion and freed their Negroes, no powerful undercurrent of emancipation ever occurred. Quaker emancipations were few and of little consequence, and the Methodist leadership was soon forced to condone the existence of slave-holding even among its traveling clergy, and to give up its proposals for emancipation.[108] As for the Anglican hierarchy,

while it too developed a powerful commitment to emancipation at the end of the eighteenth century, it took forceful Parliamentary legislation to carry out emancipation even in the West Indies. As for Virginia this emancipation movement never found echo in the local episcopal hierarchy, when the latter was finally established in 1790.[109]

The clergy of Virginia were unable to convince the planters that emancipation was a good act in the sight of God, and was to be considered a common and accepted form of pious action, as in Cuba. Nor could the morally aroused and committed clergy, of whatever denomination, convince the masters that slavery was essentially a moral evil and that on these grounds the slaves should be emancipated as soon as possible. Neither forcing emancipation on moral grounds from above, nor having it become a part of routine common practice from below, the whole emancipation movement in Virginia was at best a haphazard and distinctly minor affair. In fact, from the late seventeenth to the late eighteenth century it was to all intents and purposes outlawed by the State. By 1691 the reaction had become so intense, that the General Assembly of Virginia declared that "great inconveniences may happen to this

Gewehr, *op. cit.*, pp. 242–49; and for the Quakers see Thomas E. Drake, *Quakers and Slavery in America* (New Haven, Yale University Press, 1950).

[109] Though the Anglican church consecrated native candidates between 1784 and 1790, which enabled the Americans to establish the Protestant Episcopal Church in the United States, the new bishops were subservient to local interests and Vestry government was in no way changed. See Cross, *op. cit.*, pp. 263 ff; Clara O. Loveland, *The Critical Years, The Reconstruction of the Anglican Church in the United States of America: 1780–1789* (Greenwich, Seabury Press, 1956); Edward Lewis Goodwin, *The Colonial Church in Virginia* (Milwaukee, Morehouse Pub. Co., 1927), pp. 127ff. for the early bishops of the Diocese of Virginia.

---

[105] Leland, *op. cit.*, p. 11.

[106] *Ibid.*, p. 9.

[107] C. G. Woodson, *The Education of the Negro Prior to 1861* (New York: Putnam, 1915), chaps. vii, viii.

[108] On the failure of the Methodists, see

countrey by setting of negroes and mulattoes free," and provided under heavy penalty, that owners who emancipated their slaves had to pay for their transportation out of the country within six months.[110] Not satisfied with this restriction on the growth of the free Negro class, the legislature next made it impossible for a master to free his slaves even on his own initiative. By a law of 1721 all emancipation was prohibited "except for some meritorious services, to be adjudged and allowed by the governor and council."[111]

By these extreme measures, the free Negro population, which probably numbered around 350 in 1691, was kept for the next century to its natural increase alone; by 1782 there were only some 2,800 freedmen in the state.[112] In this year, however, under the impact of the revolution and the growth of clerical opposition, a new law permitted open emancipation at the discretion of the owner.[113] By the first federal census of 1790, the number of freedmen had increased to 12,866. Even with this increase, the free colored population represented only 4% of the total colored population. Nor did the half-century between the first federal census and the Civil War see any major change. The percentage slowly rose from decade to decade, but with almost the identical number of colored, just over 550,000 in Cuba and Virginia in 1860/1861, Virginia had only 58,042 freedmen (or 11%) to Cuba's 213,167 (or 39%).[114]

As for the development of education for the free Negroes, this was informal and haphazard in the extreme, except for one short-lived experiment. In the late 1720's, Dr. Thomas Bray, who had been commissary in the State of Maryland for the Bishop of London, helped found a group of missionaries known as "Bray's Associates" who directed considerable attention to founding schools for Negroes in the American Colonies. A leading founder of the SPG, Dr. Bray received a private donation of £900 for this purpose.[115] After setting up a successful school with the aid of Benjamin Franklin in Philadelphia in 1759, Dr. Bray helped establish a Negro school in Williamsburg in 1764. Under the direction of Commissary Dawson, local clerics, and Mrs. Ann Wager, the school soon opened its doors to 24 Negro students, and made major progress in the area.[116] It appears to have won some local support, for a local printer, Mr. William Hunter, left in his will in 1761, some £7 for the support of Mrs. Wager.[117] But despite the initial success and support granted to the school, with the death of Mrs. Wager in 1774, the school ceased to operate. In fact, in the agitation of those years all the Negro and Indian schools on the North American continent founded by Dr. Bray and his associates, as well as by the SPG, collapsed. The Williamsburg school seems to have been the model for another which lasted five years in the 1770's in Fredericksburg, but with the American Revolution, the source of English enthusiasm and funds for these schools was destroyed and local planter

---

[110] Hening, *Statues*, III, 87–88.

[111] *Ibid.*, IV, 132.

[112] John H. Russell, *The Free Negro in Virginia, 1619–1865* (Baltimore: Johns Hopkins Press, 1913), pp. 10–11.

[113] Hening, *op. cit.*, XI, 39–40.

[114] U.S. Bureau of the Census, *Negro Population 1790–1915* (Washington, Government Printing Office, 1918), p. 57, table 6. It should be noted that Virginia had the largest number and percentage of freedmen in its colored population in 1860 of any slave state in the Union except

---

Maryland, which was a unique border state.

[115] Thompson, *op. cit.*, pp. 9–19, 42–43.

[116] Mary F. Goodwin, "Christianizing and Educating the Negro in Colonial Virginia," *Historical Magazine of the Protestant Episcopal Church*, I, no. 3 (September, 1932), 148–51.

[117] *William and Mary Quarterly*, 1st Series, VII (1899), 13.

interest seems to have become exhaust-ed.[118] Apparently neither free nor slave Negroes were permitted regular educa-tion by the local county schools.

There was some attempt by the Vestries, however, to provide for the free Negroes, orphans and poor, some type of apprenticeship in which they were also taught to read and write by the person to whom they were inden-tured. The Vestry of Petsworth Parish in 1716 required that for his indenture, Mr. Ralph Bevis was to:

give George Petsworth, a mulattoe boy of the age of 2 years, 3 years' schooling, and carefully to Instruct him afterwards that he may read well in any part of the Bible, also to instruct and Learn him ye sd mulattoe boy such Lawful way and ways that he may be able after his Indented time expired to gitt his own Liveing, and to allow him sufficient meat, Drink, washing, and apparill, until the expiration of ye sd time &c. . . .[119]

But these indentured and apprentice-ship programs were for only a few free Negroes, and aside from the temporary Negro school experiment on the eve of the American Revolution, the Church seems to have made almost no serious or successful effort to educate the Virginia Negro. No Negro was ad-mitted to William and Mary College, and none appears to have been trained by the Church in local parish schools for the liberal professions, as was the case in Cuba, while in the harsh reaction which took place by the early 19th century, even basic literacy was denied the freedmen.[120]

Thus the Virginia Church, domi-nated by the planter elite, offered no educational escape opportunities either for free or slave Negroes. It totally denied the right to slave marriages, and by and large in the colonial period did not even Christianize the majority of African Negroes. Finally, the es-tablished Church in Virginia did noth-ing to enrich the community life of the Negroes. The religious brotherhoods, the pageantry and processions, the folk religious syncretization, which were such an important part of the fabric of Catholic Cuba, were alien to Anglican-ism. Although the dissenter groups in the "Great Awakening" after 1740 provided some compensation in the evangelical and revivalist meetings (which were to give birth to the future Negro church movement) these were confined to the frontier in the colonial period and involved only a few thou-sand Negro slaves. For the "Great Awakening" in Virginia was the work of only a handful of ministers and never penetrated into the Tidewater pa-rishes where the overwhelming major-ity of slaves lived under Anglican masters.

Within the great plantation areas, despite all the efforts of the Bishop of London and his commissaries, the few local clergy were hard pressed to main-tain even the established Church among the white colonists. As late as 1774, Virginia had only 104 Church of Eng-land clergymen,[121] in a total population of roughly 447,000 persons,[122] just one

---

[118] Thompson, *op. cit.*, chap. 4.

[119] *William and Mary Quarterly*, 1st Series, V (1897), 219; also see the case of Robert, son of the free Negro woman Cuba, who was bound out in Lancaster County in 1719 till his twenty-first birthday. *William and Mary Quarterly*, 1st Series, VIII (1899), 82.

[120] In 1800 the General Assembly specifically prohibited the local parishes from requiring the masters to teach the indentured free colored children to read or write, and by the 1830's the state legislature was prohibiting all types of schooling and education for even free Negroes who were willing to pay the costs. Russell, *op. cit.*, pp. 140, 144–45.

[121] Brydon, *op. cit.*, II, 608–614.

[122] Evarts B. Greene and Virginia D. Harring-ton, *American Population before the Federal Census of 1790* (New York: Columbia University Press, 1932), p. 141.

to over 4,000 colonists. Nor was this ratio unusual, for the Reverend James Ramsay in his famous attack on slavery in the British West Indies, asked for an ideal of one clergyman per 3,000 inhabitants to carry out the needed Christianization of the Negroes.[123]

Few in number, operating on provisional contracts based on the consent of the congregation, and completely subservient to the planter-dominated Vestry, and working against ingrained opposition to conversion, it is surprising that the Church of England accomplished as much as it did. Unfortunately, when moral pressure within the Church finally brought the metropolitan hierarchy to put pressure on the Crown and Parliament to override local slave legislation, it was already too late for Virginia. The antislavery crusade did not fully get under way, despite the sentiments of such early leaders as Bishop Fleetwood, until after 1783, when the colonies were no longer a part of the British Empire. Although it was to have a profound influence on the British West Indies and on the abolition of the slave trade, the severance of political ties and the establishment of an independent Episcopalian Church in Virginia rendered the North American colonies impervious to this great moral crusade. How differently events might otherwise have turned out is shown by the impact of the aroused church on the eventual education, Christianization, and emancipation of the British West Indian Negro slave.[124]

Too involved with defense of its very

position at home in the seventeenth century, the Church of England had allowed the colonists to usurp its power and authority, and to create for themselves a congregational church organization. While this allowed more religious liberty for the white colonists, and greater individual expression in this age of religious nonconformity and dissent, it was fatal to the rights of the Negroes and Mulattoes, slave and free. When the Church finally turned its attention to the issue, it was too late, and the emancipation of the colonies of the North American continent destroyed the hope of the colored peoples that the Church would protect their rights and liberties as human beings.

IV

Having compared the impact of the Church on the lives of the Negro slaves within two distinct New World colonies, we have a clearer conception of the uniqueness and the consequent differences between the two institutions of Negro slavery. As Elkins and Tannenbaum have properly pointed out, the Church was one of the most crucial institutions which had the power to intervene in the relations between master and slave and to help mold that relationship.

In Cuba, the Church took an immediate daily concern and involvement, and succeeded in molding custom and patterns, as well as commanding obedience to higher authorities. From the beginning the Church viewed its own role toward the slaves as distinct from that of the masters and succeeded in establishing its claim on the mind, soul, and time of the Negroes, free or slave. Not troubled by the belief that Christianity was incompatible with the slave status and working with establish-

---

[123] Ramsay, *op. cit.*, pp. 265–66.

[124] For the history of this struggle see Reginald Coupland, *The British Anti-Slavery Movement*, 2d Ed. (London: Frank Cass and Co., 1964), along with Frank Klingberg, *The Anti-Slavery Movement in England, A Study in English Humanitarianism* (New Haven: Yale University Press, 1926).

ed Iberian attitudes toward the Negro and his place within the Catholic society, the Cuban clergy were able to mold and modify the conditions of human bondage for the African Negro. Capable of carrying imperial and synodal edicts into immediate effect, the Cuban clergy effectively Christianized the imported slaves and freely admitted them into the Church. For the slaves this admittance provided inestimable social advantages and rights, as well as duties, and a host of concrete immediate advantages, from rest days on Sunday to the full sanctity of the family through the sacrament of marriage. In the syncretization of African religions in folk catholicism, and in the organization of *cofradías*, *cabildos*, and religious processionals, the Africans were provided with a rich cultural and community existence, which paradoxically eased their assimilation into society. Finally, the Church stood as the great potential benefactor to the exceptionally able, who, through church education, could achieve a new upper class status within society.

None of these things occurred for the Virginia Negro. Beginning with the planters' open hostility even to the admittance of Negroes into the Church, and faced by usurpation of authority by the parishioners, the fight even for minimal conversion was an uphill struggle for the Church of England. Involved with defense of the Church at home, the Anglican hierarchy allowed the Church abroad to be converted into a democratic congregational organization. It therefore had as much as it could do to guarantee church conformity among the white colonists, and had little energy to spare for the Negro, and even less for the Indian. Fully aware of the progress of the Catholic Church in these two areas, and morally sensitive

to the issues, the metropolitan Anglican hierarchy could not develop enough power and unity prior to 1776 to break down the American congregational control and overcome planter hostility toward its conversion and incipient emancipation efforts.

Unlike the Cuban Church, the Church of England could not rely on the Crown for unquestioned support on these matters, for in the organization of the Empire, control over slavery and the Negro was left exclusively to the local government. Thus the Anglican Church could not build up a panoply either of canonical or civil law to guarantee free entry of the Negroes into the Church, and even more importantly to provide them with the full rights to the sacraments. As for the local legislature, the glaring silence of Virginia law as to the religious rights and condition of the Negro slave reflects the totally marginal character of slave Christianity, where it even existed. With such hostility built up in the colonial period against conversion, it was impossible for the Church even to suggest that slaves be legally married before God, or that the family had to be protected against the economic needs of the planter.

Even in the revivalist churches of the upland parishes, the "Great Awakening" and the participation of the Negro slaves was a short-lived affair, and within a few decades of Independence, the Virginia branches of the Baptist, Methodist, and Presbyterian churches had conformed to planter opinion and had, by and large, contained slave conversion and participation to a minimum. As for the Virginia Episcopal Church, the successor after 1790 to the Church of England, its own decay and even greater dependence on planter support, made it take even less of an interest in Negroes, slave or free, than its colonial originator.

Denied the full rights of the Christian, with his family unrecognized by the Church or the state, with his previous religious experience rendered totally useless and destroyed, and his chances for self and community expression severely curtailed if not openly discouraged by the local parish, the Virginia Negro slave faced a harsh world dominated by his master, and with little possibility of protective intervention and support from an outside institution.

While the relationship of the Church to the slave was only one of several relationships, it was probably the most important nonplanter one available. Because of this, the success or failure of the Anglican or Catholic Church to mold the life and soul of the Negro slaves had a profound impact on the personality, social organization and even eventual assimilation of the Negro into Cuban and Virginian society.

ELSA V. GOVEIA

Comment on "Anglicanism, Catholicism, and the Negro Slave"

In writing his article, Mr. Klein clearly intended his particular evidence about the influence of different religions to be taken as a proof of general conclusions which would explain the different characteristics of Negro slavery in different parts of the Americas. Quite early, he suggests that his aim is to assess previous comparative studies of American slavery empirically "by subjecting to detailed analysis the slave systems of two colonial powers in the New World . . . through detailing the operation of one crucial aspect of the slave system, the relationship between infidel Negro and Christian Church, in two highly representative colonies, those of Cuba and Virginia" (p. 139*). Later, summing up his evidence about the influences of the Catholic and Anglican Churches in his chosen samples, he claims that

"having compared the impact of the Church on the lives of the Negro slaves within two distinct New World colonies, we have a clearer conception of the uniqueness and the consequent differences between the two institutions of Negro slavery" (p. 164).

However, any historian acquainted with the varying development of the Catholic colonies in the West Indies must immediately doubt that there is any necessary connection between Mr. Klein's particular evidence and his general conclusions. He himself seems to have accepted at face value Rev. James Ramsay's assertion that slaves in the French West Indies in the later eighteenth century were well treated and effectively instructed in Christian knowledge and conduct (Footnote 87). But Ramsay had his own reasons for exaggerating the contrasts between the French and British islands with respect to treatment of slaves. More recent authorities on the history of French West Indian slavery have taken a less rosy view of the prevailing attitudes

Reprinted, by permission of the Editors, from *Comparative Studies in Society and History*, vol. VIII, no. 3 (April 1966), pp. 328–330.

*Page references are to the Klein article as reprinted in this book. Eds.

towards the slaves. In fact, it appears very likely that the typical opinion for these colonies during the greater part of the eighteenth century was that expressed by Fénelon in 1764 when he remarked that "The safety of the whites, less numerous than the slaves, surrounded by them on their estates, and almost completely at their mercy, demands that the slaves be kept in the most profound ignorance."[1]

In spite of the religious differences between the Catholic French and the Protestant British in the West Indies, both their religious attitudes and their general behavior toward slaves showed striking similarities during the course of the eighteenth century, and these similarities were in marked contrast with the attitudes and behavior accepted in Cuba until that colony began to develop a great plantation system.[2] Catholicism, as such, must seem an unconvincing explanation of the characteristic treatment of slaves in Cuba when it failed to produce the same consequences in other Catholic colonies. But even in Cuba itself, as Fernando Ortiz has emphasised in his work, there were very significant differences in the development of Negro slavery in its earlier and later phases.[3] With the spread of great plantations during the

nineteenth century, Cuban slavery began to exhibit many of the characteristic rigidities and severities of plantation slavery elsewhere, even though Cuban society was too much influenced by its previous more liberal development to succumb completely to the ethics of the slave plantation.

This suggests that Mr. Klein has interpreted the influence of religion as a "crucial aspect" of his subject without giving enough attention to the evidence which indicates that it was only one influence among many, and, in itself, not so much a cause as an effect of other causes shaping the social development of the colonies that he has studied. As Fénelon's comment hints, the ratios of Negro slaves to whites can be more significant for the analysis of religion and slavery than the ratios of clergy to total population, though the two sets of facts are not unconnected. But Mr. Klein has used his statistics of population almost exclusively for the light they throw on the state of religion, neglecting what they may reveal of the state of society. He has given us, therefore, no comparative analysis of the racial distribution of slave and free population in Cuba and Virginia. Yet it is very possible that if he had done so we should find that the two colonies were "representative" not of Catholic and Anglican societies but of societies with differing proportions of Negro and white populations, reflecting differing degrees of dependence on the slave plantation as a way of life.

In the case of Virginia, Mr. Klein mentions in passing that Tidewater contained "great plantation areas" (p. 163). The frontier may have followed somewhat different patterns of settlement, and this difference may be significant in explaining an element of Negro participation in the "Great Awakening" (*ibid.*). But a society dominated by

---

[1] L. Peytraud, *L'Esclavage aux Antilles Françaises avant 1789* (Paris, 1897), pp. 193–94.

[2] The present writer has already pointed to the significance of these contrasts and resemblances in two earlier articles: E. V. Goveia, "Influence of Religion in the West Indies" in *History of Religion in the New World* (Washington, D.C., 1958), pp. 174–80, and "The West Indian Slave Laws of the Eighteenth Century," in *Revista de Ciencias Sociales*, Vol. IV, No. 1 (March 1960), pp. 75–105.

[3] The point is well made in Ortiz' early work on Cuban slavery, *Los Negros Esclavos* (Havana, 1916), and recurs in his later classical study of Cuban economic development, *Cuban Counterpoint: Tobacco and Sugar* (Eng. Ed., New York, 1947).

Tidewater plantations would be, with or without religious differences, a very different society from that of Cuba in the period before the growth of a great plantation system. Even as late as 1827, when this growth was already under way, Cuba had a very atypical racial distribution of population as compared with the older plantation colonies of the British and French West Indies. During earlier centuries, its ethnic composition and social structure were even more different, and it is therefore not surprising that Cuban society then showed a degree of tolerance and even liberality towards Negro slaves and free people of color which would have been regarded as suicidal by the ruling groups in any of the plantation colonies.

When the state of society is so fundamentally different, other differences, including differences of religious policy, flow naturally from the basic difference of social circumstances. So there is good reason to question the claim that "the attitudes and actions of the Church" ex-plain the relatively lenient treatment accorded to slaves in Cuba up to the end of the eighteenth century. It can be argued with far more justification that the factors differentiating Cuban slavery from slave systems to be found elsewhere originated in the nature and function of the slave systems themselves. The state of religion did not determine the state of slavery. It was the state of slavery which set limits to what the Catholics, Anglicans, or any of the other varieties of Christians could hope to achieve.

Negro slavery in the New World has been neither uniform nor static. For it was an economic and social institution that changed both in time and in place. Comparative study of its similarities and differences can, indeed, be profitably pursued for a long time to come. But such study will only yield sound results if it starts with a methodology which adequately defines whether or not the slave systems to be compared are of the same kind.

SIDNEY W. MINTZ

Labor and Sugar in Puerto Rico
and in Jamaica, 1800–1850

See the headnote on page 27 for bibliographical information on Sidney W. Mintz.

The islands of Puerto Rico and Jamaica, which lie roughly at the same latitude and less than 600 miles apart at their nearest points, share a number of remarkable similarities in general physical environment. Strikingly in contrast to the similarities in topography, climate, flora, and fauna are the differences in the cultures of the two islands. One of the reasons for this cultural disparity has to do not with the cultures of the colonial powers, but with the persistence of a strong peasantry in one island (Jamaica), and a relatively weak peasantry in the other (Puerto Rico). This difference stems in large part from the individual histories of the two islands, histories predominantly determined by the colonial aims and policies of, in one case, Spain and Great

Reprinted, by permission of the Editors, from *Comparative Studies in Society and History*, vol. I, no. 3 (March 1959), pp. 273–280.

Britain; in the other, Spain and the United States. The present paper purports to treat principally one brief period (1800–1850) during which a sharp divergence in the colonial objectives of the respective controlling powers affected the cultures of Jamaica and Puerto Rico accordingly. It was during this half-century that Puerto Rico repeated a historical experience which Jamaica had undergone nearly 150 years earlier: the development of a sugar plantation economy.[1]

History never repeats itself exactly, and every event is, of course, unique; but historical forces surely may move

[1] It need not be stressed that, although Spain had conquered and explored vast New World areas long before England, and had introduced sugar and slavery to the Caribbean, it was England which first developed a Caribbean sugar-and-slave empire. Not for nearly 150 years did the Spaniards repeat the English experiment. Cf. Bourne (1904).

in parallel paths at the same or at different times. The comparisons of such parallels may reveal regularities of potential scientific value. To compare Puerto Rico and Jamaica during the first half of the nineteenth century is to compare two countries which, in their historical trajectories, were passing each other in opposite directions along a single continuum: dedication to the sugar plantation economy. Between 1800 and 1850, Puerto Rico was developing such an economy, while Jamaica was abandoning it.

In colony after colony in the Antilles, the sugar plantation economy had flourished wildly, had overextended itself, overborrowed, produced less and less, and had finally died. One of the basic factors responsible for its denouement was the gutting of the land; in every case, the colony which replaced its failing predecessor was land-rich at the start, land-poor at the time of its eclipse. "Neither capital nor abundance of labor," wrote Merivale in 1839, "have ever been found to compete, in tropical cultivation, with the advantage of a new and fertile soil."[2] And Williams writes:

From Virginia and Maryland to Carolina, Georgia, Texas, and the Middle West; from Barbados to Jamaica to Saint Domingue and then to Cuba; the logic was inexorable and the same. It was a relay race; the first to start passed the baton, unwillingly we may be sure, to another, and then limped sadly behind.[3]

Jamaica and Puerto Rico were both runners in this race; the effects of the races they ran live on in the contemporary societies and economies of the two islands.

Until 1655, both islands were Spanish possessions. Jamaica fell to Britain in that year, but Puerto Rico remained Spanish until the close of the nineteenth century. Before 1655, the development of both colonies had been minimal, for after an initial period in the Antilles, Spain had concentrated her energies on the mainland. Even after Jamaica became British, it was not until the rise of the sugar industry there that the two islands began to diverge rapidly in their economic development, in the character of their settlements, and in their importance on the colonial scene. Jamaica, although colonized by the Spaniards in 1509,[4] and reputedly making sugar in 1527,[5] never became a "sugar colony" under Spain. In the year of her conquest by the British, she had but three sugar works in operation.[6] As late as 1673, Sir Thomas Lynch could write that, "If Jamaica have easy government, be defended from enemies, and be supplied with negroes and servants, and have no privateering, in six years it may produce as much sugar as Barbados."[7] In 1673, Jamaica's 57 sugar works were producing 670 tons; in the period 1671–79, the average yearly production had risen to 986 tons.[8] It was not until well into the eighteenth century, however, that Jamaica's fertile lands brought her ahead of all of her Empire competitors. Burn states:

The increase in the total population from some 87,100 in 1722 to nearly 236,000 in 1787 corresponded to the rise of Jamaica to the unchallenged leadership in sugar production among the British West Indian colonies, but its production was sluggish until it was stimulated by the increase in sugar prices in the later thirties of the eighteenth century. Then its vast reserves of virgin land told heavily in its favor.[9]

---

[2] Cited in Burn (1951), p. 34.
[3] Williams (1944), p. 8.
[4] Deerr (1949), Vol. I, p. 174.
[5] Ibid.
[6] Ibid.
[7] Cited in Burn (1951), p. 64.
[8] Deerr (1949), loc cit.
[9] Burn (1951), p. 65.

Jamaica enjoyed its golden age between the 1730's and the start of the nineteenth century. The relatively brief but rapid rise of its sugar-and-slave society has been described in rich detail by such writers as Mathieson,[10] Ragatz,[11] and Williams.[12] During the later decades of the eighteenth century, the "West Indians" in Parliament wielded power out of all proportion to their numbers;[13] Jamaica was worth more to Britain at the time than were the thirteen colonies.[14] Yet Jamaica's great importance within the Empire rested on rigid mercantilist foundations: the assurance that, whatever the consequences, the sugar market at home would be protected by the mother country from foreign competitors. At the same time, of course, Jamaica was not free to choose or to widen the markets for her sugar. The planter regime had hardly reached a pinnacle of power and wealth, in the later decades of the eighteenth century, when it began to decline. The causes were manifold: the rapid exhaustion of the soil, requiring larger-scale enterprise and heavier capitalization to make the plantation profitable; overspeculation and excessive interest rates, leading to bankruptcy and abandonment; the intensification of competition by other colonial sugar producers; and the growth of a new kind of merchant and manufacturing class in the mother country jealous of the West Indians' power, and unwilling to protect the West India interests at cost to itself.

Many writers have argued that it was Emancipation that spelled the doom of the Jamaican planters. The indications are, however, that their doom was sealed many years before. Pitman reports that in 1775, Jamaica had 775 plantations; out of every hundred, twenty-three had been sold for debt, twelve were in the hands of receivers, and seven had been abandoned.[15] This was several decades before the end of the slave trade and almost half a century before Emancipation. Pitman's figures and the materials assembled by other scholars suggest that, rather than Emancipation, it was ruined land and lack of access to capital, as well as the growth of new economic forces in the metropolis, which undermined the plantation economy in Jamaica. And it was these same factors, rather than lack of labor, which ensured the ruin of the economy in the years following Emancipation. Platt has pointed out that the introduction of East Indian contract laborers to Jamaica after Emancipation only partly alleviated the sugar industry's problems.[16] Sewell's comments, made less than fifteen years after Emancipation and based on an on-the-spot tour of Jamaica, are harshly revealing:

> . . . many proprietors are really unable to pay for labor; that, although want of labor, that is, want of such a competition as would prevent labor being tyrannical, is one cause of the island's scanty cultivation, yet another and more serious cause is want of capital. Money is the one essential thing needed by the Jamaica proprietary. They have no money; they have no credit. The post-obits, drawn in the days of a flourishing plantocracy, have been long overdue, and they exceed in amount by a thousand per cent the actual value of the property owned. Money cannot be raised in Jamaica, and without money, or its equivalent, a country in these days is without labor, life, learning, religion. Everything must be paid for. Potatoes and principles have their market

---

[10] Mathieson (1926).
[11] Ragatz (1928).
[12] Williams (1944).
[13] *Ibid.*, pp. 92–97, 108–125.
[14] Williams (1951).

[15] Cited in Williams (1944), p. 123.
[16] Platt *et al.* (1941).

value. When the millennium comes, we may hope to get things for love.[17]

The picture is almost bewildering in the swiftness with which changes occurred. Jamaica, conquered by Britain in 1655, was turned into a sugar-and-slave economy beginning in the 1670's; it climbed to a position of unparalleled power by 1775, but began to fade within decades. By the time the end of the slave trade had been decreed for the British colonies, the end of the sugar economy was already in sight—although no one would admit it. Emancipation in 1838 did little more than confirm and reinforce the ruin of the planter class.[18]

The picture of Puerto Rico from the period 1655–1838 was dramatically different from that of Jamaica. Puerto Rico remained economically undeveloped in every way until as late as the start of the nineteenth century. In 1833, Colonel Flinter could write:

Notwithstanding all the advantages of soil and situation, which nature had so lavishly bestowed on the island of Puerto Rico, it was considered, for the space of three centuries, only as a place of banishment for the malefactors of the mother country. Agriculture had scarcely emerged from its primitive state of simplicity. The inhabitants led a pastoral life, sowing only provisions barely necessrry for their support. . . . It can scarcely be said that, until these last twenty years, the fertile fields of Puerto Rico had felt the vivifying hand of cultivation.[19]

But during the span of three hundred years through which Puerto Rico had been lying undeveloped, its society had taken on a characteristic form. A substantial population had accumulated, a population which supported itself principally by squatter farming for subsistence. This population, composed of deserters from the military services, survivors of shipwrecks, colonists en route to the mainland but prevented by law or lack of opportunity from going on, the Spanish officialdom, etc., was mainly of European origin and was almost entirely free. In 1776, there were 70,260 persons in Puerto Rico, of whom only 6,487 were slaves.[20] By the start of the nineteenth century, the total population had grown considerably, but the slave population was less than 7.5 per cent of the total—13,333 out of 174,192.[21] In addition to its slave population, the island had a very large number of free men of color. Puerto Rico at the beginning of the nineteenth century was unusual in the West Indies in these regards—an island almost entirely devoted to peasant agriculture; a population which was substantially of European rather than African provenience, with a large group of free men of color; and a social system which did not rest on slavery and to which slavery was not of great economic importance. Needless to add, in all of these regards, Puerto Rico was the very opposite of Jamaica.

In 1815, Spain granted to Puerto Rico certain economic advantages which transformed the island. Spain's island possessions had been ignored almost entirely in the preceding centuries because of the vastly greater importance of the mainland colonies. But revolution on the mainland had caused the empire to shrink and the Crown, consequently, to value the Spanish Antilles more highly than before. The *Cédula de Gracias*, now famous as a turning-point in Puerto Rican history, was expressly designed to encourage the economic development of the Spanish islands. It energetically encouraged the expansion

---

[17] Sewell (1861), p. 195.
[18] Cf. Curtin (1955).
[19] Flinter (1834), pp. 1–2.

[20] Deerr (1949), Vol. II, p. 281.
[21] *Ibid.*

of the sugar industry by lowering duties and tariffs, granting new lands to sugar entrepreneurs, and otherwise favoring and facilitating sugar production.[22] The results were all that the Crown might have hoped for. Flinter was able to claim that the rich Puerto Rican soil was producing more sugar per acre than any British island,[23] and in 1833 he wrote that ". . . the number of sugar estates established within the last twenty years exceeds 200."[24] By the 1830's, there was ample evidence that Puerto Rico had embarked on her sugar-and-slave career. She would never approach the peaks achieved by Jamaica; correspondingly, however, her decline would prove less catastrophic.

As many writers have observed, Puerto Rico's economic development during the early decades of the nineteenth century was accomplished largely without the vast influx of slaves which had earlier marked a similar development in the British islands. Turnbull points out that in Jamaica, before Emancipation, the slaves formed about 90 per cent of the total island population, while in Puerto Rico in the nineteenth century the comparable figure only rarely rose slightly above 10 per cent of the total.[25] The lack of sufficient slaves meant that some other source of labor supply had to be found. It was, in the form of the coercion of free but landless citizens to work on the plantations.[26] A whole series of laws was passed during the period 1815–50 to exact more labor from landless freemen. Puerto Rico in this period presented the

curious picture of a Caribbean colony where slaves were treated little worse than landless freemen.[27] The laws of 1824, 1837, and 1849, which tied the free but landless laborer of whatever physical type ever more tightly to the plantations, were paralleled by laws directed specifically against people of color, free or slave. General Prim's infamous "Código Negro" of 1843 empowered slave-owners to punish their slaves without recourse to civil authorities and, for certain offenses such as bearing arms, made colored freemen and slaves alike subject to severe penalties.[28] It is interesting that the expansion of the economy and the consequent increased need for labor should produce one set of laws which divided the free population into those who owned land and those who did not, in order to extract labor from the landless, and another set of laws which treated slave and landless freeman alike and which were intended to prevent any weakening of the institution of slavery, from within or from without.

These developments—the increase in the number of slaves, the decline of the civil liberties of the landless, and the repressive measures against all people of color—temporarily contributed to the improvement of the *economic* situation of the country as a whole: that is to say, the amount of land in cultivation increased and the production of sugar and other crops rose; the population nearly doubled in twenty years.

Events were proceeding quite differently in Jamaica. Final emancipation in 1838 was followed by a continuing

---

[22] Cf. *Boletín Histórico de Puerto Rico*, XIV (1927), 3–24; López Dominguez (1927), p. 103; Mintz (1953), pp. 224–51.

[23] Flinter (1834), pp. 180–81.

[24] *Ibid.*, p. 175.

[25] Turnbull (1840), p. 555.

[26] Mintz (1951), pp. 134–41.

[27] The case is reminiscent of Barbados, early in its development, when indentured servants were used to produce sugar before the slave population had grown. Cf. Williams (1944), pp. 23–24.

[28] Díaz Soler (1953). Cf. also Rosario and Carrión (1939).

decline in the apparent material wealth of the island, and the continued abandonment of more and more sugar plantations, once flourishing and now ruined. The new freedmen, no longer welcome on the estates and anxious to acquire land for themselves, engaged in a mass exodus away from the large properties and sought every means for becoming small proprietors. In this process of establishing the ex-slaves as an independent peasantry, the missionary churches played a very significant role.[29] By 1844, a mere six years after Emancipation, 19,000 families had been settled on their own land in 116 communities through the agency of the missionary societies.[30] In addition to the support rendered by the missionary societies, ex-slaves were able to acquire funds by restricting their own consumption, by part-time wage labor, and through marketing.[31] No longer faced with the problem of saving funds to purchase freedom, many were able to accumulate cash for the purchase of land. Motivation to get away from the estates and all they represented must have been very high among the newly freed: in 1859, Sewell estimated that there were already approximately 50,000 colored freeholders in Jamaica.[32]

The period following Emancipation in Jamaica, then, was a period of recovery from the whole epoch of slavery, marked by the growth of an independent, largely self-sufficient peasant population. Economically, the island was now of much less importance to the metropolis; but from the point of view of the masses of the Jamaican people, life unquestionably looked much better than before. The corresponding period in Puerto Rico was one of vast economic expansion and of unquestionable prosperity for insular and metropolitan entrepreneurs. Yet the working population of Puerto Rico had no cause to rejoice. Squatter farmers were cleared from Crown and private land, and marshalled on the plantations to work in a state approximating slavery. Slaves and landless freemen alike could not leave the plantation without permission. The number of slaves increased, and colored freemen were warned to show no resistance to the stiffened control of the enslaved population. No wonder that Merivale, in comparing Puerto Rico and Jamaica in 1839, declared:

The tropical colonies of Spain were commonwealths in an epoch when those of most other nations were mere factories; they are now rapidly acquiring the degrading characteristics of factories, while ours, we may hope, are advancing toward the dignity of commonwealths.[33]

The decline of Puerto Rico's sugar industry in the late nineteenth century was not so stunning as Jamaica's had been some decades earlier. The Puerto Rican industry was still expanding after mid-century, but losing ground in the total world picture. By the last quarter of the nineteenth century, coffee had begun to eclipse sugar, and it was only the United States Occupation in 1899 which restored sugar to first place, where it has remained ever since.[34] The decline of the sugar industry in Jamaica provided the opportunity for the formation of a peasantry which is still fundamental in the island's economy and society. In the case of Puerto Rico, the demand for plantation labor in the early nineteenth century destroyed much of the peasant population

---

[29] Cf. Paget (n.d.), pp. 7–19. Cf. also Mintz (1958).

[30] Paget (n.d.).

[31] Hall (1954), pp. 149–69.

[32] Sewell (1861), p. 247. Cf. also Lopez (1948), pp. 298–301.

[33] Merivale (1928), p. 41.

[34] Crist (1948), pp. 183–84.

which previously had developed there, and the perpetuation of large-scale mechanized agricultural production by the United States, among other things, has prevented the regrowth of a peasantry of any real importance. According to the 1940 Census, there were 54,200 farmers, or an equivalent number of families, owning or renting their land in Puerto Rico, out of an agricultural labor force of 229,000.[35] In Jamaica (1943 census), out of an agricultural labor force of almost the same absolute size (221,376), 49,201 farmers were operating holdings of ten acres or less; an additional 16,972 operators had larger holdings; and a very significant proportion of the agricultural labor force listed as wage earners was simultaneously engaged in cultivating owned land in plots of less than one acre, or cultivating rented land.[36] Although the absolute numbers of laborers engaged in agriculture were approximately the same in both Puerto Rico and Jamaica for the specified years, it is important to note that the population of Puerto Rico at the time (1940) was 1,869,255; the population of Jamaica in 1943 was 1,237,063, or 632,000 less than the figure for Puerto Rico three years earlier. Other comparative data could be presented to make the picture yet sharper—but it is sharp enough. Jamaica is still substantially a country of the peasantry; Puerto Rico is not.

The present paper does not contend that the situation of the peasantries of Puerto Rico and Jamaica can be understood merely by reference to a single determining factor—the development of the sugar industry. The aim is rather to suggest that similar trends were at work in the two situations (but at dif-

ferent historical periods), resulting in certain significant similarities of process. The growth of the plantation economy in the early decades of British control over Jamaica was marked by the concomitant growth of a legally degraded society. Puerto Rico in the same period remained a yeoman colony with an internal frontier. The decline of the plantation economy in Jamaica was followed by the growth of an independent peasantry, reconstituted out of the slave population of the previous period. In Puerto Rico, the rise of the plantation system degraded slave and freeman alike, in the very years that the Jamaican people were getting their first taste of freedom. A comparison of these two cases offers compelling evidence of the relationship between economic forces and social relations. It suggests a qualification as well of the oft-cited assertion that ideological factors always ensured a humane quality to servitude in the Spanish colonies, setting them apart from their British, Dutch, and French neighbors.[37] In Puerto Rico (and much more dramatically, in Cuba), the intensification of the plantation system and the increasing centrality of that system in the nineteenth century almost made a myth of Spain's reputation for the humane treatment of the slaves. By the time the *hacendados* of Puerto Rico and Cuba were learning to apply the whip with enthusiasm, the populations of the British, Dutch, and French colonies were already free. The way men were treated in these colonial societies, physically and politically, would appear to have been determined much more by the level of economic development, than by the ideologies, of the different metropolitan powers.

---

[35] H. Perloff (1950), pp. 34–35.
[36] G. Cumper (n.d.).

[37] See, for instance, Tannenbaum (1947).

BIBLIOGRAPHY

Boletín Histórico de Puerto Rico (San Juan).

Bourne, E. G., *Spain in America, 1450–1580* (New York and London, 1904).

Burn, W. L., *The British West Indies* (London, 1951).

Crist, R., "Sugar Cane and Coffee in Puerto Rico," *American Journal of Economics and Sociology*, VII, No. 2 (January, 1948).

Cumper, G., *Social Structure of Jamaica* (Mona, Jamaica: *University College of the West Indies, Department of Extra-Mural Studies, Caribbean Affairs Pamphlets*, No. 1 n.d.).

Curtin, P., *Two Jamaicas* (Cambridge, Mass., 1955).

Deerr, N., *The History of Sugar* (London, 1949).

Díaz Soler, L., *História de la Esclavitud Negra en Puerto Rico* (Madrid, 1953).

Flinter, G., *An Account of the Present State of Puerto Rico* (London, 1834).

Hall, D., "The Social and Economic Background to Sugar in Slave Days," *Caribbean Historical Review*, III-IV (December, 1954).

Lopez, A., "Land and Labour to 1900," *Jamaican Historical Review*, I, No. 3 (December, 1948).

López Domínguez, F. A., "Origen y desarrollo de la industria azucarera de Puerto Rico," *Revista de Agricultura de Puerto Rico*, XIX, No. 3 (1927).

Mathieson, W. L., *British Slavery and its Abolition* (London, 1926).

Merivale, H., *Lectures on Colonization and Colonies* (London, 1928).

Mintz, S., "The Role of Forced Labour in Nineteenth Century Puerto Rico," *Caribbean Historical Review*, II (1951).

————, "The Culture History of a Puerto-Rican Sugar Cane Plantation, 1876–1949,"*Hispanic American Historical Review*, XXXIII, No. 2 (May 1953).

————, "The Jamaican Internal Marketing Pattern," *Social and Economic Studies*, IV, No. 1 (March, 1955).

————, "The Historical Sociology of the Jamaican Church-Founded Free Village System," *De West-Indische Gids*, XXXVIII, Nos. 1–2 (September, 1958).

Paget, H., "The Free Village System in Jamaica," *Caribbean Quarterly*, I, No. 4 (n.d.).

Perloff, H., *Puerto Rico's Economic Future* (Chicago, 1950).

Platt, R. R., et al., *The European Possessions in the Caribbean Area* (New York: *American Geographical Society, Map of Hispanic America Publication*, No. 4, 1941).

Ragatz, L. J., *The Fall of the Planter Class in the British Caribbean, 1763–1833* (New York, 1928).

Rosario, J., and J. Carrión, *El Negro* (*Boletín de la Universidad de Puerto Rico*, Serie X, No. 2, December, 1939).

Sewell, W. G., *The Ordeal of Free Labor in the British West Indies* (New York, 1861).

Tannenbaum, F., *Slave and Citizen* (New York, 1947).

Turnbull, D., *Travels in the West: Cuba; with Notices of Porto Rico and the Slave Trade* (London, 1840).

Williams, E., *Capitalism and Slavery* (Chapel Hill, N.C., 1944).

————, "The Caribbean in World History, 1492–1940" (A lecture delivered December 12, 1951, as part of the celebrations of the First Centenary of the Trinidad Public Library).

RACE

HARRY HOETINK

Race Relations in
Curaçao and Surinam

*H. Hoetink is Director of the Center for Latin American Research and Documentation at the
University of Amsterdam. He has written extensively on the Dutch colonies in the New
World. He is the author of* The Two Variants in Caribbean Race Relations
*(English edition, 1967), and of a number of other books and articles in Dutch. The
following article was originally presented at the University of Puerto Rico on April 21,
1960 under the auspices of the Institute of Caribbean Studies, and was subsequently
published in the* Revista de Ciencias Sociales. *It has been translated to English for
this collection by Victoria Ortiz, with the assistance of Laura Foner and Stephen Wangh.*

The Caribbean region, including the southern United States and the northern coast of Brazil, forms a sociological unit by virtue of its common socioeconomic history and racial composition. Because of this we also find similarities in the social institutions, in the development of social and economic structures, and in the cultural characteristics of the region. This culture is derived in part from the black population and in part from the impact that

Reprinted from Harry Hoetink, "Diferencias en Relaciones Raciales entre Curazao y Surinam," *Revista de Ciencias Sociales*, V, no. 4 (December, 1961), pp. 499–514, by permission of the author and the *Revista de Ciencias Sociales*.

the black culture had on the culture of the dominant whites.

Nevertheless, there are regional variations even within the Caribbean, and there are variations in content and function within the specified areas of similarity. For example, slavery, which existed as a legal institution throughout the Caribbean, had strong sociological variations in different areas.

Social scientist Eric Williams insists on explaining these variations (such as the gradations between mildness and cruelty in the master-slave relationship) solely by differences in economic factors. This one-sided approach has not proved very successful. Not only is a narrowly deterministic approach in itself unacceptable but it fails to account for the variations in race relations found in Brazil and the southern United States. These variations have fascinated a great number of sociologists and historians of the Caribbean, who have characterized race relations in the former as "mild" and the latter as "harsh".

Those who have been trying to explain this difference have until recently preferred to seek their explanation in the differing cultural heritages brought by the whites to the New World. For example, the European cultural heritage of the Brazilian colonists was characterized by Thomist-Catholic and precapitalist traits, Arab influences, and a long history of slavery. The North Americans, on the other hand, came from a Puritan area, where commercial capitalism flourished. Lacking a tradition of slavery, they developed one themselves based on both their economic practices and their Calvinist religion (although we need not agree with the theory of Max Weber that the two were coincidental).

The difference between race relations in Brazil and the southern United States is thus shown to be only part of a larger comparative framework: the differences between a Spanish-Portuguese "variant" in the Caribbean and a Northern and Western European "variant." (For the purpose of this discussion, we will not deal with the French "variant.") This method of examining the historico-cultural differences between the colonizers from Spain and Portugal and those from Western and Northern Europe seems to be the correct approach to use in clarifying the differences in race relations in the Caribbean, and many of the relevant points of difference between these two groups still remain to be studied.

Nevertheless, this method clearly leads to an oversimplified division of the Caribbean region and a danger of schematization and polarization: of unconsciously associating the Spanish-Portuguese Caribbean with the adjective "mild" and the North-Western European Caribbean with the adjectives "harsh" or "cruel". It is precisely to make evident this danger that we will discuss the race relations which developed in two areas, both belonging to the Western and Northern European Caribbean and both colonized by the same European nation. These are Surinam and Curaçao. The comparison we will make between these two areas will also give us the opportunity to further explain what is meant by the term "race relations."

Both territories became Dutch possessions at a time when the maritime and colonial expansion of Holland was at its height. Curaçao was won from the Spanish in 1634 during the last phase of the 80 Years War, which in 1648 brought about the formal independence of the United Provinces. Surinam was won from the British in 1667 in the second British naval war; in the Treaty of Breda of that year, the British recognized Surinam as a Dutch possession in exchange for the then much less valuable Dutch commercial colony on the island of Manhattan, New Amsterdam.

Although under the sovereignty of the Dutch Estates General, Surinam and Curaçao were both governed, until the end of the 18th century, by semi-official mercantile companies. Among those who owned shares in the company which governed Curaçao were the West India Company, the city of Amsterdam and, until 1770, the noble family van Aerssen van Sommelsdijk.

These companies appointed directors or governors who were to carry out the companies' orders. But this absentee control by the companies was frequently difficult to maintain—and not only because of deficient communications. It is important for us to be aware of this last point for, in the case of company plantations, we know that extensive instructions were sent to the colonies from Holland concerning the material and religious care of the slaves. But the local directors, claiming "inside information" and greater knowledge of the local situation, very often largely disregarded the instructions and chose to apply standards other than those recommended by authorities in the mother country. In Surinam and Curaçao, just as in other colonies, the dominant European groups had developed a world-view which, although certainly a seventeenth-century vision, differed in many respects from the vision of the dominant groups in the mother country.

The existence of slaves and company plantations in Curaçao and Surinam did not mean that the settlement of free whites was hindered. On the contrary, emigration was stimulated, soon bringing to these colonies (in Curaçao mainly after 1700, in Surinam before) numerous private merchants and planters. These free colonists did not come only from what today is Holland. Among them were Scandinavians, Scottish, British, and Germans, who, after serving in the colonial garrisons, settled permanently in the colony. (Among the Germans, we should especially mention the Moravian Brothers of Hernhutt, who, after 1735, dedicated themselves to converting the slaves and the freedmen.)

In both colonies there were also a considerable number of settlers of French origin, principally Huguenots, who, after the Revocation of the Edict of Nantes in 1685, fled to Holland and from there left for the West Indies. At the end of the seventeenth century the French, along with the Jews, formed the majority of the white population of Surinam. The Jewish settlers were Sephardic Jews of Hispano-Portuguese origin. Most of them had left Holland for Brazil, where they had devoted themselves to commerce and agriculture. After the last Dutch possession in Brazil, Pernambuco, fell to the Portuguese in 1654, they went to Surinam and Curaçao. In both colonies they constituted a large part of the population. Until the nineteenth century they were rarely less than a third of the white population. At times, in Surinam, they made up one half of the white population.

While the other European sectors of the population in the colonies were blending into one white group, the Sephardim continued to exist as a group apart. Until the late 1870's in Curaçao, they maintained the use of Portuguese in their religious services, and many of them spoke Spanish at home. Compared to the groups from Western and Northern Europe who were strongly influenced by Holland, the Jews in Curaçao and Surinam in many senses represented the Latin language and customs. We shall see how this was also manifested in their relations with the black population.

Neither in Curaçao nor in Surinam did the indigenous population, the Indians, play an important role in the social and economic development of the country after the Dutch conquest. In Curaçao the majority of the Indian population went with the Spanish soldiers to Venezuela; in Surinam a few tribes remained in the regions outside of the colonized coastal zone. Here they rapidly degenerated and became a miniscule minority compared to the imported slaves.

Let us now turn to the slaves of

Curaçao and Surinam and examine their parallel characteristics. It does not seem as if the slaves of Surinam and Curaçao came from widely separate regions of Africa; on the contrary, since the West Indian Company monopolized the slave trade to both colonies, the majority of the slaves came from the Company's establishments on the West African coast. These establishments were spread between Cabo Verde and Angola, but there were many particularly in what is today Ghana, in such places as Accra and San Jorge del Mina. The slaves came from the Congo region and from such peoples of the Guinea coast as the Dahomey, Ashanti, Yoruba and Ibo. Unfortunately, little is known about how many came from each of these.

Up to this point I have attempted to show the many parallels that are found in these two Dutch regions in the forms of government and the compositions of the populations. Now, I must point out that the relations between masters and slaves in the two regions were of a markedly different nature.

In Curaçao these were characterized as "mild," and in Surinam as "harsh," judged, naturally, by the norms of observers of the period and by those of the Caribbean. This was attested to by all the observers who compared Surinam with the surrounding colonies and all those who compared Surinam with Curaçao. In fact, because of their mild treatment the slaves of Curaçao had a bad reputation on the foreign market and were considered ill-bred. Their conduct showed an absence of severe discipline. They were not frequently punished and when they were punished, the punishments used were not as cruel as those in Surinam. Certain instruments of torture used in Surinam did not even exist in Curaçao. Finally, Curaçao always had a natural

increase of its slave population, while in Surinam the death rate was as high as the birth rate, a phenomenon due only in part to the less healthy climate there.

While van Lier goes as far as to delineate in psycho-pathological terms the mental state of masters and slaves in Surinam (he speaks of sadism and masochism as psychic features acquired in the colonial ambiance), no such explanation is necessary. For Curaçao it is enough to note that the social roles of master and slaves produced an institutionalized and mutually complementary pattern of behavior for both master and slaves.

As we have seen, the dominant white groups had more or less similar social and cultural European origins and we have no evidence to suppose that the slaves had important differences in their composition. Therefore, how do we explain these surprising differences in the conditions of the slaves of Surinam and Curaçao? We must look at the economic, geographic and demographic differences between Surinam and Curaçao and the differences in the numerical proportions of these groups in Curaçao and Surinam.

The first important difference is that Curaçao had no real plantations, no real latifundios producing for the world market. The initial efforts of the Company to cultivate cotton, sugar, and tobacco were confronted with the problem of the dry climate. Curaçao very soon developed into a mercantile colony, with heavy trade in slaves, in contraband, and in arms for the surrounding Caribbean region. What were (and are) called "plantations" were, in Curaçao, no more than large expanses of arid terrain, where a little sorghum was grown for the livestock and a piece of irrigated land on which some vegetables and fruit were grown for local and city consumption. Most of the Curaçao plantation owners were individuals who had earned their money in commerce; retired officials, leading a sober and rustic life; people who used their plantations as a country home while in the city they worked as government employees or merchants; or people who dealt in contraband from their plantations on the coast. If any of these owners had had to depend exclusively on their plantations for their incomes, they would have faced bankruptcy in a few years. More than a possession of economic value, in Curaçao a "plantation" was a status symbol.

This explains why the great majority of the slave-owners of Curaçao owned only a few slaves. Of 376 owners in 1735, only 38 owned more than 10 slaves. The largest slave-owner at that time had 120 slaves. And in 1863, the year of abolition, when 6 to 7 thousand slaves were emancipated, the great majority of owners still owned fewer than 5 slaves. The "average" slave-owner held a few slaves as coachmen, house servants, or gardeners. Only on the so-called plantations (especially in the western part of the island) were there slave-holdings of more than 50 slaves, and only rarely more than 100. In general the relation of the master to his slaves in Curaçao was one of individual contact; there was no fear on the part of the owners, and, therefore, no insecurity or sadism.

The situation was totally different in Surinam. There were vast sugar, coffee, cotton, and lumber plantations. There were large concentrations of hundreds of slaves; the "fear of the slave masses" was a phrase which was frequently repeated in the official documents. At no time did the number of whites exceed 7% of the number of slaves; at the end of the eighteenth century, in the plantation region outside the city, there was one white for

every 65 blacks, despite the repeated instructions from the authorities that there should be at least one overseer for every 25 slaves. At the end of the eighteenth century in Surinam there were about 3 thousand whites and about 5 thousand slaves. In Curaçao the number of whites was more or less the same, but there were only one-tenth as many slaves.

These statistics alone help to explain the more severe treatment of the slaves in Surinam. Naturally, there were gradations of treatment according to the "class" of slave; the domestics and the artisans led more bearable lives than the field hands. Of these latter, those living in the worst conditions in Surinam were those working on the sugar plantations (and these were in the majority), while those on the lumber plantations enjoyed an exceptional degree of independence.

The more severe, and crueler treatment of slaves in Surinam is also explained by other phenomena.

Curaçao is a small island (some 400 square kilometers) and none of the plantations there were as isolated as some of the Surinam plantations, which were several days on foot or by boat from the capital. This meant that the force of public opinion and of justice (which despite everything militated against excesses beyond the norms of the period) was felt throughout Curaçao and not in Surinam.

Furthermore, it can be assumed that the relatively low level of prosperity of the Curaçao planters stopped them from seriously mistreating their slaves.

Related to this there is another point which deserves our attention. As we have seen, Curaçao is primarily a commercial island. Doubtless, at times of economic depression many merchants left the island, while in periods of prosperity, immigration increased.

But those who owned the greatest numbers of slaves were frequently persons who belonged to the families of officials living permanently on the island, or people who, after adventurous lives as soldiers or navigators, had arrived on the island with the intention of remaining there. Thus, among the group of Curaçao planters we do not find a great desire to acquire wealth rapidly in order to return to the mother country; the *animus revertendi* which troubled Mauricius, the director of Surinam, was not found to such an extent in Curaçao.

From about 1775 on, the Jews formed the only group of white "planters" in Surinam whose stay in that country was not temporary. From about that time, the majority of the white, non-Jewish "planter" families left, beginning the period of absenteeism.

The cause of this change was the great crisis of the Amsterdam Stock Market in 1773, when the credits of the private planters were annulled and their plantations bought by companies which sent administrators and directors to Surinam to exploit them. From the available data we can estimate that, after this crisis, between 70 and 80 percent of the plantations of Surinam belonged to absentee owners living abroad.

Even without considering the low social level from which these new administrators were recruited (especially in the beginning), it is easy to suppose that, not having roots in the country and being above all eager to make a fortune, they had less compassion for the lot of the slaves and were also less susceptible to social control than the "planters" of Curaçao, who had been living on the island from generation to generation. Furthermore, the administrators of Surinam were frequently forced to satisfy the absurdly high plantation output demands of their absentee bosses.

The improvements in the conditions of the slaves in Surinam which we observe after 1800 (for example, greater help from the missionaries) can be explained by the greater interest in the well-being of the slaves after 1808 when the open slave trade was abolished.

Up until this point I have attempted to explain the reasons for the differences in the relations between masters and slaves in the two Dutch regions of Curaçao and Surinam. I noted the difference in the economy of the two areas, the geography, the type of social control and the attitude of a large part of the white "planters" toward the country in which they were living. After what has previously been said, it is curious to note that it was Curaçao and not Surinam which, in 1795, was the scene of a large slave revolt.

In Surinam the uprisings were limited to single plantations, because, according to van Lier, the discontented slaves (sometimes after killing the white master) could retreat to the forest or join earlier runaways who lived in the interior and whose lives are well-known from Herskovits' book [*Rebel Destiny*]. This is surely an important reason. Furthermore there is the possibility that the geographic isolation of many of the plantations in Surinam would have made a general uprising difficult.

As far as Curaçao is concerned, the uprising took place in the plantations in the western part of the island, and was caused by the masters having violated the previously agreed-upon working conditions (rest on Sundays, distribution of clothing and rations, etc.). Nevertheless, it is certain that the slaves were also under the influence of blacks from the French islands and that it was the rebellion in Haiti which inspired the slaves of Curaçao.

Turning to the freedmen (black and mulatto), it would seem at first sight that their respective situations in Curaçao and Surinam flowed directly from the differences we outlined between these two regions. In Curaçao the number of freedmen was always considerable. We have already seen how in this mercantile colony the slaves of the majority of the owners were used as domestic personnel, gardeners and coachmen, thus being, to a certain degree, luxury items. For this reason, the many periods of economic depression which Curaçao underwent always brought with them periods of manumission for the slaves. Their owners simply did not wish to continue supporting them.

Naturally, this economic factor also had its impact in Surinam, but the greater economic importance of the slaves there diminished this impact. Only during the crisis of 1773 do we see in Surinam a considerable increase in the number of freedmen. This number increased, from 1787 to 1812, in other words in 25 years, from 650 to more than 3000, despite the obstacles to freedom erected by the government there as well as in Curaçao.

In 1830 there were in Surinam more than 5 thousand freedmen and about 2 thousand whites; at that time in Curaçao this proportion was the same: more than 6500 freedmen and 2600 whites. Let us remember, however, that in that year the number of freedmen in Surinam was more or less 10% of the slaves, while in Curoçao it was almost 110%.

That the economic factors in Curaçao played a more important role in emancipation results also from the fact that there the freed blacks formed a majority compared to the freed

mulattoes; in Surinam the opposite was true. From this we may deduce, among other things, that in Surinam the personal preference for a mulatto concubine or servant was frequently the motive for her emancipation, while the master in Curaçao felt obligated to free his black slaves before the others.

What we cannot completely deduce from this data, and what seems at first a paradox, is the fact that, in the course of the nineteenth century, there developed in Surinam a strong mulatto middle class. This did not happen in Curaçao. This fact is of supreme importance, for it offers us the principal key to understanding the present social situation in the two regions.

Let us look first at Curaçao. The majority of the freedmen always found themselves in a miserable economic situation, often even worse than that of slaves. Some of them worked in the city as artisans or small shop-keepers, and only very few achieved some prosperity. The very small group of outstanding mulattoes were descended principally from the favorite illegitimate sons of the whites. If the father belonged to the group of white officials and planters, he could offer to his natural son a piece of arid land or a job in the government. If the father were a rich Jewish merchant, the son could find a position in the business. But the monopoly of business was predominantly in the hands of the Jews, and the monopoly of important government jobs remained in the hands of the white Protestants. It was only in the third decade of this century that for the first time the Courts named a jurist who was considered mulatto.

Let us compare this with Surinam where, in the first half of the last century, we find mulattoes in important posts—as doctors, lawyers, judges or plantation directors and administrators.

It is true that the great majority of freedmen in Surinam had a standard of living comparable to that of the freedmen of Curaçao, but despite this we see that, as opposed to Curaçao, a number of them ascended in the last century to form an intellectual and official élite.

If we wish to seek a "primary" economic cause for this phenomenon, we can point out, along with van Lier, the above-mentioned crisis of 1773. Since this crisis led to the departure of almost all the non-Jewish planter families, the exploitation of the plantations remained in the hands of administrators and directors, who were preferably unmarried. Except for the Jews, the white community of Surinam became all male.

As we have seen, this brought about a worsening in the slaves' conditions. But it also led to the growth of a mulatto élite, from the "Surinam marriage." This was a form of common-law marriage between a European and a "native" woman, which we must distinguish from the more prevalent institution of concubinage. For the "Surinam marriage" was possible only with the consent of the girl's mother, and the celebration of these marriages was accompanied by a system of "rite de passage." After 1773, this form of quasi-marriage was extended throughout the colony and was completely accepted, not only by the plantation administrators, but also by the high officials. The sons of such unions received a good education, frequently being sent to Holland for higher studies; these were the children who would later become members of the mulatto intelligentsia.

Naturally, the whites of Curaçao also had concubines. Surinam did not differ from Curaçao in the practice of race mixing, but only in the position of the mulatto mother.

In Curaçao, although there was no serious scarcity of white women, illegitimate children, especially from Jewish families, were still sometimes treated with affection and received economic help; but it was understood that the legitimate sons inherited the businesses of the Jews or the official posts of the Protestants. Even more than the white fathers, the white mothers took care of and defended the social and economic position of their own sons. At the end of the eighteenth century in Surinam, one governor even made plans to support the mulatto group financially and to help them in various ways to reach a dominant position in the country. In Curaçao such plans were unheard-of.

The new mulatto élite in Surinam was culturally strongly influenced by Holland. They began to consider Dutch their mother tongue, instead of Srnang, which was spoken by the blacks and by the lowest group of mulattoes. (Only in recent years, under the influence of a cultural nationalism, can one note among the Surinamese élite a greater tendency to appreciate Srnang.) Many of them were accepted as members of the Lutheran Church and of the Dutch Reformed Church, converting themselves, as it were, into white men and Dutchmen, also in the religious sense. Once again this was in contrast with the blacks and the lower group of mulattoes who continued to belong to the Moravian Brotherhood or later joined the Catholic Church.

This strong assimilation to Dutch culture by the distinguished mulattoes of Surinam brought with it a closeness to the government employees and officials sent by the metropolis. This produced, in the course of the nineteenth century, several "real" marriages.

How different was the situation of the few distinguished mulattoes in Curaçao in the last century!

In the religious sense, they were separated from the Jews and the Protestants by their Catholicism, since the Catholic missionaries were the only ones who, since the early nineteenth century, had devoted themselves to the task of converting them. Only a few of them adopted Dutch (under the influence of Dutch missionaries), which continued to be an exclusive language for a few white Protestant families. Some spoke Spanish, perhaps influenced by the Sephardic Jews, while the great majority spoke Papiamento, which originated as a *lingua franca* and which is still widely used. Until late in the last century there was no solid education for mulattoes in Curaçao.

Thus, the mulattoes of Curaçao, more so than those of Surinam, were separated from the dominant groups by social and cultural barriers. It is not my intention to say that in the last century the mulatto élite in Surinam did not find prejudice among the whites. The Dutch officials, for example, were certainly prejudiced. They were sent by the metropolis to spend not more than 10 years in the colony, and they considered themselves of the social élite. The mulatto government employees and intellectuals found themselves in an ambiguous marginal position with respect to these officials. On the one hand, they felt a sympathy for their norms of conduct and their ideas, but on the other hand, they felt considerable antipathy for the fact that they were considered, because of their physical characteristics, as somewhat inferior.

This same ambivalence toward the Dutch officials is noted in the group of Sephardic Jews who, after the crisis of the end of the eighteenth century, made up the only white Creole group in Surinam.

The crisis had brought about noticeable losses among the Jews, and a great number of them lived from that time on as poor businessmen and dependents. Yet, in the nineteenth century, some Jews once again reached great prosperity.

After 1824, when Jews were allowed to hold public office, they found themselves in a position of confrontation with the metropolitan Dutch, a position similar to that of the mulattoes with the administration of the colony. Despite the fact that this often led to struggles between them (which were always carried out in private), there were, nevertheless, indications that the Jews and the mulattoes frequently felt united by their common Surinamese heritage, and formed a united front against the metropolitan Dutch.

From around the second quarter of the last century the official Surinamese élite was made up of Jews and distinguished mulattoes, with the domination of first one group, then the other. The support which the Jewish group gave to the mulatto group cannot be explained only by the marginal position of both groups. It was not only strategic considerations which produced this collaboration; there were more intimate ties betweeen the two groups. Sometimes a mulatto Jew was assimilated into the Jewish group. And there were deep and affectionate social relations between some Jewish and mulatto families.

This is remarkable if we remember that intimate contact between the Dutch and the mulattoes was limited to contact between Dutch men and mulatto women, and that this contact was, as it were, necessary because of the scarcity of white women. For the Jews there was no such scarcity, for they frequently had their families with them.

In Curaçao even today, although to a lesser degree, there is still easier (though not intimate) social intercourse between the Sephardim and the mulattoes than between the mulattoes and the white Protestants.

Up until now I have attempted to point out some areas of similarity and of difference between the groups which formed the "ancient" colonial communities of Curaçao and Surinam.

Time does not allow me to speak extensively about the interesting changes which have taken place more recently in the two regions. It is enough to say that immigration to Surinam of Chinese, Javanese, and Indian workers, after the abolition of slavery, has produced an even more complex community. Since about 1930, this community has been numerically dominated by Asiatics.

Until now, thanks to an ingenious electoral system, the so-called Creoles have achieved a predominant role in politics. But as in Trinidad, the Indian population is beginning to play an important role, especially in the economic sector, but also in the intellectual professions. Only when the black and mulatto Surinamese begin to view this Indian development as a real threat will we see if the highly glorified mutual tolerance in Surinam is more than a *pax neerlandica* of the old colonial situation.

The colonial status ended for Surinam in 1955 when political autonomy was granted to Surinam and the Dutch Antilles, within the Dutch kingdom.

In Curaçao the great change occurred in 1916 when the Shell Oil Refinery was established there to refine Venezuelan oil. Thousands of foreigners now give the island a cosmopolitan atmosphere, but the old dominant groups have lost little of their influence.

Today's observers are more and more astonished by the great differences in "social character", in psychosocial characteristics, and in the attitude toward the future of their country, between the blacks and the educated mulattoes of Curaçao and Surinam.

The group from Curaçao is described as indifferent, docile, lacking in spiritual vitality and enthusiasm, while that of Surinam is seen as completely the opposite.

Up to a point, the truth of these observations can be explained by the greater economic possibilities which Surinam will offer in the future, compared with the arid Curaçao which is enjoying only a temporary "boom." We should also understand that the progress of the mulatto élite in Surinam in the past century gave the nonwhite population a social perspective which those of Curaçao have not yet achieved. They are, therefore, less frustrated.

Moreover, the influences of Catholicism on the people of Curaçao and of Protestantism on the people of Surinam might help explain the supposed greater individualism of the latter and the greater hierarchical complacency of the former.

In ending my comparison between the nature of race relations between population groups of Curaçao and Surinam, allow me to mention some points which may be useful for the discussion of the Iberian and the North-Western European Caribbean.

1) In Curaçao and Surinam, both belonging to the so-called North-Western European Caribbean, the whites were not all from Western and Northern Europe.

2) The differences in treatment of the slaves in the two regions must be attributed to economic and geographic factors and to psycho-social factors which were a function of the statistical proportions of the population.

3) The development in Surinam of a group of mulatto intellectuals in the nineteenth century cannot be explained by a difference in the attitude toward mulattoes of the Western and Northern Europeans in that country as compared with Curaçao, but precisely by the absence in Surinam of a resident European group organized on a family basis.

4) There are no indications that the slaves were generally treated better by the Sephardic Jews of Curaçao or Surinam than by the other European masters. There *are* indications that the group of mulattoes had better social contacts in both countries with the Sephardim than with the groups of Western and Northern European origins. It would be worthwhile to study to what degree the supposed differences in race relations between the Iberian and the North-Western European "variants" in the Caribbean can be reduced to different attitudes toward the mulattoes rather than toward the slaves (blacks).

5) If we agree that the Sephardim exhibit the characteristics of what we have called the Iberian "variant" in these two Dutch colonies, then we will be able to eliminate as determining factors of this variant those characteristics which the Sephardim do not share with other Iberian peoples.

BIBLIOGRAPHY

Hoetink, "Het patroon der oude Curaçaose samenleving", Assen, 1958.

Morse, "Toward a Theory of Spanish American Government", *Journal of the History of Ideas*, Vol. XV, no. 1, 1954.

Tannenbaum, "Discussion on Williams' Article", in *Caribbean Studies: A Symposium*, Ed., Vera Rubin, 1957.

Van Lier, "Samenleving in een grensgebied," Den Haag, 1949.

Wagley, "Plantation-America: a Culture Sphere", in *Caribbean Studies: A Symposium*, Ed., Vera Rubin, 1957.

Williams, "Race Relations in Caribbean Society", *idem*.

WINTHROP D. JORDAN

American Chiaroscuro:
The Status and Definition of
Mulattoes in the British Colonies

Winthrop D. Jordan is Associate Professor of History at the University of California at Berkeley. He is the author of White Over Black: The Development of American Attitudes Towards the Negro, 1550–1812 *(1968), as well as of a number of important articles.*

The word *mulatto* is not frequently used in the United States. Americans generally reserve it for biological contexts, because for social purposes a mulatto is termed a *Negro*. Americans lump together both socially and legally all persons with perceptible admixture of Negro ancestry, thus making social definition without reference to genetic logic; white blood becomes socially advantageous only in overwhelming proportion. The dynamic underlying the peculiar bifurcation of American

Reprinted from Winthrop D. Jordan, "American Chiaroscuro: The Status and Definition of Mulattoes in the British Colonies," *William and Mary Quarterly*, XIX, No. 2 (April, 1962), 183–200, by permission of the author.

society into only two color groups can perhaps be better understood if some attempt is made to describe its origin, for the content of social definitions may remain long after the impulses to their formation have gone.

After only one generation of European experience in America, colonists faced the problem of dealing with racially mixed offspring, a problem handled rather differently by the several nations involved. It is well known that the Latin countries, especially Portugal and Spain, rapidly developed a social hierarchy structured according to degrees of intermixture of Negro and European blood, complete with a complicated system of terminology to facilitate definition.[1] The English in Maryland, Virginia, and the Carolinas, on the other hand, seem to have created no such system of ranking. To explain this difference merely by comparing the different cultural backgrounds involved is to risk extending generalizations far beyond possible factual support. Study is still needed of the specific factors affecting each nation's colonies, for there is evidence with some nations that the same cultural heritage was spent in different ways by the colonial heirs, depending on varying conditions encountered in the New World. The English, for example, encountered the problem of race mixture in very different contexts in their several colonies; they answered it in one fashion in their West Indian islands and in quite another in their colonies on the continent.

As far as the continental colonies were concerned, the presence of mulattoes received legislative recognition by the latter part of the seventeenth century. The word itself, borrowed from the Spanish, was in English usage from the beginning of the century and was probably first employed in Virginia in 1666. From about that time, laws dealing with Negro slaves began to add "and mulattoes." In all English continental colonies mulattoes were lumped with Negroes in the slave codes and in statutes governing the conduct of free Negroes:[2] the law was clear that

mulattoes and Negroes were not to be distinguished for different treatment—a phenomenon occasionally noted by foreign travelers.[3]

actually created a legally separate class of persons known as "Mulattoes born of white women," and in doing so developed a severe case of legislative stuttering. The difficulty originated in 1664 when the Assembly declared that children were to follow the condition of the father (rather than the mother as in other colonies). It took 35 years to straighten out this matter, but meanwhile some provision had to be made for mulatto children of white mothers, for no one really wanted them to be slaves. The Assembly provided that they should serve until age 31. This group was sometimes treated legally as white and sometimes as Negro, a procedure which seems to have been followed only about through the 1730's. (Virginia in 1691 enacted similar provisions for this class, but apparently abandoned them five years later.) The underlying intention was that mulatto children of white mothers should be free in status, though punished for their illegitimate origin. This was not discrimination between mulattoes and Negroes but between mulattoes of two different kinds of mothers, white and black. The legal confusion and inconsistencies on this matter may be followed in Browne and others, eds., *Archives of Md.*, I, 526–527, 533–534; VII, 176, 177, 203–205; XIII, 290, 292, 304, 306–307, 308, 323, 380, 394, 529, 546–549; XIX, 428; XXII, 551–552; XXVI, 254–261; XXX, 289–290; XXXIII, 111–112; XXXVI, 275–276; XXXVIII, 39; William Kilty, ed., *The Laws of Maryland* (Annapolis, 1799–1800), II, chap. 67, sec. 14. None of the standard secondary sources on the Negro in Maryland offer a satisfactory account of this matter. For Virginia, see William Waller Hening, ed., *The Statutes at Large: Being a Collection of All the Laws of Virginia* ... (New York, Philadelphia, Richmond, 1819–23), II, 170; III, 87, 137–140, 252. A Virginia militia act of 1777 declared that free mulattoes might serve as "drummers, fifers, or pioneers" (Hening, ed., *Statutes of Va.*, V, 268), but this failure to refer to "negroes and mulattoes" was so unusual that one must suspect inadvertent omission. See also a clear case of such omission in Massachusetts: George H. Moore, *Notes on the History of Slavery in Massachusetts* (New York, 1866), 228–237.

[1] See, for example, Irene Diggs, "Color in Colonial Spanish America," *Journal of Negro History*, XXXVIII (1953), 403–427.

[2] These statements are based on an examination of what I believe to be nearly all the colonial and state statutes concerning Negroes and slaves through 1807. For the use of *mulatto* see the *Oxford English Dictionary* and the private petition to the Virginia Assembly in "The Randolph Manuscript," *Virginia Magazine of History and Biography*, XVII (1909), 232. The word was first used in a statute in 1678: William Hand Browne and others, eds., *Archives of Maryland* (Baltimore, 1883—), VII, 76. Maryland

[3] Duc de La Rochefoucault Liancourt, *Travels through the United States of North America* ... (London, 1799), I, 568; Kenneth and Anna M. Roberts, trans., *Moreau de St. Méry's American Journey, 1793–1798* (Garden City, N.Y., 1947), 301-302.

If mulattoes were to be considered Negroes, logic required some definition of mulattoes, some demarcation between them and white men. Law is sometimes less than logical, however, and throughout the colonial period only Virginia and North Carolina grappled with the question raised by continuing intermixture. In 1705 the Virginia legislature defined a mulatto as "the child, grand child, or great grand child of a negro," or, revealingly, merely "the child of an Indian." North Carolina wavered on the matter, but generally pushed the taint of Negro ancestry from one-eighth to one-sixteenth.[4] There is no reason to suppose that these two colonies were atypical, and in all probability something like these rules operated in the other continental colonies. What the matter came down to, of course, was visibility. Anyone whose appearance discernibly connected him with the Negro was held to be such. The line was thus drawn with regard to practicalities rather than logic. Daily practice supplied logic enough.

Another indication of the refusal of the English continental colonies to separate the "mixed breed" from the African was the absence of terminology which could be used to define a hierarchy of status. The colonists did, it is true, seize upon a separate word to describe those of mixed blood. They were forced to do so if they were to deal with the problem at all, even if

they merely wished, as they did, to lump "mulattoes" with Negroes. If, however, an infusion of white blood had been regarded as elevating status, then presumably the more white blood the higher the social rank. Had such ranking existed, descriptive terminology would have been required with which to handle shades of distinction. Yet no such vocabulary developed in the American colonies. Only one word besides *mulatto* was used to describe those of mixed ancestry. The term *mustee* (*mestee, mustize, mestizo, mustizoe*) was used to describe a mixture which was in part Indian, usually Indian-Negro but occasionally Indian-white. The term was in common use only in the Carolinas, Georgia, and to some extent New York, that is, in those colonies where such crosses occurred with some frequency. Its use revealed the colonists' refusal to identify Indians and Negroes as the same sort of people, a refusal underlined by their belief that the two groups possessed a natural antipathy for each other.[5] Yet while the colonists thus distinguished persons of some Indian ancestry by a separate word, they lumped these *mustees* with mu-

---

[4] Hening, ed., *Statutes of Va.*, III, 252; Walter L. Clark, ed., *The State Records of North Carolina* (Goldsboro, N. C., 1886–1910), XXIII, 106, 160, 262, 345, 526, 559, 700, 882; XXIV, 61; XXV, 283, 445; William L. Saunders, ed., *The Colonial Records of North Carolina* (Raleigh, 1886–90), VII, 605, 608, 645. In 1785–87 Virginia altered the definition to one-quarter Negro, but there was no general trend in this direction during the 19th century; see Hening, ed., *Statutes of Va.*, XII, 184; Samuel Shepard, ed., *The Statutes at Large of Virginia, from October Session 1792, to December Session 1806, Inclusive*, New Ser., being a continuation of Hening (Richmond, 1835–36), I, 123.

[5] See, for example, Hugh Jones, *The Present State of Virginia from Whence Is Inferred a Short View of Maryland and North Carolina*, ed. Richard L. Morton (Chapel Hill, N.C., 1956), p. 50; John Brickell, *The Natural History of North-Carolina* ... (Dublin, 1737), pp. 263, 273; Anne Grant, *Memoirs of an American Lady; With Sketches of Manners and Scenes in America as They Existed Previous to the Revolution*, ed. James G. Wilson (New York, 1901), I, 134; [George Milligen-Johnston], *A Short Description of the Province of South-Carolina* (London, 1770), in Chapman J. Milling, ed., *Colonial South Carolina; Two Contemporary Descriptions by Governor James Glen and Doctor George Milligen-Johnston*, South Caroliniana, Sesquicentennial Series, No. 1 (Columbia, 1951), p. 136; Parish Transcripts, Box III, bundle: Minutes of Council in Assembly (1755), p. 3, New-York Historical Society, New York City. See also Kenneth W. Porter, "Relations between Negroes and Indians within the Present Limits of the United States," *Jour. of Negro Hist.*, XVII (1932), 298–306, 322–27.

lattoes and Negroes in their slave codes. Although legislative enactments provide a valuable index of community sentiment, they do not always accurately reflect social practice. An extensive search in the appropriate sources—diaries, letters, travel accounts, newspapers, and so on—fails to reveal any pronounced tendency to distinguish mulattoes from Negroes, any feeling that their status was higher and demanded different treatment. The sources give no indication, for instance, that mulattoes were preferred as house servants or concubines. There may well have been a relatively high proportion of mulattoes among manumitted slaves, but this was probably due to the not unnatural desire of some masters to liberate their own offspring. Yet all this is largely negative evidence, and the proposition that mulattoes were not accorded higher status than Negroes is as susceptible of proof as any negative. Perhaps the usual procedure of awaiting disproof through positive evidence may be allowed.

A single exception to these generalizations stands out sharply from the mass of colonial legislation. In 1765 the colony of Georgia not only undertook to encourage immigration of free colored persons (itself a unique step) but actually provided that free mulatto and mustee immigrants might be naturalized as white men by the legislature, complete with "all the Rights, Priviledges, Powers, and Immunities whatsoever which any person born of British parents" could have, except the right to vote and sit in the Commons House of Assembly.[6] Thus a

begrudging kind of citizenship was extended to free mulattoes. That Georgia should so distinguish herself from her northern neighbors was a measure of the colony's weak and exposed condition. A small population with an increasingly high proportion of slaves and perpetual danger from powerful Indian tribes made Georgians eager for men who might be counted as white and thus strengthen the colony. The legislature went to great lengths in its search—perhaps too far, for it never actually naturalized anyone under the aegis of the 1765 law.

Only rarely in the colonial period did the subject of mulattoes receive any attention from American writers. Mulattoes were so fixed in station that their position apparently did not merit attention. The subject did come up once in the *South-Carolina Gazette*, yet even then it was casually raised in connection with an entirely different topic. An anonymous contributor in 1735 offered the public some strictures on Carolina's *nouveau riche*, the "half Gentry," and attacked especially their imitative and snobbish behavior. For illustration he turned to the character of the mulatto.

It is observed concerning the Generation of *Molattoes*, that they are seldom well beloved either by the Whites or the Blacks. Their Approach towards Whiteness, makes them look back with some kind of Scorn upon the Colour they seem to have left, while the Negroes, who do not think them better than themselves, return their Contempt with Interest: And the Whites, who respect them no Whit the more for the nearer Affinity in Colour, are apt to regard their Behaviour as too bold and assuming, and bordering upon Impudence. As they are next to Negroes, and but just above them, they are terribly afraid of being thought Negroes, and therefore avoid as much as possible their Company or Com-

---

[6] Allen D. Candler, comp., *The Colonial Records of the State of Georgia* (Atlanta, 1904–16), XVIII, 659. The wording of the act is ambiguous, and though free Negroes might have fallen under its provisions, the legislature was apparently thinking only of mulattoes and mustees.

merce: and Whitefolks are as little fond of the Company of *Molattoes*.[7]

The writer's point, of course, was not that mulattoes were in fact superior to Negroes, but that they alone thought they were. Apparently mulattoes thought white blood to be a source of elevation, a proposition which whites (and Negroes as well) were quick to deny. White blood secured one's status only if undiluted.

A somewhat different aspect of this problem came up in 1784 when it was forced on the attention of a Savannah merchant, Joseph Clay. As executor of a will Clay became responsible for the welfare of two young mulattoes, very possibly the children of his deceased friend. Because the young people were both free, Clay's letter to a gentleman in Ireland offers valuable evidence of what a combination of personal freedom and some white ancestry afforded in the way of social position in Georgia. "These young Folks are very unfortunately situated in this Country," Clay wrote, "their descent places them in the most disadvantageous situation, as Free persons the Laws protects them —but they gain no rank in Life, White Persons do not commonly associate with them on a footing of equality—so many of their own Colour (say the mixt breed) being Slaves, they too naturally fall in with them, and even the Negro Slaves claim a right to their acquaintance and Society." For Clay the situation was one of unrelieved gloom, even of horror: "thus a little reflection will present to you what their future Prospects here must be—neglected by the most respectable Class of Society, [they] are forced to intermix with the lowest, and in what that must end—we woud wish to draw a Veil—all the Care

that can be taken of them cant prevent it, it arrises from our peculiar situation in regard to these people." Clay went on to recommend as "the most eligible plan" that the children be sent to Europe if his correspondent would accept them as wards. "The Boy might be Bound to some business . . . and the Girl might make a very good Wife to some honest Tradesman." It was essential that they cross the Atlantic: "this alone can save them . . . I think they might both be made usefull Members of Society, no such distinctions interfere with their happiness on your side the Water."[8] Clay added finally that several of his friends endorsed his proposal. Apparently America offered little opportunity for blacks to become whites through intermixture. American society, wedded as it was to Negro slavery, drew a rigid line which did not exist in Europe: this was indeed "our peculiar situation in regard to these people."

The existence of a rigid barrier between whites and those of Negro blood necessarily required a means by which the barrier could on occasion be passed. Some accommodation had to be made for those persons with so little Negro blood that they appeared to be white, for one simply could not go around calling apparently white persons Negroes. Once the stain was washed out visibly it was useless as a means of identification. Thus there developed the silent mechanism of "passing." Such a device would have been un-

[7] *South-Carolina Gazette* (Charleston), Mar. 22, 1735.

[8] Joseph Clay to John Wright, Savannah, Feb. 17, 1784, in *Letters of Joseph Clay, Merchant of Savannah, 1776–1793* . . . (Georgia Historical Society, *Collections*, VIII [1913]), 203–4. Further testimony that mulattoes considered themselves superior to Negroes may be found in William Logan to Lord Granville, London, Aug. 13, 1761, Logan Papers, XI, 60, Historical Society of Pennsylvania, Philadelphia.

necessary if those of mixed ancestry and appearance had been regarded as midway between white and black. It was the existence of a broad chasm which necessitated the sudden leap which passing represented.

Fortunately it is possible to catch a glimpse of this process as it operated in the colonial period by following the extraordinary career of a family named Gibson in South Carolina. In 1731 a member of the Commons House of Assembly announced in the chamber that several free colored men with their white wives had immigrated from Virginia with the intention of settling on the Santee River. Free Negroes were undesirable enough, but white wives made the case exceptionally disturbing. "The house apprehending [this prospect] to be of ill Consequence to this Province," appointed a committee to inquire into the matter. Governor Robert Johnson had already sent for what seemed to be the several families involved, and the committee asked him to report his findings to the house.

"The people lately come into the Settlements having been sent for," Johnson duly reported, "I have had them before me in Council and upon Examination find that they are not Negroes nor Slaves but Free people, That the Father of them here is named Gideon Gibson and his Father was also free, I have been informed by a person who has lived in Virginia that this Gibson has lived there Several Years in good Repute and by his papers that he has produced before me that his transactions there have been very regular, That he has for several years paid Taxes for two tracts of Land and had seven Negroes of his own, That he is a Carpenter by Trade and is come hither for the support of his Family." This evident respectability so impressed the governor that he allowed the Gibson family to remain in the colony. "The account he has given of himself," Johnson declared, "is so Satisfactory that he is no Vagabond that I have in Consideration of his Wifes being a white woman and several White women Capable of working and being Serviceable in the Country permitted him to Settle in this Country upon entering into Recognizance for his good behaviour which I have taken accordingly."[9]

The meaning of Johnson's statement that "they are not Negroes nor Slaves but Free people" is not entirely clear. Certainly Gideon Gibson himself was colored; it seems likely that he was mulatto rather than Negro, but it is impossible to tell surely. At any rate Gideon Gibson prospered very nicely: by 1736 either he or a son of the same name owned 450 acres of Carolina land. He continued to own Negroes, and in 1757 he was described as owning property in two widely separated counties. By 1765 the status of Gideon Gibson (by this time definitely the son of the original carpenter) was such that he was appointed administrator of an estate.[10] His sister married a wealthy planter, and there is no evidence to indicate that Gibson himself was regarded by his neighbors as anything but white.[11] In 1768 he was leading a

[9] Parish Transcripts, Box II, bundle: S. C., Minutes of House of Burgesses (1730–35), 9.

[10] *South-Carolina Gazette*, Aug. 29, 1743, supplement; Nov. 26, Dec. 10, 1750; Mar. 3, 1757, supplement; "Abstracts of Records of the Proceedings in the Court of Ordinary, 1764–1771," *South Carolina Historical and Genealogical Magazine*, XXII (1921), 97, 127; see also XXIII (1922), 35; [Prince Frederick Parish], *The Register Book for the Parish Prince Frederick, Winyaw* (Baltimore, 1916), 15, 20, 32, 34.

[11] For this point I am indebted to Dr. Richard M. Brown, of Rutgers University, who is currently publishing a study of the South Carolina Regulators. He also provided information and references on the younger Gideon

band of South Carolina Regulators on the field of battle. The commander dispatched to arrest Gibson was a planter and colonel in the militia, George Gabriel Powell, who ignominiously resigned his commission when his men sided with the Regulators. This latter worthy, apparently a kind master to his own Negroes, sought vindication by attacking Gibson's ancestry.[12] The exact nature of the attack is unclear, but the matter came up on the floor of the Commons, of which Powell was a member. The prominent merchant-patriot of Charles Town, Henry Laurens, recorded the conflict in a letter written some years later. Laurens was writing from England of his own conviction that slavery ought to be brought to an end, a conviction that inevitably raised the question of color.

Reasoning from the colour carries no conviction. By perseverance the black may be blanched and the "stamp of Providence" effectually effaced. Gideon Gibson escaped the penalties of the negro law by producing upon comparison more red and white in his face than could be discovered in the faces of half the descendants of the French refugees in our House of Assembly, including your old acquaintance the Speaker. I challenged them all to the trial. The children of this same Gideon, having passed through another stage of whitewash were of fairer complexion than their prosecutor

Gibson's regulating activities and kindly pointed out to me a useful local history: Alexander Gregg, *History of the Old Cheraws* [2d Ed.] (Columbia, 1905). See this source, 72*n*, for the marriage of Gibson's sister.

[12] For the Regulators' battle, see Gregg, *Old Cheraws*, 73–74, 139–156; Charles Woodmason, *The Carolina Backcountry on the Eve of the Revolution; The Journal and Other Writings of Charles Woodmason, Anglican Itinerant*, ed. Richard J. Hooker (Chapel Hill, N.C., 1953), 176–177. For biographical information on Powell and his kindness to his slaves, A. S. Salley, ed., "Diary of William Dillwyn during a Visit to Charles Town in 1772," *S. C. Hist. and Genea. Mag.*, XXXVI (1935), 35, and n.

George Gabriel [Powell].—But to confine them to their original clothing will be best. They may and ought to continue a separate people, may be subjected by special laws, kept harmless, made useful and freed from the tyranny and arbitrary power of individuals; but as I have already said, this difficulty cannot be removed by arguments on this side of the water.[13]

Laurens showed both sides of the coin. He defended an individual's white status on the basis of appearance and at the same time expressed the conviction that colored persons "may and ought to continue a separate people." Once an Ethiopian always an Ethiopian, unless he could indeed change his skin.

Gideon Gibson's successful hurdling of the barrier was no doubt an unusual case; it is of course impossible to tell how unusual. Passing was difficult but not impossible, and it stood as a veiled, unrecognized monument to the American ideal of a society open to all comers. One Virginia planter advertised in the newspaper for his runaway mulatto slave who he stated might try to pass for free or as a "white man." An English traveler reported calling upon a Virginia lawyer who was "said to be" and who looked like a mulatto.[14] But the problem of evidence is insurmountable. The success of the passing mechanism depended upon its operating in silence. Passing was a conspiracy of silence not only for the individual but for a biracial society which had drawn a rigid color line based on visibility. Unless a white man was a white man,

[13] Henry Laurens to William Drayton, Feb. 15, 1783, in David Duncan Wallace, *The Life of Henry Laurens; With a Sketch of the Life of Lieutenant-Colonel John Laurens* (New York and London, 1915), 454. The speaker was Peter Manigault.

[14] Rind, *Virginia Gazette* (Williamsburg), Apr. 23, 1772; J[ohn] F. D. Smyth, *A Tour in the United States of America: Containing an Account of the Present Situation of that Country* . . . (London, 1784), I, 123.

the gates were open to endless slander and confusion.

That the existence of such a line in the continental colonies was not predominantly the effect of the English cultural heritage is suggested by even a glance at the English colonies in the Caribbean. The social accommodation of racial intermixture in the islands followed a different pattern from that on the continent. It was regarded as improper, for example, to work mulattoes in the fields—a fundamental distinction. Apparently they were preferred as tradesmen, house servants, and especially as concubines.[15] John Luffman wrote that mulatto slaves "fetch a lower price than blacks, unless they are tradesmen, because the purchasers cannot employ them in the drudgeries to which negroes are put too; the colored men, are therefore mostly brought up to trades or employed as house slaves, and the women of this description are generally prostitutes."[16]

Though the English in the Caribbean thought of their society in terms of white, colored, and black, they employed a complicated battery of names to distinguish persons of various racial mixtures. This terminology was borrowed from the neighboring Spanish, but words are not acquired unless they fulfill a need. While the English settlers on the continent borrowed one Spanish word to describe all mixtures of black and white, the islanders borrowed at least four—*mulatto, sambo, quadroon,* and *mestize*—to describe differing degrees.[17] And some West Indians were prepared to act upon the logic which these terms implied. The respected Jamaican historian, Bryan Edwards, actually proposed extension of civil privileges to mulattoes in proportion to their admixture of white blood.[18] Such a proposition was unheard of on the continent.

The difference between the two regions on this matter may well have been connected with another pronounced divergence in social practice. The attitude toward interracial sex was far more genial in the islands than in the continental colonies. In the latter, miscegenation very rarely met with anything but disapproval in principle, no matter how avid the practice. Sexual intimacy between any white person and any Negro (that "unnatural and inordinate copulation") was utterly condemned. Protests against the prac-

---

[15] [Thomas Tryon], *Friendly Advice to the Gentlemen-Planters of the East and West Indies* ([London], 1684), pp. 140–141; John Singleton, *A General Description of the West-Indian Islands, as far as Relates to the British, Dutch, and Danish Governments...* (Barbados, 1767), pp. 152–153; [Janet Schaw], *Journal of a Lady of Quality; Being the Narrative of a Journey to the West Indies, North Carolina, and Portugal, in the Years 1774 to 1776,* ed. Evangeline Walker Andrews, in collaboration with Charles M. Andrews, 3d Ed. (New Haven, 1939), p. 112; [Edward Long], *The History of Jamaica...* (London, 1774), II, 328–30, 332–35; William Beckford, *A Descriptive Account of the Island of Jamaica* (London, 1790), II, 322; Bryan Edwards, *The History, Civil and Commercial, of the British Colonies in the West Indies,* 3d Ed. (London, 1801), II, 18–31. The only place in the United States ever to develop an established institution of mulatto concubinage was New Orleans, where the influence of the Spanish and of French refugees from the West Indies was strong.

[16] John Luffman, *A Brief Account of the Island of Antigua, together with the Customs and Manners of its Inhabitants, as Well White as Black* (London, 1789), p. 115.

---

[17] *Mulatto* meant one-half white; *sambo,* one-fourth white; *quadroon,* three-fourths white; and *mestize* (which did not imply Indian mixture as it did on the continent), seven-eighths white. Long, *Jamaica,* II, 260–261; Edwards, *History,* II, 18; J[ohn] G. Stedman, *Narrative of a Five Years' Expedition, against the Revolted Negroes of Surinam, in Guiana* (London, 1796), II, plate opposite p. 98; *Jamaica, a Poem, in Three Parts* (London, 1777), pp. 22–23.

[18] Edwards, *History,* II, 24n.

tice were frequent.[19] A traveler in New York reported that the citizens of Albany possessed a particular "moral delicacy" on one point: "they were from infancy in habits of familiarity with these humble friends [the Negroes], yet being early taught that nature had placed between them a barrier, which it was in a high degree criminal and disgraceful to pass, they considered a mixture of such distinct races with abhorrence, as a violation of her laws."[20] About 1700 the Chester County Court in Pennsylvania ordered a Negro "never more to meddle with any white woman more uppon paine of his life." Public feeling on this matter was strong enough to force its way over the hurdles of the legislative process into the statute books of many colonies. Maryland and Virginia forbade cohabitation of whites and Negroes well before the end of the seventeenth century. Similar prohibitions were adopted by Massachusetts, North and South Carolina, and Pennsylvania during the next quarter-century and by Georgia when Negroes were admitted to that colony in 1750. Thus two Northern and all Southern colonies legally prohibited miscegenation.[21] Feeling against intercourse with

Negroes was strengthened by the fact that such activity was generally illicit; Americans had brought from England certain standards of marital fidelity which miscegenation flagrantly violated.

The contrast offered by the West Indies is striking. Protests against interracial sex relations were infrequent. Colored mistresses were kept openly. "The Planters are in general rich," a young traveler wrote, "but a set of dissipating, abandoned, and cruel people. Few even of the married ones, but keep a Mulatto or Black Girl in the house or at lodgings for certain purposes."[22] Edward Long of Jamaica put the matter this way: "He who should presume to shew any displeasure against such a thing as simple fornication, would for his pains be accounted a simple blockhead; since not one in twenty can be persuaded, that there is either sin; or shame in cohabiting with

---

[19] For a few examples: James Fontaine, *Memoirs of a Huguenot Family*, trans. and ed. Ann Maury (New York, 1872), p. 350; Eugene P. Chase, trans. and ed., *Our Revolutionary Forefathers; The Letters of François, Marquis de Barbé-Marbois during His Residence in the United States as Secretary of the French Legation, 1779–1785* (New York, 1929), p. 74; *South-Carolina Gazette*, Mar. 18, 1732; Mar. 28, 1743; May 22, 1749; Elhanan Winchester, *The Reigning Abominations, Especially the Slave Trade, Considered as Causes of Lamentation* (London, 1788), p. 22n; Klaus G. Loewald, Beverly Starika, and Paul S. Taylor, trans. and eds., "Johann Martin Bolzius Answers a Questionnaire on Carolina and Georgia," *William and Mary Quarterly*, 3d Ser., XIV (1957), 235.

[20] Grant, *Memoirs*, I, 85.

[21] Hening, ed., *Statutes of Va.*, II, 170; III, 86–87, 452–54; Browne and others, eds., *Archives*

of Md., I, 533–34; VII, 204–5; XIII, 546–49; XXII, 552; XXVI, 259–60; XXX, 289–90; XXXIII, 112; XXXVI, 275–76; Edward R. Turner, *The Negro in Pennsylvania, Slavery—Servitude—Freedom, 1639–1861* (Washington, 1911), p. 30n; *The Acts and Resolves, Public and Private, of the Province of the Massachusetts Bay* (Boston, 1869–1922), I, 578–579; *Acts and Laws of the Commonwealth of Massachusetts* (Boston, 1890–98), IV, 10; Clark, ed., *State Recs. of N. C.*, XXIII, 65, 106, 160, 195; Thomas Cooper and David J. McCord, eds., *Statutes at Large of South Carolina* (Columbia, 1836–41), III, 20; James T. Mitchell and others, eds., *Statutes at Large of Pennsylvania from 1682 to 1809* (Harrisburg, 1896–1915), IV, 62–63; also X, 67–73, and the *Pennsylvania Packet* (Philadelphia), Mar. 4, 1779; Candler, comp., *Col. Recs. of Ga.*, I, 59–60. Delaware, not considered a Southern colony or state by contemporaries, passed no outright prohibition until 1807 (repealed the next year) but provided for heavier fines in interracial bastardy cases than in such cases where only whites were involved; *Laws of the State of Delaware* (New Castle and Wilmington, 1797–1816), I, 105–9; IV, 112–3, 221.

[22] Samuel Thornely, ed., *The Journal of Nicholas Cresswell, 1774–1777* (New York, 1924), p. 39.

his slave."[23] Perhaps most significant of all, no island legislature prohibited extramarital miscegenation and only one declared against intermarriage.[24] The reason, of course, was that white men so commonly slept with Negro women that to legislate against the practice would have been merely ludicrous. Concubinage was such an integral part of island life that one might just as well attempt to abolish the sugar cane.

Mulattoes in the West Indies, then, were products of accepted practice, something they assuredly were not in the continental colonies. In the one area they were the fruits of a desire which society tolerated and almost institutionalized; in the other they represented

an illicit passion which public morality unhesitatingly condemned. On the continent, unlike the West Indies, mulattoes represented a practice about which men could only feel guilty. To reject and despise the productions of one's own guilt was only natural.

If such difference in feeling about miscegenation has any connection with the American attitude toward mulattoes, it only raises the question of what caused that difference. Since the English settlers in both the West Indies and the continental colonies brought with them the same cultural baggage, something in their colonial experiences must have caused the divergence in their attitudes toward miscegenation. Except perhaps for climatic disimilarity, a factor of very doubtful importance, the most fundamental difference lay in the relative numbers of whites and Negroes in the two areas. On the continent the percentage of Negroes in the total population reached its peak in the period 1730–65 and has been declining since. It ranged from about 3 per cent in New England, 8 to 15 per cent in the middle colonies, 30 to 40 in Maryland and Virginia, 25 in North Carolina, 40 in Georgia, to a high of some 60 per cent in South Carolina. The proportion of Negroes in the islands was far higher: 75 per cent in Barbados, 80 in the Leeward Islands, and over 90 in Jamaica.[25]

---

[23] Long, *Jamaica*, II, 328.

[24] The exception was Montserrat; the law was probably disallowed: Colonial Office Papers, Ser. 391, LXIX, 51 (Feb. 16, 1762), Public Record Office, London, for which reference I am indebted to Frank W. Pitman, *The Development of the British West Indies, 1700–1763* (New Haven, 1917), p. 27, where the citation is given as C.O. 391/70, p. 51 (Feb. 16, 1762). This statement on the absence of antimiscegenation laws is based on a reading of the statutes of the various islands which, from the nature of the sources, is probably less complete than for the continental colonies. For obvious reasons only those islands settled primarily by Englishmen have been included: those captured from the French had a different cultural heritage. An act applying to all the Leeward Islands declared that no "Free Person" should be married to "any Slave," but this provision was in a section regulating the conduct of free Negroes and almost certainly applied only to them; *Acts of Assembly, Passed in the Charibbee Leeward Islands. From 1690, to 1730* (London, 1734), pp. 138–39. Bermuda in 1663 acted against miscegenation, but this fact merely gives additional confirmation to the pattern outlined above, since the island at the time had fairly close contact with Virginia and never became like the Caribbean islands in economic structure, proportion of Negroes, or social atmosphere. See J. H. Lefroy, comp., *Memorials of the Discovery and Early Settlement of the Bermudas or Somers Islands, 1515–1685* (London, 1877–79), II, 190.

[25] Population statistics for the colonial period are at best merely rough estimates in most cases. I have compiled tables showing the proportion of Negroes in the total population for the principal colonies settles by Englishmen, with figures drawn largely from the following sources: U. S. Bureau of the Census, *A Century of Population Growth, from the First Census of the United States to the Twelfth, 1790–1900* (Washington, 1909); Evarts B. Greene and Virginia D. Harrington, *American Population before the Federal Census of 1790* (New York, 1932); *Calendar of State Papers, Colonial Series, America and West Indies*, 37 vols. (London, 1860———); Alan Burns, *History of*

These figures strongly suggest a close connection between a high proportion of Negroes and open acceptance of miscegenation. South Carolina, for example, where Negroes formed a majority of the population, was alone among the continental colonies in tolerating even slightly conspicuous interracial liaisons.[26] Thoroughly disparate proportions of Negroes, moreover, made it inevitable that the West Indies and the continental colonies would develop dissimilar societies. The West Indian planters were lost not so much in the Caribbean as in a sea of blacks. They found it impossible to re-create English culture as they had known it. They were corrupted by living in a police state, though not themselves the objects of its discipline. The business of the islands was business, the production of agricultural staples; the islands were not where one really lived, but where one made one's money. By contrast, the American colonists maintained their hold on the English background, modifying it not so much to accommodate slavery as to winning the new land. They were numerous enough

the British West Indies (London, 1954), pp. 401, 454, 461, 465, 499, 500, 510, 511, 514, 515; Vincent T. Harlow, A History of Barbados, 1625–1685 (Oxford, 1926), p. 338; C. S. S. Higham, The Development of the Leeward Islands under the Restoration, 1660–1688; A Study of the Foundations of the Old Colonial System (Cambridge, Eng., 1921), pp. 145, 148; Pitman, West Indies, pp. 48, 370, 374, 378; Edwards, History, II, 2. My figures are in substantial agreement with those which may be calculated from a table recently compiled by Stella H. Sutherland in U. S. Bureau of the Census, Historical Statistics of the United States, Colonial Times to 1957 (Washington, 1960), p. 756, except in the case of North Carolina where her figures yield a proportion nearly 10 per cent higher than mine.

[26] For a New Englander's comment on miscegenation in South Carolina see Mark Anthony DeWolfe Howe, ed., "Journal of Josiah Quincy, Junior, 1773," Massachusetts Historical Society, Proceedings, XLIX (Boston, 1916), 463.

to create a new culture with a validity of its own, complete with the adjustments necessary to absorb non-English Europeans. Unlike the West Indians, they felt no need to be constantly running back to England to reassure themselves that they belonged to civilization. Because they were conscious of the solid worth of their own society, forged with their own hands, they vehemently rejected any trespass upon it by a people so alien as the Negroes. The islanders could hardly resent trespass on something which they did not have. By sheer weight of numbers their society was black and slave.

This fundamental difference was perhaps reinforced by another demographic factor. In the seventeenth century the ratio of men to women had been high in America and higher still in the West Indies, where the ratio was about three to two, or, as the sex ratio is usually expressed, 150 (males per 100 females). In the following century it dropped drastically. New England's sex ratio went below 100 as a result of emigration which was as usual predominantly male. Elsewhere on the continent the bounding birth rate nearly erased the differential: in 1750, except on the edge of the frontier, it was probably no more than 110 and in most places less. Perhaps not so well known is the fact that the same process occurred in most of the English islands. Emigration sapped their male strength until Barbados had a sex ratio in the 80's and the various Leeward Islands were balanced in the neighborhood of 100. A significant exception was Jamaica, where in mid-eighteenth century a plentiful supply of land maintained a sex ratio of nearly two to one.[27]

[27] Tables of the sex ratios in the various colonies have been calculated from the sources given in the previous note and, in addition, Pitman, West Indies, pp. 371–82; Long, Jamaica, I, 376.

Male numerical predomination was surely not without effect on interracial sexual relations. Particularly where the white population was outnumbered by the black, white women formed a small group. Their scarcity rendered them valuable. The natural reaction on the part of white men was to place them protectively upon a pedestal and then run off to gratify passions elsewhere. For their part white women, though they might propagate children, inevitably held themselves aloof from the world of lust and passion, a world associated with infidelity and Negro slaves. Under no circumstances would they have attempted, nor would they have been allowed, to clamber down from their pedestal to seek pleasures of their own across the racial line. In fact the sexual union of white women with Negro men was uncommon in all colonies. When it did occur (and it did more often than is generally supposed) it was in just those areas to which the demographic factors point—America north of South Carolina, especially in New England, where white women even married Negroes. Such a combination, legitimized or not, was apparently unknown in the West Indies.[28]

If a high sex ratio contributed to the acceptability of miscegenation, it may well have enhanced the acceptablity of mulatto offspring. For example, there is the striking fact that Jamaica, the only colony where the sex ratio continued high, was the only colony to give legislative countenance to the rise of mulattoes. In 1733 the legislature provided that "no Person who is not above Three Degrees removed in a lineal Descent from the Negro Ancestor exclusive, shall be allowed to vote or poll in Elections; and no one shall be deemed a Mulatto after the Third Generation, as aforesaid, but that they shall have all the Privileges and Immunities of His Majesty's white Subjects of this Island, provided they are brought up in the Christian Religion."[29]

---

[28] I have found no cases of white women sleeping with colored men in the West Indies. For this combination on the continent, see extracts from the Court of General Sessions of the Peace [Suffolk County, Mass.], Apr. 4, 1704, Oct. 2, 1705, Apr. 6, 1708, July 4, 1710, Apr. 6, 1714, in Parish Transcripts, Box XVI; James Bowdoin to George Scott, Boston, Oct. 14, 1763, in Bowdoin-Temple Papers, XXVIII, 56, Mass. Hist. Soc., Boston in which Bowdoin wrote that "My Man Caesar has been engaged in an amour with some of the white ladies of the Town. . . ." so he was sending him to Grenada in exchange for produce or another Negro boy; W. H. Morse, "Lemuel Haynes," *Jour. of Negro Hist.*, IV (1919), 22; [Daniel Horsmanden], *A Journal of the Proceedings in the Detection of the Conspiracy Formed by Some White People, in Conjunction with Negro and other Slaves, for Burning the City of New-York in America, and Murdering the Inhabitants* (New York, 1744), pp. 2, 4; *Boston News-Letter*, June 25, 1741; Arthur W. Calhoun,

A Social History of the American Family from Colonial Times to the Present (Cleveland, 1917–19), I, 211; Helen T. Catterall, ed., *Judicial Cases Concerning American Slavery and the Negro* (Washington, 1926), I, 89–91; II, 12; IV, 28, 32; *Maryland Gazette* (Annapolis), Aug. 19, 1746; James H. Johnston, Race Relations in Virginia and Miscegenation in the South, 1776–1860 (unpubl. Ph.D. diss., University of Chicago, 1937), pp. 199–202; John H. Franklin, *The Free Negro in North Carolina, 1790–1860* (Chapel Hill, N. C., 1943), pp. 37, 39; Saunders, *Col. Recs. of N. C.,* II, 704; "Johann Martin Bolzius," p. 235. For this combination in actual marriage, see Lorenzo J. Greene, *The Negro in Colonial New England, 1620–1776* (New York, 1942), pp. 201–2; Morse, "Lemuel Haynes," p. 26; Grant, *Memoirs,* I, 86; Calhoun, *Family,* I, 211; Catterall, ed., *Judicial Cases,* II, 11; La Rochefoucault Liancourt, *Travels,* I, 602; *Maryland Gazette,* July 31, 1794; and the case of Gideon Gibson discussed above. A causal connection between the sex ratio and miscegenation has been suggested by Herbert Moller, "Sex Composition and Correlated Culture Patterns of Colonial America," *William and Mary Quarterly,* 3d Ser., II (1945), 131–37, but some of his conclusions must be treated with caution.

[29] *Acts of Assembly, Passed in the Island of Jamaica; from 1681, to 1737, inclusive* (London, 1738), pp. 260–61; see also Long, *Jamaica,* II, 261, 321. This same definition of a mulatto was retained in 1780; *Acts of Assembly, Passed in the Island of Jamaica; from 1770 to 1783, inclusive* (Kingston, 1786), p. 174.

In this same period Barbados was barring any person "whose original Extract shall be proved to have been from a Negro" from voting and from testifying against whites.[30] Beginning in the 1730's the Jamaican legislature passed numerous private acts giving the colored offspring (and sometimes the colored mistress) of such and such a planter the rights and privileges of white persons, especially the right to inherit the planter's estate. There was objection to this blanching of mulattoes, however, for in 1761 the Assembly restricted the amount of property a planter might leave to his mulatto children, saying that "such bequests tend greatly to destroy the distinction requisite, and absolutely necessary to be kept up in this island, between white persons and negroes, their issue and offspring. . . ." The law failed to destroy the acceptability of the practice, however, for the private acts continued.[31] It was in

Jamaica, too, that Bryan Edwards called for extension of civil privileges to mulattoes. And Edward Long, in his history of the island, wrote that those beyond the third generation were "called English, and consider themselves as free from all taint of the Negroe race."[32] Thus Jamaica, with the highest proportion of Negroes and highest sex ratio of all the English colonies, was unique in its practice of publicly transforming Negroes into white men.

The American continental colonist refused to make this extension of privilege. He remained firm in his rejection of the mulatto, in his categorization of mixed-bloods as belonging to the lower caste. It was an unconscious decision dictated perhaps in large part by the weight of Negroes on his society, heavy enough to be a burden, yet not so heavy as to make him abandon all hope of maintaining his own identity, physically and culturally. Interracial propagation was a constant reproach that he was failing to be true to himself. Sexual intimacy strikingly symbolized a union he wished to avoid. If he could not restrain his sexual nature, he could at least reject its fruits and thus solace himself that he had done no harm. Perhaps he sensed as well that continued racial intermixture would eventually undermine the logic of the racial slavery upon which his society was based. For the separation of slaves from free men depended on a clear demarcation of the races, and the presence of mulattoes blurred this essential distinction. Accordingly he made every effort to nullify the effects of racial intermixture: by classifying the mulatto as a Negro he was in effect denying that intermixture had occurred at all.

---

[30] *Acts of Assembly, Passed in the Island of Barbados, from 1648, to 1718* (London, 1721), pp. 112, 153, 171, 213, 226, 267; Richard Hall, comp., *Acts, Passed in the Island of Barbados. From 1643, to 1762, inclusive* (London, 1764), p. 256.

[31] *Acts of Assembly, Passed in the Island of Jamaica, from the Year 1681 to the Year 1769 inclusive.* 2 vols. in 1, with an *Appendix: Containing Laws Respecting Slaves* (Kingston, 1787), I, Table of Acts, 18, 20–25, 30-31; II, Table of Acts, 3, 7–11, 14–15; II, 36–39; *Acts of Assembly, Passed in the Island of Jamaica; from 1770, to 1783, inclusive,* Table of Acts, 8, 11, 13, 16, 18, 20, 22, 24, 26, 28, 30–31; *Acts of Assembly, Passed in the Island of Jamaica, from the Year 1784 to the Year 1788 inclusive* (Kingston, 1789), Table of Acts, vi-viii, xi, xv-xvi; *The Laws of Jamaica: Comprehending all the Acts in Force, Passed between the Thirty-Second Year of the Reign of King Charles the Second, and the Thirty-Third Year of the Reign of King George the Third* (St. Jago de la Vega, 1792), I, Table of Acts, no pagination; *The Laws of Jamaica, Passed in the Thirty-Third Year of the Reign of King George the Third* (St. Jago de la Vega, 1793), Table of Acts, no pagination; *The Laws of Jamaica, Passed in the Thirty-Fourth Year of the Reign of King George the Third* (St. Jago de la Vega, 1794), Table of Acts, no pagination. See also Long, *Jamaica,* II, 320–23; Edwards, *History,* II, 22–23.

[32] Long, *Jamaica,* II, 332. This general picture of Jamaica is borne out by a work on a somewhat later period; Philip D. Curtin, *Two Jamaicas: The Role of Ideas in a Tropical Colony, 1830–1865* (Cambridge, Mass., 1955), chaps. 1–3.

SPECIAL PROBLEMS

EUGENE D. GENOVESE

The Treatment of Slaves in Different Countries: Problems in the Applications of the Comparative Method

Eugene D. Genovese is Chairman of the Department of History at the University of Rochester. He is the author of The Political Economy of Slavery: Studies in the Economy and Society of the Slave South *(1965) and of a number of articles. He is currently working on a general study of the Negro slave in the antebellum South. The following selection is published here for the first time.*

After a long and often discouraging struggle, the comparative method is finally beginning to triumph over parochialism in the study of Afro-American slavery. As it is extended, almost every question relevant to Southern slavery will take on a new and richer meaning, but only if considerable rigor is brought to our analyses. To demonstrate the possibilities and pitfalls let us consider the seemingly narrow and simple problem of the treatment of slaves in the several New World plantation systems.

When scholars discuss the treatment of slaves, they ought to make clear the meaning of the word "treatment," but they rarely do. As a result, there has been much waste of time, effort, and good temper. In such circumstances comparative analysis tends to obscure rather than illuminate. We ought to distinguish carefully the different meanings of the word, for there are at least three. Once proper distinctions have been made, many quarrels disappear. Ulrich Phillips was right in thinking that Southern slaves were better treated than others, and Gilberto Freyre was right in thinking that Brazilian slaves were: They were talking about quite different things. No wonder so fine a scholar as C. R. Boxer has scoffed at the claims. Without close definition all such statements reduce themselves to romantic speculations.

The three basic meanings of "treatment" are:

1. *Day-to-day living conditions:* Under this rubric fall such essentially measurable items as quantity and quality of food, clothing, housing, length of the working day, and the general conditions of labor.
2. *Conditions of life:* This category includes family security, opportunities for an independent social and religious life, and those cultural developments which, as Elkins has shown, can have a profound effect on the personality of the slave.
3. *Access to freedom and citizenship:* This is the meaning for "treatment" that is implied in the work of Frank Tannenbaum and those who follow him closely. It ought to be immediately clear that there is no organic connection between this and the first category and only an indirect connection between this and the second.

When Ulrich Bonnell Phillips insisted that Southern slaves were the best treated, he meant in terms of the first category. Those who have argued in favor of the proposition that Brazilian slaves were the best treated have meant in terms of the third category and sometimes the second; occasionally, as in Freyre's case, they have also argued in terms of the first, but in doing so, they have certainly talked nonsense.

Tannenbaum, in his seminal essay, *Slave and Citizen*, accepts Freyre's assertion that Brazilian slaves were better treated than others, but his celebrated thesis requires only that they had greater access to freedom and citizenship. There was in fact no necessary relationship between good treatment in Tannenbaum's sense, which describes primarily the treatment of the black slave as a black man, and good treat-

ment in the sense of day-to-day conditions of life. When Davis writes that the ease and frequency of manumission provides the "crucial standard in measuring the relative harshness of slave systems," he creates unnecessary difficulties and is in danger of confusing the extent to which a slave society is closed with the extent to which it deals severely with its slaves on a day-to-day basis. Often, a slave system, as Davis himself notes, is harsh in one sense, but mild in the other.[1] Davis' ambiguity is usually nothing more than a certain carelessness —the more striking since his book is a model of careful work—in the use of the appropriate terms. It nonetheless contributes to his unfortunate insistence that we cannot make a judgment on the relative severity of the slave systems. We can, but only if we compare specific kinds of treatment and their consequences, instead of trying to use a single standard of judgment.

The relationship among these different meanings may be observed in such matters as miscegenation and manumission. In some ways miscegenation and the doctrine that "money whitens the skin," which is often taken as indicative of good treatment, damaged the standard of living of those who remained field slaves. Brazilian planters took the precaution of locking up their allegedly well-treated slaves, including house slaves, every night. (What Southern slave-holder had to do that?) In order to do so, the Brazilians had to build tight, often windowless, escape-proof cabins. Thus, Brazilian slave quarters were generally inferior to those in the United States. These precautions were made necessary by the enormous free colored population in Brazil, where racial bars were minimized and where

---

[1] David Brion Davis, *The Problem of Slavery in Western Culture*, (Ithaca, N. Y., 1966), p. 54.

even blacks were often presumed to be free men. The resultant ease with which runaway slaves could pass for free men made necessary greater police control of the plantations. Similarly, with respect to the practice of manumission, it was much easier for Brazilian than for American masters to liberate their slaves and thereby escape their patriarchal responsibilities. There is evidence that at least some of Brazil's vaunted voluntary manumissions were of this kind.

If we consider such matters as slave food supplies, we may see at a glance how good treatment in one sense implies bad treatment in another. In the United States masters generally provided slaves with food; individual garden plots were supplementary and inessential. In the British West Indies and elsewhere slaves had to raise their own food on special provision grounds. As a result, the slaves in the United States received the better treatment in two ways: their food supply was steady and generally adequate at least in bulk; and their free time was their own. In the West Indies slaves had to choose between a good deal of extra work after field hours and on weekends and seeing their families go without sufficient nourishment. Yet, these same circumstances represented better treatment for the West Indian slaves—more favorable conditions of life—in the second of our senses of the word. Although not supported at law, the system of provision grounds became so well established in custom that the slaves developed a strong sense of private property, which was almost always respected by the masters. The system required that slaves be allowed to travel into town on "market Sundays" to sell their produce and buy items they could not grow on their particular land. West Indian slaves thereby developed a much

freer social life and a much stronger sense of independence.

Similarly, with respect to clothing and the condition of the quarters, Southern masters appear to have taken far greater pains than West Indians to guarantee adequate supplies and to police for cleanliness and order. In so doing they could pride themselves on providing the better treatment in the first, purely material, sense and yet unwittingly plead guilty to the greater throttling of their people's independence and personality development.

By separating the different categories of treatment we can begin to measure those features which lend themselves to measurement, as well as to assess more easily those which require qualitative judgment. Having done that much we can study the different kinds of treatment to see to what extent they were mutually enouraging, directly contradictory, or merely compatible. In general, for example, it is a striking fact that the marked improvement in the day-to-day conditions of American slave life proceeded during the nineteenth century hand in hand with the rapid disappearance of the possibilities for escaping the system.

A comparative analysis of treatment, in any of its meanings, must take place on at least two different levels simultaneously. First, conditions must be measured or assessed at a given historical moment. Race relations or working conditions must be evaluated for Cuba, Brazil, Jamaica, Saint-Domingue, and Virginia for a certain year or decade, for each slave system reflected the exigencies of the world market at any given moment in time. Second—more difficult but probably more important —conditions must be measured or assessed according to corresponding points of historical development. The second half of the seventeenth century in Barbados, for example, must be compared and contrasted with the second half of the eighteenth century in Saint-Domingue or the middle of the nineteenth century in Cuba. One sugar boom has to be measured in economic and social effects against another. These two sets of investigations, undertaken with care in their particulars and a reasonable degree of historical imagination in their combination, should lay bare the details of life in time and place with due attention to the state of the world market and the technological level of each section of the slave economy.

The work of Gilberto Freyre provides a good opportunity for a review of the methodological problems inherent in comparative analysis in general and a comparative analysis of the treatment of slaves in particular. The notion that Brazilian slaves received better treatment than others stems principally from his work, in which it has been a running thread for more than forty years. In his youthful paper on "Social Life in Brazil in the Middle of the Nineteenth Century," he asserted simply that slaves were well fed, well housed, well clothed, and generally well treated.[2] He attributed the belief that they were victims of cruelty to British-inspired antislavery crusaders and to the propagandistic zeal of Brazilian abolitionists. Gross exaggerations, he argued, reinforced guilt feelings to convince Brazilian public opinion that this distortion was the historical reality, whereas that reality was in fact another matter: "The Brazilian slave lived like a cherub if we contrast his lot with that of the English and other European factory workers in the middle of the last cen-

tury." Cruelty did exist, of course, but it was exceptional. Freyre added to these judgments a perceptive and essential observation: He noted that the cruelty of masters to slaves must be evaluated in the light of the cruelty of fathers to children, which in patriarchal Brazil was common. In the patriarchal setting of a quasifeudal colony, the word and whim of the father was absolute law. Children were punished severely and even killed for disobedience. The evidence of cruelty to slaves to some degree indicates the extension of the brutal side of family relations to the wider social family. In this way Freyre inadvertently showed how cruel treatment in one sense could imply good treatment in another.

Freyre extended these judgments back into the sixteenth and seventeenth centuries in his most famous work, *The Masters and the Slaves*,[3] but he said too much in defense of his thesis. When, for example, he noted that slaves could and did become artists, entertainers, dentists, barbers, teachers, and so forth—that they were well treated in several senses of the word—he failed to note that the very possibility of escape from the rigors of gang labor necessarily made the lot of the overwhelming majority the more unbearable. Fluidity of caste, under certain conditions, might have rendered the Brazilian slaves, as a class, more rebellious, dissatisfied, and alienated from the plantation community than were the slaves of the Old South.

Freyre's argument wavers when considered over time. On the one hand, he insists that Luso-Brazilian patriarchalism, with its medieval and Moorish ideas of family and society, guaranteed

---

[2] Gilberto Freyre, "Social Life in Brazil in the Middle of the Nineteenth Century," *Hispanic American Historical Review*, V (November, 1922), 597–628.

[3] Gilberto Freyre, *The Masters and the Slaves: A Study in the Development of Brazilian Civilization*, (2nd English language Ed., New York, 1956).

the slaves protection during the sixteenth and seventeenth centuries,
whereas the inroads of urbanization,
industrialization, and increased production for the world market undermined
patriarchalism during the second half
of the eighteenth and especially during
the nineteenth century. On the other
hand, he insists on maintaining his
thesis for the mid-nineteenth century as
well. Specifically, he is forced—in *The
Mansions and the Shanties* and retrospec-
tively in *Ordem e Progresso*[4]—to proclaim
the patriarchalism of the mineowners
of Minas Gerais and of the parvenu
coffee *fazendeiros* of Sao Paulo and
Rio de Janeiro. Yet, in order to
accent the patriarchalism of the sugar
fazendeiros of the Northeast, he repeatedly contrasts them with the cruder, more
avaricious men of Southern Brazil.
Since the center of slave-holding shifted
away from the Northeast during the
nineteenth century the admission grave-
ly compromises his thesis.

In *The Portuguese and the Tropics*,
Freyre replies to Lewis Hanke's criticism by asserting that his own thesis has
not been effectively challenged by
contrary evidence.[5] As a matter of fact,
it has been challenged by many writers.
Ironically, Freyre dedicates this book
to C. R. Boxer, whose own work,
particularly *Salvador de Sa and the
Struggle for Brazil and Angola* and *The
Golden Age of Brazil*, demolishes much of
Freyre's argument. One looks in vain
in Freyre for evidence, but more important, one looks in vain for definite
criteria by which treatment may be

judged good or bad, kind or cruel.
Freyre's evidence amounts mostly to
generalizations about Portuguese and
Brazilian national character, which are
objectionable not because they are not
measurable, for Freyre's poetic insights
give his sociology a depth that only the
most superficial positivists could ignore;
they are objectionable because he has
not applied to them available tests of
objective analysis. If, for example, he
is right in asserting in his essay, *O
Mundo que o Português crious* that the
Portuguese colonizer carried with him
a special kind of Christian sympathy
for allegedly inferior races, then this
sympathy ought to show up in specific
circumstances of master-slave relations.[6]

As we review Freyre's argument,
numerous methodological problems
emerge, and we may therefore use it to
begin to establish criteria for comparative analysis. By good treatment he
usually means day-to-day treatment—
food, shelter, work routine, leisure, and
the like—but often he defends his thesis
with reference to treatment in the other
two senses. In an absolute sense these
can be measured reasonably well. But
how useful would comparisons of absolute levels be? For example, suppose
we could establish that slaves in the
United States received more and better
food, had bigger and more comfortable
cabins, and were better clothed than
those in Brazil. We should then have
proven one of Freyre's contentions
wrong, but not necessarily another and
more significant one. For, if at the same
time we found that the material gap
between masters and slaves was greater
in the United States than in Brazil, then
his thesis of a more developed patri-

---

[4] Gilberto Freyre, *The Mansions and the
Shanties: The Making of Modern Brazil*, (New
York, 1963), *Ordem e progresso: Processo de dis-
integração das sociedades patriarcal e semipatriarcal
no Brasil sob o regime de trabalho livre* . . . , 2 vols.
(Rio de Janeiro, 1962).

[5] Gilberto Freyre, *The Portuguese and the Tropics*,
(Lisbon, 1961), p. 283.

[6] Gilberto Freyre, *O Mundo que o portugues criou
& Uma Cultura ameaçada: a Luso-Brasileira*,
(Lisbon, 1940).

archalism in Brazil might obtain. Since American slavery existed within a more advanced technological and economic national framework than did the Brazilian, the American slaves could have been the more comfortable and yet the more exploited simply because they produced a greater surplus. Kenneth M. Stampp errs in his discussion of this problem and in his criticism of the work of Ulrich B. Phillips. Stampp writes, "If . . . the quantity of labor were compared with the compensation the inevitable conclusion would be that most slaves were overworked."[7] And more to the point:

The slave's labor was controlled labor: his bargaining power was, by design, severely circumscribed. His labor was cheap labor: his compensation was, also by design, kept at a minimum. The free worker was, inevitably, more independent, more often successful in his efforts to increase his material comforts; and as a rule his labor was therefore more expensive.[8]

And again:

The Southern master's capitalization of his labor force has caused more confusion than anything else about the comparative cost of free and slave labor. This capital investment was not an added expense; it was merely the payment in a lump sum of a portion of what the employer of free labor pays over a period of years. The price of a slave, together with maintenance, was the cost of a lifetime claim to his labor; it was part of the wage an employer could have paid for a free laborer.[9]

Since this viewpoint has been criticized elsewhere[10] we may limit ourselves to

a brief reply. The cost of purchase, which Phillips incisively analyzed as contribution toward the "overcapitalization of labor," roughly corresponds to the capitalists' investment in plant and equipment, whereas the cost of maintenance precisely corresponds to the wage bill. To measure the extent to which labor's product was being appropriated by capital—Marx's "rate of exploitation"[11]—we need to divide the surplus (the total product less the wage bill) by the wage bill or investment in living labor (Marx's "variable capital"). It will be easily perceived that the entire relationship cannot be fruitfully examined without consideration of the productivity of labor and, specifically, that the low costs of maintenance may and often do produce dear, not cheap, labor. The less comfortable Brazilian slaves might have been, in this sense, less exploited and perhaps as a result, less alienated in a sociological and psychological sense, from their masters. Freyre's claim of greater patriarchalism might not fall with the appearances of negative evidence on living standards.

Several questions bear on the establishment of standards of judgment: Were the slaves of the Southern United States materially better off than those of Barbados, Cuba, or Brazil? Was the material gap between the classes greater or less than in other countries? What was the relationship between the standards of treatment and the technological possibilities inherent in the national and international economy at particular moments? Did slaves fare much worse than the depressed peasants of Eastern Europe, or the more advanced peasants of Western Europe, of the factory workers of England and New Eng-

---

[7] Kenneth M. Stampp, *The Peculiar Institution*, (New York, 1956), p. 750.

[8] *Ibid.*, p. 282.

[9] *Ibid.*, pp. 403–4.

[10] Eugene D. Genovese, *The Political Economy of Slavery*, (New York, 1965), esp. Chs. I and II.

[11] Karl Marx, *Capital*, 3 Vols. (Moscow, 1961), Vol. I, Ch. 18.

land?[12] These are quite different questions, requiring detailed research, but they only begin the discussion.

Let us consider the bearing of economic conditions, narrowly considered, on these questions. Boxer notes the appalling accident rate on the Brazilian sugar *engenhos*. If that rate was—as seems evident—significantly higher than the rate in Louisiana, then the slaves were less safe and worse treated in Brazil. But Louisiana developed its sugar later and under radically different conditions. First, the later development made it possible to introduce safer and more efficient machinery. Second, it occurred on virgin land, produced higher profits during the nineteenth century, and facilitated a more comfortable life for the laborers without special sacrifice on the part of the planters. Third, the location of the Louisiana sugar industry within a relatively advanced country offered masters and slaves alike more products and services at lower costs than were possible in Brazil. In short, in strictly economic terms, time and circumstance favored the American over the Brazilian slaves in the sugar districts. We might also note parenthetically that the national economic structure of the United States greatly facilitated the provision of food supplies for slaves, whereas that of Brazil inhibited it.[13]

Or, let us consider another set of economic and demographic data: those bearing on the importation of African slaves. Examination of data on living conditions in French Saint-Domingue, the British Caribbean, Cuba, Brazil, and the Southern United States reveals a common pattern. So long as the slave trade remained open, slaves were greatly abused in all systems. Conversely, the shutting off of the slave trade and the sources of cheap labor generally stimulated increased attention to the health and comfort of the slaves. For Brazil and Cuba, the continuation of an active slave trade into the middle of the nineteenth century militated against kind treatment, however defined. Demographic analyses of Brazil demonstrate that the death rate of slaves probably ran ahead of the brith rate during the nineteenth century. For Cuba, and indeed for many of the sugar islands at one time or another, an open slave trade, when combined with the rapid expansion of the sugar market, greatly increased the tendency toward brutality and dehumanization. The evidence from the Caribbean, whether British, French, or Spanish, is clear and decisive.[14]

---

[12] Raimondo Luraghi has recently made an estimate: "Questa era la schiavitù nel sud; e bilanciadone tutti gli aspetti, non si può negare che la condizione degli schiavi fosse indubbiamente nel suo complesso assai meno crudela che quella dei lavoratori liberi d'Europa quale ci e descritta per esempio da Friedrich Engels nelle *Condizioni della classe operai in Inghilterra*, o da Rodolfo Morandi nella sua *Storia della grande industria italiana*; e certamente meno dura di quella che ancora per anni sarebbe esistita nella compagni italiane, tra i braccianti, quale la possiamo veder descritta nelle terribili pagine della *Inchiesta agraria Jacini*." *Storia della guerra civile americana* (Torino, 1966). Luraghi adds that the average conditions—he means the material conditions of our first category—were "certainly better" than those of the East European and South Italian peasants and even perhaps of those of the economically advanced Po Valley.

[13] This point has been made by Celso Furtado, *The Economic Growth of Brazil*, (Berkeley, 1963), p. 128. The generalization, however, needs to be subjected to a more careful analysis than has yet been provided.

[14] Cf. Furtado, *Economic Growth*, pp. 127–29; C. R. Boxer, *Portuguese Society in the Tropics: The Municipal Councils of Goa, Bahia, and Luanda, 1510–1800*, (Madison, 1965), p. 130; Caio Prado Junior, *História Económica do Brasil*, 7th Ed. (São Paulo, 1962), esp. Chs. 10–18. For a perceptive and suggestive discussion of the relationship between commercialization of

These data raise another problem, which existed in Brazil as well as in the Caribbean. Almost invariably male slaves greatly outnumbered female. Stein has shown that this imbalance was especially serious on the coffee *fazendas* of southern Brazil. To take several local illustrations: in Sao Paulo in 1797, white females outnumbered males 47,053 to 42,270, but black males outnumbered females 20,699 to 17,971; as late as 1872 in Rio Grande do Sul, male slaves outnumbered female 35,686 to 32,705.[15] We might then ask how the resultant sexual deprivation of the male slaves ought to be weighed in the pros and cons of good treatment. It is difficult to assess the effects of promiscuity and loosely structured mating patterns on the slaves, but Orlando Patterson's book, *The Sociology of Slavery*,[16] which analyzes in depth similar patterns in Jamaica, suggests grave short- and long-run consequences. In any case, what are we to make of those hymns to slave family life in the Hispanic countries in the face of these data?

We are led again, even by our economic data, to the social plane. Tannenbaum also argues that Brazilian slaves were better treated than American, but unlike Freyre he restricts himself to two sets of related questions: those relating to the possibilities of escape from slave status altogether and those relating to the possibilities for absorbing the freed men into the national culture. Freyre himself did pioneering work on these questions, and had he, like Tannenbaum, left matters there, he would have remained on strong ground.[17] The image of Brazil as a "racial democracy" is being subjected to hard blows by a growing number of scholars who are making intensive sociological investigations. There is no longer any doubt that Brazil, too, has had a color problem since slavery times and that Negroes still suffer from considerable discrimination and prejudice. Yet, there is also no doubt that these problems exist on a different level from those in the United States, that Brazil has avoided the extreme forms of racism characterizing the American experience, and that the older view popularized by Freyre needs to be qualified,

---

agriculture and the deterioration of institutional arrangements designed to protect Caribbean slaves see the review-essay by Sidney W. Mintz of Elkins' *Slavery* in *American Anthropologist*, LXIII (June 1961), 579–87, esp. p. 582. Herbert Klein, *Slavery in The Americas*, (Chicago, 1967), which contrasts the experience of Virginia and Cuba, supports Elkins' view and insists on the continued vitality of Cuban institutions during the sugar boom. Yet, even if Klein is right, the appearance of a strong counter-tendency cannot be denied. An older, less defensible but still suggestive treatment may be found in Hubert H. S. Aimes, *A History of Slavery in Cuba*, (New York, 1907), p. 266.

[15] Roger Bastide and Florestan Fernandes, *Brancos e negros em São Paulo*, 2nd Ed., rev. (São Paulo, 1959), p. 16; Cardoso, *Capitalismo e escravidão*, p. 78.

[16] H. Orlando Patterson, *The Sociology of Slavery*, (London, 1967).

[17] These criticisms hardly add up to a general assessment. His great contributions, which alone make *The Masters and the Slaves* a masterpiece, have been his penetrating studies of the ways in which slavery resulted in the amalgamation of whites and Negroes, not only biologically but on every level of culture. It is therefore pointless to berate him for concentrating on house slaves and for judging the life of the field slaves by the standards of the Big House. His primary concern has been the interpenetration of diverse peoples, and it is merely a matter of qualification to argue that the majority of the slaves did not participate immediately and in a comfortable way. The essential point was the effect of racial interpenetration on the consciousness of whites and blacks; the full participation of both races was not decisive here. Frank Tannenbaum is therefore correct in demanding that American historians reassess Southern slavery along Freyre's lines of inquiry.

not discarded.[18] David Brion Davis, for example, skillfully juxtaposes an admission that Hispanic peoples have been more tolerant, and therefore more able to assimilate colored peoples, to the plausible assertion that slave systems have generally come to rest on one or another kind of discrimination.[19]

Care in definition of terms and precision in comparison of the strictly comparable should take us a long way toward the solution of many problems, the ramifications of which far transcend

the study of slavery. Once we have brought order to the subject of slave treatment—once we have made separate estimates of its several meanings— we can begin to evaluate in more than an abstract way the quality and significance of paternalism and patriarchalism in the several slave-holding classes. Such an evaluation should provide an essential ingredient for the construction of a history of the intersection of bourgeois and prebourgeois social formations in the modern world. A proper comparative study of treatment will simultaneously lead us into another question that extends by implication into every historical period and that has particular importance for our own: In what ways do the particular circumstances of the lower classes and their treatment (in each particular sense) by the individuals and classes in power condition their consciousness and perception of reality? condition the extent and form of their acquiescence in oppression and the extent and form of their will to revolution?

---

[18] For critical appraisals of Brazilian race relations see especially, Bastide and Fernandes, *Brancos e negros;* Fernando Henrique Cardoso and Octavio Ianni, *Côr e mobilidade social em Florianópolis,* (São Paulo, 1960); Roger Bastide, "The Development of Race Relations in Brazil," Ch. I of Guy Hunter, ed., *Industrialisation and Race Relations: A Symposium,* (London and New York, 1965); and Oracy Nogueira, "Skin Color and Social Class," in *Plantation Systems of the New World: Papers and Discussion Summaries of the Seminar Held in San Juan, Puerto Rico,* (Washington, D.C., 1959), pp. 164–78.

[19] Davis, *Problem of Slavery,* p. 53.

H. ORLANDO PATTERSON

The General Causes of
Jamaican Slave Revolts

Horace Orlando Patterson teaches sociology at the University of the West Indies, Jamaica. He studied at the University of the West Indies and the London School of Economics. By the time he received his Ph. D. in 1965 from the London School (at the age of 25), he had already published two novels, The Children of Sisyphus *(1964) and* An Absence of Ruins *(1965), as well as essays and short stories.* The Sociology of Slavery, *from which the following selection is taken, is based on his doctoral dissertation and appeared in 1967.*

With the possible exception of Brazil, no other slave society in the New World experienced such continuous and intense servile revolts as Jamaica. During the seventeenth and eighteenth centuries the slaves of Barbados and the Leeward Islands were remarkably docile compared with those of Jamaica, only two mild disturbances taking place in all the latter islands during this time.[1] Aptheker "found records of ap-

Reprinted from H. Orlando Patterson, *The Sociology of Slavery* (London: MacGibbon & Kee Ltd., 1967), pp. 273–83, by permission of the publisher. (*The Sociology of Slavery* is to be published Winter 1969 in the United States by A.S. Barnes & Co., Inc.)

[1] Elsa Goveia, *Slave Society in the British Leeward Islands, 1780–1800,* Unpublished Ph.D. Thesis, University of London, p. 6.

proximately 250 revolts and conspiracies in the history of American Negro slavery."[2] But his definition of a revolt was rather liberal[3] and in any case, when these 250 cases are spread over the much greater slave population of America and over the much longer period of slavery there, the Jamaican record is far more impressive. In addition, the scale of the average Jamaican revolt was far greater and more dangerous than that of the average American. The most serious revolt in the latter country—that of Nat Turner—involved only 70 slaves. The average number of slaves in the Jamaica

[2] Aptheker, *American Negro Slave Revolts,* p. 162.
[3] *Ibid.,* p. 10, A minimum of ten slaves, etc.

211

revolts of the seventeenth and eighteenth centuries was approximately 400, and the three most serious revolts of the island—the first Maroon war; the 1760 rebellion; and the 1832 rebellion—each involved over a thousand slaves.

For this greater spirit of rebellion among the Jamaican slaves compared with those of the other British slave societies of the New World several causes may be given. First, there was the ratio of masters to slaves. On average, there were, during the seventeenth and eighteenth centuries over ten slaves to every white person in the island; and in the nineteenth century, over thirteen slaves to every white.[4] In Barbados, on the other hand, the average ratio during the entire period of slavery was very close to four slaves to one white,[5] and although after 1724 the number of slaves increased greatly in the Leeward Islands, with the exception of Antigua, it was never more than eight Negroes to one white. In the case of the American South we find that of the fourteen slave states only two—South Carolina and Mississippi—had slave populations which slightly outnumbered the whites. In nine of the other states the slave population varied between 1.5 and 33 per cent; and in three, between 44 per cent and 47 per cent of the total population.[6] Thus, of all the British slave societies Jamaica had by far the highest ratio of slaves to whites. A brief comparative analysis is enough to demonstrate a positive correlation between the density of the slave population and the frequency of servile revolts. If we take the most famous of the slave revolts of ancient times—that of the Sicilian revolt of 134–32 B.C.—we find that it

was that area of the Roman Empire which had the highest proportion of slaves in the population which broke into rebellion, Sicily being, according to Mommsen, "the chosen land of the plantation system."[7] In the case of the Leeward Islands we find that the only two serious conspiracies took place in Antigua in 1736[8] and Tortola in 1790[9] both of which had the two highest ratios of slaves to whites in their population.[10] And with regard to the United States Aptheker has noted that "areas of dense Negro population, particularly areas showing a recent accession, were very frequently the centers of unrest."[11] It is not unreasonable to conclude therefore, that the greater density of the Jamaican slave population partly accounts for its larger number of slave revolts in comparison with other slave societies of the New World.

The second general cause accounting for the frequency of Jamaican slave revolts is to be found in the ratio between creole and African slaves. Naturally, a slave population which had a higher proportion of slaves who were born freemen and were enslaved only as adults would exhibit a greater tendency to revolt than one in which there was a higher proportion of creoles who were born into the system and socialized in it. It is significant that almost every one of the revolts of the seventeenth and eighteenth centuries was instigated and carried out by African slaves (and their children born in the rebel camps). The agent for Jamaica in England wrote after the 1776 revolt that the planters had been "more particularly alarmed

---

[4] See Chapter 4 on Slave population; also, Pitman, *The Development of the B.W.I.*, pp. 373–74.

[5] *Ibid*, pp. 372–73.

[6] K. Stampp, *The Peculiar Institution*, p. 41.

[7] T. Mommsen, *The History of Rome*, vol. III, pp. 306–10; see also W. L. Westermann, *The Slave Systems of Greek and Roman Antiquity*, p. 65.

[8] Pitman, *op. cit.*, pp. 59–60.

[9] Goveia, *op. cit.*, p. 247.

[10] Pitman, *op. cit.*, pp. 379–80, 383.

[11] Aptheker, *op. cit.*, p. 114.

on Account of many of the Creole Negroes being concerned in it, who never
were concerned in former rebellions."[12]
In an earlier chapter we have estimated the African sector of the slave
population in the middle of the eighteenth century at about a half; at the
end of the eighteenth century at a little
more than a quarter; and in the last
decade or so of slavery, at about a little
less than a quarter. The reason for the
persistence of the African sector was
the failure of the slave population to
reproduce itself in Jamaica. On the
other hand, we may infer from the
more successful attempts at reproduction both in Barbados[13]* and the
United States[14] that the creole slaves
formed a much greater proportion of
those populations at a much earlier
period than they did in Jamaica. This
factor, in turn, partly accounts for the
greater frequency of slave revolts in
Jamaica.

Thirdly, there was the quality of the
slaves bought by the Jamaican planters.
It is remarkable that almost every one
of the serious rebellions during the
seventeenth and eighteenth centuries
was instigated and carried out mainly
by Akan slaves who came from a highly
developed militaristic régime, skilled
in jungle warfare.[15] Yet a bill to restrain
their entry into the island after the 1765
revolt was defeated.[16] It is significant

that modern researches on the descendants of the maroon rebels reveal a
marked degree of Akan cultural sur-
vivals mong them.[17]

A fourth general cause of these revolts lies in the character of the
Jamaican whites—their inefficiency (especially in military matters) and
general smugness. Goveia explains the
absence of any serious slave revolt in
the Leewards in terms of the rigid
execution of the slave laws which were
"expressly designed to make formal
organization virtually impossible."[18]
Jamaica too, had many severe laws
in this respect but they were made
useless by the planters' lack of vigilance.
The planters' attitude toward slave
revolts oscillated between extreme
hysteria and unbelievable smugness.
Corbett wrote near the middle of the
eighteenth century that:

One would imagine that Planters really
think that Negroes are not of the same
Species with us, but that being of a different
Mould and Nature as well as Colour, they
were made entirely for our Use, with
Instincts proper for that Purpose, having
as great a propensity to subjection as we
have to command and loving slavery as
naturally as we do liberty; and that there
is not need for Management, but that of
themselves they will most pleasantly to hard
labour, hard Usages of all kinds, Cruelties
and Injustice at the Caprice of one white
man—such one would imagine is the
Planter's Way of thinking.[19]

He bemoans the neglect of the slave
laws, and on the hysteria of the planters
in time of danger he comments: "As no
People are more thoughtless of Danger
at a Distance, so I must own they are
apprehensive of it enough when it is

---

[12] Fuller to Board of Trade, 27/10/1776:
C.O. 138/27.

[13] See Pitman, "Slavery on British West
India Plantations in the 18th Century," in
Journal of Negro History, 11, 584–668.

[14] Stampp, *op. cit.*, p. 305; the U.S. slave
population grew by natural increase at a rate
of 23 per cent each decade.

[15] See W. W. Claridge, *A History of the Gold
Coast and Ashanti*, vol. 1, pt. 3–4.

[16] Long, *op. cit.*, Bk. 3, p. 470.

* Thus, in 1817 there were 71,777 creole
(345 of them from other islands) and only
5,496 African slaves in Barbados. See BPP, Vol.
xvi, 1818, p. 111.

[17] J. J. Williams, *The Maroons of Jamaica*,
(1938).

[18] Goveia, *op. cit.*, p. 245.

[19] Corbett, *Essay Concerning Slavery*, p. 19.

at hand."[20] The vacillation of the planters was particularly marked during the nineteenth century. Between 1800 and 1825—due largely to the successful slave revolt in the neighboring island of Haiti—the responses and fears of the planters in respect of conspiracies or suspected plots were out of all proportion to what did in fact take place among the slaves which, in the words of the governor, often amounted to little more than "a very active spirit of enquiry which may be naturally accounted for without attributing to them any criminal intentions."[21] On the other hand, by 1831 the planters had, to use Corbett's phrase, relating to the mid-eighteenth century "took T'other Turn and fell quietly flat a-sleep again." The abolition debate was openly discussed by them in front of their slaves without the slightest awareness of the impact it was having on them. One of them, an assemblyman, even went so far as to write that "Our Slave Population have been too long habituated to hear discussed the details of the question of slavery and emancipation, for us to entertain any alarm from their recollections on this subject."[22] And a visitor to the island during the period of the rebellion wrote that:

The greater part of the inhabitants of Jamaica had indeed been lulling themselves into a fancied and fatal security, while, in fact, they were sleeping on a mine; and any one who suspected the probability of an insurrection was looked upon as a timid alarmist (even after the preparatory notes of insubordination had been sounded).[23]

It was in vain that the governor pleaded with them to be more discreet in their denunciation of the abolitionists.[24] One can well understand then, why the masters had no hint of the widespread rebellion that broke out after Christmas 1831 until a few days before it actually began,[25] although the secrecy with which the slaves kept their plans must be borne in mind.

A fifth cause of slave revolts in the island was to be found in the treatment and maintenance of the slaves. A historian of ancient slavery has noted that "in any slave system the slave group has definite rights—not legal, but actual, and sanctioned by custom. These rights the slaves both accept and insist upon;"[26] and he gives this as "the primary cause of the first Sicilian slave revolt."[27] It has already been pointed out in our chapter on the slave laws that the Jamaican slave, like his American and Sicilian counterpart, had certain minimum customary rights which he insisted upon. Without becoming involved in the rather tired controversy as to which area of the New World had the most severe form of slavery—a controversy which Professor Harris, has, not unreasonably, dismissed as "a waste of time"[28]—it may be suggested that there was one feature of Jamaican slave society which may well have encouraged the greater infringement of the minimal customary rights of the slaves. This was the excessive degree of absenteeism which was greater than in any other slave colony in the New World. Pitman makes the cogent

[20] *Ibid.*

[21] *Report of the Secret C'ttee at Close of Sessions, 1824.*

[22] A. H. Beaumont, "Compensation-Manumission, etc." enclosed in C.O. 137/179.

[23] T. Foulks, *Eighteen Months in Jamaica*, etc. (1833).

[24] Belmore to Board of Trade, 6/8/1831 in C.O. 137/179.

[25] Belmore to Board of Trade, Jan. 6, 1832, C.O. 137/181.

[26] W. L. Westermann, 'Slave Maintenance and Slave Revolts, in *Classical Philology*, Vol. 40, 1945, p. 8.

[27] *Ibid.*, p. 9.

[28] Marvin Harris, *Patterns of Race in the Americas*, p. 72.

observation that the period during which the whites suffered most from the rebels and general desertion from the estates—i.e., between 1730 and 1739—was that in which the profits from sugar had greatly declined, in which large numbers of whites were leaving the island and those supervising the slaves were making excessive demands on their labor in addition to reducing their supplies of clothing and food.[29]

Another factor explaining the revolts of the island was its geography. The mountainous interior of the country with its intricate, innumerable ravines, naturally concealed mountain passes, precipices and forests, was ideal for guerrilla warfare. In this respect the African slaves, used to the jungle warfare of their own country, had an insurmountable advantage over their British masters. It was their knowledge of the interior country and the guerrilla tactics they evolved[30] in it which more than compensated for the inferiority of the Maroons in arms and numbers against the whites. The latter sought to redress the balance in their favor by importing Mosquito Indians in the 1720's[31] and specially trained Cuban bloodhounds in 1795,[32] but there is no evidence that either of these measures proved of any use. After 1740, however, with the Maroons on the side of the whites, the opportunities offered by the interior of the country were cut off to future rebels.

Finally, between 1770 and 1832, rebellions in Jamaica were caused partly by the impact of certain social, religious, and political forces current at

that time, on the slave. The agent for Jamaica in England suggested that the American Revolution may have been partly responsible for the slave revolt of 1776, the first in which the creole slaves played a significant part.[33] And Balcarres, Governor of Jamaica, insisted that the second Maroon war of 1795 was largely instigated by professional revolutionaries from Haiti, France, and the United States.[34] So much did the planters fear the contagious revolutionary spirit of the Haitian Negroes who had successfully revolted against their masters, that an entire regiment of soldiers who had been recruited from among the slaves to augment the troops of an ill-fated attack on Haiti was refused readmittance into the island. They were disbanded in Haiti and "numbers of them joined the enemy."[35]

The abolition movement also played its part in inciting the slaves to revolt. Its influence, however, was due largely to the misinterpretation (sometimes deliberately) by the slaves of the debates they heard among their masters and—in a few cases—read in local or foreign newspapers.[36] Large numbers of slaves who joined the various conspiracies of the nineteenth century were convinced that the King, or some other benefactor abroad, had sent their "free-paper" but that the planters were maliciously keeping it from them. When the slave trade was abolished in 1807 it was generally believed among the slaves that they had been emancipated. Related to

---

[29] Pitman, *op. cit.*, 1917, p. 115.
[30] For a description of these tactics, see Dallas, *op. cit.*, vol. I, pp. 39–40.
[31] *Ibid.*, p. 38; also, Lawes to Board of Trade, C.O. 137/13, f. 93.
[32] Edwards, *Proceedings*, pp. IXV-IXXXI, also Dallas, *op. cit.*, vol. II, letters 9–12.

[33] Fuller to Lords, 27/10/1776: C.O. 138/27.
[34] Earl of Balcarres to the Duke of York, 20/5/1795, in *The Maroon War*, p. 7.
[35] Gardner, *op. cit.*, p. 225.
[36] See Evidence of Rev T. Stewart, "Papers Relating to Rebellion 1832": C.O. 137/181; Evidence of Lieut. Col. Codrington, *ibid.*; Viscount Goderich to Earle of Belmore, *ibid.*, Bleby, *op. cit.*, pp. 138–42.

the abolition movement were the activities of the missionaries who had begun to preach among the slaves with some effect since the last decade of the eighteenth century. While these preachers strenuously denied ever inciting the slaves to revolt, there can be little doubt that the latter saw in the egalitarian aspects of Christianity part of the justification they needed to rebel against their masters. When a popular preacher left for a short stay in England in 1831 his return was anxiously awaited as it was the general opinion that he would be returning with "the gift" or their "free-paper."[37] Indeed, the rebellion of 1831–32 was dubbed the "Baptist war" by the Negroes.[38]

As in Jamaica, the American Revolution,[39] the Haitian slave revolution,[40] the abolition movement,[41] as well as rumor of the King having sent orders to set them free and debates about emancipation all played their part in inciting the American slaves to revolt. The Haitian revolution—the only completely successful slave revolt in the New World—was directly inspired and made possible by the French Revolution. There are also instances in ancient slavery where rumors regarding their emancipation incited agitation among slaves, for example, the possible disturbances created in Asia Minor by the rumor of the emancipation of the slaves in Pergamum during the First Century B.C.[42]

The final question to be answered is why was it that despite the favorable conditions discussed above, the Jamai-

can slaves failed to overthrow their masters? The first answer is the divisions within the slave group itself. These were of two types: firstly, that between the African slaves. Due partly to the deliberate policy of the masters, and, more important, to the nature of the supply of slaves, it was the unusual estate which had all, or even the majority of its slaves from one tribal stock. And it would seem that the different tribal groups hated "one another so mortally that some of them would rather die by the Hands of the English than join with other Africans in an Attempt to shake off their yoke."[43] The second major division was that between the creole slaves and the Africans. We have already discussed the animosity which the creoles bore for the Africans, and it is inconceivable that any of them would allow themselves to be led in a rebellion by an African.

A second reason for the slaves' lack of success was, paradoxically, their early successes against the whites. The whites, having been obliged to come to terms with the Maroons in 1739, then proceeded to use them to prevent or subdue further uprisings. It was unfortunate for the slaves that Cudjoe—the rebel chief with whom the first treaty was signed—should have been as obsequious in his relation with the whites as he was, since the position from which he negotiated with them was not weak. Several of his commanding officers disagreed with the treaty to the extent of rebelling against his authority and attempting to incite the slaves on the plantations to revolt.[44]

Finally, there was the military strength of the whites. It is true that the militia was an inefficient body but,

[37] B. M. Senior, *Jamaica, As it was, As it is, and as it May be*, (1835) pp. 183–84.
[38] T. Foulks; *op. cit.*, p. 112.
[39] Aptheker, *op. cit.*, p. 87.
[40] *Ibid.*, pp. 97–100.
[41] *Ibid.*, pp. 79, 81.
[42] Westermann, "Slave Maintenence and Slave Revolts," *op. cit.*, pp. 9–10.

[43] Leslie, *A New History*, p. 311.
[44] See "Cudjoe's Fidelity," C. E. Long Papers, B.M. *op. cit.*

however incompetent its members were, they had at least some semblance of up-to-date military training and a more than adequate supply of arms. Against these the relatively primitive African rebels could never hope to win in an open engagement, and when the possibility of compensating for their disadvantage by resorting to guerrilla warfare was cut off, the chances of a successful revolt became very thin. This was, of course, as long as the whites remained united. Thus, if we compare the Jamaican situation with that of Haiti it will be found that the crucial difference lies in the hopeless division of the master class during the course of the successful rebellion in the latter country.[45] The French Revolution created fatal divisions between the loyalists, radical revolutionaries, and bourgeois revolutionaries among the Haitian planter-class, and, what was worse, the political state of the mother country made it impossible for her to assist the planters until it was too late.

Selfish and incompetent though they were, the Jamaican planters always managed at least to present a united front against the rebels and there was never any question of losing the support of the mother country. Thus, when assistance was asked for during the first Maroon war, two regiments of soldiers from Gibraltar were promptly sent to the island, having an immediate impact on those slaves who were not in revolt.[46] Throughout the remainder of the period of slavery there were always at least two regiments stationed on the island. In addition, Jamaica was a frequent port of call for squadrons of the British navy which, on several occasions (not

always to the best effect) offered their services in quelling revolts.[47] It is quite possible too, that the terrible reprisals of the whites after they had subdued a rebellion deterred other slaves from rebelling.[48]

This chapter has attempted to explain the reasons for the frequency and intensity of the resistance of the Jamaican slaves to their exploitation, and the reasons why they did not, like their Haitian neighbors, completely succeed. We have seen that most of this resistance came from among that section of them which had already experienced freedom. But in the last days of slavery even the creole slaves, who had never known what it was to be free, began to organize revolts against their masters, and the last and most damaging of all the rebellions remains a living memory of their struggle for something they had never experienced but for which they felt a need sufficiently strong for which to die.

What then, accounts for the presence of this need which seems to survive under conditions which in every way conspire to smother it? Every rebellion, Camus has written, "tacitly invokes a value." This value is something embedded deep in the human soul, a value discovered as soon as a subject begins to reflect on himself[49] through which he inevitably comes to the conclusion that "I *must* become free—that is, that my freedom must be won."[50] In the final analysis it is the discovery of this universal value which justifies

---

[45] See C. L. R. James, *The Black Jacobins*, pp. 27–61; 174–98.

[46] Hunter to Board of Trade, 13/11/1731: C.O. 137/19.

[47] Hunter to Board of Trade, C.O. 137/20, f. 165; Swanton to Hunter, *ibid.*, f. 184; Extract out of Lieut. Swanton's Journal Rel. to Expedition against the Rebel Negroes, *ibid.*, f. 192–93; Gardner, *op. cit.*, p. 145.

[48] See Review of Rebellions above.

[49] Gabriel Marcel, *The Existential Background of Human Dignity*, p. 87.

[50] *Ibid.*

and stimulates the most tractable of slaves to rebel. As Camus pointed out: "Rebellion cannot exist without the feeling that somewhere, in some way you are justified. It is in this way that the rebel slave says yes and no at the same time. He affirms that there are limits and also that he suspects—and wishes to preserve—the existence of certain things beyond those limits. He stubbornly insists that there are certain things in him which are worth while . . . and which must be taken into consideration."[51]

[51] Albert Camus, *The Rebel*, p. 19.

III

On the Debate

This last part of the book contains three selections that, in different ways, try to evaluate the ideological and philosophical issues in the debate and to assess the present state of empirical work. Magnus Mörner's article is the only one in this volume that has been cut, for the first part deals with ethnic demography and racial mixture. We have included only the section on slavery, race relations, and abolition. Genovese's article takes up the two general tendencies presented in Part One and suggests a materialist viewpoint opposed to that of Williams and Harris and the economic determinists. Finley's essay on Davis' *Problem of Slavery* concludes this part of the book and fittingly closes the book as a whole. Finley, probably the world's foremost authority on ancient slavery, brings his wide learning to bear on a number of problems concerning modern slavery and simultaneously criticizes certain idealist and mechanistic tendencies that have persisted throughout the discussion.

MAGNUS MÖRNER

The History of Race Relations
in Latin America:
Some Comments on the
State of Research

Magnus Mörner is Professor of History at Queens College of the City University of New York. He earned his Ph.D. degree at Stockholm University and served for thirteen years as Director of the Library and Institute of Latin American Studies in Stockholm. He has published and edited a number of books and articles on Latin American history, including The Expulsion of the Jesuits from Latin America *(1965) and* Race Mixture in the History of Latin America *(1967).*

THE MESTIZAJE IN THE LEGISLATION AND SOCIAL STRATIFICATION OF COLONIAL SPANISH AMERICA

Reflecting the dichotomy between the Spanish conquerors and the vanquished Indians, colonial legislation at first did not reckon with the appearance of a third group, the mestizos. Intermarriage, which was clearly sanctioned in

1514 in accordance with canonical rules, legally opened the way for the admission of mestizos into the ranks of the *españoles*. The idea that the Crown promoted intermarriage (e.g., Barón Castro, 1946, p. 799*) has been dispelled by Konetzke (1946 b, p. 216). The dualistic concept of the two Republics, that of Spaniards and that of Indians, became the guideline of municipal organization. The continued existence of two parallel communities, both of

Reprinted from Magnus Mörner, "The History of Race Relations in Latin America: Some Comments on the State of Research," *Latin American Research Review*, I, No. 3 (Summer, 1966), 23–44, by permission of the editor.

* Complete references are given in the bibliography at the end of this selection. Eds.

221

them stratified, was taken for granted (see, e.g., Góngora, 1951, pp. 78ff). On a theoretical level, this would have been compatible with a high degree of equality between Spaniards and Indians, though it is difficult to share with the Chilean historian Vial Correa (1964) a great appreciation of the equalitarian spirit of the early sixteenth century.

The dualistic legal theory was soon challenged by two important facts: the immense majority of the mestizos were illegitimate; and the African slaves brought to the Indies in spite of severe prohibitions also took part in the process of miscegenation. The stigma thus attached to persons of mixed origin did affect the legal as well as the social attitude. Mestizos born out of wedlock and free people of African descent were subject to legal discrimination by the fact that the fictitious dualism ignored their existence for a long time. In addition, they were also subjected to specific discriminatory laws. This discrimination was rather slight against the mestizos, much harsher against "free" Negroes, mulattoes, and zamboes; yet the separate legal statutes established for these different groups remained rather incomplete. The whole matter used to be studied only on the basis of the *Recopilación de Leyes de los Reinos de las Indias* of 1680. It is now becoming much better known especially because of the source collection and studies published by Richard Konetzke (1953–62; 1960). A special aspect of the legislation, that which imposed residential dualism and separation excluding non-Indians from settling among Indians, is the subject of my own research (1961 a, b; 1962 a, b; 1963; 1964 a, b; 1965). A study of Puebla highlights this policy in the urban sector (Marín Tamayo, 1960).

Blurring the border between social

legislation and social reality is still a weakness of certain historians of the *Hispanidad* persuasion (e.g., Barón Castro, 1946). It is nevertheless apparent that the relationship between the two deserves great attention. Referring to the triumph of the Spanish Crown over feudalistic tendencies in the New World during the *Conquista*, Konetzke states that "metropolitan legislation was an essential factor in molding colonial society" (1953–62, I, p. vii; 1951). His view is shared by Juan Beneyto, for example (1961, p. 232). In the concrete case of the legal status of the mixed bloods, however, it seems that the role of the Crown was largely passive. It was greatly influenced by pressures from special interests and by prevailing prejudice.

Accounts of colonial society have often suffered from oversimplification. Undoubtedly the coincidental circumstance that the contemporary term for mixed-bloods happened to be *casta* has induced some students to classify it erroneously as a "Caste Society" (see Corominas, 1954, I, pp. 722–24). As Lyle McAlister points out in his perceptive study of the social structure in New Spain (1963), society in the Indies was the result of the transfer of the hierarchical, estate-based, corporative society of late medieval Castile to a multiracial, colonial situation in the New World. The location of the existing ethnic groups within the hierarchical structure gave rise to what A. Lipschutz (1944, p. 75; 1963) has called "pigmentocracy." In accordance with "the law of the spectrum of racial colors," he states that the privileged group tried to justify its own position in terms of physical or racial characteristics. As time went on, racial differences between the exploiters and the exploited continued to be invoked although they no longer existed. That prejudice thus helped to maintain and strengthen the established hierarchical order is not at all surprising.[1] The Iberian concept of *limpieza de sangre* (see Sicroff, 1960) was easily transformed in the colonial situation to exclude those of illegitate or slave origin. The corporative structure offered excellent opportunities for effective discrimination (see, e.g., Konetzke, 1949 b; Carrera Stampa, 1954, pp. 223–44; Leal, 1963, pp. 310–33). Many historians, especially those of the Hispanidad persuasion, have made tenacious efforts to prove that prejudice and discrimination in the Indies were social and religious, not racial in character. Konetzke (1946 b, p. 237) also makes this point. Others, on the contrary, approach the issue somewhat anachronistically and condemn Spanish American society as "racist" (e.g., Dusenberry, 1948). Even if one does not accept the Marxist position that prejudice is merely an invention with which to defend economic self-interest (Bagú, 1952, p. 54), this controversy seems to be utterly sterile. What matters is the precise relationship that existed in Spanish America between social (and even legal) status and the color of the skin.

To what extent did the different strata of the *Régimen de castas* fulfill special social functions? Both Marxist and non-Marxist students have tried to identify the castas in functional terms (see, e.g., Chavez Orozco, 1938, pp. 24–25; Aguirre Beltrán, 1946, pp. 270–71).[2] But the results of their efforts are hardly convincing in view of the bewildering complexity of the social reality that we find in the documenta-

tion. A more thoroughgoing study of this social reality has only been initiated. The interesting facts about Negro slavery in the Indian "ghetto" of Lima presented by Emilio Harth-Terré (1861) exemplify what a scholar may uncover. Was the Régimen de castas a kind of veil draped over a reality of economic classes (Bagú, 1952, p. 23)? We still lack information about wealth, income, and occupation that would be essential for a meaningful discussion of the issue. To the extent that members of different ethnic groups were found within the same occupation, for example, were there discriminatory wage rates? Of the scattered evidence that we possess, certain sources indicate that there were (Jara, 1959, p. 74), others that there were not (Harth-Terré and Márquez Abanto, 1962, p. 39 and *passim*). Whereas economic classes can be discerned in colonial society, especially during the later period and in the rural sector, it seems reasonable to regard them, in McAlister's terms (1963, pp. 362–63), "as an incipient situation." He believes that "the value systems" corresponding to economic classes "were lacking or at best rudimentary." It was the Régimen de castas that supplied the social values until the end of the colonial period, and this order was sanctioned in law.

On the assumption that the Régimen de castas reflected a social reality, the struggles that took place between different social strata in the course of the colonial period and within the framework of the Wars of Emancipation need not be explained only or even mainly in terms of class exploitation and conflict. They may also have derived from frustration engendered by the different forms of discrimination imposed by the Régimen de castas. Eric Wolf (1962, pp. 236ff) has given an eloquent account of the alienation of the mestizo

---

[1] The obligatory work on prejudice is Allport (1950).

[2] A paper by J. Comas at the Race and Class Conference in 1965, analyzed the elaborate scheme presented by E. Molina Enríquez in "Grandes Problemas Nacionales."

and of his becoming a rootless "power seeker." Mestizo frustration also manifested itself in revolts against the established order (see, e.g., Guthrie, 1945; Lopez Martínez, 1965). When studying these various conflicts, Marxist historians are faced with a dilemma. Thus Federico Brito Figueroa (1961, p. 85 with reference to F. Engels) admits that ethnic and juridical elements related to different social groups did influence the class struggle and sometimes even gave it external form. Consequently the economic origin of the aspirations of the contending parties has been obscured.

The Régimen de castas is sometimes presented as an almost static phenomenon. Much more attention should be paid to its gradual development and decline. The life story of an Inca-descended mestizo by Ella Temple (1948) shows, for example, how late-sixteenth-century mestizos of good status found themselves gradually downgraded to a casta. On the other hand, the military organization of the eighteenth century enabled *pardos* to rise from their low status and even share certain privileges of the military establishment (McAlister, 1957, chapter IV). When introduced in the Indies, the marriage regulations of 1776 were changed to place the mestizos in a better position that the mulattoes (Konetzke, 1953–62, III, p. 477). Toward the end of the colonial era, cultured and wealthy mulattoes were also sometimes able to obtain legal recognition as "whites." We owe the first study of these *cédulas de gracias al sacar* to James F. King (1951; compare Lanning, 1944). A systematic investigation of this matter would be of great interest. In the late sixteenth and early seventeenth century, mestizo had been almost synonymous with illegitimate. It seems that the frequency of marriage

in the middle strata increased as time passed and that neighboring castas were likely to intermarry. But the subject, with its obvious importance for changing social attitudes, remains to be investigated. A study on the Norte Chico in Chile shows that one-fourth of the children recorded in the books of baptism between 1690 and 1800 were illegitimate (Carmagnani, 1963, p. 30; see also Gutierrez Pineda, 1963).

The Régimen de castas was above all undermined by the continuation of the process that had been responsible for its creation—the *mestizaje*. The terminological proliferation illustrates this fact. A number of famous series of eighteenth-century paintings representing the various castas provide complex terminologies that have always attracted considerable attention (León, 1924; Blanchard, 1908–10; Rosenblat, 1954; Woodbridge, 1948; Varallanos, 1962, pp. 66–70). In fact, as Aguirre Beltrán (1946, pp. 175–78) points out, they should not be taken too seriously because they express erudite imagination and genealogical concern rather than social reality. The complex terminologies do highlight the increasing absurdity of a genealogical criterion for social classification in a multiracial environment. Furthermore, in the case of individuals who were often illegitimate, how could their genealogy possibly be traced? On the other hand, the variations in phenotype could only allow for a few, vague distinctions. In administrative practice we encounter only about five to eight different "racial" terms. Parish priests in New Spain, for example, kept three different sets of books, for Spaniards, Castas, and Indians (Konetzke, 1946 a, p. 585). These three categories are the only ones that McAlister (1963, pp. 356–57) is willing to recognize "as elements in a definable social structure" possessing "definable social and juridical statuses." Aguirre Beltrán (1946, pp. 270–71), on the other hand, finds six identifiable groups. It seems to me that the differences, legally and socially, between the mestizos and the castas of African descent were sufficiently significant to permit at least a four-group pattern.

It is important to notice that even the borders between the basic ethnic groups tended to blur. The self-interest of individuals encouraged "passing." Nor was it necessarily a question of "upwards" passing within the "pigmentocratic" social structure. Whereas the Indian might wish to pass for a mestizo in order to escape paying tribute, the mestizo might find it convenient to present himself as an Indian to escape the jurisdiction of the Inquisition (Greenleaf, 1965, pp. 149–53; compare Gibson, 1964, pp. 144, 147). Even as early as 1600 the mestizo phenotype and Indian dress of the same individual made it difficult to classify him (Jara, 1959, p. 60). Later, as we emphasized in the discussion of demography, many colonial officials recognized the futility of the classification they were carrying out. As the arbitrary designations in the parish records were not legally valid, on the eve of Emancipation, recourse to the courts was considered the only means of establishing the certain status of an individual (Konetzke, 1946 a). It is clear that socioracial prejudice increased during the Bourbon period as a defense mechanism on the part of the higher strata (see, e.g., King, 1953 a). At the same time, upward mobility between neighboring strata seems to have become increasingly frequent. Downward mobility is exemplified by the so-called *blancos de orilla* (Brito Figueroa, 1961, pp. 78–80). The whole complex of phenomena related to the decline of the Régimen de castas deserves considerable research.[3]

The constitutional and legal aspects of the breakdown of the Régimen de castas in the course of Emancipation do not seem to require very great efforts of historians. A succinct account of the situation in Argentina has been presented by O. Carracedo (1960). The texts of the laws and constitutions are usually sufficiently clear, and the legislative debates preceding them have in part been made available in modern editions. Apart from the constitutions enacted in Latin America, the Cádiz constitution of 1812 is also worthy of attention in this respect because so many Spanish American deputies participated in its formulation. As J. F. King (1953 b) has indicated, the ethnic composition of the overseas population became a key issue during the discussions of what form popular representation of a constitutional Spanish monarchy should take.

Deprived of its legal framework and shaken by revolutionary upheaval, the Régimen de castas did not survive the lengthy Wars of Emancipation, although the traces it left have been profound. How social attitudes and conditions, apart from the legal aspect, were changed in the process is still imperfectly known. Charles Griffin's studies present the current state of research (1949, 1961, 1962).

THE EVOLUTION OF NEGRO SLAVERY AND THE PROCESS OF ABOLITION IN LATIN AMERICA

Since J. F. King surveyed the state of research (1944 a, 1944 c), considerable progress has taken place in historical

[3] A seemingly interesting study by González Sánchez (1963) has not been available for consultation.

and sociological research on Negro slavery in Spanish America and Brazil. New documentation has been brought to light and new interpretations have been advanced. A great deal more is known about slave traffic in the importation stage than about the internal trade and distribution.[4] Mellafe (1964) gives a general idea of the state of our present knowledge on slavery in Spanish America.

Slavery in the Iberian Peninsula prior to and parallel with slavery in Latin America has been explored by Charles Verlinden (1955), A. Domínguez Ortiz (1952), E. Correia Lopes (1944) and Vicenta Cortés (1964). It would now be possible to examine F. Tannenbaum's (1947) well known thesis about the importance of the regulations of slavery and serfdom in *Las siete Partidas*. Of even greater interest is that under the impact of the sixteenth century commercial revolution, the plantation came into being on the islands settled by the Iberians off the coast of the peninsula and Northern Africa (Verlinden, 1964?). The combination of plantation and Negro slavery would soon be carried to the New World.

Indian slavery had preceded Negro slavery in the New World. But in the case of Spanish America, at least, Indian slavery, condemned by the influential ecclesiastical pressure group, declined and disappeared rather early. Konetzke (1949a) provides the best account. At the same time, Negro slavery was never seriously challenged (cf. Konetzke, 1965, p. 80). Why did this ambivalence exist? Verlinden (1964?) suggests that it was primarily because Indian slavery constituted a threat against colonial peace. In Africa,

on the other hand, European colonial ambitions were very limited, and the local effects of enslavement did not really matter.

Granting that the plantation provided the principal framework for slavery in the New World, another major problem arises. Why have Negro-White relations taken such a different course in Anglo and Latin America (e.g., Brazil), if the point of departure were the same? Were the differences already present during the time of slavery despite the common plantation framework? Or are they mainly a result of postabolition conditions? Students who believe that Latin American slavery per se was different from and more benign than Anglo-Saxon slavery include Gilberto Freyre (1951 a, 1963 a), Frank Tannenbaum (1947), M. W. Williams (1930) and Stanley Elkins (1959). Evidence presented by M. Cardozo (1961) also lends itself to such an interpretation. This school relies on "national character," religion, and legislation to support its thesis. At a 1957 seminar on the plantations in the New World, the rapporteur concluded (PAU, 1959, p. 187) that to solve the problem posed by the different trends in race relations one needs to look beyond economic factors to "law, for one, or better . . . religion."

The idealization of the Portuguese approach to slavery and race relations in general is especially evident in Freyre's later works (e.g., 1963 a.) This thesis has naturally provoked adverse criticism (e.g., Stein, 1961). Examining Portuguese behavior in different overseas territories, C. R. Boxer (1963) gives a picture which is in striking contrast to that of Freyre.

It is probable that the universalist approach of Catholicism per se was better fitted to influence and humanize slavery than the approach of exclusivist

---

[4] One of the few exceptions: Sempat Assadourian (1965).

Protestant churches (W. Jiménez Moreno in IPGH, 1961, p. 82). But it remains to be proved that the Catholic Church did more to improve the situation of the slaves than Protestant churches did. With regard to abolition it seems that the Church in Brazil and elsewhere in Latin America played an insignificant role if any at all (Stein, 1957, pp. 138–39; cf Siqueira, 1964).

That legislation in Latin America had a humanizing impact of some importance on slavery also needs to be proved. The reconstruction of social reality on the basis of legal documents is notoriously risky under any circumstances, and particularly in the case of slave codes that limited the rights of an owner of human property. Furthermore, the picture that one gets of early Spanish slave regulations (Konetzke, 1953–62; Vial Correa, 1947)[5] is not exceedingly bright. The "humane" Spanish slave code of 1789, which played an important role in Tannenbaum's (1947) argumentation, has proved to be a rather complex issue, inspired as it was by the French *Code Noir* of 1685 (Malagón, 1956; Torre Revello, 1932). With regard to the application of the code, conflicting evidence has been presented (Petit Muñoz, 1947, pp. 79–89; Jaramillo Uribe, 1963, pp. 79–89; cf King, 1943 b, p. 310). Finally, the code should be placed in the context of Bourbon efforts to liberalize trade and promote commercial agriculture (King, 1942; Villalobos, 1962).

The frequency of voluntary manumissions among the Spaniards and Portuguese has often been used as an argument supporting the humanity of slavery in Latin America. But Federico Brito Figueroa (1960, pp. 108–14) has shown that these acts can sometimes be explained by the economic convenience of the ex-owners. A study on early nineteenth-century slavery in Mendoza, Argentina (Masini, 1962, p. 40 and *passim*), illustrates the different categories of manumission. It is also clear that certain categories of slaves were in a better position to purchase their freedom than others. The whole problem of the extent and nature of manumissions should, as we stated in the discussion on demography, receive a systematic investigation.

The growing opposition to the Freyre-Tannenbaum school prefers to explain the nature of slavery on the basis of the economic function displayed by the enslaved manpower. Both the rise and the decline of slavery can be interpreted in purely economic terms, as Eric Williams did in his treatise on the British West Indies (1944). Consequently, the treatment of enslaved manpower also obeys primarily economic motives. The slaves working in a profitable enterprise tend to be harshly exploited, while those held partly for noneconomic motives, i.e., servants and others, will usually receive more lenient treatment. They will also be able to purchase their freedom more easily. Thus the degree of rentability of slave labor rather than the nationality of the slave-holder or the character of legislation are held responsible for the character of slavery. Sidney Mintz's (1959) comparative study of slavery in Jamaica and Puerto Rico provides facts that support this view.[6] It is also quite possible that the somber picture Stein (1957) presents of slavery in the coffee district of the Paraíba Valley and Freyre's (1951 a) much brighter por-

---

[5] With regard to Brazil, see Boxer (1963, pp. 101–4).

[6] See also Mintz's review of Elkins (1959) in *American Anthropologist*, XLIII (1961), 579–87 and Morse (1964).

trayal of slavery on the sugar *fazendas* of the Northeast reflect the contrast between a booming, more efficient economy and an old-fashioned, decaying one. The significant contributions of Florestan Fernandes (1965) and his fellow sociologists in São Paulo (Ianni, 1962; Cardoso, 1962; Cardoso and Ianni, 1960) on slavery and abolition in southern Brazil also fit into the theory briefly summarized here. It should, of course, be kept in mind that slavery is primarily an *economic* institution whereas the juridical aspect stressed by Tannenbaum and others is of a secondary character. There is a risk, however, that a strictly Marxist interpretation of the funtional theory will lead to an oversimplification of historical reality.

In the new approach to the problem of slavery, comparisons will be meaningful only insofar as the whole economic context is considered and similar categories of slaves are compared. This recognition increases the urgency of investigating the economic functions that slavery fulfilled in different regions. In addition to Ortiz's (1916) classical work on slavery in Cuba, other good regional studies are those of Díaz Soler (1953) on Puerto Rico, of Goulart (1949) on Brazil, of Jaramillo Uribe (1963) on eighteenth-century Colombia and of Inge Wolff on Alto Peru during the period 1545–1640 (1964). Zelinsky's (1949) useful survey should also be mentioned. Surveys of slavery within specific occupational sectors in the whole or parts of Latin America remain to be written.

It is obvious that Gilberto Freyre (1951 a-b) often talks about slaves used as domestic servants. These slaves, frequently held as status symbols as well as for practical reasons, seem to have formed a large percentage of the slaves in Spanish America. They constituted the slave elite.

Urban slaves often made profits for their owners by being let out or being allowed to work on their own in exchange for a rent to the master (Carneiro, 1964, pp. 8–10; Harth-Terré and Márquez Abanto, 1962, pp. 46–48). They consequently had good opportunities to buy their freedom.

Slaves used as cattle hands also seem to have enjoyed a comparatively high degree of freedom of movement within their condition of bondage. At least Cardoso (1962, pp. 136–39) draws this conclusion in his study of slavery in Rio Grande do Sul. Our knowledge of Negro slave cowboys in the southern United States (Durham and Jones, 1965, pp. 16–17) points in the same direction.

In mines, due to the high cost, Negro slave labor was used only when Indian labor was not abundantly available. Through C. R. Boxer's writing (1962, pp. 173–78) we know a little about the harsh conditions under which slave labor exploited the mines of Minas Gerais during the eighteenth century. Other recent contributions of interest in this respect include that of I. Wolff on Alto Peru (1964, pp. 162–64) and that of M. Acosta Saignes (1956) on Venezuela.

Plantation slavery, finally, constitutes such a vast area of research that general conclusions of value are not easily reached. As Stanley Stein (Wagley, 1964, p. 100) puts it, comparisons between plantation slavery in different areas require the use of comparable criteria, such as the phase and trend of agricultural development, size, function and location of the plantations and slave labor as well as the availability of slave supply. The studies of the historically oriented sociologist S. Mintz (1953, 1959) and Stein's own *Vassouras* (1957) are especially noteworthy. Many similar studies are needed.

Functionally and regionally focused

studies of slavery in Latin America will undoubtedly help to explain the strength or weakness of the institution in the course of history. It will also be possible to place Latin American slavery within a global or hemispheric context. In addition to the bibliography on the United States and the Caribbean, the study by van Lier (1949) on Surinam offers material for comparison. Those who out of romanticism or nationalism want slavery in their countries to have been better than and different from that of others will probably be dissatisfied with the results of this comparative analysis. Slavery by definition has been an inhumane institution everywhere. Gilberto Freyre himself, in an excellent but little known monograph (1963 b, p. 220) on the descriptions in Brazilian newspapers of runaway slaves, has indicated the frequency of scars and mutilations on their bodies.[7] The repression of the family institution within slavery is another universal feature. A puzzling question arises in this context. Was the rate of reproduction of the slave population in Brazil, for example, lower than that in the American South? If it were so, as Brazilian economist Celso Furtado concludes (1965, pp. 127–29), this would indicate that the living conditions of the slaves were probably worse.

Negro rebellions were a normal feature in both Spanish America and Brazil as they were in all slave-holding societies. They were characterized by mutual savagery. Runaway slaves often formed small "independent" communities—*quilombos* in Brazil, *palenques* or *cumbes* in Spanish America—as did the Maroons in Jamaica and the Bush Negroes in Guiana. These dramatic

aspects of slavery have been highlighted in a number of recent contributions (Acosta Saignes, 1961; Arcaya, 1949; Carneiro, 1958; Guillot, 1961; Jaramillo Uribe, 1964, pp. 42–50).

During the Wars of Emancipation Negro slaves and Indians often provided a major part of the fighting forces on both sides. Their role was a "passive" one, completely subordinated to aims dictated by the white leadership. Their history should be written in these terms, but it should not be forgotten as it has been in the past. In literature, for instance, there are surprisingly few references to the fact that about a third of San Martín's army at Maipú and Chacabuco were Negroes. The recruitment of Negro slaves provided the way to freedom, but the casualties they suffered were heavy. The rapid decrease in the percentage of slaves and the corresponding increase in that of the free Negroes, as well as the absolute diminution of the African element in continental Spanish America during the early nineteenth century, must be seen against this background. Students like Masini (1962), Rodríguez Molas (1961), and Pereda Valdés (1940, 1941)[8] stress this point. During the civil wars that followed Independence, Negroes continued to enlist in the armies.

During the period from the 1820's to 1888 slavery was abolished in country after country in Latin America, and suppression of the slave trade had preceded abolition. Expectably, both steps were taken sooner in the countries where slaves were few and slavery of little economic importance, such as Central America, than in countries where it constituted a basic element within the economy, as in Cuba and

---

[7] Stein (1960, p. 259) also refers to A. Ramos, "Castigos de escravos," *Revista do Arquivo Municipal de São Paulo*, IV, 42 (1938), 79–104.

[8] Though loosely constructed, the study of Molinari (1963) also contains interesting facts.

Brazil. Both the suppression and the abolition of the slave trade have received considerable attention from historians. J. F. King's (1944 b) article on Great Britain and the suppression of the slave trade in the Spanish American countries and Alan Manchester's (1933) treatment of the same matter with regard to Brazil are noteworthy. A brief comment by E. Carneiro (1964, pp. 91–94) interprets the suppression of the slave trade to Brazil as favorable to the slave-holders themselves because they evaded their debts to the slave dealers.

With regard to the process of abolition itself, monographs are numerous but often of a rather poor quality. The best ones dealing with Spanish America are probably one by Feliú Cruz (1942) on Chile and another by H. Bierck (1953) on Gran Colombia. The principal legislative texts have also been made available, for example, in the bulky compilation on Colombia by E. Posada and C. Restrepo Canal (1933; Restrepo Canal, 1938).⁹ With regard to Brazil, the literature is rather abundant (see Stein, 1960, pp. 259–60, 275–77). Monographs on the abolition in different Brazilian states have also appeared. But only the recent contributions of the São Paulo group of sociologists have seriously tried to present more than a rather superficial compilation of abolitionist speeches and laws.¹⁰

During a transitional period in some countries, the *libertos* enjoyed a peculiar status that is worth studying. In Argentina they were even sold "for the

years of service stipulated by law" (Masini, 1962, p. 53).¹¹

Historians seem to lose all their interest in the Negro in Spanish America as soon as the abolition is over. He disappears almost completely from historical literature after that juncture. One of the few exceptions is a study by R. O. Hudson on the Negro in Northern South America until 1860 (1964), but its conclusions are vague. In the case of Brazil, Gilberto Freyre has to some extent followed up his famous interpretation of plantation slavery from *Casa Grande and Senzala* with ideas about postabolition conditions (1959). But only the São Paulo sociologists have really attacked the complex problem of how the Negro fared after abolition. Stanley Stein's concluding remarks in his *Vassouras* (1957) are also enlightening. The Race and Class Conference in New York in 1965 contributed considerably to the study of this whole problem, as the publication of the papers by R. Graham on Brazil, G. Aguirre Beltrán on Mexico, C. Rama on Uruguay, and F. Fernandes on immigrants and race relations in São Paulo will show.

The manner in which final abolition was achieved and the relative number of slaves freed by this act compared with earlier manumissions seem to have been important in conditioning future race relations. Were there already a great number of Negroes and mulattoes within the free labor sector when final abolition occurred? Or did the former slaves have to compete primarily with immigrants and "poor whites" (Harris, 1964, pp. 83–89)? It may be possible to discern a correlation between the growth of racial prejudice and the com-

---

⁹ See also Díaz Soler (1953), Nuñez Ponte (1954), Martínez Durán and Contreras (1962), Tobar Donoso (1959). Compare, for an example of the reintroduction of slavery, Chavez Orozco (1961).

¹⁰ Villela Luz (1948) has not been available for consultation. Fernandes (1965), Ianni (1962), Cardoso (1962), Cardoso and Ianni (1960).

---

¹¹ Compare with the *amparo* system in eighteenth-century Paraguay, Carvalho Neto (1962, pp. 44, 49).

petition for jobs in the case of Latin America as in other areas. It is not surprising that abolition easily creates the need to substitute a mythical racial inequality for the previous legal inequality (Cardoso and Ianni; Cardoso, 1962, p. 282; Ianni, 1962, pp. 244–47). In many Latin American environments, however, the former slaves and their descendants have evidently been absorbed within the lower strata of the population with a minimum of friction (Stein, 1964, p. 100; Cardoso, 1962, pp. 299–305).

Insofar as the historian shares the curiosity of his social scientist colleagues in the problems raised by the comparative study of race relations in the New World, he will undoubtedly have to rely on them for part of the answer. If, as is probable, the answer must be sought in postabolition rather than preabolition conditions, the subject matter would also be more easily within their reach. Subtle circumstances that are properly within the domain of the

social psychologist seem to play a considerable role.[12] In the past the Negro has received the greatest attention in scholarly research; now the historian would probably do well to focus more attention on the mulatto and his position in society.[13] It is well known that general recognition of the fact of miscegenation and of the mulatto rather than the attitude toward the Negro has made Brazil something of a contrast to Anglo America in the realm of interethnic relations.

[12] The importance of the white elite's own "somatic norm image" is stressed by Hoetink (1962). Psychological factors probably count for the paradox indicated by T. Matthews, IPGH (1961), 94. As long as slavery lasted, continuous imports of slaves into the Caribbean was needed to prevent diminution of the Negroes. After abolition, their numbers increased though no one continued to be interested in their increase. A recent contribution on the role of religion is Warren (1965).

[13] R. Morse, for example, criticizes O. Ianni (1962) for not having distinguished clearly between the free Negro and the free mulatto in *American Anthropologist*, XLVI (1964), 179.

BIBLIOGRAPHY

Acosta Saignes, Miguel
  1956 Vida de negros e indios en las minas de Cocorote durante el siglo XVII. Estudios antropológicos . . . en homanaje al Dr. Manuel Gamio. Mexico.
  1961 Los negros cimarrones de Venezuela. El movimiento emancipador de Hispanoamérica. Actas y ponencias, 3: 353–398.
Aguirre Beltran, Gonzalo
  1946 La población negra de México, 1519–1810. Estudio etnohistórico. Mexico.
Allport, Gordon W.
  1950 The Nature of Prejudice. Garden City.
Arcaya, Pedro M.
  1949 Insurrección de los negros de la Serranía de Coro. Caracas.
Bagu, Sergio
  1952 Estructura social de la colonia: Ensayo de historia comparada de América Latina. Buenos Aires.
Baron Castro, Rodolfo
  1946 Política racial de España en Indias. Revista de Indias, 7: 781–802.
Beneyto, Juan
  1961 Historia social de España y de Hispanoamérica. Madrid.

Bierck, Harold A.
1953   The Struggle for Abolition in Gran Colombia. The Hispanic American
       Historical Review, 33: 365–386.
Blanchard, R.
1908–1910 Les tableaux de métissage au Mexique. Journal de la Société des
       Américanistes de Paris, N.S. 5: 59–66; 7: 37–60.
Boxer, C. R.
1962   The Golden Age of Brazil, 1695–1750. Berkeley and Los Angeles.
1963   Race Relations in the Portuguese Colonial Empire, 1415–1825. Oxford.
Brito Figueroa, Federico
1960   Ensayos de historia social venezolana. Caracas.
1961   La estructura social y demográfica de Venezuela colonial. Caracas.
Cardoso, Fernando Henrique
1962   Capitalismo e escravidão no Brasil Meridional. São Paulo.
Cardoso, Fernando Henrique and Ianni, Octávio
1960   Côr e mobilidade social en Florianópolis. São Paulo.
Cardozo, Manoel
1961   Slavery in Brazil as Described by Americans, 1822–1888. The Americas,
       17: 241–260.
Carmagnani, Marcelo
1963   El salariado minero en Chile colonial: su desarrollo en una sociedad pro-
       vincial: el Norte Chico, 1690–1800. Santiago.
Carneiro, Edison
1958   O Quilombo dos Palmares. 2nd ed. São Paulo.
1964   Ladinos e crioulos. Estuds sobre o negro no Brasil. Rio de Janeiro.
Carracedo, Orlando
1960   El régimen de castas, el trabajo y la Revolución de Mayo. Anuario del
       Instituto de Investigaciones Históricas, 4: 157–186, Rosario, Argentina.
Carrera Stampa, Manuel
1954   Los gremios mexicanos. La organización gremial en Nueva España, 1521–
       1861. Mexico.
Chavez Orozco, Luis
1938   Historia económica y social de México. Mexico.
Corominas, Juan
1954   Diccionario crítico etimológico de la lengua castellana, 1, Madrid.
Correia Lopes, A.
1944   A escravatura: subsídios para sua história. Lisbon.
Cortes, Vicenta
1964   La esclavitud en Valencia durante el reinado de los Reyes Católicos
       (1479–1516). Valencia.
Diaz Soler, L. M.
1953   Historia de la esclavitud negra en Puerto Rico, 1492–1890. Madrid.
Dominguez Ortiz, Antonio
1952   La esclavitud en Castilla durante la edad moderna. Estudios de historia
       social de España, 2, Madrid.
Durham, Philip and Jones, Everett L.
1965   The Negro Cowboys. New York.
Dusenberry, W. H.
1948   Discriminatory Aspects of Legislation in Colonial Mexico. The Journal of
       Negro History, 3: 284–302.

Elkins, Stanley
  1959   Slavery: A Problem in American Institutional and Intellectual Life.
         Chicago.

Feliu Cruz, Guillermo
  1942   La abolición de la esclavitud en Chile. Santiago.

Fernandes, Florestan
  1965   A integração do negro à sociedade de classes. São Paulo.

Freyre, Gilberto
  1951   a) Introdução história da sociedade patriarcal no Brasil. I. Casa-grande
         and senzala. Formação da família brasileira sob o regime de economia
         patriarcal. 6th ed., Vols. 1–2. Rio de Janeiro and São Paulo.
         b) Introdução . . . II. Sobrados e mucambos. Decadencia do patriarcado
         rural e desenvolvimento do urbano. 2nd ed., Vols. 1–3. Rio de Janeiro and
         São Paulo.
  1959   Introdução . . . III. Ordem e progresso. Processo de desintegração das
         sociedades patriarcal e semi-patriarcal no Brasil sob o regime de trabalho
         livre: aspectos de um quase meio século de transição do trabalho escravo
         para o trabalho livre; e da Monarquia para a República. Vols. 1–3. Rio
         de Janeiro.
  1963   a) New World in the Tropics. New York.
         b) O escravo nos anúncios de jornais brasileiros do século XIX. Tentativa
         de interpretação antropológica, através de anúncios de jornais, de carac-
         terísticas de personalidade e de deformação de corpo de negros . . . Recife.

Furtado, Celso
  1965   The Economic Growth of Brazil: A Survey from Colonial to Modern Times.
         Berkeley and Los Angeles.

Gibson, Charles
  1964   The Aztecs Under Spanish Rule. A History of the Indians of the Valley of
         Mexico, 1519–1810. Stanford.

Gongora, Mario
  1951   El estado en el deracho indiano. Epoca de fundación, 1492–1570. Santiago.

Goulart, Maurício
  1949   Escravidão africana no Brasil (das origens à cessão do tráfego). São Paulo.

Greenleaf, Richard E.
  1965   The Inquisition and the Indians of New Spain: A Study in Jurisdictional
         Confusion. The Americas, 22: 138–166.

Griffin, Charles
  1949   Economic and Social Aspects of the Era of Spanish American Independence.
         The Hispanic American Historical Review, 43: 349–370.
  1961   Aspectos económico-sociales de la época de la Emancipación hispanoameri-
         cana: una bibliografía selecta de la historiografía reciente, 1949–1959. El
         Movimiento Emancipador de Hispano-América. Actas y Ponencias, 1:
         347–360.
  1962   Los temas sociales y económicos en la época de la independencia. Caracas.

Guillot, Carlos Federico
  1961   Negros rebeldes y negros cimarrones. Perfil afroamericano en la historia del
         Nuevo Mundo durante el siglo XVI. Buenos Aires.

Guthrie, Chester L.
  1945   Riots in Seventeenth Century Mexico City: A Study of Social and Eco-
         nomic Conditions. Greater America: Essays in Honor of H. E. Bolton,
         243–258, Berkeley and Los Angeles.

Gutierrez de Pineda, Virginia
1963   La familia en Colombia, 1. Trasfondo histórico. Bogotá.
Harris, Marvin
1964   Patterns of Race Relations in the Americas. New York.
Harth-Terre, Emilio
1961   El esclavo negro en la sociedad indoperuana. Journal of Inter-American
       Studies, 3: 297–340.
Harth-Terre, Emilio and Marquez Abanto, A.
1962   Perspectiva social y económica del artesano virreinal en Lima. Revista del
       Archivo Nacional del Perú, 26.
Hudson, Randall O.
1964   The Status of the Negro in Northern South America, 1820–1860. The
       Journal of Negro History, 49.
Ianni, Octávio
1962   As metamorfoses do escravo: apogeu e crise da escravatura no Brasil
       Meridional. São Paulo.
Instituto Panamericano de Geografia e Historia. Comision de Historia
1961–1962   El mestizaje en la historia de Ibero-América. Also in: Revista de Historia
       de América, 53/54: 127–218.
Jara, Alvaro
1959   Los asientos de trabajo y la provisión de mano de obra para los no-
       encomenderos en la ciudad de Santiago, 1586–1600. Santiago.
Jaramillo Uribe, Jaime
1963   Esclavos y señores en la sociedad colombiana del siglo XVIII. Anuario
       Colombiano de Historia Social y de la Cultura, 1: 1: 3–62, Bogotá.
1964   La población indígena de Colombia en el momento de la Conquista y sus
       transformaciones posteriores. Anuario Colombiano de Historia Social y de
       la Cultura, 1: 2: 239–293.
King, James F.
1942   Evolution of the Free Slave Trade Principle in Spanish Colonial Admin-
       istration. The Hispanic American Historical Review, 22: 34–56.
1943   Negro Slavery in New Granada. Greater America. Essays in Honor of
       H. E. Bolton. Berkeley and Los Angeles.
1944   a) Negro History in Continental Spanish America. Journal of Negro History,
       29: 7–23.
       b) The Latin American Republics and the Suppression of the Slave Trade.
       The Hispanic American Historical Review. 24: 387–411.
       c) The Negro in Continental Spanish America: A Select Bibliography. The
       Hispanic American Historical Review. 24: 547–559.
1951   The Case of José Ponciano de Ayarza: A Document on "Gracias al Sacar."
       The Hispanic American Historical Review, 31: 641–647.
1953   a) A Royalist View of the Colored Castes in the Venezuelan War of In-
       dependence. The Hispanic American Historical Review, 33: 526–537.
       b) The Colored Castes and American Representation in the Cortes of Cádiz.
       The Hispanic American Historical Review, 33: 526–537.
Konetzke, Richard
1946   a) Documentos para la historia y crítica de los registros parroquiales en las
       Indias. Revista de Indias, 7: 581–586.
       b)El mestizaje y su importancia en el desarrollo de la población His-
       panoamericana durante la época colonial. Revista de Indias, 7: 7–44, 215–
       237.

1949   a) La esclavitud de los indios como elemento en la estructuración social de Hispanoamérica. Estudios de historia social de España, 1: 441–479, Madrid.

1951   Estado y sociedad en las Indias. Estudios Americanos, 3: 33–58.

1960   Los mestizos en la legislación colonial. Revista de Estudios Políticos, 112: 113–129, Madrid.

1965   Die Indianerkulturen Altamerikas und die spanisch-portugiesische Kolonialherrschaft. Fischer Weltgeschichte, 22, Frankfurt am Main.

Konetzke, Richard (ed.)
1953–1962 Colección de documentos para la historia de la formación social de Hispanoamérica, 1493–1810. Vols. 1–3: 2. Madrid.

Lanning, John T.
1944   The Case of José Ponciano de Ayarza: A Document on the Negro in Higher Education. The Hispanic American Historical Review, 24: 432–451.

Leal, Ildefonso
1963   Historia de la Universidad de Caracas (1721–1827). Caracas.

Leon, Nicolás
1924   Las Castas del México colonial. Mexico.

Lipschutz, Alejandro
1944   El indoamericanismo y el problema racial en las Américas. 2nd ed. Santiago.

1963   El problema racial en la conquista de América y el mestizaje. Santiago.

Lopez Martinez, Héctor
1965   Un motín de mestizos en el Perú (1567). Revista de Indias, 24: 367–381.

McAlister, Lyle N.
1957   The "Fuero Militar" in New Spain, 1764–1800. Gainesville.

1963   Social Structure and Social Change in New Spain. The Hispanic American Historical Review, 43: 349–370.

Malagon, Javier
1956   Un documento del siglo XVIII para la historia de la esclavitud en las Antillas. Miscelánea de estudios dedicados a Fernando Ortiz, 2: 951–968, Havana.

Manchester, Alan
1933   British Preeminence in Brazil: Its Rise and Decline. Chapel Hill.

Marin Tamayo, Fausto
1960   La división racial en Puebla de los Angeles bajo el régimen colonial. Puebla.

Masini, José Luis
1962   La esclavitud negra en Mendoza: época independiente. Mendoza, Argentina.

Mellafe, Ricardo
1964   La esclavitud en Hispanoamérica. Buenos Aires.

Mintz, Sidney
1953   The Culture History of a Puerto Rico Sugar Cane Plantation, 1876–1949. The Hispanic American Historical Review, 33: 224–251.

1959   Labor and Sugar in Puerto Rico and in Jamaica, 1800–1850. Comparative Studies in Society and History, 1: 273–281.

Mörner, Magnus
1961   a) Teoría y práctica de la segregación racial en la América Colonial española. Boletín de la Academia Nacional de la Historia, 44: 278–295, Caracas.

1962   a) La afortunada gestión de un misionero del Perú en Madrid en 1578. Anuario de Estudios Americanos, 19: 247–275.

1963 Las comunidades de indígenas y la legislación segregacionista en el Nuevo Reino de Granada. Anuario Colombiano de Historia Social y de la Cultura, 1: 63–88.

1964 a) La política de segregación y el mestizaje en la Audiencia de Guatemala. Revista de Indias, 24: 137–151.

b) Das Verbot für die Encomenderos unter ihren eigenen Indianern zu wohnen. Jahrbuch für Geschichte von Staat, Wirtschaft und Gesellschaft Lateinamerikas, 1: 187–206, Cologne.

1965 Separación o integración? En torno al debate dieciochesco sobre los principios de la política indigenista en Hispano-América. Journal de la Société des Américanistes, 54: 1: 31–45, Paris.

Ortiz, Fernando
1916 Hampa afro-cubana. Los negros esclavos. Estudio sociológico y de derecho público. Havana.

Pan American Union
1959 Plantation Systems of the New World. Washington.

Pereda Valdes, Ildefonso
1940 Negros esclavos, pardos libres y negros libres en Uruguay. Estudios Afro-cubanos, 4: 121–127, Havana.

1941 Negros esclavos y negros libres: Esquema de una sociedad esclavista y aporte del negro en nuestra formación nacional. Montevideo.

Petit Muñoz, E., Narancio, E. and Traibel Nelcis, J. M.
1947 La condición jurídica, social, económica y política de los negros durante el coloniaje en la Banda Oriental, 1, Montevideo.

Posada, Ernesto and Restrepo Canal, Carlos
1933 La esclavitud en Colombia. Leyes de manumisión. Bogotá.

Restrepo Canal, Carlos
1938 La libertad de los esclavos en Colombia o leyes de manumisión. Bogotá.

Rodriguez Molas, Ricardo
1961 Negros libres rioplatenses. Revista de Humanidades, 1: 1: 99–126, Buenos Aires.

Rosenblat, Angel
1954 La población indígena y el mestizaje en América. 1–2. Buenos Aires.

Sicroff, Albert A.
1960 Les Controverses des statuts de pureté de sang en Espagne du XVe au XVIIe siècle. Paris.

Siqueira, Sónia Aparecida
1964 A escravidão negra no pensamento do bispo Azeredo Coutinho. Contribuicão ao estudo da mentalidade do último Inquisidor. Revista de Historia, 28: 141–198, São Paulo.

Stein, Stanley
1957 Vassouras: A Brazilian Coffee County, 1850–1900. Cambridge.

1960 The Historiography of Brazil, 1808–1889. The Hispanic American Historical Review, 40: 234–278.

1961 Freyre's Brazil Revisited. The Hispanic American Historical Review, 41: 111–113.

1964 Latin American Historiography: Status and Research Opportunities. See WAGLEY: 1964: 86–124.

Tannenbaum, Frank
1947 Slave and Citizen. The Negro in the Americas. New York.

Temple, Ella Dunbar
  1948   Azarosa existencia de un mestizo de sangre imperial incáica. Documenta. Revista de la Sociedad Peruana de Historia, 1: 1: 112–156, Lima.

Torre Revello. José
  1932   Origen y aplicación del Código Negrero en la América española (1788–94). Boletín del Instituto de Investigaciones Históricas, 15: 42–50, Buenos Aires.

Van Lier, Rudolf
  1949   Samenleving in een grensgebied. Sociaal-historische studie van de Maatschappij in Suriname. The Hague.

Varallanos, José
  1962   El cholo y el Perú. Buenos Aires.

Verlinden, Charles
  1955   L'esclavage dans l'Europe médiévale. I. Péninsule Ibérique, France. Bruges.
  1964   Esclavage médiéval en Europe et esclavage colonial en Amérique. Cahiers de l'Institut des Hautes Etudes de l'Amérique Latine, 6: 29–45.

Vial Correa, Gonzalo
  1947   El africano en el reino de Chile. Ensayo histórico-jurídico. Santiago.
  1964   Teoría y práctica de la igualdad en Indias. Historia, 3: 87–163, Santiago.

Villalobos, Sergio
  1962   El comercio extranjero a fines de la dominación español. Journal of Inter-American Studies, 4: 517–544.

Wagley, Charles (ed.)
  1964   Social Science Research on Latin America. New York and London.

Williams, Eric
  1944   Capitalism and Slavery. Chapel Hill.

Williams, M. W.
  1930   The Treatment of Negro Slaves in the Brazilian Empire. A Comparison with the United States of America. Journal of Negro History, 15: 315–333.

Wolf, Eric
  1962   Sons of The Shaking Earth. Chicago.

Wolff, Inge
  1964   Negersklaverei und Negerhandel in Hochperu, 1545–1640. Jahrbuch für Geschichte von Staat, Wirtschaft und Gesellschaft Lateinamerikas, 1: 157–186, Cologne.

Woodbridge, H. C.
  1948   Glossary of Names Used in Colonial Latin America for Crosses Among Indians, Negroes and Whites. Journal of the Washington Academy of Sciences, 38: 353–362.

Zelinsky, Wilbur
  1949   The Historical Geography of the Negro Population of Latin America. The Journal of Negro History, 34: 153–221.

EUGENE D. GENOVESE

Materialism and Idealism
in the History of Negro Slavery
in the Americas

See the headnote on page 202 for bibliographical information on Eugene D. Genovese.

The study of Negro slavery in the United States is verging on a new and welcome development as historians begin to appreciate the need for a hemispheric perspective. In 1950, Allan Nevins entitled the appropriate chapter of his *Emergence of Lincoln* "Slavery in a World Setting," and in 1959 Stanley M. Elkins rescued the work of Frank Tannenbaum from an undeserved obscurity. It was Tannenbaum's remarkable essay, *Slave and Citizen* (1947) that first demonstrated the sterility of treating Southern slavery in national isolation, although the point had been made previously. Oliveira Lima, as early as 1914, had discussed the profound differences between Brazilian and North

American race relations and historical experiences with slavery, and Gilberto Freyre has been offering suggestive comparisons since the 1920's.[1] Without claiming for Tannenbaum an originality beyond reasonable limits, we may credit him with having been the first to show that only a hemispheric treatment could enable us to understand the relationship between slavery and race relations and the social and political

---

[1] Allan Nevins, *The Emergence of Lincoln*, 2 vols. (New York, 1950); Frank Tannenbaum, *Slave and Citizen: The Negro in the Americas* (New York, 1946); Manoel de Oliveira Lima, *The Evolution of Brazil Compared with that of Spanish and Anglo-Saxon America* (Stanford, 1914); Roy Nash, *The Conquest of Brazil* (New York, 1926); Gilberto Freyre, "Social Life in Brazil in the Middle of the Nineteenth Century," *Hispanic American Historical Review*, V (Nov., 1922), 597–628.

Reprinted from the *Journal of Social History* (October, 1968), by permission of the publisher.

dynamics of the transition from slavery to freedom. Simultaneously, the questions Tannenbaum posed and the method he suggested wiped out the line between history and the social sciences; Elkins' controversial book illustrates how quickly the discussion must pass into considerations of psychology and anthropology. The improved prospects for comparative analysis derive in part from the advances being made by Spanish American and especially Brazilian historians, sociologists, and anthropologists and in part, as Magnus Mörner suggests, from the excellent work done recently on slavery in the Iberian peninsula itself.[2]

Under the circumstances it is appropriate that the first sweeping assault on Tannenbaum's thesis should come from Marvin Harris, an anthropologist, and equally appropriate that the assault implicitly should accept Tannenbaum's main point—that slavery and race relations must be studied hemispherically.[3] The argument has been joined on two levels: on such specific questions as the significance of different slave codes, the degree of paternalism in the social system, and the daily treatment of slaves; and on such general questions of method and philosophy as reflect the age-old struggle between idealist and materialist viewpoints. The specific questions will hopefully be settled in

due time by empirical research; the second are likely to stay with us. Since empirical research will necessarily be conditioned by contending viewpoints we must make every effort to clarify the methodological and philosophical issues or risk wasting a great deal of time and effort talking past each other and chasing solutions to spurious problems. The value of Harris' book, apart from specific contributions to our knowledge, is that it extends the discussion in a fruitful way. Presumably, its deficiencies of style will not deny it a hearing. Unlike Harris' *The Nature of Cultural Things*, which comes close to being unreadable, *Patterns of Race in the Americas*, despite lapses into unnecessary jargon and some regrettable rhetoric, is straightforward and vigorous. Unfortunately, it is marred by savage polemical excursions. Harris appears to be a man of strong and, to me, admirable social views, but I fear that he is among those who confuse ideological zeal with bad manners. As a result, his harsh attacks on opposing scholars, some of whom are deservedly respected for their fairness and generosity to others, often result in unjust and arbitrary appraisals of their work and, in any case, leave the reader with a bad taste.

I propose to discuss Harris' demand for a materialist alternative to the idealist framework of Tannenbaum, Freyre, and Elkins and to avoid, so far as possible, discussions of specific differences about data. Those differences may be left to specialists and will not be resolved without much more work by scholars in several disciplines. I propose, too, to ignore Harris' illuminating work on the highland Indian societies. Since the book has much to offer on these and other themes it should be understood that no balanced review is intended here. Even if

[2] Magnus Mörner, "The History of Race Relations in Latin America: Comments on the State of Research," *Latin American Research Review*, I (Summer, 1966), 17–44. Pages 35–44 contain an excellent bibliography.

[3] Marvin Harris, *Patterns of Race in the Americas* (New York, 1964). Since Harris published, David Brion Davis has brought out his remarkable *The Problem of Slavery in Western Culture* (New York, 1966), which takes up a critical stance toward Tannenbaum. His criticisms, which will be noted briefly below, are tangential to the main task of his book. Harris' book is, so far, the only attempt to replace the full burden of Tannenbaum's argument.

the book suffers from as grave weaknesses of method and assumption as I believe, it would retain considerable value on other levels and may properly be evaluated more fully elsewhere.

Tannenbaum divides the slave systems of the Western Hemisphere into three groups—Anglo-Saxon, Iberian, and French. The Anglo-Saxon group lacked an "effective slave tradition," a slave law, and religious institutions concerned with the Negro; the Iberian had a slave tradition and law and a religious institution imbued with the "belief that the spiritual personality of the slave transcended his slave status"; the French shared the religious principles of the Iberian but lacked a slave tradition and law.[4] Tannenbaum, to his cost, ignores the French case and does not, for example, discuss the *Code Noir*. Were he to do so, he might reflect further on the significance of the Iberian codes, for the *Code Noir* was notoriously a dead letter in Saint-Domingue.

The burden of Tannenbaum's argument rests on his estimate of the strength of the Catholic Church is relation to the landowners and on the extent to which the law could be or was enforced. He undoubtedly takes too sanguine a view of Brazilian slavery and simultaneously greatly underestimates the force of community pressure and paternalism in reducing the harshness of the Southern slave codes. He risks broad generalizations and necessarily sacrifices much in the process; many of his generalizations, with qualifications, nonetheless obtain. The essential point is not that Brazilian slaves received kinder treatment buy that they had greater access to freedom and once free could find a secure place in the developing national culture. Tannenbaum, accepting the

authority of Gilberto Freyre, does suggest a correlation between class mobility, the absence of weakness of racism, and kind treatment, but he does so tentatively, and it forms no essential part of his argument.

Tannenbaum demonstrates that the current status of the Negro in the several societies of the New World has roots in the attitude toward the Negro as a slave, which reflected the total religious, legal, and moral history of the enslaving whites. From this assertion he proceeds to a number of theses of varying value. When, for example, he relates the acceptance of the "moral personality" of the Negro to the peaceful quality of abolition, we may well wonder about Haiti, or about Brazil, where the peaceful abolition followed decades of bloody slave insurrections and social disorders,[5] or about the British islands, where peaceful abolition followed a denial of that moral personality. We may, accordingly, take the book apart; it was intended to open, not close, the discussion of an enormously complicated subject. The essentials of the viewpoint remain in force: (1) Slavery was a moral as well as a legal relationship; (2) where tradition, law, and religion combined to recognize the moral personality of the slave, the road to freedom remained open, and the absorption of the freedmen into the national culture was provided for; (3) the recognition of moral personality flowed from the emergent slave-holders' legal and religious past, the extent and nature of their contact with darker peoples, and their traditional view of man and God —of their total historical experience and its attendant world view. Tan-

---

[4] Tannenbaum, *Slave and Citizen*, p. 65, n. 153.

[5] Richard Graham, "Causes of the Abolition of Slavery in Brazil: An Interpretive Essay," *Hispanic American Historical Review*, XLVI (May 1966), 123–37.

nenbaum draws the lines much too tightly. As David Brion Davis shows, the duality of the slave as man and thing always created problems for enslavers, who rarely if every were able to deny the slave a moral personality.[6] We may nonetheless note a wide range of behavior and attitude within such recognition, and Tannenbaum's problem therefore remains with us.

The great weakness in Tannenbaum's presentation is that it ignores the material foundations of each particular slave society, and especially the class relations, for an almost exclusive concern with tradition and cultural continuity. Tannenbaum thereby avoids essential questions. How, for example, did the material conditions of life in the slave countries affect their cultural inheritance? Tannenbaum implies the necessary victory of the inheritance over contrary tendencies arising from immediate material conditions. Thus, Harris can label his viewpoint idealist and insist, as a materialist, that material conditions determine social relations and necessarily prevail over countertendencies in the historical tradition. The special usefulness of Harris' book lies in the presentation of an alternative, materialist interpretation and the concomitant attention paid to many problems that Tannenbaum avoids or obscures. Unfortunately, his materialism, like that of such earlier writers as Eric Williams, is generally mechanical and soon reveals itself as a sophisticated variant of economic determinism. It is, in short, ahistorical.

Harris vigorously attacks Freyre for asserting that Brazil has been a virtual "racial paradise," but his discussion actually reinforces Freyre's argument.

Harris, like Charles Wagley,[7] insists on a close relationship between class and race and insists that Brazilian Negroes have always faced intense discrimination because of their lower-class status. Brazil's racial paradise is occupied only by "fictional creatures"; the real Negroes of Bahia and elsewhere suffer immensely as members of the lower classes in a country in which the rule of thumb alleges a correlation between class and race.[8]

Harris slips into a position that Wagley largely avoids. Wagley, too, attacks Freyre by drawing attention to the class dimension of race relations. He denies the absence of racism and refers to the "widely documented color prejudice in almost every part of the nation."[9] Yet, Wagley properly adds that despite prejudice and discrimination Brazilian racial democracy is no myth. Brazilians happily do not usually put their racial chatter into practice; continuing miscegenation undermines racial lines; and the doctrine that "money whitens the skin" prevails. In these terms, so different from those which might be applied to the United States, we may see Brazilian racial democracy as reality relative to other societies or as myth relative to national standards and pretensions and fully appreciate the force of Octavio Ianni's reference to "the intolerable contradiction between the myth of racial democracy and the actual discrimination against Negroes and mulattoes."[10]

The admirable work of C. R. Boxer at first glance supports Harris against Freyre, but that glance proves decep-

---

[6] Davis, *Problem of Slavery, passim.* This point is one of the leading theses of Davis' book.

[7] Charles Wagley, *An Introduction to Brazil* (New York, 1963), p. 132.

[8] Harris, *Patterns of Race*, p. 64.

[9] Wagley, *Introduction to Brazil*, p. 238; cf pp. 140–42.

[10] Octavio Ianni, *Raças e classes sociais no Brasil* (Rio de Janeiro, 1966), p. 15.

tive. Boxer dismisses as "twaddle" the notion that no color bar exists in the Portuguese-speaking world and brings us back to earth from Freyre's flights of romantic fancy, but he does not overthrow the essentials of his argument.[11] What Boxer does show is how painful a struggle has had to be waged and how much racism has persisted. The strides toward racial democracy that he describes in *Race Relations in the Portuguese Colonial Empire*, *Portuguese Society in the Tropics*, *The Golden Age of Brazil*, and elsewhere remain impressive when considered against Anglo-Saxon models. The question is what accounts for the greater "plasticity" (to use Freyre's word) of the Portuguese. The economic and demographic features of colonization, stressed almost exclusively by Harris, played a great role, but the careful research of so skeptical and cautious a historian as Boxer shows the force of legal, moral, religious, and national traditions. Viewed polemically, Boxer's work destroys the propagandistic nonsense of Dr. Salazar's court historians but only qualifies the main lines of argument in Freyre and Tannenbaum.

In asserting a racial paradise all Freyre could possibly mean is that considerable racial mobility exists and that discrimination is held within tolerable bounds. The criticisms of Wagley, Harris, Boxer, and others demonstrate the existence of an acute class question with a racial dimension; they do not refute Freyre's main claim that society is not racially rent by the standards of the Anglo-Saxon countries. Freyre is undoubtedly open to criticism, for he slides impermissably from race to class. He insists that miscegenation "never permitted the endurance in

absolute antagonisms of that separation of men into masters and slaves imposed by the system of production. Nor the exaggerated development of a mystique of white supremacy nor of nobility."[12] When he writes that miscegenation negated the class antagonism of master and slave, he talks nonsense; but when he writes that it inhibited—he does not say prevented—a mystique of white supremacy, he is surely correct.

Freyre, possibly in response to criticism of his earlier exaggerations, tries to qualify his lyrical praise of Luso-Brazilian racial attitudes and practices. Sometimes, although by no means consistently even in his most recent work, his evaluations are so well balanced as virtually to accept the criticisms and qualifications offered on all sides:

Not that there is no race or color prejudice mixed with class prejudice in Brazil. There is. . . . But no one in Brazil would think of laws against interracial marriage. No one would think of barring colored people from theatres or residential sections of a town.[13]

The main point for Freyre is not that race prejudice has been absent but that "few Brazilian aristocrats were as strict about racial impurity as the majority of the Anglo-Saxon aristocrats of the Old South were";[14] and that the Brazilian Negro "has been able to express himself as a Brazilian and has not been forced to behave as an ethnic

---

[11] C. R. Boxer, *Salvador de Sá and the Struggle for Brazil and Angola, 1602–1686* (London, 1952), p. 235.

[12] Gilberto Freyre, *O Mundo que o portugues criou & Uma Cultura ameaçada: A Luso-Brasileira* (Lisbon, 1940), p. 41.

[13] Gilberto Freyre, *New World in the Tropics: The Culture of Modern Brazil* (New York, 1963), p. 8. At that, he underestimates the extent of prejudice and discrimination. See, e.g., the important sociological studies of Fernando Henrique Cardoso and Octavio Ianni, *Côr e mobilidade social em Florianópolis* (São Paulo, 1960); and Roger Bastide and Florestan Fernandes, *Brancos e negros em São Paulo*, 2nd Ed. (São Paulo, 1959).

[14] Freyre, *New World*, p. 82.

and cultural intruder."[15] Harris writes: "Races do not exist for Brazilians. But classes do exist both for the observer and *for* the Brazilians."[16] These words surrender the argument.

Law, Church, and cultural tradition are not viewed by Tannenbaum, or even Freyre, as unambiguous forces for racial equality; they appreciate the internal conflicts and are concerned with the different outcomes of these conflicts in different cultures. "The colonial governments, the Spaniards, and the *criollos* treated the mestizo as an inferior human being."[17] Much race prejudice, Tannenbaum adds, existed and exists against Indians and Negroes throughout Latin America. He notes too, in a striking comment on class and race, that United States Negroes can and do advance themselves personally in the economic, social, and political arenas with greater ease than do Latin American Negroes, for whom class rigidities and the economic backwardness of society present severe limitations.[18] The distance between rich and poor, cultured and uncultured in Latin America "is obviously not racial, not biological, nor based on color of skin or place of origin, but it is perhaps even more effective as a dividing line, and perhaps more permanent. It is an ingrained part of the total scheme of things."[19]

[15] *Ibid.*, p. 144.
[16] Harris, *Patterns of Race*, p. 64. Original emphasis.
[17] Frank Tannenbaum, *Ten Keys to Latin America* (New York, 1965), p. 43.
[18] *Ibid.*, pp. 49–51.
[19] *Ibid.*, p. 52. Similarly, Stanley M. Elkins draws attention to Hispanic race prejudice and discrimination against Negroes. "Was there squalor, filth, widespread depression of the masses? Much more so than with us—but there it was the class system and economic 'underdevelopment,' rather than the color barrier, that made the difference." *Slavery: A Problem in American Institutional and Intellectual Life* (Chicago, 1959), p. 79.

Harris rejects on principle the idea that Portuguese tradition, law, and religion could overcome the counterpressures inherent in Brazilian slavery. He makes some strange assumptions in his often admirable discussion of political relations of Church, state, and landowner in highland and lowland America. He properly portrays each as a separate entity, struggling for control of material resources, but he portrays them as only that. Apart from a grudging phrase here and there (and we find a touch of sarcasm even there), he leaves no room for landowners who on many matters would follow the advice and teaching of the Church simply out of religious commitment, nor for a state apparatus deeply infused with Catholic ethics, nor for a Church with a genuine sense of responsibility for the salvation of souls. Instead, he offers us three collective forms of economic man. Harris repeatedly dismisses as romantic nonsense and the like arguments appealing to Catholic sensibility or inherited values. He misses much of Tannenbaum's implicit schema of a society resting on a balance of power between state, church, and family-based economic interests, and he misses Elkins' acute restatement of Tannenbaum's schema as descriptive of a precapitalist society in which minimal room is provided for unrestrained economic impulse.

The burden of Harris' criticism lies in his badly named chapter, "The Myth of the Friendly Master." He begins by asserting, "Differences in race relations within Latin America are at root a matter of the labor systems in which the respective subordinate and superordinate groups become enmeshed . . . . A number of cultural traits and institutions which were permitted to survive or were deliberately encouraged under one system were discouraged or suppressed in the other . . . ."[20] He contrasts his view with those of Tannenbaum and Freyre: "It is their contention that the laws, values, religious precepts, and personalities of the English colonists differed from those of the Iberian colonists. These initial psychological and ideological differences were sufficient to overcome whatever tendency the plantation system may have exerted toward parallel rather than divergent evolution."[21] Tannenbaum and Freyre may be read this way but need not be; Harris has reduced their position to its most idealist and superficial expression. Harris is not alone among social scientists of deserved reputation in caricaturing their ideas. K. Oberg, for example, hails *Patterns of Race in the Americas* for having demolished the supposedly prevalent notion that these patterns could be traced to "the Iberian soul or the inherent racism of the Anglo-Saxon."[22] For polemical purposes this reading scores points, but it does not get us very far. Tannenbaum and Freyre may be—and in my opinion ought to be—read another way, for each in effect describes the historical formation of slave-holding classes.

It is easy but unenlightening to dismiss discussions of psychology and ideology as if they were mere prejudices of romantics when laid against material interests. Harris, like every sensible man, rejects "simplistic economic determinism" and single-factor explanations,[23] but on close inspection he

rejects the simplistic rather than the economic determinism. "From the standpoint of an evolutionary science of culture," he writes, "it matters not at all if one starts first with changes in the technoenvironmental complex or first with changes in the institutional matrix; what matters is whether or not there is a correlation."[24] For him, however, the correlation reduces itself to an ideological reflection of the material reality. What Harris' materialism, in contradistinction to Marxian materialism, fails to realize is that once an ideology arises it alters profoundly the material reality and in fact becomes a partially autonomous feature of that reality. As Antonio Gramsci says about Marx's more sophisticated and useful comments on the role of ideas in history: "The analysis of these statements, I believe, reinforces the notion of 'historical bloc,' in which the material forces are the content and ideologies the form—merely an analytical distinction since material forces would be historically inconceivable without form and since ideologies would have to be considered individual dabbling without material forces."[25] This understanding of ideology and economics as reciprocally influential manifestations of particular forms of class rule may be contrasted with Harris' mechanistic and economistic view. He replies to a friendly critic who seeks to defend him against the charge of economic determinism by embracing it proudly: "I share with all economic determinists the conviction that in the long run and in most cases, ideology is swung into line by material conditions—by the evolution of technoenvironmental and

---

[20] Harris, *Patterns of Race*, p. 65.
[21] *Ibid.*, pp. 65–66.
[22] K. Oberg, Comment on Harris' article, "The Cultural Ecology of India's Sacred Cattle," *Current Anthropology*, VII (Feb., 1966), 62.
[23] Cf Marvin Harris, "The Economy Has No Surplus?" *American Anthropologist*, LXI (April, 1959), 188.

[24] *Ibid.*, p. 194.
[25] Antonio Gramsci, *Il Materialismo storico e la filosofia di Benedetto Croce* (Turin, 1949), p. 49.

production relationships."[26] Psychology and ideology are, however, as much a part of class formation as economic interest. Harris implies that ideology simply reflects material interests, which fluctuate sharply, but the ideology of a ruling class ought to be understood as its world view—the sum of its interests and sensibilities, past and present. An essential function of the ideology of a ruling class is to present to itself and to those it rules a coherent world view that is sufficiently flexible, comprehensive, and mediatory to convince the subordinate classes of the justice of its hegemony. If this ideology were no more than a reflection of immediate economic interests, it would be worse than useless, for the hypocrisy of the class, as well as its greed, would quickly become apparent to the most abject of its subjects.[27]

Harris admits that the Portuguese in Portugal exhibited little race prejudice but adds, "This datum can only be significant to those who believe that discrimination is caused by prejudice, when the true relationship is quite the opposite."[28] He argues, especially for Brazil, along the lines that the Marxists, Eric Williams, and C.L.R. James have argued for the Caribbean and that American Marxists and non-Marxists like Herbert Aptheker and the Handlins have argued for the United States.[29]

Unhappily, Harris asserts what needs to be proven, and the assertion exposes the fundamental weakness in his ideological armor: He insists on principle that the relationship must be one way and makes the case for materialism rest on this dogma. "If, as asserted, the Iberians initially lacked any color prejudice, what light does this shed upon the Brazilian and other lowland interracial systems?"[30] According to this view, the past plays no vital role in the present except for transmitted technology. If the case for materialism rests on a denial of the totality of human history and on the resurrection of an economic determinism brought to a higher level of sophistication, materialism has poor prospects.

It is easy to dismiss as idealism or subjectivity the view that prejudice existed prior to discrimination, but the tenacious defense of this position by such sober and diverse scholars as Carl Degler, Juan Comas, Arnold A. Sio, and David Brion Davis ought to give us pause. Davis recounts the various origins of anti-Negro prejudice in Europe. "The fact that Africans had traditionally been associated with Noah's curse of Canaan," he notes for example, "may have disposed some Europeans to regard them as fit for bondage."[31] Winthrop D. Jordan has made a simple point to present us with a complex reality. He has persuasively traced the origins of anti-Negro prejudice in New England to the prior existence of slavery, discrimination, and

---

[26] Marvin Harris, Reply to Criticism, appended to his article, "The Cultural Ecology of India's Sacred Cattle," *Current Anthropology*, VII (Feb., 1966), 64.

[27] The most suggestive discussions of the problem from a Marxian point of view are to be found in Gramsci's *Opere*, but see also John M. Cammett's excellent introduction to Gramsci's life and thought, *Antonio Gramsci and the Origins of Italian Communism* (Stanford, Calif., 1967).

[28] Harris, *Patterns of Race*, p. 67.

[29] Cf Eric Williams, *Capitalism and Slavery* (New York, 1961) and *The Negro in the Caribbean*

(Manchester, England, 1942); Herbert Aptheker, *American Negro Slave Revolts* (New York, 1943); Oscar and Mary F. Handlin, "Origins of the Southern Labor System," *William and Mary Quarterly*, 3rd Series, VII (April, 1950), 199–222; C. L. R. James, *The Black Jacobins: Toussaint L'Ouverture and the San Domingo Revolution*, 2nd Ed. (1963).

[30] Harris, *Patterns of Race*, p. 68.

[31] Davis, *Problem of Slavery*, p. 281.

racism in Barbados.[32] Thus, we may obediently agree on the materialist formulation   exploitation → discrimination → prejudice and find ourselves nowhere except on the further ahistorical assumption that ideas, once called into being, have no life of their own.[33] As M. I. Finley observes:

... For most of human history labor for others has been involuntary.... Slavery in that context must have different overtones from slavery in a context of free labor. The way slavery declined in the Roman Empire... illustrates that. Neither moral values nor economic interests nor the social order were threatened by the transformation of slaves and free peasants together into tied serfs. They were—or at least many powerful elements in society thought they were—by proposals to convert slaves into free men.

What sets the slave apart from all other forms of involuntary labor is that, in the strictest sense, he is an outsider. He is brought into a new society violently and traumatically; he is cut off from all traditional human ties of kin and nation and even his own religion; he is prevented from creating new ties, except to his masters, and

in consequence his descendants are as much outsiders, as unrooted, as he was. . . .

Dr. [Eric] Williams holds that "slavery was not born of racism, rather racism was the consequence of slavery." One wishes profoundly that one could believe that. However, the slave-outsider formula argues the other way, as does the fact that as early as the 1660's Southern colonies decreed that henceforth all Negroes who were imported should be slaves, but whites should be indentured servants and not slaves. The connection between slavery and racism has been a dialectical one, in which each element reinforced the other.[34]

The most balanced and suggestive statement on the Portuguese remains Boxer's: "One race cannot systematically enslave members of another on a large scale for over three centuries without acquiring a conscious or unconscious feeling of racial superiority."[35] The good sense of this observation enables us to grasp the necessarily racist influence of Negro slavery on European cultures without destroying our ability to distinguish between levels of influence and without compelling us to turn our backs on either historical-traditional or ecological processes.[36] The work of the distinguished Brazilian Marxian scholar, Caio Prado Junior, may be cited as an illustration of the way in which the force of the historical inheritance can be taken into account

---

[32] Carl Degler, "Slavery and the Genesis of American Race Prejudice," *Comparative Studies in Society and History*, II (Oct., 1959), 49–66; Juan Comas, "Recent Research on Racial Relations—Latin America," *International Social Science Journal*, XIII, No. 2 (1961), 271–99, esp. p. 291; Arnold A. Sio, "Interpretations of Slavery: The Slave Status in the Americas," *Comparative Studies in Society and History*, VII (April, 1965), 289–308; Winthrop D. Jordan, "The Influence of the West Indies on the Origins of New England Slavery," *William and Mary Quarterly*, 3rd Series, XVIII (April, 1961), 243–50.

[33] In another essay Jordan gropes for a formulation that would subsume both prejudice and discrimination instead of relating them to each other causally. His answer is neither clear nor convincing, but he has presented the problem in a sensitive and illuminating way. See "Modern Tensions and the Origins of American Slavery," *Journal of Southern History*, XXVIII (Feb., 1962), 18–30.

[34] M. I. Finley, review of Davis, *The Problem of Slavery* in *New York Review of Books*, VIII (Jan. 26, 1967), 10.

[35] C. R. Boxer, *Race Relations in the Portuguese Colonial Empire, 1415–1825* (Oxford, 1963), p. 56.

[36] Regrettably, even Boxer slights the historical dimension. It is noteworthy that he begins his survey, *Race Relations*, with the conquest of Ceuta in 1415 and leaves aside the racial conditioning of Portuguese life that preceded it. For an excellent statement of the intersection of tradition and economic milieu in the formation of Brazilian attitudes see Roger Bastide, "Race Relations in Brazil," *International Social Science Bulletin*, IX, No. 4 (1957), 495–512, esp. 495–96.

in a materialist analysis. For Prado the historical conditioning stressed by Freyre and Tannenbaum played its part precisely because the material basis of life and especially the class relationships provided room for it to breathe, but, given this room, it seriously affected that basis and those relationships.[37]

Harris's failure to grasp the historical and class nature of Tannenbaum's argument appears most strikingly in his reference to English law. Tannenbaum notes that England had long lacked slavery and a slave code and therefore had no legal tradition to humanize the practice of colonial slavery. "Why this legal lacuna should have been significant for the course run by slavery in the United States is quite obscure."[38] There is nothing obscure about it, and Harris could find the answer in Elkins' discussion of a slave system's rise amidst an "uncontrolled capitalism." Here again, idealists or no, Tannenbaum and Elkins have greatly deepened our understanding of the processes by which specific slave-holding classes were formed, and those processes are, or ought to be, the central concern of a materialist interpretation of history.

"At one point, and one point only," Harris writes, "is there a demonstrable correlation between the laws and behavior, the ideal and the actual, in Tannenbaum's theory: the Spanish and Portuguese codes ideally drew no distinction between the ex-slave and the citizen, and the actual behavior followed suit."[39] This one point kills Harris' argument since Tannenbaum set out to explain the absorption of

former slaves into the national culture in Brazil and the extreme difficulties in the United States. Harris has much to offer to complement the work of Freyre and Tannenbaum; in particular, he is strong on the economic and material exigencies of colonial Brazil and their influence in promoting race patterns. Instead of seeing a two-fold process within which colonial conditions reinforced tradition and allowed it to expand and within which tradition altered, however secondarily, material conditions, he insists dogmatically on either/or. "One can be certain that if it had been materially disadvantageous to the Latin colonists, it would never have been tolerated—Romans, *Siete Partidas*, and the Catholic Church notwithstanding."[40] Harris may be certain; others may be permitted some doubt. Had such a divergence occurred, the outcome would have been determined by the strength of the contending forces, with Church and state opposing slave-holders and with the conscience and consciousness of the slave-holders split among various commitments. Harris' crystal ball gazing constitutes not materialism but fatalism, not history but a secular equivalent of theology.

Harris misunderstands and misrepresents Tannenbaum as arguing that Negro slaves were better treated in Brazil than in the United States. Tannenbaum does express such an opinion, but he merely accepts Freyre's probably erroneous judgment; it forms no essential part of his thesis. Tannenbaum could live comfortably with evidence that Brazilian slaves were treated more harshly than American, for his case rests on the degree of class and race mobility. Harris, by identifying Tannenbaum with Freyre here and by

[37] Caio Prado Junior, *Formação do Brasil contemporaneo: Colonia*, 7th Ed. (São Paulo, n.d.), pp. 103–4; *Evolução política do Brasil e outros estudos*, 4th Ed. (São Paulo, n. d.), pp. 46–47.

[38] Harris, *Patterns of Race*, p. 70.

[39] *Ibid.*, p. 79.

[40] *Ibid.*, p. 81.

merging two separate theses in Freyre, confuses the issues. Elkins argues quite sensibly that Hispanic slaves could have been more severely mistreated than American "without altering the comparison." Harris replies, in one of his most inexcusable polemical outbursts, with sarcasm and personal abuse; he does not reply to the argument.[41]

Harris' discussion of demographic and economic forces in the formation of a mulatto population and a class of free blacks is a solid contribution, notwithstanding some statistical juggling, but the methodological difficulties reappear. He insists that Brazilian slave-holders "had no choice but to create a class of half-castes" to function as soldiers, cattlemen, food-growers, and intermediaries of various kinds.[42] Unlike the United States, he notes, Brazil lacked a white population large enough to serve as a middle class and to provide a political and military establishment. Brazilian slave-holders consequently smiled on the elevation of the mulattoes. Winthrop D. Jordan also questions the emphasis on national characteristics by pointing out that in the British West Indies, where conditions similar to those in Brazil existed, Anglo-Saxon hostility toward miscegenation was much softened and a much greater respect for the mulatto emerged.[43] Yet, the juxtaposition of the British West Indies, the United States, and Brazil favors a qualified version of Tannenbaum's argument, for what emerged in the islands was not the Brazilian pattern but a compromise: a three-caste system in which "coloreds"

were set apart from both whites and blacks. The material conditions of life had indeed prevailed over the purely ideological-institutional inheritance, as materialists would expect, but that inheritance significantly shaped and limited the force of those conditions.

Harris cites the work of Fernando Ortiz to show that law and tradition fared badly in Cuba against economic pressure. Here again, however, he assumes a fatalistic stance. Sidney W. Mintz also cited the Cuban case as especially instructive, but he does so with greater perception and caution: Cuba, he writes, shows what happens to "those rosy institutional arrangements which protected the slave, once slavery became part of the industrial plantation system . . . . Institutional restrictions may have hampered the maturation of slave-based agricultural capitalism in Cuba; but . . . could not prevent it. In the mid-nineteenth century, Cuban slavery dehumanized the slaves as viciously as had Jamaican or North American slavery." Mintz notes that Tannenbaum and Elkins "circumvent critical evidence on the interplay of economic and ideological forces." Elsewhere he writes that the way men were treated in colonial Caribbean societies was "determined much more by the level of economic development than by the ideologies of the different metropolitan powers."[44] The words "much more than" leave considerable room for the autonomous force of ideology. If Harris were to restrict himself within the limits of Mintz' critique, he might help develop the work of Freyre, Tan-

---

[41] Elkins, *Slavery*, p. 77; Harris, *Patterns of Race*, p. 75.

[42] Harris, *Patterns of Race*, p. 86.

[43] Winthrop D. Jordan, "American Chiaroscuro: The Status and Definition of Mulattoes in the British Colonies," *William and Mary Quarterly*, 3rd Series, XIX (April, 1962), 183–200.

[44] Sidney W. Mintz, review of Elkins' *Slavery* in *American Anthropologist*, LXIII (June, 1961), 579–87; "Labor and Sugar in Puerto Rico and in Jamaica, 1800–1850," *Comparative Studies in Society and History*, I (March, 1959), 273–83; quote from p. 283. On the effects of commercialization see Sio, *Comparative Studies in Society and History*, VII (April, 1965), 298–308.

nenbaum, and Elkins along materialist lines; instead he declares ideological war. Mintz' remarks on the intersection of ideology and economics constitute the beginning of a new departure, although I should prefer to assume both within a synthetic analysis of social classes that avoids compartmentalizing their constituent human beings. Social classes have historically formed traditions, values, and sentiments, as well as particular and general economic interests. Harris, like Mintz, Eric Williams, and others, refers to the components of the slave-holders' world view and the possible divergence between economic interests and traditional commitments. The solution of these problems awaits empirical research. A materialist interpretation must account for the full range of possibilities, but it can do so only if it eschews economic determinism and a narrow ecology for a concern with the historical formation of class interests and antagonisms under specific geographic and technological conditions.[45]

Harris makes much of the philosophical idealism of Freyre, Tannenbaum, and Elkins but does not analyze it. Since Freyre has written at some length on his method and viewpoint Harris ought to examine them specifically instead of contenting himself with the application of labels. That Freyre, Tannenbaum, and Elkins may be safely classed as idealists I do not deny, but their superb work ought to warn their philosophical opponents that the subject matter resists simplistic materialist schemata. A review of Freyre's methodological comments will lay bare not only the weakness of idealist interpretations, but also the elusiveness of the reality which makes such interpretations possible and even enormously helpful.

Freyre's critique of historical materialism is especially suggestive, for he rejects it without hostility and indeed with considerable appreciation. "However little inclined we may be to historical materialism," he writes, "which is so often exaggerated in its generalizations—chiefly in the works by sectarians and fanatics—we must admit the considerable influence, even though not always a preponderant one, exerted by the technique of economic production upon the structure of societies and upon the features of their moral physiognomies. It is an influence subject to the reaction of other influences, yet powerful as no other. . . ."[46] Freyre's words

---

[45] The limits of the ecological viewpoint are brought out with great skill by Clifford Geertz. Several passages from his book, *Agricultural Involution: The Processes of Ecological Change in Indonesia* (Berkeley, Calif., 1963) are especially useful: "How much of the past growth and the present state of Indonesian culture and society is attributable to ecological processes is something to be determined, if at all, at the end of inquiry, not at the beginning of it. And as political, stratificatory, commercial, and intellectual developments, at least, seem to have acted as important ordering processes in Indonesian history, the final awarding of prepotency to ecological developments seems no more likely than that they will turn out to have been inconsequential" (p. 11). On the contrast between Japanese and Javanese society: "Given, then, all the admittedly background differences, one can hardly forbear to ask when one looks at these two societies: 'What has happened in the one which did not happen in the other?' A satisfactory answer to such a question would involve the whole eco-

nomic, political, and cultural history of the two civilizations . . ." (p. 131).
"A search for the true diagnosis of the Indonesian malaise takes one, thus, far beyond the analysis of ecological and economic processes to an investigation into the nation's political, social, and cultural dynamics" (p. 154—the last sentence in the book.)
[46] Gilberto Freyre, *The Masters and the Slaves: A Study in the Development of Brazilian Civilization*, 2nd English language Ed. (New York, 1956), p. xxvii.

strike sharply at economic determinism, which has roots in Marxism, where it clutters up rich fields, and strike at certain schools of ecology, but they are generally consistent with a properly understood dialectical materialism. What is primarily missing in Freyre's organic view of society is a suitable concern for class antagonisms as the historical motor force, but that is precisely what is missing from Harris' materialism.

Freyre's objections to historical materialism rest largely on his narrow economic reading of Marxian theory. In *The Mansions and the Shanties* he refers to an essay by Lefebvre des Nöettes in which it is asserted that moral suasion proved helpless against slavery until technological developments gave it room to expand. Freyre asks, "Does this mean the absolute dependence of moral progress on material progress, as narrowly sectarian 'historical materialists' claim . . . ?"[47] He answers negatively, citing the United States as proof that slavery and technological progress could coexist. I doubt that the United States would offer him much evidence to refute even vulgar-Marxism on this point, but we need not discuss the specific questions now. The main point is that he sees Marxism as an economic and technological determinism; in effect, he describes it in terms much more appropriate to certain schools of ecology. If it is Marxism, then certainly it is the kind that once drove Marx to protest, "*Je ne suis pas un marxiste.*" The class element has somehow disappeared, but without it historical materialism is a senseless abstraction.

If historical materialism is not a theory of class determinism, it is nothing, but to be a theory of class determinism it must accept two limitations. Certain social classes can only rise to political power and social hegemony under specific technological conditions. The relationship of these classes, from this point of view, determines the contours of the historical epoch. It follows, then, that changes in the political relationship of classes constitute the essence of social transformations; but this notion comes close to tautology, for social transformations are defined precisely by changes in class relationships. What rescues the notion from tautology is the expectation that these changes in class relationships determine—at least in outline—the major psychological, ideological, and political patterns, as well as economic and technological possibilities; that changes in class structure constitute the most meaningful of all social changes. To argue that they constitute the only meaningful changes is to reduce historical materialism to nonsense and to surrender its dialectical essence.

Freyre's idealism appears most crudely in his discussion of Portuguese colonization. He refers to the "task" of colonization as being "disproportionate to the normal resources of the population, thereby obliging the people to maintain themselves in a constant state of superexcitation, in the interests of large-scale procreation."[48] Lapses into teleology and mysticism abound in his writings, and one could, if one wished, put them side by side to prove him quaint or foolish. He who wastes time doing so will be the loser, for Freyre's thought is too rich for us to focus on its weak side. To see where Freyre is going we need to analyze his notion of the "creative image."

In writing of Brazilian patriarchal

---

[47] Gilberto Freyre, *The Mansions and the Shanties: The Making of Modern Brazil* (New York, 1963), p. 305.

[48] Freyre, *Masters and Slaves*, p, 262.

society and of the intersection of Indian, Negro, and European cultures Freyre "was trying to accomplish a pale equivalent of what Picasso has masterfully accomplished in plastic art: the merging of the analytic and the organic approaches to man: what one of his critics has called 'a creative image.' "[49] Freyre seeks to use methods and data of the physical, biological, and social sciences to assist in what is essentially an artistic project, for only through artistic image can the wholeness of man and his world be glimpsed. He admits the large role assigned to intuition in his work.[50] In a passage, which seems to me to reflect a strong Sombartian influence, he writes, "The truth really seems to be that only 'within' the living whole of human development can the relations between what is arbitrarily considered rationality and irrationality in human behavior, or between different human cultures, be fully understood."[51] Properly disciplined, this concern with getting "within" a society should mean a concern with its spirit— its dominant ideology, system of values, and psychological patterns. Freyre's effort can and should be assimilated into a historical view of social classes, for it is essentially an attempt to grasp the wholeness of a society's world view, including its self-image. Only two steps are required to place Freyre's viewpoint on materialist ground. The first takes us to the realization that society's world view must necessarily be essentially the view of its ruling class; the second to the realization that, in order to rule, a ruling class must be sufficiently wise and flexible to incorporate much from the manners and sentiments of the classes being ruled.

Freyre is therefore not toying with us when he writes that he endeavors to be "almost entirely objective" but that at certain points he introduces an "objective-introspective" method. His purpose is to be able to feel life as lived by his long-dead subjects in all its "sensual fullness of outline."[52] This attempt at psychological reconstruction, he wisely observes, depends less on "the strictly psychological approach of academic psychologists than that of novelists who have found it necessary to add a psychological time to the conventional chronological one, in novels otherwise historical in their substance . . . ."[53] In this spirit he constructs, for example, a historical-psychological model of Indian and African personality traits, as absorbed into Brazilian culture.[54] So far as possible, he strives to discover the roots of these divergent patterns in social and technical modes of life. The problem lies in the elusiveness of a full explanation. The mechanisms and the extent of the inheritance of acquired group characteristics continue to elude us and may to some degree always do so. Recognition of this elusiveness and of how few definite, scientifically demonstrated conclusions we can borrow from psychologists or from other social and biological scientists throws Freyre and

---

[49] *Ibid.*, p. xxi.
[50] *Ibid.*, p. xxi.
[51] *Ibid.*, p. xxii.

[52] *Ibid.*, p. lviii.
[53] *Ibid.*, p. lxix. Perhaps the most straightforward illustration of Freyre's method is, appropriately, *Mother and Son: A Brazilian Tale* (New York, 1967), which he describes as a seminovel and in which fictional situations are meant to represent historical and social reality, apparently on the principle of *se non e vero, e ben' trovato*. As the narrator writes of a character about whom he planned to write and who suddenly appears before him in real life (p. 4): "I must be aware that she had existed before I had imagined her; if she had not, I would not have tried to conjure her up."
[54] Freyre, *Masters and Slaves*, pp. 284–85.

the rest of us back on our own fragile ability as social historians to reach for everything at once. Poetry, for us as well as for the ancient Greeks, remains truer than history. As Freyre reminds us:

The human being can only be understood—insofar as he can be understood—in his total human aspect; and understanding involves the sacrifice of a greater or lesser degree of objectivity. For in dealing with the human past, room must be allowed for doubt, and even for mystery. The history of an institution, when undertaken or attempted in keeping with a sociological criterion which includes the psychological, inevitably carries us into zones of mystery where it would be ridiculous for us to feel satisfied with Marxist interpretations or Behaviorist or Paretist explanations, or with mere description similar to those of natural history.[55]

Freyre's willingness to speak approvingly of intuition, "mystery," and the sacrifice of objectivity opens him to attack and even ridicule from those who are content to ignore the challenge. Yet Freyre's intuition, like the passionate opposition to racial and social injustice that informs all of Harris' work, has its place. As Gramsci observes, "Only passion sharpens the intellect and co-operates to render intuition clearer."[56] Freyre, sensing the elusiveness of historical truth and the dangers of strict rationalism, has raised serious objections to materialist theory, and only superficial mechanists could fail to realize as much. Since a full reply would entail an effort beyond the editor's and reader's patience, I should like to restrict myself to a few observations.

The strength of Marxian materialism, relative to other materialisms, is its

dialectic, which gives it, or ought to give it, the flexibility and wholeness Freyre demands. The principle of interrelatedness is fundamental to Hegelian and Marxian dialectics and cannot be sacrificed to convenient notions of simple causation. If dialectical materialism is taken seriously, it must assert historical continuity as well as discontinuity. Every historical event necessarily embraces the totality of its components, each of which brings to that event the product of its total historical development. For this reason alone, a failure to respect the force of a people's tradition and historically developed sensibility will always prove fatal to materialist thought and betray it into mechanism. The task of those who would confront Freyre's idealism with a convincing materialism is to account for the complexity of societies in their historical uniqueness and for the special manifestations of the human spirit embodied in each such society.

Freyre's recourse to an idealist stance results from an irresponsible attitude toward the complex reality he seeks to explain. In his methodological preface to his study of postmonarchical Brazil, he identifies his subject as a society entering the modern world with a persistent tradition of patriarchalism; and he identifies his method as less the historical than the anthropological and psychological.[57] Life, he insists, is a process of development of values and lends itself only partially to scientific

---

[55] Freyre, *Mansions and Shanties*, p. xxix.

[56] Quoted by Cammett, *Antonio Gramsci*, p. 197.

[57] Gilberto Freyre, *Ordem e progresso: Processo de disintegração das sociedades patriarcal e semipatriarcal no Brasil sob o regime do trabalho livre . . .*, 2 vols. (Rio de Janeiro, 1962), pp. xxiv. I deliberately pass over Freyre's extension of his psychological method in his theory of Luso-Tropicalism. This extension raises a different set of problems, beyond the scope of this paper. See Freyre, *The Portuguese and the Tropics* (Lisbon, 1961), esp. p. 9.

analysis.[58] Perhaps so, but as Marx, Freud, and Weber, among others, have argued, it is both necessary and possible to deal rationally with the irrational and to develop, at least in approximation, a disciplined approach to a reality so rich that we shall certainly never fully grasp it. The most attractive inheritance of Marxism from the Hegelian dialectic is the simultaneous assertion of progress toward essential knowledge and yet the ultimate elusiveness of the whole; it is this inheritance that makes Marxian philosophy, when it is not trampled on by political imbeciles, enthusiastically embrace the experimental sciences without fear of losing its dogmatic virginity. Freyre's weakness lies in his unwillingness to try to discipline his many-sided viewpoint. I do not suggest that he ought to tell us which "factor" in the social organism he analyses is "primary"—I cannot imagine what a "historical factor" is, and the assignment of primacy would do violence to the spirit of his work. I do suggest that we need some clue to the motor force of social change. Freyre fails us here, hence the sharpness of Harris' critique.[59]

Freyre's failure—like Harris'—emerges most clearly from his friendly reply to an author who "would place responsibility for the principal defects in our social, economic, and moral development upon slavery . . . where I am inclined to put the blame upon monoculture and the latifundia. . . ."[60] The difference, Freyre argues, is one of emphasis, and each emphasis does fall on the material conditions of life. Ironically, Harris' position is close to Freyre's, although more rigid, for Freyre himself often slides into a narrow mechanism when he discusses specific historical problems rather than theoretical and methodological ones. He does not, for example, pay nearly enough attention to the feudal-Catholic tradition in his discussions of morality, sexual relations, sadism in pedagogy, and some other matters.[61] The advantage of emphasizing slavery rather than monoculture lies not in the superior virtue of one "factor" over the other, but in the focus on human relationships. The special quality of master-slave relationships in Brazilian slavery lies in their being a special case in a broad pattern of quasifeudal, paternalistic relationships brought from Portugal and reinvigorated on the virgin soil of Bahia and Pernambuco. Freyre himself contributes much toward such an

---

[58] Freyre, *Ordem e progresso*, pp. xxxii-xxxiii; It is only a short step from this attitude to a romanticization of the Brazilian past. Stanley J. Stein is harsh but not unjust when he rebukes Freyre for transforming hypotheses advanced in *Masters and Slaves* into "facts" simply by restating them in later books. See Stein, "Freyre's Brazil Revisited: A Review of *New World in the Tropics: The Culture of Modern Brazil*," *Hispanic American Historical Review*, XLI (Feb., 1961), 113.

[59] There is also, apparently, a political and ideological component to this sharpness. Freyre's writings on Angola and Mozambique have come close to apologetics for Dr. Salazar's imperialist policies. Harris sees a direct line between Freyre's point of view on Brazilian colonization and his recent political pronouncements. As one who has seen the ravages of Portuguese imperialism first hand and who has done good work in exposing them, Harris is incensed. I agree that there is a direct line between the two sets of

views, but I also think that Freyre's polite criticisms of Portuguese racial policies as "un-Portuguese" ought to be given due weight. His views of past and present can be related to a general ideological commitment that looks to me—he would probably deny it—like a sophisticated greater-Brazilian nationalism. In any case, we dare not permit criticisms of Freyre's politics to blind us to the value of his contributions to history and sociology. His formulations on Brazilian history and culture must be examined strictly on their merits.

[60] Freyre, *Masters and Slaves*, pp. 64–65, n. 176; cf *O Mundo que o portugues criou*, p. 108.

[61] Cf *Masters and Slaves*, pp. 368, 401, 416–17, n. 34.

analysis in at least two ways: by treating the slave plantation as an integrated community and by seeing that community as a projection of the traditional family unit. Tannenbaum's early formulation of the problem remains one of the best:

It is better to speak of a slave society rather than of slavery, for the effects of the labor system—slave or free—permeate the entire social structure and influence all of its ways. If we are to speak of slavery, we must do it in its larger setting, as a way of life for both master and slave, for both the economy and the culture, for both the family and the community.[62]

What needs to be explored is the relationship between this peculiar class structure and the prevalent psychological and ideological patterns in society.

A parallel weakness in Freyre's attempt at synthetic analysis may be found in his discussion of the economic ills of monoculture. These surely were not absolute; if they crippled society at a certain point, they did so because they badly compromised the ruling class and hampered its ability to rule with that even-handedness without which the successful exercise of social hegemony would be impossible. Whether slavery or monoculture caused soil exhaustion is not an especially useful question, for they were functionally related. More to the point, they represented social and economic aspects of a specific form of class rule. In economic experience, as in the psychology of the leading strata, the relationship of master to slave proved decisive: it set limits to labor productivity, the flexibility of organization, the growth of the home market, and the accumulation of capital; it determined, in essential respects, the

sensibilities of those who could and did place their imprint on society.[63]

Of the planters Freyre writes that they "represented, in the formation of Brazilian society, the most typical of Portuguese tendencies: namely, settledness, in the sense of patriarchal stability. A stability based upon sugar (the plantation) and the Negro (the slave hut)... I would merely set alongside the purely material or Marxist aspect of things or, better, tendencies the psychologic aspect. Or the psychophysiologic."[64] Harris has not yet answered this challenge satisfactorily. We need not choose between Freyre's eclecticism and Harris' version of materialism. The historical task, to which a properly understood materialism seems to me to offer the best solution, is two-fold: to relate satisfactorily the psychological, "material," and other aspects of a society to each other in such a way as to present reality as an intergrated social process; and to avoid a sterile functionalism by uncovering the fundamental pattern of human relationships conditioning both material and spiritual life. To fulfill this task we need to examine historical continuity, with its cumulative traditions and ways of thought, as well as ecology, more narrowly understood.

Freyre's idealism may, as Harris alleges, weaken his work, but neither Freyre nor any of us could be expected to do better by rejecting a concern for the whole man in a social setting that links part to present. At his best Freyre is marvellously dialectical, as in his

---

[62] Frank Tannenbaum, "A Note on the Economic Interpretation of History," *Political Science Quarterly*, LXI (June, 1946), 248.

[63] The most suggestive starting point for a psychology of slave-holding may be found in G. W. F. Hegel, *The Phenomenology of Mind*, 2 vols. (London, 1910), I, 183ff. I have tried to sketch, in a preliminary way, the slave-holding experience in the United States: *The Political Economy of Slavery* (New York, 1965), pp. 31–34.

[64] Freyre, *Masters and Slaves*, p. xl.

pregnant remarks on the Brazilian adaptation of the Portuguese language,[65] or in his discussion of the psychology of the Portuguese colonizer, which he relates to the "intimate unity" of Portuguese culture as "a consequence of the processes and of the conditions of Portuguese colonization."[66]

The sad part of Harris' book, which is so impressive in many of its particular analyses, is the implicit conflict between his denigration of ideas, ideals, and values and his passionate plea for racial and social justice. How ironical that he should end his book with an exhortation—to whom to do what is not clear:

The backwardness of vast multitudes of the New World peasantry, illiterate, unskilled, cut off from the twentieth century and its brilliant technological advances did not simply happen by itself. These millions, about whose welfare we have suddenly been obliged to concern ourselves, were trained to their role in world history by four centuries of physical and mental conditioning. They were deliberately bottled up. Now we must either pull the cork or watch the bottle explode.[67]

In the context of his book these words are puzzling and might easily be dismissed, were it not for the obvious personal sincerity and social urgency they suggest. One is tempted to reply to Harris in the words Tannenbaum used many years ago to reply to Eric Williams:

It is hard to be a child of the Renaissance and a high priest of economic interpretation. If slavery was merely economic, and if economic forces are the only conditioning factor in shaping human institutions, then why all the indignation and the sarcasm? Why the appeal to moral forces, to justice, and to humanity?[68]

Harris, by attempting to construct a materialism that bypasses the ideological and psychological elements in the formation of social classes, passes over into a variant of vulgar Marxism. In so doing, he ranges himself much further from a consistent and useful materialism than do the idealists themselves, for he turns away from everything living in modern materialism— its dialectics and sense of historical process—and offers us the dead bones of a soulless mechanism.

---

[65] *Ibid.*, p. 348.
[66] Freyre, *O Mundo que o portugues criou,* p. 39; *New World in the Tropics,* p. 54.
[67] Harris, *Patterns of Race,* p. 99.

---

[68] Tannenbaum, *Political Science Quarterly,* LXI (June, 1946), 252.

MOSES I. FINLEY

The Idea of Slavery:
Critique of David Brion Davis'
The Problem of Slavery
in Western Culture

Moses I. Finley is Reader of Ancient Social and Economic History at the University of Cambridge, England (Jesus College), and is widely recognized as one of the world's leading authorities on slavery in the ancient world. His books include Studies in Land and Credit in Ancient Athens, 500–200 B.C. *(1951),* The World of Odysseus *(1954),* Slavery in Classical Antiquity: Views and Controversies *(1960), and* The Ancient Greeks *(1963). In the early 1950's Professor Finley taught at Rutgers University which had the privilege of firing him for refusing to cooperate with a Congressional investigating committee.*

In the year A.D. 61 the prefect of the city of Rome, Pedanius Secundus, was murdered by one of the slaves in his town house. Under the law, not only the culprit but all the other slaves in the household had to be executed, in this instance numbering four hundred. There was a popular outcry and the Senate debated the question. Some senators rose to plead clemency, but the day was carried by the distinguished jurist, Gaius Cassius Longinus, who argued that all change from ancestral laws and customs is always for the worse. When a mob tried to prevent the sentence from being carried out, the emperor personally intervened on the side of the law, though he rejected another proposal that Pedanius' ex-slaves should also be punished by banishment. That, he said, would be unnecessary cruelty.

The emperor was Nero and it has

Reprinted from *The New York Review of Books*, Vol. III, No. 1, pp. 7–10, Copyright © 1967 *The New York Review.*

been suggested that one of the unsuccessful advocates of mercy may have been his closest adviser, the Stoic philosopher Seneca, in whose writings there are some powerful passages calling for the treatment of slaves as fellow humans. Not once, however, did Seneca suggest that the institution itself was so immoral that it ought to be abolished. For that radical idea the western world still had to wait more than 1500 years, while philosophers, moralists, theologians, and jurists—save for an isolated voice here and there to whom no one listened—discovered and propagated a variety of formulas which satisfied them and society at large that a man could be both a thing and a man at the same time. This ambiguity or "dualism" is the "problem of slavery" to which Professor Davis has devoted a large, immensely learned, readable, exciting, disturbing, and sometimes frustrating volume, one of the most important to have been published on the subject of slavery in modern times.

The genesis of the book was a modest one. Professor Davis set out to make a comparative study of British and American antislavery movements. Gradually he began to appreciate that "the problem of slavery transcended national boundaries" in ways he "had not suspected." Slavery was brought to the New World at a time when it had disappeared from most of Europe; yet there were no hesitations, no gropings, because the heritage of the Bible, classical philosophy, and Roman law provided a ready-made set of regulations and a ready-made ideology. Differences within the New World, between the Anglo-Saxons in the north and the Latins in the south, between Protestant and Catholic colonies, appeared, on closer examination, to be tangential and far less significant than "their underlying patterns of unity." On this particular topic Professor Davis has now come forward with powerful support for a recent trend in scholarship running counter to the romantic idealized image of Latin American slavery, and in particular of race relations in the southern hemisphere, which had long prevailed, a view perhaps best known from the works of the Brazilian Gilberto Freyre and from Frank Tannenbaum's seminal little book *Slave and Citizen.* In short, Professor Davis came to the conclusion that "there was more institutional continuity between ancient and modern slavery than has generally been supposed" and that "slavery has always raised certain fundamental problems that originated in the simple fact that the slave is a man."

From this conclusion a new and fundamental question followed. If the "legal and moral validity of slavery was a troublesome question in European thought from the time of Aristotle to the time of Locke," why was it that not until the 1770's were there "forces in motion that would lead to organized movements to abolish . . . the entire institutional framework which permitted human beings to be treated as things"? This development, he rightly says, "was something new to the world." Slavery had declined markedly in the later Roman Empire, not as a result of an abolitionist movement but in consequence of complex social and economic changes which replaced the chattel slave by a different kind of bondsman, the *colonus,* the *adscriptus glebi,* the serf. Modern slavery, in contrast, did not become slowly transformed. It was abolished by force and violence. Attempts to picture "antislavery and efforts to Christianize and ameliorate the condition of slaves as parts of a single swelling current of humanitarianism" falsify the historical record. "All such dreams and hopes ran aground on the simple and solid fact, which for centuries had been obscured by philosophy and law, that a slave was not a piece of property, nor a half-human instrument, but a man held down by force."

The book Professor Davis started to write was thus converted into a large project of which this is the first volume (though a self-contained one) carrying the story from antiquity to the early 1770's. The story, it must be stressed, is essentially one in the history of ideas. "A problem of moral perception" is how he himself phrases it.

This book . . . makes no pretense of being a history of slavery as such, or even of opinion concerning slavery . . . I have been concerned with the different ways in which men have responded to slavery, on the assumption that this will help us to distinguish what was unique in the response of the abolitionist. I have also been concerned with traditions in thought and value from which both opponents and defenders of slavery could draw. I hope to demonstrate that slavery has always been a source of social and psychological tension, but that in Western culture it was associated with certain religious and philosophical doctrines that gave it the highest sanction.

As an essay in the history of ideas—more precisely, of ideology, a word which Professor Davis curiously shies away from—the book is brilliant, filled with detail yet never losing control of the main threads, subtle and sophisticated and penetrating. Even the relatively brief and derivative first part, on ancient and medieval thinking, has some fine insights. Then, with the discovery of America, Professor Davis comes into his own. No man, surely, has read so much or so deeply on the subject: the footnotes provide the most complete bibliography we have; too complete indeed, and one wishes he had

been more discriminating in his selection of titles. It is impossible in a review to survey the ground covered or the multiplicity of fresh ideas and suggestions. But an example or two will indicate how complicated is the counterpoint that is woven throughout around the "dualism" concept. Early on the *leitmotif* emerges. The question is posed as to why in the later Roman Empire and the early Middle Ages, when "slavery all but disappeared from most parts of Europe," we do not find "the Church turning away from its compromises with the Roman world and using its great moral power to hasten a seemingly beneficial change." Professor Davis answers:

The most plausible explanation would seem to lie in the complex network of mental associations, derived from antiquity, which connected slavery with ideas of sin, subordination, and the divine order of the world. To question the ethical basis of slavery, even when the institution was disappearing from view, would be to question fundamental conceptions of God's purpose and man's history and destiny. If slavery were an evil and performed no divinely appointed function, then why had God authorized it in Scripture and permitted it to exist in nearly every nation? If slavery violated the natural law of equality and the divine law of human brotherhood, could not the same be said of the family private property, social orders, and government?

The heretical sects were a threat all the time, for they seized on those ideas implicit in Christianity "that were potentially explosive when torn from their protective casings and ignited in the charged atmosphere of class rivalry and discontent." They had to be contained, and they were. Not until the middle of the eighteenth century did an English sect finally take a firm official stand against slavery (while the Church of England remained indifferent). The

Quakers came to that after a long period of inner conflict on the subject, but by then society had been so transformed that the moral issues acquired new practical implications.

In a period of intense soul-searching, of desire for self-purification and of concern over their image in the eyes of others, a decision to refrain from dealing in slaves was a means of reasserting the perfectionist content of their faith. It was a way of prescribing a form of selfish economic activity without repudiating the search for wealth; ... a way of affirming the individual's moral will, and the historic mission of the church, without challenging the basic structure of the social order.

So bald a summary invites the charge of mere cynicism, but nothing would be more unjust. Behind the summaries lie meticulous accounts of the intense intellectual and moral struggles that went on in the search for a moral position. In all societies which are characterized by class or national conflicts and divergence of interests, ideology is necessarily ambivalent. No account is adequate which fails to reveal how ideology serves both to criticize and to preserve the social order at the same time, and the careless or blinkered observer automatically dismisses as cynicism any analysis which gives due weight to the second function. On the subject of slavery, the crowning paradox is that the rationalist attack on Christian theology in the eighteenth century brought the slave no nearer to freedom. Locke had already shown how a defense of slavery could be reconciled with natural rights. Now, "insofar as the Enlightment divorced anthropology and comparative anatomy from theological assumptions, it opened the way for theories of racial inferiority."

And yet, at the point where this book ends, antislavery *had* become a program and eventually it was to become a successful major political issue. Slavery *was* finally abolished in the West. Why? It is on that decisive question that I find Professor Davis' account frustrating. "For some two thousand years men thought of sin as a kind of slavery. One day they would come to think of slavery as sin." Who are "they"? "By the early 1770's a large number of moralists, poets, intellectuals, and reformers had come to regard American slavery as an unmitigated evil." It is only a little unfair to remind Professor Davis of Jim Farley's remark, towards the close of Adlai Stevenson's first presidential campaign. Someone at a party was being jubilant over the fact that nearly all intellectuals were for Stevenson. "All sixty thousand of them," retorted Farley. Moralists, poets, intellectuals, and reformers did not destroy slavery. The Civil War did that, and Professor Davis himself has, as a byproduct, delivered a crushing blow against the "unnecessary conflict" school of historians. I do not, of course, wish to deny the essential role of several generations of abolitionists. But nothing did or could happen until their moral fervor became translated into political and military action, and how that came about cannot be answered by the history of ideas. Nothing is more difficult perhaps than to explain how and why, or why not, a new moral perception becomes effective in action. Yet nothing is more urgent if an academic historical exercise is to become a significant investigation of human behavior with direct relevance to the world we now live in.

It would be gross injustice to call this book an academic historical exercise or to suggest that Professor Davis is unaware of the central question. Throughout the volume there are sharp comments very much to the point. In a brief note on the rather mechanical economic explanations in Eric Williams' *Capitalism and Slavery*, Davis joins the opposition but then adds that one cannot "get around the simple fact that no country thought of abolishing the slave trade until its economic value had considerably declined." He knows and uses the most recent discussions (down to Eugene Genovese's *Political Economy of Slavery*, published in 1965) of the profitability of slavery and its effects on economic growth. He agrees that it is "theoretically possible" that such divergences with respect to freed slaves as existed between North and South America "had less to do with the character of slavery in the two countries than with economic and social structures which defined the relations between colored freedmen and the dominant white society." He mentions the wars of the eighteenth century and the changes in the balance of power, which "brought a growing awareness of the instability and inefficiency of the old colonial system." And it may be that what I am looking for will find its proper place in the next volumes.

Yet the fact remains that the comments I have just quoted are really asides, often relegated to footnotes, and I do not think it is a sufficient defense that a man has a right to choose his own subject, in this case the history of ideas. Slavery is not an autonomous system; it is an institution embedded in a social structure. It is no longer the same institution when the structure is significantly altered, and ideas about slavery have to be examined structurally too. Only by remaining in the realm of abstractions can Professor Davis lay so much emphasis on the "institutional continuity" between ancient and modern slavery. He is in consequence led astray on several important aspects. His account of slavery among the Hebrews and other ancient Near Eastern societies suffers from precisely the weakness he has so effectively exposed in the case of Latin American slavery. He has allowed his authorities to mislead him into taking at face value pious hopes which he penetrates easily when they appear in Seneca or modern writers. And he has misjudged the social ambience by failing to appreciate sufficiently that for most of human history labor for others has been involuntary (quite apart from compulsions exercised by either family or wage-earning, which are of a different order from the kind of force that is the final sanction against slaves, serfs, peons, debt bondsmen, coolies, or untouchables). Slavery in that context must have different overtones from slavery in a context of free labor. The way slavery declined in the Roman Empire, to repeat an example I have already given, illustrates that. Neither moral values nor economic interests nor the social order were threatened by the transformation of slaves and free peasants together into tied serfs. They were—or at least many powerful elements in society thought they were—by proposals to convert slaves into free men.

What sets the slave apart from all other forms of involuntary labor is that, in the strictest sense, he is an outsider. He is brought into a new society violently and traumatically; he is cut off from all traditional human ties of kin and nation and even his own religion; he is prevented, insofar as that is possible, from creating new ties, except to his masters, and in consequence his descendants are as much outsiders, as unrooted, as he was. The final proof of nonstatus is the free sexual access to slaves which is a fundamental condition of all slavery (with complex exceptions in the rules regarding access of free females to slave males). When Professor

Davis writes, "Bondwomen have always been the victims of sexual exploitation, which was perhaps the clearest recognition of their humanity," he has stood the situation on its head. Sexual *exploitation* is a denial, not a recognition, of a woman's humanity, whether she is slave or free.

I have stated the slave-outside formula schematically and therefore too rigidly. Structural differences emerge clearly when one considers how much societies have differed with respect to the freed slave. At one extreme stood Rome, which not only allowed almost unlimited rights to individual masters to free their slaves but which also automatically enrolled the freedmen as citizens if their owners were citizens. At the other extreme was the American South. Professor Davis produces evidence that by 1860 there were more free Negroes, even in the South, than is often realized. Nevertheless, the emancipation process was hemmed in by very stringent regulations. And the fate of the freed slave in the United States hardly needs spelling out. What does need a careful look is the question of color, which is too central to be evaded out of sentimentality and on which Professor Davis has an important chapter (as usual, in the realm of ideas). Dr. Williams holds that "slavery was not born of racism, rather, racism was the

consequence of slavery." One wishes profoundly that one could believe that. However, the slave-outsider formula argues the other way, as does the fact that as early as the 1660's Southern colonies decreed that henceforth all Negroes who were imported should be slaves, but whites should be indentured servants and not slaves. The connection between slavery and racism has been a dialectical one, in which each element reinforced the other.

Racism has already outlived slavery by a century. Why, we are entitled to ask, did the "revolutionary shift in attitudes towards sin, human nature, and progress," which we may concede to have been a necessary condition of antislavery, not extend to racism? Is slavery any more a sin than the denial of civil rights, concentration camps, Hiroshima, napalm, torture in Algeria, or apartheid in South Africa or Rhodesia? Why did the new moral perception succeed in wiping out one sin and not the others? It is that question which makes this book a profoundly disturbing one. There is cold comfort here for anyone who trusts to the slow ameliorative process of a growing humanitarianism, of the "progressive development of man's moral sense" which Thomas Jefferson found in history. In Professor Davis' lapidary phrase, "faith in progress smothered [Jefferson's] sense of urgency" when it came to slavery.

Bibliography

GENERAL AND COMPARATIVE

Alexander, H.B., "Brazilian and United States Slavery Compared," *Journal of Negro History*, VII (1922), 349–64.

Bastide, Roger, *Les Amériques noires: Les Civilisations africaines dans le nouveau monde* (Paris, 1967).

Berghe, Pierre L. van den, *Race and Racism. A Comparative Perspective* (New York, 1967).

*Davis, David Brion, *The Problem of Slavery in Western Culture* (Ithaca, 1966).

Deerr, N., *The History of Sugar*, 2 vols. (London, 1945).

*Elkins, Stanley M., *Slavery: A Problem in American Institutional and Intellectual Life* (Chicago, 1959).

Frazier, E. Franklin, *Race and Culture Contacts in the Modern World* (Boston, 1957).

Harris, Marvin, *Patterns of Race in the Americas* (New York, 1964).

Herskovits, Melville J., *The Myth of the Negro Past* (Boston, 1941).

Hoetink, H., *The Two Variants in Caribbean Race Relations: A Contribution to the Sociology of Segmented Societies* (London, 1967).

Klein, Herbert, *Slavery in the Americas: A Comparative Study of Virginia and Cuba* (Chicago, 1967).

---

* Works of particular importance.

Kloosterboer, W., *Involuntary Labour Since the Abolition of Slavery* (Leiden, Neth., 1960).

*Lane, Ann J., ed., *Slavery and Personality: The Elkins Thesis and Its Critics*, (Baton Rouge, forthcoming).

Mintz, Sidney W., "The House and the Yard among Three Caribbean Peasantries," *Extrait des actes du VIᵉ Congrès International des Sciences Anthropologiques et Ethnologiques*, Tome II, Vol. I (Paris, 1960), pp. 591–96.

*Mörner, Magnus, *Race Mixture in the History of Latin America* (Boston, 1967).

Morse, Richard M., "The Heritage of Latin America," Ch. V of Louis Hartz, et al., *The Founding of New Societies* (New York, 1964).

Nieboer, H.J., *Slavery as an Industrial System. Ethnological Researches* (The Hague, 1900).

Oliveira Lima, Manoel de, *The Evolution of Brazil Compared with that of Spanish and Anglo-Saxon America* (Stanford, Calif., 1914).

Pan American Union, *Plantation Systems of the New World* (Washington, 1959).

Rubin, Vera, ed., *Caribbean Studies: A Symposium* (Seattle, 1960).

Saco, José Antonio, *Historia de la esclavitud desde los tiempos mas remotos hasta nuestros días*, 2nd Ed., 4 vols. (Havana, 1936–45).

Tannenbaum, Frank, "A Note on the Economic Interpretation of History," *Political Science Quarterly*, LXI (1946), 245–52.

*――――, *Slave and Citizen: The Negro in the Americas* (New York, 1947).

Williams, Mary M., "The Treatment of Slaves in the Brazilian Empire; a Comparison with the United States," *Journal of Negro History*, XV (1930), 313–36.

Wyndham, H.A., *The Atlantic and Slavery* (London, 1935).

――――, *The Atlantic and Emancipation* (London, 1937).

SLAVERY IN THE OLD WORLD, ANCIENT TO MODERN

For an excellent introduction to the literature see Part One of David Brion Davis, *The Problem of Slavery in Western Culture* and the footnotes thereto. Among the indispensable titles for an understanding of modern Afro-American slavery are:

Cortes, Vincenta, *La Esclavitud en Valencia durante el reinado de los reyes católicos, 1479–1516* (Valencia, Spain, 1964).

Domingues Ortiz, Antonio, *La Esclavitud en Castilla durante la edad moderna* (Madrid, 1952).

Finley, M.I., ed., *Slavery in Classical Antiquity: Views and Controversies*, (Cambridge, Eng., 1960), esp. Finley's own essay "Was Greek Civilization Based on Slave Labour?" See also the excellent bibliography.

Mendelsohn, Isaac, *Slavery in the Ancient Near East*, (New York, 1949).

*Verlinden, Charles, *L'Esclavage dans l'Europe médiévale* (Bruges, Belgium, 1955).

Westermann, William L., *The Slave Systems of Greek and Roman Antiquity* (Philadelphia, 1955).

AFRICA AND THE AFRICAN SLAVE TRADE

*Davidson, Basil, *Black Mother: The Years of the African Slave Trade* (Boston, 1961).

Donnan, Elizabeth, *Documents Illustrative of the History of the Slave Trade to America*, 4 vols. (Washington, 1930).

DuBois, W.E.B., *The Suppression of the African Slave Trave to the United States of America, 1638–1870*, (Cambridge, Mass., 1896).

Duignan, Peter, and Clarence Clendenen, *The United States and the African Slave Trade, 1619–1862* (Stanford, Calif., 1963).

Howard, Warren S., *American Slavers and the Federal Law, 1837–1862* (Berkeley, Calif., 1963).

Lloyd, Christopher, *The Navy and the Slave Trade: The Suppression of the African Slave Trade in the Nineteenth Century* (London, 1949).

Mannix, Daniel P. and Malcolm Cowley, *Black Cargoes: A History of the Atlantic Slave Trade, 1518–1865* (New York, 1962).

Martin, Gaston, *Nantes au XVIIIe siècle: l'ère des Négrières, 1714–1744* (Paris, 1936).

Mathieson, William Law, *Great Britain and the Slave Trade* (London, 1929).

Mauro, Frédéric, *L'Atlantique portugais et les esclaves, 1570–1670* (Lisbon, 1956).

——, *Le Portugal et l'Atlantique au XVIIe siècle, 1570–1670* (Paris, 1960).

Ohe, Enrique and Conchita Ruiz-Burruecos, "Los Portugueses en la trata de esclabos negros de las postrimerias del siglo XVI," *Moneda y Crédito, LXXXV* (Madrid, 1963), 3–40.

Polanyi, Karl, *Dahomey and the Slave Trade: An Analysis of an Archaic Economy* (Seattle, 1966).

Pope-Hennessy, James, *Sins of the Fathers: A Study of the Atlantic Slave Traders, 1441–1807* (New York, 1968).

Rinchon, Père Dieudonné, *Le Trafic négrier, d'après les livres de commerce du capitaine gantois Pierre-Ignace-Livien Van Alstein* (Brussels, 1938).

Rodney, Walter, "African Slavery and Other Forms of Social Oppression on the Upper Guinea Coast in the Context of the Atlantic Slave-Trade," *Journal of African History*, VII (1966), 431–43.

Scelle, Georges, *La Traite négrière aux Indes de Castille*, 2 vols. (Paris, 1906).

Spears, John R., *The American Slave Trade* (New York, 1900).

BRAZIL

*Bastide, Roger, *Religions africaines au Brésil* (Paris, 1960).

Boxer, C.R., *The Dutch in Brazil* (London, 1960).

——, *Four Centuries of Portuguese Expansion, 1415–1825: A Succinct Survey* (Johannesburg, South Africa, 1965).

*——, *The Golden Age of Brazil, 1695–1750: Growing Pains of a Colonial Society* (Berkeley, Calif., 1964).

——, *Salvador de Sá and the Struggle for Brazil and Angola* (London, 1952).

——, *Race Relations in the Portuguese Colonial Empire, 1415–1825* (Oxford, Eng., 1963).

——, *Portuguese Society in the Tropics: The Municipal Councils of Gray Macao, Bahia and Luanda, 1510–1800*, (Madison, Wisc., 1965).

——, tr. and ed., "Negro Slavery—Brazil: A Portuguese Pamphlet, 1764," *Race*, V (1964), 38–47.

Cardoso, Fernando Henrique, *Capitalismo e escravidão no Brasil meridional* (São Paulo, 1962).

Cardozo, Manoel, "Slavery in Brazil as Described by Americans, 1822–1888," *Americas*, XVII (1961), 241–60.

Carneiro, Edison, *O Quilombo dos Palmares*, 2nd Ed. (São Paulo, 1958) (also in Spanish: *Las Guerras en Palmares*).

Costa, Viotta da, *Da Colonia à senzala* (São Paulo, 1966).

Dean, Warren, "The Planter as Entrepreneur: The Case of São Paulo," *Hispanic American Historical Review*, XLVI (1966), 138–52.

Ennes, Ernesto, ed. *As Guerras nos Palmares: Documentos* (Rio de Janeiro, 1937).

Etienne, l'abbé Ignace, "La Secte musulmane des Malès du Brésil et leur révolte en 1835," *Anthropos*, IV (1909), 99–105, 405–415.

Fernandes, Florestan, *A Integracão de negro à sociedade de classes*, (São Paulo, 1965).

*Freyre, Gilberto, *The Masters and the Slaves: A Study in the Development of Brazilian Civilization*, 2nd Ed. (New York, 1956).

*——, *The Mansions and the Shanties: The Making of Modern Brazil* (New York, 1963).

——, *New World in the Tropics: The Culture of Modern Brazil* (New York, 1963).

——, *O Escravo nos anuncios de jornais brasileiros do século XIX*, (Recife, Brazil, 1963).

——, *O Mundo que o portugues criou e Uma Cultura amaceada: A Luso-brasileia* (Lisbon, n.d.).

Furtado, Celso, *The Economic Growth of Brazil* (Berkeley, Calif., 1965).

Goulart, Mauricio, *Escravidão africana no Brasil (das origens à cessão do trafego)* (São Paulo, 1949).

*Graham, Richard, "Causes for the Abolition of Negro Slavery in Brazil: An Interpretive Essay, "*Hispanic American Historical Review*, XLIV (1966), 123–37.

*Ianni, Octavio, *As Metamorfoses do escrevo: Apogeu e crise da escravatura no Brasil meriodional*, (São Paulo, 1962).

*——, *Raças e classes sociais no Brasil* (Rio de Janeiro, 1966).

Kent, R.K., "Palmares: An African State in Brazil," *Journal of African History*, VI (1965), 161–75.

Martin, Percy Alvin, "Slavery and Abolition in Brazil," *Hispanic American Historical Review*, XIII (1933), 151–96.

Nina Rodriques, R., *Os Africanos no Brasil*, 3rd Ed. (São Paulo, 1945).

Pierson, Donald, *Negroes in Brazil* (Chicago, 1942).

*Prado Junior, Caio, *The Colonial Background of Modern Brazil* (Berkeley, Calif., 1967).

——, *Historia económica do Brasil*, (7th ed.; Rio de Janeiro, 1962).

Ramos, Arthur, *The Negro in Brazil* (New York, 1945).

Stein, Stanley J., "Freyre's Brazil Revisited," *Hispanic American Historical Review*, XLI (1961), 111–13.

*——, *Vassouras: A Brazilian Coffee County, 1850–1900* (Cambridge, Eng., 1957).

SPANISH AMERICA, EXCLUDING CUBA

Aguirre Beltrán, Gonzalo, *La Población negra de México, 1519–1810* (México, D.F., 1946).

Bierck, Harold A., "The Struggle for Abolition in Gran Columbia," *Hispanic American Historical Review*, XXXIII (1953), 365–86.

Borah, Woodrow, "Race and Class in Mexico," *Pacific Historical Review*, XXIII (1954), 331–42.

Brito Figueroa, Féderico, *Las Insurrecciones de los esclavos en la sociedad colonial venezolana* (Caracas, 1961).

Davidson, David M., "Negro Slave Control and Resistance in Colonial Mexico, 1519–1650," *Hispanic American Historical Review*, XLVI (1966), 235–53.

*Díaz Soler, L.M., *Historia de la esclavitud negra en Puerto Rico, 1493–1890* (Madrid, 1953).

Feliu Cruz, Guillermo, *La Abolición de la esclavitud en Chile* (Santiago, 1942).

Guillot, Carlos Federico, *Negros rebeldes y negros cimarrones. Perfil afroaméricano en la historia del Nuevo Mundo durante el siglo XVI* (Buenos Aires, 1961).

Hudson, Randall O., "The Status of the Negro in Northern South America," *Journal of Negro History*, XLIX (1964).

*Jaramillo Uribe, Jaime, "Esclavos y señores en la sociedad colombiana del siglo XVIII," *Anuario colombiano de historia social y de la cultura*, I (Bogota, 1963).

King, James F., "Negro History in Continental Spanish America," *The Journal of Negro History*, XXIX (January, 1944).

*Mellafe, Rolando, *La Esclavitud en Hispano-América* (Buenos Aires, 1964).

Parry, J.H., *The Spanish Seaborne Empire* (New York, 1966).

Prince, Howard, "The Spanish Slave Code of 1789," in *Columbia Essays in International Affairs: Vol. II, The Dean's Papers, 1966*, ed. Andrew W. Cordier (New York, 1967), pp. 157–68.

Romero, Fernando, "The Slave Trade and Negro in South America," *Hispanic American Historical Review*, XXIV (1944).

*Saco, José Antonio, *Historia de la esclavitud de la raza africana en el nuevo mundo y en especial en los países américo-hispanos* (Barcelona, 1879).

CUBA

Aimes, Hubert H.S., *A History of Slavery in Cuba* (New York, 1907).

Armas y Céspedes, F. de, *De la Esclavitud en Cuba* (Havana, 1866).

Cepero Bonilla, Raul, *Obras históricas: Azúcar y abolición* (Havana, 1963).

Ely, Roland T., *Cuando reinaba su majestad el azúcar* (Buenos Aires, 1963).

Foner, Philip S., *A History of Cuba and Its Relations with the United States*, 2 vols. (New York, 1962–63).

Friedlander, H.E., *Historia económica de Cuba* (Havana, 1944).

*Guerra y Sanchez, Ramiro, *Sugar and Society in the Caribbean* (New Haven, Conn., 1964).

Humboldt, Alexander von, *The Island of Cuba* (New York, 1856).

Ortiz, Fernando, *Cuban Counterpoint* (New York, 1947).

*———, *Hampa afro-cubana: Los Negros esclavos* (Havana, 1916).

FRENCH CARIBBEAN AND LOWER CANADA

Debien, Gabriel, *Les Engagés pour les Antilles, 1634–1715* (Paris, 1951).

———, *Etudes antillaises, XVIIIe siècle* (Paris, 1956).

*James, C.L.R., *The Black Jacobins: Toussaint L'Ouverture and the San Domingo Revolution*, 2nd Ed. (New York, 1963).

Leyburn, James G., *The Haitian People*, 2nd Ed. (New Haven, Conn., 1966).

*Martin, Gaston, *Histoire de l'esclavage dans les colonies françaises* (Paris, 1948).

Peytraud, Lucien, *L'Esclavage aux Antilles françaises avant 1789* (Paris, 1897).

Rigaud, Odette Mennesson, "Le Role du Vaudou dans l'indépendence d'Haiti," *Présence Africaine*, no. 17–18 (février-mai, 1958), 43–67.

Schoelcher, Victor, *Esclavage et colonisation* (Paris, 1948).

Stoddard, T. Lothrop, *The French Revolution in San Domingo* (Boston, 1914).

Trudel, Marcel, *L'Esclavage au Canada française; histoire et conditions de l'esclavage* (Quebec, 1960).

*Vaissière, P. de., *Saint-Domingue, 1629–1789. La Société et la Vie créoles sous l'ancien régime* (Paris, 1909).

BRITISH CARIBBEAN AND UPPER CANADA

*Bennett, J. Harry, *Bondsmen and Bishops: Slavery and Apprenticeship on the Codrington Plantations of Barbados, 1710–1838* (Berkeley, Calif., 1958).

*Curtin, Philip, *Two Jamaicas* (Cambridge, Eng., 1955).

*Edwards, Bryan, *The Civil and Commercial History of the British Colonies in the West Indies*, 5th Ed., 5 vols. (Philadelphia, 1819; first edition in two volumes, 1793).

*Goveia, Elsa V., *Slave Society in the British Leeward Islands at the End of the 18th Century* (New Haven, Conn., 1965).

Hall, Douglas, "Slaves and Slavery in the British West Indies," *Social and Economic Studies*. III (1962).

Harlow, V.T., *History of Barbados, 1624–1685* (Oxford, Eng., 1926).

Jordan, Winthrop D., "The Influence of the West Indies on the Origins of New England Slavery," *William and Mary Quarterly*, XVIII (1961).

Long, Edward, *The History of Jamaica*, 3 vols. (Jamaica, 1774).

Mathieson, W.L., *British Slavery and Its Abolition, 1823–1838* (London, 1926).

*Pares, Richard, *Merchants and Planters* (Cambridge, Eng., 1960).

————, *War and Trade in the West Indies, 1739–63* (Oxford, Eng., 1936).

————, *A West India Fortune* (London, 1950).

Patterson, H. Orlando, *The Sociology of Slavery* (London, 1967).

Phillips, Ulrich B., "An Antigua Plantation," *North Carolina Historical Review*, III (July, 1926).

————, "A Jamaican Slave Plantation," *American Historical Review*, XIX (April, 1914).

Pitman, Frank Wesley, "Slavery on the British West India Plantations in the 18th Century," *Journal of Negro History*, XI (1926), 584–668.

*Ragatz, Joseph Lowell, *The Fall of the Planter Class in the British Caribbean* (Washington, 1928).

Ragatz, Joseph Lowell, *A Guide for Study of British Caribbean History, 1763–1834 . . .* (Washington, 1932).

*Williams, Eric, *Capitalism and Slavery* (Chapel Hill, N.C., 1944).

DUTCH, DANISH, SWEDISH, CARIBBEAN

Boxer, C.R., *The Dutch Seaborne Empire, 1600–1800* (New York, 1965).

[Documents], "Petition for Compensation for the Loss of Slaves by Emancipation in the Danish West Indies," *Journal of Negro History*, II (January, 1917).

Herskovits, M.J., and F. Herskovits, *Surinam Folk-Lore* (New York, 1936).

Lannoy, Charles de, *A History of Swedish Colonial Expansion* (Newark, Department of History and Political Science, University of Delaware, 1938).

Pendleton, Leik Amos, "Our New Possessions—the Danish West Indies," *Journal of Negro History*, II (July, 1917), 267–88.

Stedman, J.G., *Narrative of a Five-Year Expedition against the Revolted Negroes of Surinam in Guiana, 1772–1777* (2 vols.; London, 1796).

Westergaard, Waldemar, *The Danish West Indies under Company Rule* (New York, 1917).

THE UNITED STATES

The literature on slavery in the United States is vast and growing. The two indispensable works, which present opposite interpretations, remain:

*Phillips, Ulrich Bonnell, *American Negro Slavery* (New York, 1918; 1967).
*Stampp, Kenneth M., *The Peculiar Institution* (New York, 1956).